T0385132

CLASSICAL MYTHOLOGY A TO Z

CLASSICAL MYTHOLOGY A TO Z

AN ENCYCLOPEDIA OF GODS & GODDESSES, HEROES & HEROINES, NYMPHS, SPIRITS, MONSTERS, AND PLACES

❖ ANNETTE GIESECKE ❖

ILLUSTRATED BY

JIM TIERNEY

BLACK DOG
& LEVENTHAL
PUBLISHERS
NEW YORK

Text copyright © 2020 by Annette Giesecke

Cover design by HEADCASE DESIGN
Illustrations by JIM TIERNEY
Cover copyright © 2020 by Hachette Book Group, Inc.

Hachette Book Group supports the right to free expression and the value of copyright. The purpose of copyright is to encourage writers and artists to produce the creative works that enrich our culture.

The scanning, uploading, and distribution of this book without permission is a theft of the author's intellectual property. If you would like permission to use material from the book (other than for review purposes), please contact permissions@hbgusa.com. Thank you for your support of the author's rights.

BLACK DOG & LEVENTHAL PUBLISHERS
Hachette Book Group
1290 Avenue of the Americas
New York, NY 10104

www.hachettebookgroup.com
www.blackdogandleventhal.com

First Edition: October 2020

Black Dog & Leventhal Publishers is an imprint of Perseus Books, LLC, a subsidiary of Hachette Book Group, Inc. The Black Dog & Leventhal Publishers name and logo are trademarks of Hachette Book Group, Inc.

The publisher is not responsible for websites (or their content) that are not owned by the publisher.

The Hachette Speakers Bureau provides a wide range of authors for speaking events. To find out more, go to www.HachetteSpeakersBureau.com or call (866) 376-6591.

Illustrations by JIM TIERNEY

Print book interior design by PAUL KEPPLE and MAX VANDENBERG at HEADCASE DESIGN · www.headcasedesign.com
Production design by Liz Driesbach

Library of Congress Cataloging-in-Publication Data has been applied for.

ISBNs: 978-0-7624-7001-3 (hardcover); 978-0-7624-9713-3 (ebook)

Printed in China
1010

10 9 8 7 6

CONTENTS

·ILLUSTRATIONS

INTRODUCTION

This book is a collection of the gods, heroes, and monsters that populate Classical mythology as well as of the places that feature in stories told about them. The number of myths that have been preserved in the works of ancient authors is enormous, and the numbers of characters and places appearing in them vast. While *Classical Mythology A to Z* is an encyclopedia of myth, it is not comprehensive. Rather, it is limited to those Greek and Roman characters and places that appear in Edith Hamilton's classic work, *Mythology: Timeless Tales of Gods and Heroes*, for which it has been designed as a companion. In her own words, it was Hamilton's hope that by reading her book, those unfamiliar with the Greco-Roman world would "gain in this way not only a knowledge of the myths, but also some little idea of what the writers were like who told them—who have been proved, by two thousand years and more, to be immortal" (Preface, *Mythology*, 1942). She indisputably achieved her goal, doing so by telling the myths of Classical antiquity in a manner that was faithful to the original sources and, at the same time, fresh, relatable, and timeless in terms of language and expression. For this reason, Hamilton's work continues to serve as an authoritative and accessible introduction to Classical mythology in all its complexities over three quarters of a century beyond its original publication.

While Hamilton's *Mythology* established this book's scope, its contents will be useful to all those wishing to dig more deeply into the world of myth out of curiosity about individual characters' genealogies, their exploits, and places they inhabited. Greco-Roman mythology has persisted for millennia beyond its origins, retaining its ancient meanings and accruing new ones while serving as a foundation of cultural memory that has been alluded to in myriad ways and in all manner of creative media. For this reason, *Classical Mythology A to Z* will be indispensable to anyone looking to verify, clarify, or connect mythological characters and places to any number of literary, musical, artistic, or even pop culture references. This is a companion to Hamilton, but also so much more.

Entries in this collection have been grouped into four basic categories: deities, humans, monsters, and places. The first category includes immortal gods and goddesses as well as mortal ones. Nymphs, for example, were spirits that were believed to inhabit trees, bodies of water, and other components of the natural world, but they were subject to decline and death. The second category, which focuses on humans, encompasses individual heroes and heroines as well as groups of people, such as the female warriors called the Amazons. Characters of prodigious size and hybrid creatures are here all classed as monsters, regardless of whether they were benign or fearsome; in this case, "monster" is conceived of in the sense of its Latin etymology, *monstrum*, a thing or person that is strange but not necessarily evil. Landmarks, regions, bodies of water, mountains, and cities are naturally categorized as places. One particularly interesting aspect of mythological characters and places is the degree to which they resist strict categorization. Inevitably, the categories overlap, as in cases where a human hero becomes divine, or a river is conceived of both as a geographic feature and as a divine personification of the river. Hercules and Asclepius are examples of the former; the Peneus and Achelous rivers are examples of the latter. Gaia was the earth and also the earth goddess. The hunter Orion was a giant, being in this respect a prodigy or monster, but he was neither entirely mortal nor was he entirely divine. Satyrs, hybrid creatures that most would classify as monsters, were, at the same time, woodland spirits. And so on. A system of cross-referencing ensures that entries appropriate to multiple categories can be found in all of them.

Just as categorization poses challenges, so too does the spelling of names. The spellings here follow those used in Hamilton's work, although an effort has been made to indicate alternate spellings as well. The issue of spelling is complicated by several factors. One of them is the transmission of names from the original Greek to Latin and then to English, at least in many cases. An example is Ouranos, Greek god of the heavens. For the Romans, he was Uranus, and this is the spelling with which most speakers of English will be familiar. The Greeks had no letter "c," but the Romans used "k" only infrequently; as a consequence, the Greek god Kronos became Cronus in Latin. Another factor influencing spelling is inconsistency among the ancient authors, even those writing in the same language.

Varying spellings of a given character's name went hand in hand with varying, sometimes conflicting traditions concerning their lives and exploits. The myths themselves, as well as the characters in them, evolved over millennia. When confronted with variants and conflicts, it is important to remember that many or most myths were transmitted orally at some stage, being influenced by cultural shifts and factors such as depictions in art. One example is the cycle of myths surrounding the Trojan War. It has long been known that these tales had their origins in the Bronze Age (very roughly 1800–1150 BCE), the time of the Trojan War itself—and, yes, there was a Trojan War, or, more properly, a number of Trojan wars. Aspects of the story of Achilles, as well of his comrades and adversaries, so familiar from Homer's *Iliad*, were, at the time when it was committed to writing—perhaps 750 BCE or later—hundreds of years old, having been passed on orally previously, and doubtless altered at least to some degree with each telling. In those hundreds of years, the Greek world had changed dramatically, witnessing the flowering and fall of powerful kingdoms, a Dark Age, and the birth of city-states no longer governed by monarchs.

Not all variants of the myths surrounding the characters and places featured in this book have been documented here. The particular details included are derived from what today are the best-known sources of Greek and Roman myths, among them Homer, Hesiod, Apollonius of Rhodes, Virgil, and Ovid, all of them authors of epic poetry; the lyric poets Sappho, Stesichorus, Pindar, and Bacchylides; the tragedians Aeschylus, Sophocles, and Euripides; the historian Herodotus; the geographer Strabo; the travel writer and ethnographer Pausanias; the natural historian Pliny the Elder; and the mythographers Apollodorus and Hyginus. All of the ancient sources referenced in this book, complete with biographical details, have been assembled in a bibliography for quick reference. A number of these authors recorded more than one version of a given myth, even when they themselves were skeptical about some of them. In the spirit of Diodorus Siculus (first century BCE), who relates several alternate versions of the origins of the Pillars of Hercules—namely that Hercules created them to memorialize his extraordinary journey to the edges of the world, as a means by which to prevent sea monsters from penetrating the Mediterranean from the ocean beyond, or to create a channel allowing ships to pass between the seas—I invite readers of this book to select the versions most entertaining, credible, or far-fetched.

PART

I

GODS

GODDESSES

SPIRITS

AND

NYMPHS

THE
PRINCIPAL GODS

after Hesiod's Theogony (Origin of the Gods)

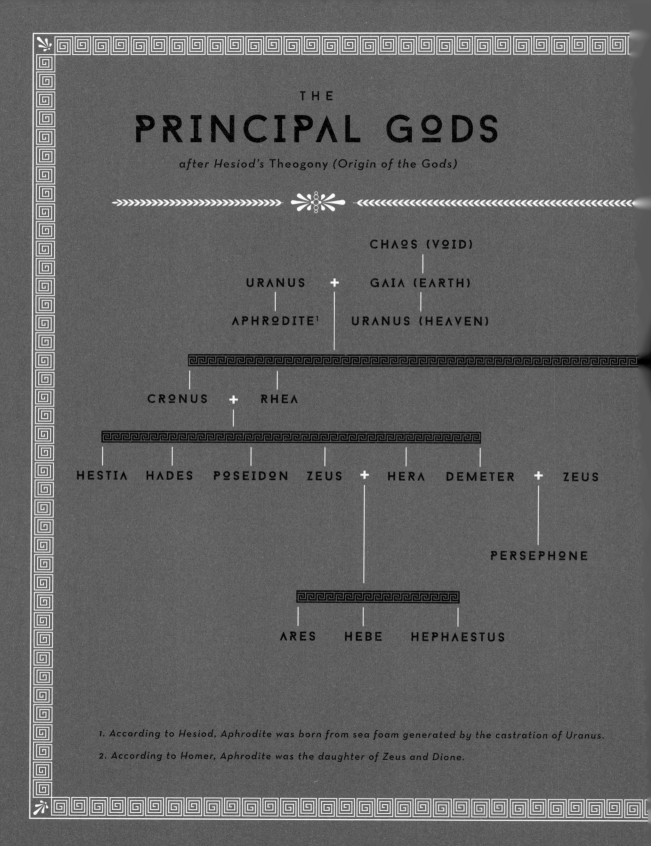

CHAOS (VOID)

URANUS + GAIA (EARTH)

APHRODITE[1] URANUS (HEAVEN)

CRONUS + RHEA

HESTIA HADES POSEIDON ZEUS + HERA DEMETER + ZEUS

PERSEPHONE

ARES HEBE HEPHAESTUS

1. According to Hesiod, Aphrodite was born from sea foam generated by the castration of Uranus.

2. According to Homer, Aphrodite was the daughter of Zeus and Dione.

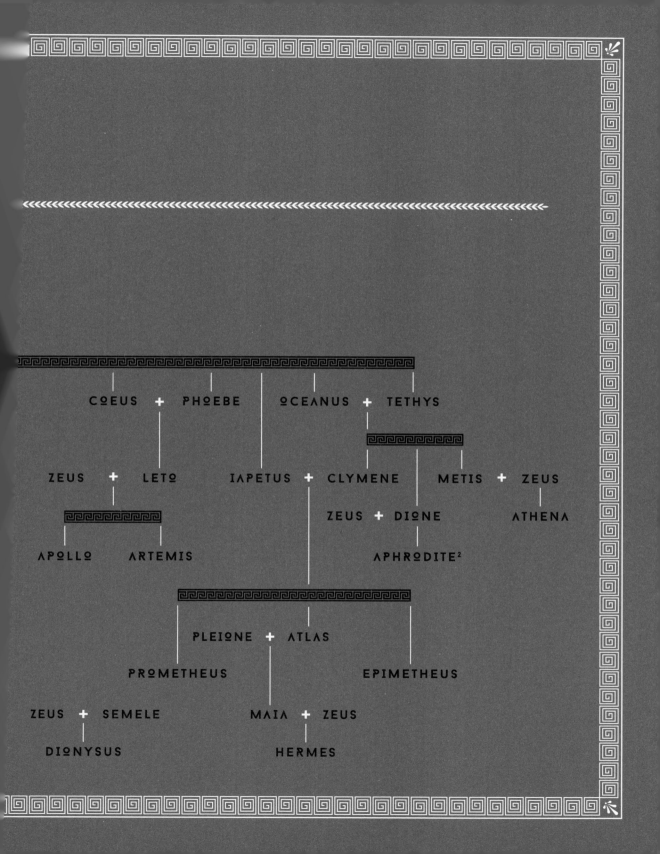

COEUS + PHOEBE   OCEANUS + TETHYS

ZEUS + LETO   IAPETUS + CLYMENE   METIS + ZEUS

APOLLO   ARTEMIS   ZEUS + DIONE   ATHENA

APHRODITE[2]

PLEIONE + ATLAS

PROMETHEUS   EPIMETHEUS

ZEUS + SEMELE   MAIA + ZEUS

DIONYSUS   HERMES

ACHELOUS Achelous was a river and, at the same time, the god of that river, which was one of the longest and most voluminous in Greece. While on the one hand associated with a specific river, this god could be invoked when making reference to rivers (and their gods) in general. In other words, he could be invoked as the god of all rivers. According to the Greek poet Hesiod, Achelous, along with a host of other rivers, was a child of the elemental Titan gods Oceanus and Tethys. His own children included the lovely voiced but monstrous Sirens as well as a number of Nymphs who were said to draw their water from him. These included Castalia, spirit of the Castalian Spring near Delphi, a fount sacred to the Muses; and Pirene, spirit of the Corinthian spring Pirene, whose waters Pegasus caused to burst from the earth when he struck it with his hoof.

Achelous is perhaps best known for his involvement with the hero Hercules, who wrestled with him for the hand of Deianeira, daughter of Oeneus, king of Calydon. Although Achelous changed his shape into a serpent and then a bull, Hercules prevailed nonetheless and broke off one of his horns. This horn, according to the Roman poet Ovid, became the Horn of Plenty, for the Naiad nymphs took it and filled it with fruits and flowers, the bounty of the earth made possible by Achelous's waters. According to an alternate tradition, Hercules returned Achelous's horn, and Achelous, in exchange, gave him the horn of Amaltheia, a goat that had provided milk for baby Zeus, and it was this that became the Horn of Plenty.

(See also Achelous [place], Calydon, Castalian Spring [the], Corinth, Deianeira, Delphi, Muses [the], Naiads [the], Nymphs [the], Oceanus, Oeneus, Pirene, Sirens [the], Titans [the], *and* Zeus.)

ADRASTEA The nymph Adrastea (also spelled Adrasteia or Adrastia) inhabited the Dictaean Cave on the island of Crete. The mythographer Apollodorus reports that since Cronus had swallowed all of his children at their birth so as to avoid a prophecy that he would be overpowered by one of his own progeny, Rhea, his consort and sister, went clandestinely to Crete when on the verge of delivering Zeus, her last child by Cronus. There Rhea entrusted her newborn child to Adrastea and her sister Ida, as well as to the Curetes, semi-divine beings who sang and clashed their weapons to hide the baby's cries.

(*See also* Cronus, Curetes [the], Nymphs [the], Rhea, *and* Zeus.)

AEGINA The nymph Aegina was a daughter of Asopus, a Sicyonian river god, and Metope, a daughter of the river Ladon, who together produced two sons and twenty daughters, of whom Aegina was one. The lovely Aegina was carried off by Zeus to the island Oenone, where he bedded her. When Asopus went in search of his daughter, he came to Corinth and learned from Sisyphus, who ultimately received terrible punishment for offering this information, that Aegina's abductor was Zeus. Asopus went in pursuit of the god, who hurled thunderbolts at him and drove him back to his own streams. Meanwhile, Aegina gave birth to a son named Aeacus, and Zeus renamed the island Oenone—now called Aegina—after her.

(*See also* Aeacus, Aegina [place], Corinth, Nymphs [the], Sisyphus, *and* Zeus.)

AEOLUS When Aeolus, "Lord of the Winds," first appeared in the literary tradition, he was a mortal favored by the gods and living on the island of Aeolia with his family. It was there that the hero Odysseus encountered him, according to Homer. In the passage of time, however, Aeolus came to be viewed as a god who controlled all of the winds.

(*See also* Aeolus [hero] *and* Odysseus.)

AESCULAPIUS Aesculapius is a variant spelling of Asclepius, name of the Greek god of healing.

(*See* Asclepius.)

AGLAIA Aglaia (or Aglaea), whose name means "Gleaming One" or "Resplendent One," was one of the three (or more) Charites ("Graces"), who were generally said to be daughters of Zeus and were embodiments of beauty, joy, and grace. Aglaia (or Aglaea) was the youngest of the three Charites and, according to the Greek poets Hesiod and Pindar, was married to the god Hephaestus. This Aglaia is to be distinguished from the mortal Aglaia, who was the mother of the twins Acrisius and Proetus.

(*See also* Acrisius, Aglaia [heroine], Charites [the], Graces [the], Hephaestus, *and* Zeus.)

AIDOS Aidos was a female personification of the Greek *aidos*, which connotes modesty, shame, reverence, and respect for others. The poet Pindar refers to her as a daughter of the second-generation Titan Prometheus and the source of joy and valor. In his description of the devolution of humanity from a virtuous Race of Gold to one of iron that was prone to all manner of vices, the poet Hesiod writes that the age of Iron-Race humans would be marked by the flight of Aidos and Nemesis from the earth so that they might reside instead with the deathless gods. Consequently, bitter sorrows were left for us humans, and there was no remedy for evil.

(*See also* Nemesis, Prometheus, *and* Titans [the].)

ALECTO Alecto (or Allecto), "The Implacable One," was one of the Erinyes, or Furies, as they were known to the Romans. She played a significant role in Virgil's epic the *Aeneid*, where she is described as a denizen of the Underworld "born of Night," a shape-shifter, an instigator of violence and wars, and a creature so awful that she is hated even by her father, Pluto. Under orders from an angry Juno, she caused Queen Amata to fly into a rage and incite the populace of the Italian town of Laurentum to war against Aeneas and his band of Trojans, who had recently arrived in Italy. Amata had already been upset that her husband, Latinus, was considering giving their daughter Lavinia in marriage to Aeneas and not to Turnus, prince of the Italian Rutulians; the queen became more maddened still when Alecto cast a serpent into her breast. Alecto dealt similarly with Turnus, whom she inflamed by hurling a firebrand at him. Turnus consequently marched on Latinus. Alecto next incited the dogs of Ascanius, Aeneas's son, into frenzied pursuit of a prize stag that had been a pet to the maiden Silvia; when Ascanius killed it, Silvia summoned the countryside's farmers to arms against the Italians, Alecto herself broadcasting the call to arms.

(*See also* Aeneas, Amata, Ascanius, Erinyes [the], Furies [the], Juno, Latinus, Lavinia, Pluto, Rutulians [the], Silvia, Turnus, *and* Underworld [the].)

ALPHEUS Alpheus (or Alpheius) was both a river and god of the river Alpheus, which he personified. The Alpheus, the longest and most voluminous river in the Peloponnese, flows through Arcadia and Elis. As a mythological character, Alpheus is best known for his pursuit of the nymph Arethusa from Arcadia all the way to Sicily, where she fled, emerging there as a spring that bears her name.

(*See also* Alpheus River [the], Arcadia, Arethusa, *and* Sicily.)

AMMON Ammon was the Greek iteration of Amun, the chief god of the Egyptians, god of the sun as well as a creator and fertility god. As king of the gods, Ammon became identified with Zeus and was known as Zeus Ammon. It was the oracle of Ammon in Libya that Cepheus, the father of Andromeda, consulted before offering her as a sacrifice to the sea monster that was plaguing his kingdom of Ethiopia. The same oracle reputedly declared Alexander the Great to be the son of Zeus. As regards appearance, Zeus Ammon was represented as a mature, bearded male, like Zeus, but with the ram's horns of Amun.

(*See also* Andromeda, Cepheus, Ethiopia, *and* Zeus.)

AMPHITRITE Amphitrite was a sea goddess whose name was often used as a metonym for the sea. She was said to be a daughter of Tethys and the river Oceanus (an Oceanid), or a Nereid, daughter of the sea god Nereus and the

Oceanid Doris. The mythographer Apollodorus writes that Poseidon married her and that she bore to him both the sea god Triton and Rhode, a personification of the island of Rhodes, an important center of Sun worship. According to the mythographer Hyginus, Amphitrite did not willingly become Poseidon's consort, instead fleeing the god's pursuit to take shelter with Atlas. Poseidon sent a certain Delphinus to plead his cause, a task that he carried out so effectively that the god rewarded him by transforming him into a star. The travel writer Pausanias describes a painting in the Theseion, or Theseus-sanctuary, in Athens that depicted an episode in the life of the Athenian king Theseus: the king Minos of Crete had challenged Theseus to prove that he was Poseidon's son, and threw his signet ring into the sea in the expectation that Theseus would not be able to recover it from the briny depths. But Theseus *did* retrieve the ring and emerged from the waves wearing a golden crown from Amphitrite, further proof of his divine parentage. According to a late, post-classical source, twelfth-century CE Byzantine Greek writer John Tzetzes, it was Amphitrite who turned the once-lovely maiden Scylla into a monster out of jealousy of Poseidon's interest in her.

(*See also* Atlas, Athens, Minos, Nereids [the], Nereus, Oceanids [the], Oceanus, Poseidon, Scylla, Theseus, *and* Triton.)

ANTEROS

Anteros, "Reciprocated Love," was the god of requited love and, as a consequence, he also punished those who scorned love and avenged unrequited love. Anteros, like his brother and companion Cupid (or Eros), was called both the son of Venus alone or, alternatively, of Venus and Mars.

(*See also* Cupid, Mars, *and* Venus.)

APHRODITE

Aphrodite was the Greek goddess of erotic love, sexuality, and beauty. One of the twelve Olympian gods, she was associated with the fertility of humans and animals, the fertility of the soil, and the productiveness of plants. To the Romans she became known as Venus.

There are two accounts of Aphrodite's birth. Homer reports that she was the child of the relatively obscure Titan goddess Dione by Zeus. The poet Hesiod, meanwhile, recounts a very different and dramatic tale of her birth in his *Theogony* (*Origin of the Gods*). Seeking to take vengeance upon his father Uranus for mistreating his mother, Gaia, Cronus castrated him, and Uranus's severed genitalia fell from the heavens into the sea, causing the waters to churn and froth. Reflecting the etymology of her name, which means "gift of the foam," Aphrodite arose fully grown from the waves' froth. Roses were said to have sprung from the sand, suffusing the earth with color, when Aphrodite first stepped ashore, and the Graces offered her branches of fragrant myrtle to hide her nakedness. Some believed that the location where this took place was the island of Cythera, which earned the goddess the title "Cytherean" or "Cytherea." Others, meanwhile, claimed her "birthplace" to have been Cyprus, whence the goddess was also called "Cyprian" or "Cypris."

Aphrodite was one of the most important deities in the Greek pantheon, her worship being extremely widespread in the Greek world. Material evidence of her cult has been found in Northern Greece, especially Thebes; in Attica, both in the city of Athens and in the city's territory; and in Megara and Corinth. It has been found, too, in the Peloponnese—Sicyon, Hermione, Epidaurus, Argos, Arcadia, Elis; in the islands, including Cyprus, Crete, and Cythera; at Greek colonies in Asia Minor; and in other places with close ties to Greece, including Sicily, Italy, Naucratis in Egypt, and Saguntum in Spain. Nonetheless, it was suspected even in antiquity that Aphrodite was not actually native to Greece. While the origins of Aphrodite and her cult are less than clear, it is generally conceded that Cyprus played a significant role in her genesis, likely the result of fusing Greek and Near Eastern influences. Through migrations and trade the region was exposed to new forms of fertility cult from Anatolia and the Levant during the Bronze Age (roughly 2500–1050 BCE): cults of the goddesses Ishtar and Astarte, both descended from the Mesopotamian Inanna. Aphrodite was likely a syncretization of these and, as such, adopted by the Greeks into their pantheon. The early importance of her sanctuaries on the Cyprus and Cythera in particular certainly influenced tales of the goddess's birth.

Being the goddess of love and desire, Aphrodite was not only responsible for the romantic entanglements of numerous gods and mortals but also had a number of love affairs herself. Aphrodite was married to Hephaestus, god of the forge, but in his absence, she repeatedly sought the embrace of Ares, god of war. To the latter she bore Eros, who was known to the Romans as Amor or Cupid; Deimus ("Fear"); Phobus ("Panic"); and Harmonia ("Harmony"), who would later marry Cadmus, king of Thebes. To the god Hermes, whose advances she long rejected, Aphrodite bore Hermaphroditus. By some accounts Aphrodite was also the mother of the fertility deity Priapus by the god Dionysus and of the Sicilian king Eryx by the god Poseidon. Among the best known of her mortal loves was the handsome Adonis, who was the product of an incestuous relationship between the princess Myrrha and her father, King Cinyras of Cyprus. Notably, that relationship was the result of Aphrodite's punishment of the young princess, one of several incidents demonstrating that Aphrodite's gifts were not always a blessing and could, instead, be a formidable punishment.

Those whom the goddess assisted in their amatory pursuits included the heroes Hippomenes, who was smitten with the swift-footed huntress Atalanta; Jason, who so badly needed the help of the sorceress Medea to secure the Golden

PLATE I
Aphrodite: Goddess of fertility and lust, born of sea foam

Fleece; and the Trojan prince Paris, who awarded her the golden apple that in turn earned him the beautiful Helen and thus became the cause of the Trojan War. Aphrodite's victims, on the other hand, included Theseus's son Hippolytus and his stepmother Phaedra, whom Aphrodite caused to fall tragically in love with him; Tyndareus, king of Argos, whose daughters—most infamous of them Clytemnestra, who killed her husband Agamemnon in his bath—all betrayed their husbands; the Cretan queen Pasiphae, who was overcome with lust for a bull; and the women of Lemnos, who would murder their male relatives.

As for Aphrodite's attributes and symbols, these included plants that featured in her mythology: the fragrant rose and myrtle; the apple, a fleshy fruit associated with love and procreation; and the poppy (or poppy anemone), which was the flower that sprang from the blood of Adonis. In the animal kingdom, doves, sparrows, swallows, geese, swans, hares, goats, rams, dolphins, and even tortoises were sacred to her, some being symbols of love or fertility and others being associated with her watery birth.

(*See also* Adonis, Aeneas, Agamemnon, Anchises, Arcadia, Argos, Atalanta, Athens, Cinyras, Clytemnestra, Corinth, Crete, Cronus, Cupid, Cyprus, Dione, Dionysus, Gaia, Graces [the], Harmonia, Helen, Hephaestus, Hermes, Hippolytus, Hippomenes, Jason, Lemnian Women [the], Medea, Megara, Myrrha, Olympus [Mount], Paris, Pasiphae, Phaedra, Priapus, Thebes, Theseus, Titans [the], Troy, Tyndareus, Uranus, Venus, *and* Zeus.)

APOLLO Apollo was the Greek god of prophecy, healing, archery, music, and poetry. By the fifth century BCE, he also became equated with the sun god Helios, whose functions he assumed. While Apollo was one of the most important of the gods and was well established by the time of Homer and Hesiod in the eighth century BCE, his origins are obscure. Among his many names and cult titles were Phoebus, "Bright One," a name that is not well understood; Hekebolos, "He Who Strikes from Afar," which highlights his role as archer-god; Pythian, an allusion to his slaying of the monstrous Python; Hiator ("Healer"); Mousagetes ("Leader of the Muses"), a title underscoring his close ties with the Muses; and Daphnephoros ("Laurel-Bearer"), a reference to the bay laurel, a plant that was sacred to him. Apollo was worshipped throughout Greece, but his sanctuary at Delphi, which was the site of his most important oracle, as well as that on the island of Delos were the most significant.

One of the twelve Greek Olympian gods, he was the son of Zeus and the second-generation Titan goddess Leto. Artemis, goddess of the wild and of hunting, was his twin sister. Apollo and Artemis (but by some accounts, only Apollo) were born on the island of Delos, their mother clutching a palm tree during delivery. It was not Leto, however, who nursed the infant Apollo, but rather the goddess Themis, who fed him ambrosia and nectar. According to the so-called *Homeric Hymn* in his honor, he established his oracle at Delphi upon slaying the serpent Python that resided there. The god had many loves and many children. Those who spurned his advances were the nymph Daphne and the Trojan princess Cassandra. Daphne became a laurel tree in order to escape him, but he remained devoted to her, designating laurel as his most sacred plant. As for Cassandra, she had been offered the gift of prophecy in exchange for accepting the god's affection, but when she rejected him, he ensured that although she could foretell the future, nobody would believe her. His best-known children were Asclepius, to whom he taught the art of healing, as well as the divine bards Orpheus and Linus. As was usual in the Greek world, Apollo had both male and female love interests, his notable attachments having been to Hyacinth, whom he accidentally killed with a discus, and to Cyparissus, who pined away in grief over the death of his beloved deer. Apollo allowed Cyparissus to grieve forever by transforming him into a cypress, the tree of mourning. Where Hyacinth died, there grew the flower that thereafter bears his name. Those who incurred Apollo's wrath included the Satyr Marsyas and Pan, both of whom challenged the god to music contests. Marsyas himself suffered a terrible punishment, but in the case of the contest with Pan, it was Midas, the judge, who was punished. The Trojans, too, were subjected to Apollo's enmity during the Trojan War because their earlier king Laomedon had failed to pay the god for building the city's walls. The Thessalian king Admetus, on the other hand, enjoyed Apollo's favor, for he had treated the god with kindness when, as punishment for slaying the Cyclopes, Zeus made him Admetus's indentured servant.

Apollo's cult was introduced to Rome by the fifth century BCE at the incidence of a plague, and he was accordingly called upon specifically as a healer. Although his mythology was certainly known and exploited by Roman authors and artists, healing remained his main cultic function in the Roman world. While Apollo was ultimately overshadowed by Asclepius as healer, he assumed particular importance during the age of Augustus, since the emperor adopted him as his personal deity.

In terms of identifying characteristics, Apollo was represented as youthful, athletic, and unbearded. The lyre and cithara were his favored instruments, and his weapons of choice were the bow and arrow. His sacred trees were above all the bay laurel and palm but also cypress.

(*See also* Admetus, Artemis, Asclepius, Cassandra, Cyclopes [the], Cyparissus, Daphne, Delos, Delphi, Helios, Hyacinth, Laomedon, Leto, Linus, Marsyas, Midas, Muses [the], Orpheus, Pan, Python, Rome, Satyrs [the], Thessaly, Titans [the], Troy, *and* Zeus.)

AQUILO Aquilo is the Romans' name for the Greek god Boreas, the personified north wind. His best-known exploits include the abduction of the Athenian princess Orithyia and the near-destruction of the Trojan Aeneas's ships at the behest of an angry Juno, who had bribed the winds' lord Aeolus to help her.

(*See also* Aeneas, Aeolus, Athens, Boreas, Juno, Orithyia, *and* Troy.)

ARES Ares was the Greek god of war and, as such, was associated with the violence of war, bloodlust, panic, and the screams of the dying. He was attended by Phobos ("Fear") and Deimos ("Dread"), two of his children, according to the Greek poet Hesiod. Athena, too, was a war deity, but of a different sort: her particular realm was defensive war waged in the interest of safeguarding the city. Accordingly, Ares was feared as well as revered and had a limited presence in religion and cult in comparison with his siblings. One of the twelve Olympian gods, Ares was the son of Zeus and Hera. He himself fathered a number of children with a variety of partners. His most famous liaison was with the goddess Aphrodite, wife of Hephaestus, who used his skills as god of the forge in order to trap the lovers while in bed. With Aphrodite, he reputedly became father not only to Deimos and Phobos but also to Eros ("Love"), Anteros ("Requited Love"), and Harmonia ("Harmony"). His other children included the warlike Cycnus, the Thracian Diomedes, the godless Tereus, the Amazon Penthesileia, and Parthenopaeus, one of the Seven Against Thebes.

As for artistic representations of Ares, these are relatively few, and, logically, he is shown armed with helmet, shield, and sword or spear. In the Roman world, Ares was identified with the Italian war god Mars.

(*See also* Amazons [the], Anteros, Aphrodite, Athena, Cycnus, Diomedes, Eros, Hera, Mars, Olympus [Mount], Parthenopaeus, Penthesileia, Seven Against Thebes [the], Tereus, *and* Zeus.)

ARETHUSA Arethusa was a nymph who would give her name to a spring on the island of Ortygia in the Sicilian harbor of Syracuse. While there were in reality a number of springs and nymphs by this name, it is the Sicilian Arethusa whose mythology is best known; her dramatic tale is vividly told by the Roman poet Ovid. The exceedingly lovely Arethusa was born in Arcadia and spent her days at the hunt. One hot day on her way home, she decided to refresh herself in the streams of the river Alpheus. When the river's god, Alpheus, saw her, he desired her fervently. Arethusa leaped out of the water and ran, and Alpheus ran in pursuit. At last, when she was exhausted, Arethusa cried out to the goddess Artemis for help, and the goddess obliged, surrounding her in a mist. Then, suddenly, she became liquid—a stream of water—and the river found her in this new form; changing his shape from that of a human to a river, he tried to mingle his waters with hers. Now Artemis caused the earth to split, and Arethusa dove through the crack to re-emerge in Sicily. Even there, however, Alpheus found her, plunging under the earth's surface after her.

(*See also* Alpheus [god and place], Artemis, Nymphs [the], *and* Sicily.)

ARISTAEUS Aristaeus was a rustic deity credited with instructing humans in agricultural pursuits. The Greek poet Apollonius of Rhodes writes that he was the son of the shepherdess Cyrene, who was abducted and impregnated by Apollo. The god rewarded her by transforming her into a nymph and making her immortal. Apollo then took the baby Aristaeus to be reared by the wise Centaur Chiron. When he was grown, the Muses found him a bride, taught him in his father's arts of healing and prophecy, and made him shepherd of their extensive flocks. In Virgil's *Georgics*, he is presented as a practitioner of agriculture, viticulture, and the keeping of bees (apiculture) whose bees have suddenly and inexplicably died. When this occurred, Aristaeus went to his mother's spring, the spring Cyrene that feeds the Peneus River, to ask for her assistance. She instructed him to seek out the changeable sea deity Proteus, and Aristaeus learned from him that the bees' death had been caused by Orpheus and the Dryad sisters of the nymph Eurydice, whose death he had inadvertently caused. Cyrene then told her son that he must make sacrifice to the nymphs, Orpheus, and Eurydice in atonement. Then, from the carcasses of the sacrificed oxen there emerged bees that repopulated Aristaeus's hives.

Aristaeus was also named as the father of Actaeon by the Theban king Cadmus's daughter Autonoe, and according to the poet Pindar, it was the Horai ("Hours") and Gaia who made him immortal.

(*See also* Actaeon, Apollo, Autonoe, Cadmus, Centaurs [the], Chiron, Cyrene [heroine], Dryads [the], Eurydice, Gaia, Muses [the], Orpheus, Peneus, Proteus, *and* Thebes.)

ARTEMIS Artemis was the Greek goddess of the wild, residing in the mountains and glens where she kept the company of Nymphs. She was a huntress, a protector of animals and also of hunters, who were fully aware that they were taking lives of other creatures in order to sustain their own, their activities requiring thanks to animal and goddess alike. Artemis, who was one of the twelve Olympian gods, also presided over childbirth among animals and humans, protecting birthing mothers and also their offspring. At the same time, she could bring sudden death during childbirth with her golden arrows. While herself a virgin, she was a goddess of transitions, presiding over rites of passage to adulthood for young women but also young men. Insofar as their powers and realms of influence overlapped, especially with respect to childbirth, the Greek goddesses Eileithyia, Hecate, and Selene became identified with her, as did the Roman goddess Diana, who adopted Artemis's mythology.

Artemis was a daughter of Zeus and the second-generation Titan goddess Leto, whose pregnancy Hera cruelly extended in jealousy of Zeus's affair with her. By some accounts, both Artemis and her twin brother, Apollo, were born on the island of Delos, where Leto clung to a palm tree while giving birth. According to the Roman historian Tacitus, however, Artemis was born in a cypress grove at Ortygia near Ephesus, which would become an important site of her worship and the location of a temple built in her honor that was considered one of the Seven Wonders of the ancient world. Other authors, meanwhile, cite Crete as her birthplace. As for the historical origin of this goddess, this is less than clear. There is some evidence to suggest that she may have been an import to Greece from Anatolia, but in any event, she was known since the Bronze Age, a period extending from circa 3000 to 1150 BCE. Sanctuaries of Artemis could be found throughout the Greek world, some of the most prominent being at Brauron in the territory of Athens and at Sparta: the first was the site of initiation ceremonies for young girls, who dressed as bears, and the second was linked with the ritualized process by which Spartan boys became warriors and citizens.

The many mythological tales involving Artemis featured various aspects of her complex persona. She and her brother, Apollo, armed with bow and arrows, avenged their mother when the Lydian princess Niobe boasted that, on the grounds that she had more children than Leto, she was more deserving of worship than that goddess. Artemis's other victims included the hunter Actaeon, whose hunting dogs she turned upon him in consequence of his catching sight of her naked. According to the mythographer Hyginus, it was not Hera but Artemis who transformed her companion Callisto into a bear as punishment for becoming pregnant by Zeus, although the pregnancy was the result of rape. The hunter Orion she killed for challenging her at quoits (ring toss), and with Apollo, she set upon Tityus for his unwanted pursuit of their mother. Her best-known devotee was the chaste but tragically flawed Hippolytus, son of the Amazon queen Hippolyta, and she demanded the sacrifice of Agamemnon's daughter Iphigeneia in compensation for that king's killing of a deer sacred to her. By some accounts, Iphigeneia met her end on Artemis's altar, but by others, the goddess saved her, bringing her to the barbarian land of the Taurians, where she became Artemis's priestess, being tasked with preparing the victims of human sacrifice.

As for distinguishing attributes, Artemis was represented in Greek art as armed with a bow, quiver, and arrows. She sometimes also, like Hecate and Eileithyia, carries a torch or torches. All animals were sacred to her, but deer, bear, and boar especially. As was the case with her brother, Apollo, the palm and cypress were among her most sacred plants.

(*See also* Actaeon, Agamemnon, Amazons [the], Apollo, Athens, Callisto, Delos, Diana, Eileithyia, Hecate, Hera, Hippolyta, Hippolytus, Iphigeneia, Leto, Niobe, Olympus [Mount], Orion, Ortygia, Selene, Sparta, Taurians [the], Titans [the], Tityus, *and* Zeus.)

ASCLEPIUS

Asclepius (or Aesculapius) was a son of Apollo and a healing hero who became divinized, thus being known more generally as god of healing and medicine. According to the Greek poet Hesiod, his mother was a mortal woman named Arsinoe, a daughter of Leucippus, but the more usual tale of his origins names his mother as Coronis, daughter of the Thessalian Phlegyas. Of his birth there are also several versions. Either Coronis gave birth to Asclepius while in Epidaurus with her father, who was unaware of her pregnancy, and exposed the infant in the wild. There Asclepius was suckled by goats and guarded by the dog of a herdsman who later came upon him. As lightning flashed from the child upon his approach, the terrified herdsman left him where he lay. Alternatively, the pregnant Coronis took a mortal lover, and an enraged Apollo (or his sister Artemis) killed her. However, Hermes was instructed to snatch the baby from his mother's womb as her body lay on the lit funeral pyre. Asclepius was given to the noble Centaur Chiron to rear and educate in the arts of healing. The mythographer Apollodorus writes that Asclepius became so skilled in his profession that he not only saved lives but even revived the dead by use of Gorgon's blood given him by Athena. Hyginus offers a different account of Asclepius's ability to raise the dead, a tale also told of the seer Polyidos: when Asclepius was ordered to restore Glaucus, son of Minos, to life and was considering what to do, a snake wound its way up the staff that he was holding. Asclepius killed the snake, but soon afterward another snake appeared, this one with an herb in its mouth, which it placed on the head of its deceased mate. Both snakes then fled the place, and Asclepius used the same herb on Glaucus to bring him back to life. Fearing that the distinction between the immortal gods and mortal humans would forever be compromised, Zeus struck Asclepius with a thunderbolt, and an angry Apollo killed the Cyclopes, makers of the thunderbolts, for which vengeful crime he was required to be servant to a mortal, Admetus, for a year. Asclepius, for his part, was placed by Zeus among the stars at Apollo's request.

While the most important center of Asclepius's worship was Epidaurus in the northeastern Peloponnese, his sanctuaries—the so-called Asclepeia, forerunners to modern hospitals, to which people made pilgrimages in order to be healed—could be found throughout the Greek world and beyond; in Rome the worship of Asclepius was introduced from Epidaurus in 293 BCE in order to avert the plague. What was unique about Asclepius and his worship was the relative uniformity of the layout of his sanctuaries and the rituals practiced therein. The sanctuaries, which comprised a temple, an altar, and a dormitory, tended to lie outside settlements and close to sources of water. Asclepius's sacred animals, snakes and dogs, were kept in Asclepeia, and goats, sacred to the god insofar as they nursed him while a baby, could not be sacrificed, nor could goat meat be consumed in the sanctuaries' confines. The actual "healing" took place during incubation, while the patients were lying down and asleep. Asclepius, or one of his representatives, would appear to patients in a dream and either perform cures or communicate remedies for their ailments. As for representations of Asclepius, he was generally shown wearing a long mantle and holding a snake-entwined staff.

(*See also* Admetus, Apollo, Arsinoe, Athena, Centaurs [the], Chiron, Coronis, Cyclopes [the], Gorgons [the], Hermes, Leucippus, Minos, Polyidos, Thessaly, *and* Zeus.)

ASTRAEA Astraea (or Astraia) was a personification of Justice, who became the constellation Virgo, according to the *Phaenomena* (*Celestial Phenomena*) of Aratus and Roman authors influenced by this work on the constellations. Astraea was thus acknowledged as both Virgo and Dike (Justice), and she was variously known as the daughter of the second-generation Titan god Astraeus with Eos, goddess of the dawn, and as daughter of Zeus with Themis ("Sacred Law"). For the Roman authors Ovid, Hyginus, and others, Astraea departed the earth for the heavens in horror when humans became a wicked Race of Iron in the course of their devolution from a Race of Gold, then of silver, and subsequently of bronze.

(*See also* Dike, Eos, Themis, *and* Zeus.)

ATE Ate was a feminized personification of reckless folly. According to the poet Hesiod, she was the daughter of Eris, "Strife," and Homer calls her a daughter of Zeus. The goddess has no mythology to speak of but was invoked in numerous sagas as the cause of a given character's wildly imprudent or delusional and ruinous actions. These characters include the Mycenaean king Agamemnon, who blamed Ate for his decision to take the lovely Briseis from Achilles, which deed caused the latter to withdraw from fighting at a critical point in the Trojan War; Agamemnon's wife, Clytemnestra, who counted folly as one of the reasons why she murdered her husband; and Orestes and Electra, who recklessly killed their mother in vengeance for their father's death.

(*See also* Achilles, Agamemnon, Briseis, Clytemnestra, Electra [heroine], Eris, Mycenae, Orestes, *and* Zeus.)

ATHENA Athena was the Greek goddess of war, wisdom, and crafts, and she was the protectress of cities, especially Athens. As a war goddess, her character was very different from that of Ares, who represented aggression and the violence of war. Athena, by contrast, was the goddess of wars that were defensive, necessary, and not waged on impulse. As patroness of crafts and craftspeople, she had particularly strong associations with women's crafts of spinning and weaving, but her oversight of crafts extended to carpentry and metalworking, overlapping in this regard with Hephaestus, with whom she was linked in cult. Prominent among her numerous cult titles were Ergane ("Craftswoman" or "Maker"), Nike ("Victorious"), Promachos ("Who Fights in the Front Lines"), Polias or Poliouchos ("Protectress of Cities"), and Parthenos ("Maiden"), in which guise she was housed in the Athenian Parthenon. Athena was also often called "Pallas Athena" or simply "Pallas," a name that ancient authors derived from a close companion of the goddess whom she accidentally killed or a giant whom she killed on purpose. As for the origins of Athena and of her name, there is no consensus, though it appears that an early form of her name was known in Greece in the Bronze Age, the period extending from roughly 3000 to 1150 BCE. It is also not known whether the name of Athens, the city most sacred to her, predated her own.

Regarding Athena's mythology, she was the daughter of Zeus and his first wife, Metis, a personification of wisdom. As the Greek poet Hesiod recounts, Zeus swallowed Metis when she was about to give birth, for he had learned from the gods Gaia and Uranus that she was destined to bear children who would threaten his position as king of the gods: first a wise and mighty daughter and then a bold and strong son. In due course, Zeus developed a terrible headache and requested the assistance of Hephaestus, who struck his head with an axe. From the cleft in his skull sprang Athena, fully grown and fully armed. Athena remained unmarried and a virgin, but she did become the foster mother of the legendary Athenian king Erichthonius, the snake-man born from semen spilled on the earth when Hephaestus attempted to rape her. A number of heroes enjoyed her support and protection, among them Perseus, to whom she gave a polished shield with which he could locate Medusa without having to look at her directly. In thanks for helping him, Perseus gave her Medusa's head, which she fixed to her breastplate. The clever Odysseus, too, was a favorite of hers, for, as Homer writes, of all humans, he was the closest to her in terms of mental acuity. Athena was also a defender of the Mycenaean prince Orestes, acquitting him of matricide. Those who came to feel the full brunt of the goddess's anger included Arachne, the skilled weaver who arrogantly claimed to be more talented than the goddess, her teacher. And although their city contained one of her sanctuaries, Athena hated the Trojans, for she, like the goddess Hera, remained angry over the Trojan prince Paris's judgment of Aphrodite as the fairest of the three goddesses.

The most important myth involving Athena, apart from the tale of her miraculous birth, was the account of her contest with Poseidon for patronage of Athens. Poseidon struck the Acropolis with his trident to produce a saltwater spring, a symbol of naval power, and Athena produced an olive tree. The goddess won this contest, as the olive, which became a mainstay of the Athenian economy, was judged the more valuable gift.

As for Athena's attributes, she was depicted armed, wearing a helmet as well as a snake-fringed breastplate, the so-called *aegis* ("goatskin") that had the head of Medusa affixed to it, and carrying a shield and lance or spear. Animals sacred to her were the snake and owl, a symbol of wisdom, and her most sacred plant was the olive.

The Romans equated their goddess Minerva with Athena.

(*See also* Acropolis [the], Aphrodite, Arachne, Athens, Erichthonius, Gaia, Hephaestus, Medusa, Metis, Minerva, Mycenae, Odysseus, Orestes, Pallas, Paris, Perseus, Poseidon, Troy, Uranus, *and* Zeus.)

ATLAS Atlas was a second-generation Titan god, from a patrilineal perspective. He was the child of the first-generation Titan Iapetus and Clymene, a daughter of Iapetus's brother Oceanus (an Oceanid). With his Oceanid aunt Pleione he sired the Pleiades, the Hyades (whose mother is also named as Aethra, another Oceanid), and Calypso. With Hesperis, daughter of the Evening Star Hesper, he produced the Hesperides. Atlas's brothers were Prometheus, Epimetheus, and Menoetius.

The mythographer Hyginus reports that as a consequence of his leadership role in the power struggle between the Olympian gods and the Titans, Zeus punished him by placing the heavens on his shoulders. Atlas was said to live by the garden of the Hesperides, on the westernmost shores of the river Oceanus, in Libya, or in the distant North (or East), where the Hyperboreans resided.

Hercules enlisted Atlas's assistance when he went to fetch the apples of the Hesperides: Hercules asked Atlas to retrieve the apples in exchange for giving Atlas a break from holding up the heavens by shouldering the burden himself. But Atlas, apples in hand, attempted to protract the reprieve from his onerous task by offering then to deliver the apples to Eurystheus, at whose behest Hercules was performing the task. Hercules tricked him into taking the heavens back by asking him to hold up the burden momentarily while he looked for a pillow to cushion his shoulders. Needless to say, Hercules did not resume the burden. Atlas also played a role in the saga of the hero Perseus. As retribution for not having offered him hospitality, Perseus, holding up Medusa's severed head, transformed Atlas into the mountains that still bear his name.

(*See also* Calypso, Clymene, Epimetheus, Eurystheus, Hercules, Hesper, Hesperides [the], Hyades [the], Hyperboreans [the], Oceanids [the], Oceanus [place], Perseus, Pleiades [the], Prometheus, *and* Titans [the].)

ATROPOS   Atropos, the "Unturnable One," was one of the three Fates, or Moirae, goddesses that portioned out or allotted a person's destiny. As Atropos's name suggests, it was generally the case that the Fates' determination could not be altered once they had spun and cut the thread of an individual's life.

(*See also* Fates [the] *and* Moirae [the].)

AURORA   Aurora is the Roman name for Eos, goddess of the dawn.

(*See* Eos.)

AUSTER   Auster was the Roman equivalent of Notus (or Notos), the south wind.

(*See* Notus.)

BACCHUS   Bacchus was another name for the god Dionysus. This name was originally used as a title or descriptor of Dionysus, with particular reference to his being a god inducing ecstatic frenzy. The name Bacchus could also be used to designate a male worshipper of Dionysus who was in such an ecstatic state or was an initiate of the mysteries of the god, however. Similarly, Bacchantes were celebrants of the god.

(*See also* Bacchantes [the] *and* Dionysus.)

BELLONA   Bellona, whose name was derived from *bellum*, the Latin word for war, was the Roman goddess of war and was identified with the Greek war goddess Enyo. Representations of her in art show her wearing a helmet. Her other attributes include a shield, a sword or spear, and a trumpet, with which to sound the call to battle, as well as Gorgon-like snake-hair. Because she personified the destructive aspects of war, her temple "in" Rome was located outside the city's *pomerium*, its religious and legal boundary.

(*See also* Enyo *and* Gorgons [the].)

BOREAS Boreas was the personification of the north wind and the deity of that wind. He, along with Notus, the south wind, and Zephyr, the west wind, were children of Eos, goddess of the dawn, and Astraeus, a second-generation Titan. His home, according to the Greek poet Pindar, was beyond the land of the Hyperboreans, who were untouched by his frozen, wintry breath. Boreas's bride, whom he abducted as she was gathering flowers by the Ilissus River, was Orithyia, daughter of the legendary Athenian king Erechtheus. With her he became father to twin sons, Zetes and Calais, who would accompany Jason and the Argonauts on their quest for the Golden Fleece, and to two daughters, Chione and Cleopatra. His children collectively were known as Boreads.

Boreas and his brothers were depicted as winged and sometimes even as horses. Indeed, there were legends to the effect that Boreas and his siblings sired particularly swift horses. Among them were colts born to the mares of the Trojan king Erichthonius. The Romans identified Boreas as Aquilo.

(*See also* Aquilo, Argonauts [the], Athens, Erechtheus, Erichthonius, Hyperboreans [the], Ilissus River [the], Jason, Notus, Orithyia, Troy, Zephyr, *and* Zetes.)

BROMIUS Bromius (or Bromios) was a name used for Dionysus and is translated as the "Thunderer" or "Loud/Boisterous One." This name describes the loud and boisterous nature of the god's worship, which involved ecstatic dancing and ritual shouting. This title is also a nod to the thundering Zeus, Dionysus's father, and, at the same time, to the fact that Dionysus could change his shape at will into that of a roaring beast, among others.

(*See also* Dionysus *and* Zeus.)

CALLIOPE Calliope, the "Beautiful-Voiced" goddess, was one of the Muses and was sometimes described as their leader. She became known as the Muse of epic poetry but was also considered a patroness of poetry more generally. According to the mythographer Apollodorus, Calliope bore two sons to the Thracian king Oeagrus (or to Apollo): the famed musician Linus, whom his pupil Hercules killed, and another son, Orpheus, who with his music could move trees and stones. Even Homer was called her son, though likely in a symbolic sense.

(*See also* Apollo, Hercules, Linus, Muses [the], Orpheus, *and* Thrace.)

CALYPSO Calypso, whose name means "I will hide you," was, according to Homer in his *Odyssey*, a goddess and a daughter of the second-generation Titan Atlas. Calypso was a nature or earth goddess who lived in a cave surrounded by luxurious vegetation: trees, burgeoning vines, and thick meadows. By the time Odysseus arrived on her island of Ogygia, he was alone, his ships having been destroyed and all his companions lost. The goddess loved and cared for him for seven years and offered to make him immortal, but Odysseus missed his wife and home. While Calypso was nurturing, she also posed a threat to Odysseus and his homecoming, which was intimated by the presence of particular species of plants and animals surrounding her cave: black poplars, alders, cypresses, violets, owls, gulls, and hawks, all mentioned by Homer, had symbolic associations with death. Knowing the threat Calypso posed, the goddess Athena prevailed on Zeus to send Hermes to convince Calypso to release Odysseus. This she did and, with her perhaps surprising knowledge of technology, assisted him in making a raft.

(*See also* Athena, Atlas, Hermes, Odysseus, Titans [the], *and* Zeus.)

CAMENAE, THE
The Camenae were four (or three) Roman goddesses who became identified with the Greek Muses, goddesses presiding over the sciences, poetry, and the arts. The nymph or goddess Egeria was sometimes included in their number. According to the ancient biographer Plutarch, the legendary second king of Rome, Numa Pompilius, established a sacred grove for them in Rome and also declared as holy the spring that watered this location, designating use of its waters by the Vestal Virgins (priestesses of Vesta) for the purpose of purifying their temple.

(*See also* Egeria, Muses [the], Numa, Nymphs [the], *and* Vesta.)

CASTOR
Castor (or Kastor) and his brother Pollux (or Polydeuces) were known as the Dioscuri, twin "Sons of Zeus." According to some Classical sources, Castor's father was actually the Spartan king Tyndareus while Pollux's was Zeus, both of whom had lain with Leda, queen of Sparta, on the same day. While both brothers were associated with horses, it was Castor who was called an expert horseman and a tamer of horses by the Greek poet Alcman. His brother, by contrast, excelled at boxing. Following a number of adventures, the twins were transformed into stars central to the constellation Gemini.

(*See also* Dioscuri [the], Gemini, Leda, Pollux, Sparta, Tyndareus, *and* Zeus.)

CEPHISSUS
Cephissus was the name both of several rivers in Greece and of the gods of those rivers, one in Boeotia, two in the territory of Athens, and one in the territory of Argos. The deity personifying the Boeotian Cephissus was said to be the father of the lovely youth Narcissus, who pined away out of love for himself. The deity of the Argive Cephissus, for his part, was reputedly one of the judges in the contest between Hera and Poseidon for patronage of Argos, a contest in which Hera prevailed.

(*See also* Argos, Athens, Boeotia, Cephissus River [the], Hera, Narcissus, *and* Poseidon.)

CERES Ceres, whose name could be used as a word for grain or bread, was an ancient Italian goddess of agriculture upon whom the growth of crops depended. Her origins are obscure, but early on, she became identified with the Greek goddess Demeter, to whom she was inherently similar and whose mythology she assumed. In Roman cult, Ceres was associated with Liber, the ancient Italian god of fertility and wine who was the Roman counterpart of Dionysus, and with Tellus, the Roman goddess Earth.

(*See* Demeter, Dionysus, *and* Liber.)

CHAOS In his *Theogony* (*Origin of the Gods*), the earliest surviving account of the origin of the Greek gods, the poet Hesiod writes that Chaos, a great Void, was first to come into being, followed by Gaia, the Earth; Tartarus, the earth's deepest recess; and Eros, Desire. Thereafter, the Darkness of Erebus and Night came to being from the elemental Chaos, and Night then gave rise to Aether, the bright upper atmosphere, and Day, both of whom she conceived by lying in love with Erebus. Gaia, for her part, first bore Uranus (or Ouranos), the Heavens, and then the mountains (Ourea) and sea (Pontus) that "shaped" her physically. Gaia and Uranus then produced several groups of children between them, and so on. This theogony is clearly also a cosmogony, an account of the origins of the universe and its components; the first deities to come into being are elemental, but they are also to some degree personified, with personification increasing the narrative progresses.

(*See also* Erebus, Eros, Gaia, Tartarus, *and* Uranus.)

CHARITES, THE The Graces, goddesses embodying beauty, joy, and grace, were called Charites ("Graces") by the Greeks. According to the poet Hesiod, they were the children of Zeus and the lovely Eurynome, a daughter of Oceanus, and their names were Aglaia ("The Resplendent One"), Euphrosyne ("Good Cheer"), and Thalia ("Blooming One").

(*See also* Graces [the], Oceanus [god], *and* Zeus.)

CHARON In Greco-Roman mythology, Charon was the ferryman of the dead. He conveyed those who were deceased and had received proper burial across the river Acheron (or Styx) in his skiff and thus from the world of the living to the Underworld. The god Hermes was responsible for leading the souls of the dead to the Acheron's banks, where they were met by Charon. The fare of an obol (an ancient Greek coin having the equivalent weight of a cooking spit) secured passage across the river, and for this reason the dead were buried with a coin in their mouths. Only a few had been able to persuade Charon to ferry them into the land of the dead while alive: the heroes Theseus, Pirithous, Hercules, and Aeneas. The most vivid description of Charon is the poet Virgil's in the *Aeneid*, where he is grim, aged, fearsome, and squalid, having a matted beard, a filthy mantle, and eyes that blaze like fire.

It is thought that Charon, a minor deity, was originally a personification of death. Interestingly, he was honored in cult as a healing deity, according to the geographer Strabo.

(*See also* Acheron [the River], Aeneas, Hercules, Hermes, Pirithous, Styx [the River], Theseus, *and* Underworld [the].)

CIRCE

Circe was a goddess possessing a sorceress's powers. She is described by Homer as the sister of Aeetes, king of the barbarian people of Colchis, and the daughter of the sun god Helios and Perse, a daughter of Oceanus. Circe lived on the island of Aeaea in a house built of well-polished stone. Her companions were nymphs as well as wolves and lions that she had enchanted. She entertained those of Odysseus's men who had been sent to explore her island, offering them drugged wine. When she then struck them with her wand, they turned into swine, a transformation that Odysseus was later able to compel her to reverse. Odysseus himself escaped transformation only because the god Hermes had supplied him with an herb, moly, that served as an antidote to Circe's potion, which he, too, was served. Odysseus and his men stayed with Circe for a year, at which point she instructed the hero to travel to the land of the dead at the ends of the earth, there to consult the seer Teiresias about how to achieve his homecoming. By Odysseus, Circe became the mother of Telegonus (or Nausithous, Agrius, and Latinus), according to post-Homeric traditions.

Other heroes or mythological figures who had encounters with Circe included the sea god Glaucus, who wanted to obtain a love potion from her but whose love interest, Scylla, Circe turned into a monster out of jealousy. Circe also featured in tales surrounding her niece Medea, who, accompanied by the hero Jason, visited her in hopes (ultimately unrealized) of being purified of the murder of Apsyrtus, Medea's brother.

(*See also* Aeaea, Aeetes, Apsyrtus, Colchis, Glaucus, Helios, Hermes, Jason, Medea, Oceanus [god], Odysseus, Scylla, *and* Teiresias.)

CLIO Clio (or Cleio), "The Praiser," was one of the nine Muses, patron goddesses of literature and the arts. Clio's particular realm of influence was rhetoric and history, especially works that recounted noteworthy deeds of persons and achievements or initiatives of towns. The mythographer Apollodorus records a disturbing episode in which Clio mocked Aphrodite for her infatuation with Adonis. Aphrodite punished Clio by causing her to fall in love with Pierus, to whom she bore the handsome Hyacinth, who in turn was loved by the bard Thamyris and Apollo, and met a tragic end.

(*See also* Adonis, Aphrodite, Hyacinth, Muses [the], Pierus, *and* Thamyris.)

CLOTHO Clotho, "The Spinner," was one of the three Moirae, or Fates. What Clotho spun was the "thread of life" that she and her sisters subsequently measured and cut to a determined length.

(*See also* Fates [the] *and* Moirae [the].)

CLYMENE The best-known Clymene in the extant body of Classical myth was an Oceanid (daughter of Oceanus) and a second-generation Titan, as she was born of Oceanus and Tethys, who were first-generation Titan gods. The Greek poet Hesiod calls her the mother of Atlas, Epimetheus, and Prometheus; and according to the Roman poet Ovid, she was mother to the tragic figure Phaethon by Helios (Apollo in the guise of sun god).

(*See also* Apollo, Atlas, Epimetheus, Helios, Oceanids [the], Oceanus, Phaethon, Prometheus, Tethys, *and* Titans [the].)

COEUS Coeus was one of the Titans, a group of twelve gods born to Gaia ("Earth") and Uranus ("Heaven"). He was known primarily as joining with his sister Phoebe to produce the second-generation Titan goddesses Asteria ("the Starry One"), future mother of Hecate, and Leto, who in turn would become mother to the divine twins Apollo and Artemis.

(*See also* Apollo, Artemis, Gaia, Hecate, Leto, Phoebe, *and* Uranus.)

CORA Cora (or Kora and Kore), translated as "The Maiden," was a name or title used for Persephone, daughter of the harvest goddess, Demeter.

(*See also* Demeter *and* Persephone.)

CORYBANTES, THE The Corybantes were divine beings who became confused and conflated with the Curetes. They were variously said to be children of the Muse Thalia with Apollo, as according to the Greek poet Hesiod; sons of Helios and Athena; of Zeus and the Muse Calliope; or of

Cronus and Rhea. The Corybantes were priests and attendants of the Phyrgian Great Mother Goddess Cybele, whom they worshiped in orgiastic dance, and it was due to the identification of Cybele with Rhea that the Corybantes in turn became identified with the Curetes. As the Curetes had been guardians of the infant Zeus, so the Corybantes were said to have been guardians of the infant Dionysus.

(*See also* Apollo, Athena, Calliope, Cronus, Curetes [the], Cybele, Dionysus, Helios, Muses [the], Rhea, Thalia, *and* Zeus.)

CRONUS

Cronus (or Kronos) was a son of the primeval elemental deities Gaia ("Earth") and Uranus ("Heaven"), whose children were the twelve Titan gods, of whom Cronus was the youngest, as well as the monstrous Hecatoncheires ("Hundred-Handers") and Cyclopes. Uranus hated his malformed offspring and pressed them back into their mother, causing her much suffering. According to the Greek poet Hesiod in his account of the origins of the gods, Gaia asked her remaining children for help, but only Cronus was willing. She supplied him with a sickle of adamant as a weapon, and at nightfall, when Uranus came to lie with Gaia, Cronus ambushed and castrated him. Uranus's severed genitals yielded Aphrodite and the Erinyes, spirits of vengeance. Cronus dethroned his father and became king of the gods. Largely following Hesiod, the mythographer Apollodorus writes that after releasing the Cyclopes and Hecatoncheires, Cronus again imprisoned them in the earth, deep in Tartarus, and took his sister Rhea as wife. From his parents he learned that he, in turn, would be dethroned by one of his children, and, as a consequence, he swallowed each of them as they were born, apart from Zeus, whom Rhea saved by giving Cronus a stone wrapped in swaddling clothes to swallow instead. A decade-long battle between the older-generation Titan gods and Zeus and his siblings, the so-called Olympian gods, raged until Zeus, with the aid of the Cyclopes and Hecatoncheires, prevailed. The Titans were then imprisoned in Tartarus, and Zeus became king of the gods.

According to a different poem attributed to Hesiod, the *Works and Days*, a golden race of mortals inhabited the earth while Cronus was king of the gods, and this golden race would later be replaced by a race of silver and then races of bronze and iron—the current, sinful race. The reign of Cronus thus became viewed as a Golden Age, a notion that appears also in Roman myths of Saturn, Cronus's Roman equivalent. An additional detail about Cronus is added by Plato, who presents the dethroned Cronus as a later king of Elysium.

(*See also* Aphrodite, Cyclopes [the], Elysium, Erinyes [the], Gaia, Hecatoncheires [the], Olympus [Mount], Rhea, Saturn, Tartarus, Titans [the], Uranus, *and* Zeus.)

CUPID Cupid was the Roman name for the Greek god of love, Eros. As in the case of Eros, he was a personification of desire, which in Latin is *cupído*.

(*See also* Eros.)

CURETES, THE According to the Greek historian Diodorus Siculus, the Curetes were divine beings, nine in number. By some accounts, they were born of the earth, and they lived in mountainous, thickly wooded places that offered them good shelter. They taught humankind animal husbandry, beekeeping, hunting, and communal living, all being arts that they discovered. They were also said to have invented swords and helmets, with which they danced and made noise when they were entrusted by Rhea with the safekeeping of the infant Zeus either on Mount Ida or Mount Dicte on Crete. The Curetes became confused and conflated with the Corybantes, attendants of the goddess Cybele.

These divine Curetes are to be distinguished from the people of the same name who became embroiled with the hero Meleager in the course of the hunt for the Calydonian Boar.

(*See also* Corybantes [the], Crete, Ida [Mount], Cybele, Meleager, Rhea, *and* Zeus.)

CYBELE Cybele, who was also called the Great Mother (*Meter Megale* in Greek, and *Magna Mater* in Latin), was a western-Asiatic fertility goddess whose wide-ranging powers and realms of influence included healing, prophecy, and the protection of settlements and cities. Acknowledged by the Greeks and Romans as a foreign deity, she was introduced to Greece by at least the sixth century BCE from Phrygia, but her roots extended deeper still: to Mesopotamia. In Greece, Cybele was equated with the goddess Rhea, mother of Zeus, Hera, Poseidon, Hades, Demeter, and Hestia. She also had close ties with the goddesses Demeter, Artemis, and Aphrodite insofar as their realms of influence overlapped.

Cybele's cult was ecstatic and orgiastic in nature, involving dancing and chanting to the wailing of the flute and beat of cymbal and drum. Cybele's priests were called *galli* ("roosters"), and some of their number were eunuchs, having undergone voluntary castration following the model of Cybele's mythological "consort" or love interest, Attis, who castrated himself. As for the Romans, they imported the Great Goddess in the form of her cult image, a great meteoritic stone, in the year 205/204 BCE, when they were hard pressed by war with the Carthaginian general Hannibal. The resolution to bring the goddess from Phrygia was made on the basis of codified utterances of the prophetic Sibyl of Cumae, and, according to Roman legend, it was through the efforts of the noble matron Claudia Quinta that the stone entered Rome. The hull of the barge carrying this stone had become stuck in the Tiber's bottom at the river's mouth. As the Roman poet Ovid records, Claudia easily dislodged the barge with a gentle tug on a rope affixed to it, this act serving as testimony to her chastity, which a vicious rumor had put into question.

The best-known myth involving Cybele is the account of her birth and love for Attis. According to the travel writer Pausanias, there was an occasion on which a drop of Zeus's semen fell upon the ground, and after a time, the earth produced a deity called Agdistis, who had both male and female reproductive organs. In fear of this most fortunate and powerful daemon, the gods cut off the male organ, leaving their victim a female goddess, Cybele. Meanwhile, an almond tree grew from the severed penis. This tree's fruit fell into the lap of Nana, daughter of a local river god, and from its contact with her, Nana gave birth to a handsome baby boy called Attis. When he was grown, Cybele fell in love with him, but her affections were not returned. When, on Attis's marriage day, Cybele appeared at the wedding ceremony in place of his intended bride, a crazed Attis castrated himself. At Cybele's request, he became immortal and was transformed into a pine tree. There were, of course, other legends associated with Cybele, too. She played a role in the tale of the young lovers Hippomenes and Atalanta, who thoughtlessly defiled her temple and whom she consequently transformed into the lions that pulled her chariot. Another tradition made Cybele the mother of the overly fortunate king Midas, known for his golden touch. The ships of the hero Aeneas, who traveled from a fallen Troy to Italy so as to found the Roman race, were reputedly from a pine grove sacred to her on Mount Ida.

Given the orgiastic nature of her worship, she became linked with Dionysus and his entourage. As a counterpart to the Greek goddess Rhea, who called upon the Curetes to care for the infant Zeus, Cybele's mythical celebrants included warrior Corybantes, with whom the Curetes were confused.

As regards Cybele's appearance and attributes, she was regularly represented seated on a throne flanked by lions or in a chariot drawn by them. On her head she wore a basket or a crown in the shape of a turreted city wall, while holding a bowl for the pouring of liquid offerings or a ritual drum.

(*See also* Aphrodite, Artemis, Atalanta, Carthage, Corybantes [the], Curetes [the], Dionysus, Hades, Hera, Hestia, Hippomenes, Ida [Mount], Midas, Phrygia, Poseidon, Rhea, Rome, Sibyl of Cumae [the], Troy, *and* Zeus.)

CYNTHIA Cynthia, which literally means "of or relating to Mount Cynthus," was an epithet of and name for Artemis, the goddess of the wild, who was said to have been born on the island of Delos, where Mount Cynthus is located.

However, in cult, even the goddess Hera could be called "Cynthia," specifically in reference her worship at her temple on that mountain.

(*See also* Artemis, Cynthus [Mount], Delos, *and* Hera.)

CYPRIAN GODDESS, THE
The goddess Aphrodite was sometimes called "Cyprian" or "Cypris," which names or epithets were an allusion to the island of Cyprus and its claim to have been the land where the goddess first stepped ashore after her watery birth. The same claim was also made by the island of Cythera, among other places.

(*See also* Aphrodite, Cyprus, *and* Cythera.)

CYTHEREA
Cytherea was named for Aphrodite as a direct reference to the island of Cythera's claim to have been the place where the goddess first stepped on land after her birth from the waves of the sea.

(*See also* Aphrodite *and* Cythera.)

DEMETER
Demeter was the Greek goddess of grain, the harvest, and agriculture more generally. The earth's fertility depended on her good will and that of her daughter, Persephone, with whom she was closely linked in cult. Demeter's origins as a goddess are disputed, as is the derivation of her name, a combination of the word for mother (*meter*) and, perhaps, the word for earth or barley. One of the Olympian gods, Demeter was, according to the Greek poet Hesiod, a child of the Titan gods Rhea and Cronus, her siblings being Hestia, Hera, Poseidon, Hades, and Zeus. The most significant myth relating to Demeter was the abduction of her daughter, Persephone, by Hades, who wished to make her his bride and queen of the Underworld. As detailed in the *Homeric Hymn to Demeter*, when Persephone was abducted, Demeter wandered the earth for nine days in search of her until she learned that Hades was responsible. In anger at Zeus and the gods of Olympus, she changed her form to that of an old woman and was taken in by King Celeus of Eleusis, in whose palace she became the nurse of his infant son Demophoon. When the child's mother, Metaneira, saw that Demeter had placed him in the embers of a fire, she cried out in terror, not knowing that the nurse was a goddess and placement in embers a means to make her son immortal. Demeter dropped the boy and shed her disguise, revealing herself in her full divinity. She commanded Celeus and the people of Eleusis to build a temple and altar in her honor, which they did. Demeter, however, did not relent from her despair and anger over the abduction of Persephone, refusing the offer of all manner of gifts from the gods. Instead, she remained in mourning for a full year, during which time no crops of any kind grew. People starved, and the

gods ceased to receive sacrifices. At this point Zeus intervened, persuading Hades to release Persephone. To this Hades agreed, but by tricking his bride into eating pomegranate seeds, he ensured that she would be compelled to spend at least a portion of the year—the months of winter—with him in the Underworld.

Demeter's mythology was closely tied to the rituals associated with her. The most famous of these were the Eleusinian Mysteries, initiation into which offered the promise of a felicitous afterlife and prosperity in the present. While a great deal about the Mysteries is necessarily not known, they involved ritual bathing and piglet sacrifice on the part of those participating, a procession in which sacred objects were conveyed from Athens to Eleusis, and a re-enactment of the abduction and search for Persephone. Another of Demeter's festivals was the Thesmophoria, an autumn festival that was celebrated by women to ensure agricultural fertility but that also was related to the establishment of law in conjunction with the introduction of agriculture.

As for Demeter's attributes, she was variously represented holding poppy capsules, which were many-seeded and thus symbols of fertility; sheaves of grain; a bowl for pouring libations; and torches, by the light of which she sought her daughter. On her head, she could wear a wreath of grain stalks or myrtle.

The Romans identified their goddess of agriculture, Ceres, with Demeter.

(*See also* Athens, Celeus, Ceres, Cronus, Demophoon, Eleusis, Hades, Hera, Hestia, Metaneira, Olympus [Mount], Persephone, Poseidon, Rhea, Titans [the], *and* Zeus.)

DIANA The Roman goddess Diana, the "Bright One," was very early on identified with the Greek goddess of the hunt and wild places, Artemis, whose mythology and attributes she assumed.

(*See* Artemis.)

DIKE Dike was a personification of justice and the guarantor of the rights upheld by custom and law in the human realm. The poet Hesiod describes her as a daughter of Zeus and Themis, a Titan goddess who embodied divinely established law and order. With Zeus in his capacity as a civic god she sat in judgment over mortals. Her sisters were Eunomia, "Good Order," and Eirene, "Peace." She is logically associated also with the Erinyes, goddesses of retribution for blood crimes against family members, and Nemesis, wrathful retribution.

(*See also* Erinyes [the], Nemesis, Themis, Titans [the], *and* Zeus.)

DIONE Not a great deal is known about the goddess Dione, although she appears to have been an important deity. There is reason to believe that she was the god Zeus's original consort, as Homer and other sources name her as the mother of Aphrodite, and she was worshipped alongside Zeus at his famous oracular site of Dodona in northwestern Greece. According to Homer, after being wounded by the hero Diomedes at Troy, Aphrodite went to see Dione, who comforted and healed her daughter, brushing away the *ichor* (divine blood) that had been drawn and making the injured arm whole again.

(*See* Aphrodite, Diomedes, Dodona, Troy, *and* Zeus.)

DIONYSUS The god Dionysus was also called Bacchus. As the god of wine, he was held in highest esteem, being paired with Demeter as providing basic sustenance for humankind. Although Dionysus is known primarily as the god of wine, he was a great deal more than that, however. He was one of the oldest Greek gods, his name having been identified in inscriptions dating to the Bronze Age, circa 1250 BCE. The tragedian Euripides's play *The Bacchae* offers the most comprehensive information about Dionysus and the nature of his worship, especially in the earliest period in Greece. While Dionysus was among Greece's oldest identifiable deities, he was not originally Greek. In all likelihood, he was a Near Eastern deity, from Lydia or Phrygia, who made his way to Greece via Thrace and Macedonia or via the Greek islands. He was originally, and first and foremost, a god of liquid life, in particular of the life-sustaining fluids in plants. It was he who was responsible for plant growth and, for this reason, was called Dendrites ("Tree God"), Anthios ("Bloom-Producing"), and Karpios ("Bringer of Fruit"). By extension, he became the god of liquids made from plants as well as issuing from other sources in nature, including wine, milk, and honey. Dionysus enjoyed great popularity in Greece, his worship spreading like wildfire—reasonably so, as he was the most democratic god of all. He was the god of blurred distinctions, an effeminate shape-shifter, doubtless to some degree an effect of his sacred wine. As such, he was the opposite of his half brother, Apollo, the god of order, but with whom he shared the sacred mountain of Parnassus. Everyone was equal in Dionysus's eyes: male and female, young and old, slave and free, even human and animal. His worship was most popular among women, whose place was in the home and whose movements were greatly restricted in Greek society. The worship of Dionysus was considered an essential release from daily routine, and in the case of women, who constituted the greater number of his worshippers, it provided a welcome opportunity to leave behind the shuttle and loom. Partly by consuming him in the form of wine and partly through ecstatic dancing, Dionysus's celebrants would achieve communion with the god, becoming enthusiastic Bacchant(e)s and maenads ("manic ones"), literally having the god inside them, *en-theos* in Greek. They headed for the mountain wilderness, there to be "one" with nature. Small or young animals would be seized, torn apart, and consumed raw, their blood being viewed as another incarnation of the deity. While such rituals continued into historic times, especially in rural areas, the city of Athens transformed the worship of Dionysus into performances in the theater, which were staged in his honor. Dionysus thus also became the patron god of the theater.

As regards Dionysus's own mythology, he was a son of the philandering Zeus and the Theban princess Semele. As was so often the case, Hera was jealous of her husband's roving eye and caused Semele to doubt that it was a god with whom she was sleeping. When Zeus next visited her, Semele asked for a favor, which Zeus was bound to grant; she asked him to appear to her in his full divinity, and as a result, she was incinerated. Zeus rescued the unborn Dionysus and placed him in his thigh. After nine months, Dionysus emerged and was taken to the Nysaean Nymphs to raise. According to an alternate myth, Dionysus was raised by his mother's sister Ino. When grown, Dionysus took a sea voyage, wishing to travel to Naxos, but was taken captive by pirates, who wrongly believed that their princely cargo would yield a handsome ransom. Only the pirates' captain, Acetes, acknowledged that they were in the presence of divinity and was deferential. Dionysus caused the ship to become immobile, covered with grapevines, eerie flute music filling the air. Next to Dionysus appeared phantom tigers, lynxes, and panthers, causing the pirates, apart from Acetes, to jump overboard in fear. The god and his attendants faced more challenges when he arrived in Thrace, there being attacked by Lycurgus, who was duly punished. When he reached Thebes, his "birthplace," Dionysus met resistance from his cousin, Pentheus, the young regent, who refused to acknowledge his divinity. As a consequence of his arrogance, Pentheus was torn to pieces by his own mother and her sisters while they were in a Bacchic trance on Mount Cithaeron, mistaking Pentheus for a young lion. Not all of Dionysus's exploits were violent, however: his bride was King Minos of Crete's daughter Ariadne, whom he rescued from Naxos, where she had been abandoned, and made immortal.

As for Dionysus's attributes and symbols, the grapevine and ivy, a plant emblematic of eternal life, were especially sacred to him. His typical companions were Satyrs and Silens, lusty hybrid creatures, as well as Maenads, his female followers. The god and his followers appear frequently in Greek art, especially on cups and pitchers used for wine. There Dionysus is depicted regularly with long hair, bearded, wreathed with ivy, wearing the skin of a fawn, and holding a wine cup in his hands.

The Romans identified Dionysus with their wine god Liber.

(*See also* Acetes, Apollo, Ariadne, Athens, Bacchantes [the], Bacchus, Cithaeron [Mount], Crete, Hera, Ino, Liber, Lycurgus, Lydia, Maenads [the], Minos, Naxos,

Nysaean Nymphs [the], Parnassus [Mount], Pentheus, Phrygia, Satyrs [the], Semele, Silens [the], Thebes, Thrace, *and* Zeus.)

DIOSCURI, THE

There were two primary sets of Dioscuri, twin "Sons of Zeus," in Classical myth and thought: Castor and Pollux of Sparta, and Zethus and Amphion of Thebes. The more important of these were Castor and Pollux (or Polydeuces), and it is they who are typically known as "the" Dioscuri. Castor and Pollux are variously described as sons of Tyndareus, king of Sparta (by Homer, for example), and, more frequently, as having mixed parentage, their mother, Leda, having lain with both the god Zeus and her husband on the same day, the result being children sired by different fathers: Castor and his sister Clytemnestra by Tyndareus, therefore being mortal; Pollux and the beautiful Helen by Zeus, thus being immortal. Their adventures were numerous, among them the rescue of their sister Helen when she was abducted by the Athenian hero Theseus. The Dioscuri reputedly took part in the hunt for the Calydonian Boar, and also joined Jason and the Argonauts in the quest for the Golden Fleece; in the course of this second undertaking, Pollux, availing himself of his skills as a boxer, defeated and killed the hostile Amycus, king of the Bebryces, a tribe that lived near the eastern end of the Sea of Marmara. When Castor and Pollux attended the wedding of their cousins Idas and Lynceus to the daughters of Leucippus (the Leucippides), who were also their cousins, they carried off the brides. This infamous episode became known as "the rape of the Leucippides." The Dioscuri were pursued by the bridegrooms, and a fight ensued in which Castor and Lynceus were slain, while Idas was killed by Zeus with a thunderbolt. According to the mythographer Apollodorus, Zeus wished then to transport Pollux to the heavens, but he refused to accept immortality while his brother Castor was dead. Consequently, Zeus permitted them both to be among the gods and among mortals every other day. By some accounts this meant that the brothers would take turns being on Olympus or among humans (on earth or in Hades, where deceased mortals normally went). There was an alternate tradition according to which Castor and Pollux came to blows with their cousins over a collaborative cattle raid in which they felt they did not receive their fair share.

As deities, the Dioscuri Castor and Pollux were often represented as horsemen. When they were transported to the heavens, they became stars, specifically those of the constellation Gemini. They were called upon to bring help to those in distress at sea and appeared as stars or as the atmospheric phenomenon known as St. Elmo's fire. Their power as saviors extended beyond the sea to battles fought on land.

(*See also* Amphion, Calydon, Castor, Clytemnestra, Gemini, Hades [place], Helen, Leda, Leucippus, Olympus [Mount], Pollux, Sparta, Thebes, Tyndareus, Zethus, *and* Zeus.)

DIS Dis, or Dis Pater ("Father Dis"), was the Roman equivalent of the Greek god of the Underworld, Hades, who was also called Pluto. As in the case of Pluto, his name was derived from the word for wealth, *divitiae*, or its adjectival form, wealthy (*dives*). The lord of the Underworld was considered wealthy, since all things and everyone came to him eventually but also, and perhaps more importantly, because the earth was the source of bounty, especially agricultural. As was the case with Dis's Greek counterpart, his name became a toponym, thus being synonymous with the Underworld itself.

(*See also* Hades [god and place], Pluto, *and* Underworld [the].)

DORIS Doris was a sea nymph and one of the Oceanids, daughters of the Titan god Oceanus and his sister Tethys. With the sea god Nereus, she became mother to the fifty Nereid nymphs, the best known of whom were Galatea, whom the Cyclops Polyphemus loved; Thetis, who became mother to the hero Achilles; and, by some accounts, Amphitrite, who was pursued by the god Poseidon and bore his children Triton and Rhode.

(*See also* Achilles, Amphitrite, Cyclopes [the], Galatea, Nereids [the], Nereus, Oceanids [the], Oceanus [god], Polyphemus, Poseidon, Rhode, Tethys, Titans [the], *and* Triton.)

DRYADS, THE Dryads were a specific kind of nymph, nymphs being female nature deities or "spirits" who were thought to inhabit and animate various parts or components of the natural world, including bodies of water (Naiads), mountains (Oreads), and trees. Nymphs could possess powers of prophecy and, unusually for deities, were mortal. Dryads were tree nymphs, often associated with oaks in particular, though the Greek word *drys* was used to designate trees in general as well as oaks. Dryads were distinguished from Hamadryads, who were also tree nymphs, but in the latter's case, the nymphs' lives were dependent on and "one with" the life of their trees.

(*See also* Hamadryads [the], Naiads [the], Nymphs [the], *and* Oreads [the].)

ECHO The nymph Echo became nothing but a disembodied voice that repeated only the last words that someone else had spoken. How this occurred is explained by the Roman poet Ovid in his *Metamorphoses*. It had been Echo's task to divert Juno's attention when Jupiter was dallying with various mountain nymphs, and this she did by chatting with her. For this Juno punished her by limiting her speech to repetition of snippets of others' words. It was Echo's further misfortune to fall in love with Narcissus, who spurned her along with all others. As a result of her love-sickness and his inattention, she wasted away to become nothing but her voice.

(*See also* Juno, Jupiter, Narcissus, *and* Nymphs [the].)

EGERIA Egeria was a nymph or goddess of springs and was associated both with prophecy and childbirth. In Roman tradition she was best known as lover, wife, and/or counselor of Numa Pompilius, the legendary second king of Rome, the dates of whose rule are given as 715–673 BCE. The Roman historian Livy recounts that, on assuming the crown, Numa set out to provide Rome with a set of laws and customs whereby to subdue and civilize its bellicose people. Importantly, this effort involved establishing cults, priesthoods, and religious rites. In order to lend credence to these cultic institutions and to instill in the populace fear of the gods, Numa made it known that he had been meeting with the nymph Egeria at night, and that his actions were based on her advice. From the poet Ovid we learn that, grief-stricken upon Numa's death, a despondent Egeria fled from the City to the forests of Aricia and dissolved in a flood of tears. Taking pity on her, the goddess Diana transformed Egeria into a spring near her sanctuary near Aricia in Latium.

In cult, Egeria was associated both with Diana and the Camenae, at whose grove in the city of Rome she was worshipped.

(*See also* Camenae [the], Diana, Latium, Numa, Nymphs [the], *and* Rome.)

EILEITHYIA Eileithyia (or Ilithyia), "The One Who Comes to Help," was the Greek goddess who assisted women with childbirth. She is described by the poet Hesiod as a child of Zeus and Hera, but there are mentions of two aspects of her, or even multiples of her, in other sources: one Eileithyia who brought relief and hastened childbirth and another who delayed it, causing discomfort and pain. These two iterations (or functions) of the goddess, together with Eileithyia's close relation to Hera, patron goddess of women as wives, are illustrated by the well-known tale of Hercules's birth, in which instance she hastened the birth of Eurystheus to Nicippe, a daughter of Pelops, and delayed that of Hercules to Alcmena. This she did at Hera's command, since it had been prophesied that a child of Zeus's bloodline would soon be born and become the ruler of all the territory of Argos. As Hercules was her husband Zeus' own child, while Eurystheus was more distantly related, a jealous Hera wished to prevent this boon from falling to Hercules.

Eileithyia was sometimes invoked as an aspect of the goddesses Artemis and Hera in their function as goddesses of childbirth. Her Roman counterpart was Lucina.

(*See also* Argos, Artemis, Eurystheus, Hera, Hercules, Lucina, Pelops, *and* Zeus.)

ELECTRA Two minor deities were named Electra. One was a daughter of the sea deities Oceanus and Tethys. With Thaumas, a son of Pontus and Gaia, she became mother to Iris, goddess of the rainbow, and to the dread Harpies. Another Electra was one of the Pleiades. She was pursued by Zeus, who successfully made advances toward her, even though she had taken refuge at a statue of Athena. Impregnated by the god, she bore Dardanus, an ancestor of the Trojans, and Iasion, with whom the goddess Demeter would fall in love.

These Electras are to be distinguished from the daughter of the Mycenaean king Agamemnon of the same name.

(*See also* Agamemnon, Athena, Dardanus, Demeter, Electra [heroine], Gaia, Harpies [the], Iris, Oceanus [god], Pleiades [the], Tethys, Thaumas, Troy, *and* Zeus.)

ENYO Enyo was a Greek goddess and personification of war, especially of close combat. In Homer's *Iliad*, she accompanied both Ares, god of war and its horrors, and Athena, goddess of defensive war. In the work of later authors, she is named as the mother, nurse, and even sister of Ares, and is described as blood-covered, grim, torch-bearing, and, like the Erinyes, snake-haired. The Romans conflated and identified her with their war goddess Bellona.

(*See also* Ares, Athena, Bellona, *and* Erinyes [the].)

EOS Eos was the goddess of the dawn and, by extension, of daylight. To the Romans, Eos was known as Aurora. Homer famously describes her as "rosy-fingered," "saffron-robed," "golden-throned," and "early-born." According to the Greek poet Hesiod, Eos was a second-generation Titan, being the child of the Titan gods Theia and Hyperion. Her siblings were Helios ("the Sun") and Selene ("the Moon"), and her original consort was said to be another second-generation, Astraeus, to whom she bore the wind gods Zephyr, Boreas, and Notus as well as the other stars in the heavens, including Eosphorus (Lucifer), the Morning Star.

Eos had human lovers as well, however, and she abducted those mortals who caught her fancy. One of them was the newly married Cephalus, who prayed to be released and restored to his young wife, Procris. In anger, Eos set in motion the tragic events that caused Procris's death at Cephalus's hands. Another was the hunter Orion. A third was the handsome Tithonus, a son of the Trojan king Laomedon and brother of the later king of Troy, Priam. According to the so-called Homeric *Hymn to Aphrodite*, Eos asked Zeus that he make Tithonus immortal, a request that the god readily granted, but she had forgotten to ask that Tithonus also remain eternally youthful. So long as he remained young, Eos and her beloved lived happily beside the river Ocean (Oceanus), but as soon as he began to age, she no longer permitted him inside her bedroom, though she fed him ambrosia, the food of the gods, and gave him lovely clothes. When, in the passage of time, he became so feeble that he could no longer move and only babbled endlessly, she locked him in a chamber. By a tenth-century, post-classical account, he became a cicada.

Eos's sons by Tithonus were Emathion, a king of Arabia whom Hercules killed, and Memnon, whom Achilles slew at Troy and at whose death Eos reputedly left the earth in darkness for a day.

(*See also* Achilles, Boreas, Cephalus, Helios, Hercules, Laomedon, Notus, Oceanus [place], Orion, Priam, Procris, Selene, Titans [the], Tithonus, Troy, *and* Zephyr.)

ERATO Erato was one of the Muses and, as her name "The Lovely One" (who is thus desired) suggests, her sphere of influence was lyric poetry focusing on the theme of love. Given her realm, it is especially striking that the poet Virgil calls on her for inspiration at the midpoint of his epic poem the *Aeneid*, the latter half of this poem being given over to war incited by love and lovers wronged, central to which are the Carthaginian queen Dido, the Rutulian prince Turnus, and the Italian princess Lavinia.

(*See also* Carthage, Dido, Lavinia, Muses [the], Rutulians [the], *and* Turnus.)

ERINYES, THE The Erinyes were spirits of vengeance whose greatest concern was blood crimes against family members. In his account of the origin of the gods, Hesiod writes that the Erinyes, together with the Giants, were produced by Gaia ("Earth"), when drops of blood from the castration of Uranus fell on her; in the sense that she, too, resulted from this violence against Uranus, Aphrodite was their sister. According to the mythographer Apollodorus, the Erinyes were named Megaera ("Envious One"), Tisiphone ("Avenger of Murder"), and Alecto ("Implacable One"). The Erinyes play a large role in the myths of Oedipus and of the matricide Orestes, son of King Agamemnon and Clytemnestra, whom he killed in vengeance for Agamemnon's death. The tragedian Aeschylus describes the Erinyes, who pursued Orestes until he was purified of his crime by Apollo and by Athena, as similar in appearance to the Gorgons and Harpies, having snakes as hair but having no wings. They dripped gore from their eyes, were dressed in squalid garments, and their snores emitted fetid breath. At the culmination of Orestes's tribulations, the goddess Athena transformed the fearsome Erinyes into Eumenides ("Kindly Ones"), spirits that promoted the fertility of flocks, fields, and humans alike and went to live beneath the Areopagus ("sacred Hill of Ares") in Athens. It is as the Eumenides that Oedipus, blinded and exiled from Thebes for his crimes, encountered them, having accidentally stepped into an area sacred to them at Colonus in the territory of Athens. This trespass compounded Oedipus's guilt, but he was expiated of this recent crime by the Athenian king Theseus, in compensation for which favor Oedipus would protect Athens from his place of burial at Colonus even after his death.

For the Romans, the Erinyes were known as Furies.

(*See also* Agamemnon, Alecto, Aphrodite, Apollo, Athena, Athens, Clytemnestra, Colonus, Eumenides [the], Furies [the], Gaia, Giants [the], Gorgons [the], Harpies [the], Oedipus, Orestes, Thebes, Theseus, *and* Uranus.)

ERIS Eris, the personification of strife, was a goddess chiefly known for her role in the Trojan War. It was, in fact, she who was that war's ultimate cause. All the gods had been invited to the wedding of the hero Peleus and the sea goddess Thetis, except the disagreeable Eris. For this slight she would have her revenge. Eris appeared at the wedding to deliver a gift: a golden apple inscribed with the words "for the fairest." Three goddesses came forward to claim this prize: Athena, Hera, and Aphrodite. The individual thought best qualified to judge this beauty contest was Paris, the prince of Troy, handsomest of men, who was tending a flock of sheep on Mount Ida. The goddesses did not leave his decision to chance, each of them offering him a bribe. Hera offered him wide rulership, Athena offered him success in war, and Aphrodite, knowing him best, offered him the most beautiful woman in the world. Paris chose Aphrodite and set sail for Sparta to claim his prize, Helen, wife of the Spartan king Menelaus. By some accounts, Helen left for Troy with Paris willingly, by others not. In any event, Menelaus and his brother Agamemnon, king of Mycenae, assembled a fleet of 1,000 ships manned by the best warriors that Greece had to offer and headed for Troy, where they would battle over Helen for a decade.

(*See also* Agamemnon, Aphrodite, Athena, Hera, Ida [Mount], Menelaus, Mycenae, Peleus, Sparta, Thetis, *and* Troy.)

EROS Eros, who was known as Cupid and Amor to the Romans, was the Greek personification of sexual desire. He was originally conceived of as a primeval, physical, and elemental force that was absolutely essential to the genesis of the gods and the various components of the universe. In the *Theogony*, the Greek poet Hesiod's account of the origins of the gods, Eros arose out of the great Void (Chaos) together with Gaia ("Earth") and Tartarus ("earth's depths"), and he is there characterized as the most beautiful or handsome of the gods, with the ability to overpower humans and gods alike. For the Greek lyric poets he was beautiful, young, golden-haired and golden-winged, and wreathed with flowers, but, armed with a bow and arrow with which to induce love, he was also capricious and sometimes cruel. As the notion of him as an anthropomorphized fertility deity prevailed over his guise as a cosmic "force of nature," he was viewed as the son of Ares and the love goddess Aphrodite, whom he accompanied together with Pothos ("Longing") and Himeros ("Desire"), the Charites ("Graces"), and Peitho ("Persuasion").

In terms of mythology, Eros played a role in a great many myths, causing one character to fall in love with another: the sorceress Medea with Jason, the god Apollo with Daphne, and the hard-hearted Hades with Persephone. But Eros, too, could fall in love, as he did with the lovely Psyche.

(See also Aphrodite, Ares, Chaos, Charites [the], Cupid, Daphne, Gaia, Hades [god], Himeros, Jason, Medea, Persephone, Psyche, and Tartarus.)

EUMENIDES, THE The Eumenides, whose name means "Kindly Ones," were the benign counterparts of the Erinyes, Spirits of Vengeance. The Eumenides, who were responsible for the fertility of flocks, fields, and humans, were worshipped at a range of sites in Greece, among them the Athenian sanctuary at Colonus. That site was made famous by Oedipus, who, prior to being absolved of his sins, accidentally trod on the Eumenides's sacred ground, thereby polluting it.

(See also Athens, Colonus, Erinyes [the], and Oedipus.)

EUPHROSYNE Euphrosyne, whose name means "Joy" or "Good Cheer," was one of the three Graces, or Charites as they were known in Greece, goddesses embodying beauty, joy, and grace.

(See Graces [the].)

EURUS Eurus, or Euros in Greek, was a personification and deity of the east wind. In his account of the origin of the gods, in which he describes the birth of the winds Boreas, Notus, and Zephyr, Hesiod makes no mention of Eurus. The Roman architect Vitruvius writes that Eurus derives his name from the fact that he develops from the morning breezes, and for encyclopedist Pliny the Elder, Eurus's dry and warm properties are conducive to beehives' and vineyards' productiveness if exposed to him.

(See also Boreas, Notus, and Zephyr.)

EURYDICE The best-known Eurydice was a Dryad nymph married to the Thracian bard Orpheus. Her tale is told most vividly by the Roman poets Virgil and Ovid. When the famed herdsman and beekeeper Aristaeus pursued her, she fled and, as she ran, fell victim to a lurking snake's venomous bite. A grief-stricken Orpheus sang of his love for her day and night, and entered the

Underworld in search of her. There, even the shades of the dead were mesmerized by his song, and Proserpina, Hades's queen, granted Eurydice's release to the world above on the condition that, while leading her back, Orpheus did not look back. But, overcome by worry that she may have fallen behind, he did look back, and Eurydice vanished from sight, returning to the dead. For nine months Orpheus wandered, lamenting all the while. When, at last, he was seen and desired by some Thracian Bacchantes, he repulsed their advances, and they tore him limb from limb. Orpheus's remains were swept along the currents of the Hebrus River, and as it was carried along, his severed head continued to lament Eurydice.

The nymph Eurydice is to be distinguished from the wife of the Theban regent Creon, who committed suicide upon the death of Antigone and her son Haemon.

(*See also* Antigone, Aristaeus, Bacchantes [the], Creon, Dryads [the], Eurydice [heroine], Hades, Haemon, Hebrus River [the], Orpheus, Proserpina, Thebes, *and* Thrace.)

EURYNOME Eurynome, "Good Cheer," was the mother of the three (or more) Graces, goddesses who embodied beauty, joy, and grace.

(*See also* Graces [the].)

EUTERPE Euterpe, "Bringer of Delight," was one of the Muses, daughters of Zeus and Mnemosyne. Euterpe's particular realm of responsibility became the music of the flute. She and her sisters Calliope and Clio were all three named as mothers of the Thracian king Rhesus.

(*See* Calliope, Mnemosyne, Muses [the], Rhesus, Thrace, *and* Zeus.)

FATES, THE The Fates were goddesses of prophetic destiny. Their name, as well as the word "fate," is derived from the Latin word "to speak": *for, fari, fatum* (I speak, to speak, it has been spoken). Thus speech, taking the form of decreeing or foretelling what will happen, is central to the concept of fate. For the Greeks, the Fates, generally thought of as being three in number, were known as Moirae, and for the Romans, Parcae. In both Greek and Roman traditions there is tension between the Fates and the gods: sometimes the gods could influence fate, and at other times it appears they could not.

(*See also* Moirae [the] *and* Parcae [the].)

FAUNS, THE Fauns were woodland spirits of hybrid form, predominantly anthropomorphic but having goats' tails, ears, and horns.

(*See* Fauns [Hybrid Creatures].)

FAUNUS Faunus was an Italian nature deity who was associated with forests and wild places and was responsible, too, for the fertility of flocks and fields. He became conflated or identified with the Greek god Pan, as a consequence borrowing the latter's goatlike physical features. In addition to being a nature and fertility deity, Faunus possessed prophetic powers. In Virgil's epic *The Aeneid*, for example, Latinus, the king of Latium in Italy, goes to consult the oracle of Faunus, which is located in a sacred grove: he needs to know the true meaning of the sudden presence of a swarm of bees in his citadel's sacred laurel and of his daughter's hair bursting into flames. The oracle reveals to him that Latinus's daughter is not destined to marry the Rutulian prince Turnus but rather someone from afar. This foreigner was the hero Aeneas. For Virgil, Faunus is a son of the agriculture god Picus and a grandson of Saturn.

(*See also* Aeneas, Latinus, Latium, Pan, Picus, Rutulians [the], Saturn, *and* Turnus.)

FAVONIUS For the Romans, Favonius was a personification and deity of the west wind, who was also known as Zephyr. Favonius, a warm and gentle wind, was considered a god of spring responsible for the rebirth of dormant plant life.

(*See also* Zephyr.)

FLORA Flora was the goddess of flowering crops and plants, and as such, a fertility goddess. She appears to have been a native Italian deity, not an import from Greece. She was closely linked with Ceres, goddess of the harvest, and with Ceres's daughter Proserpina (Persephone), with whom she was sometimes identified. A festival in her honor, the Floralia, was celebrated annually from April 28 to early May.

In the Roman poet Ovid's *Fasti*, Flora herself describes the divine powers given her and why. She was once a nymph called Chloris ("Greenery") who was pursued and seized by the god of the west wind, Zephyr. This god subsequently made her his bride, and she became Flora, "mistress of flowers," who lived in perpetual spring and surrounded with gardens burgeoning with all manner of blossoms. The Horae ("Hours") came to pick her flowers, and with these flowers, the Graces plaited garlands for their hair. The earth, she says, had been only one color until she scattered varied seeds. It was she, by her account, who transformed the youths Hyacinth, Narcissus, Attis, Crocus, and Adonis into the flowers that, apart from the violet (formerly Attis) and anemone (Adonis), still bear their "human" names. She was responsible, too, for the birth to Hera of the god Mars, an ancient god of agriculture. Her speech concludes with a summary of flowering plants over which she wields power: grain, grapes, olives, beans, lentils, clover, violets, and thyme all fall under her sway.

(*See also* Adonis, Ceres, Graces [the], Hera, Hyacinth, Mars, Narcissus, Persephone, Proserpina, *and* Zephyr.)

FURIES, THE The Furies were Roman deities known also as Dirae, "Dreadful Ones," and were equated with the Greek Erinyes. The name of the Furies, Furiae in Latin, reflected their fearsome nature: ancient authors derived the name from *furere* ("rage") and *furia* ("fury, anger"). Like the Erinyes, the Furies were spirits of vengeance. In literature and art, they are variously represented as Gorgon-like, having snakes as hair, or as having snakes wrapped around their arms and bodies. They could also be shown as winged and bearing torches and whips. Of the three Furies, Tisiphone and Alecto are the best known. Tisiphone guarded the portals of Tartarus, the region of the Underworld where sinners resided, while Alecto played a significant role in ensuring that there would be armed conflict between the people of Italy and the Trojan Aeneas when he arrived from Troy.

(*See also* Aeneas, Alecto, Erinyes [the], Gorgons [the], Tartarus, Tisiphone, *and* Troy.)

GAEA Gaea, also written Gaia or Ge, was the goddess of the earth and a personification of the planet Earth.

(*See* Gaia.)

GAIA Gaia (also called Ge and Gaea) was the goddess of the earth, a primeval elemental deity personified to varying degrees. To the Romans she was known as Tellus. Both Gaia's antiquity and her importance in religious thought cannot be overemphasized. She is the Greek incarnation of an earth-mother goddess that had been widely worshipped in Greece, the Near East, and elsewhere for millennia by the time that she made her appearance, complete with a mythology, in the works of Homer and Hesiod. In the so-called *Homeric Hymn* in her honor, Gaia is the mother of all living things and the oldest of all the gods. She is the source of nourishment, too, for all creatures, and as such, she is the mainstay of human civilization and prosperity. It is the case that all or most goddesses are refractions of her in her omnipotence: she was the first, and those who came after each had a portion of her powers.

Given her importance, it is not surprising that Gaia was honored in cult throughout the Greek world. The travel writer Pausanias makes particular mention of a sanctuary of Gaia in Achaia and a Gaia-altar consisting of ashes at the earlier site of her oracle within the sacred precinct of Olympia. With respect to the oracle, it should be noted that Gaia's powers extended to the realm of prophecy: her prophecies, it was thought, issued from within the earth, through clefts in the rock or otherwise. While there are a number of stories around how the god Apollo acquired, or seized, control of the famous oracle at Delphi, these are in agreement that the oracle first belonged to Gaia solely or in part. It was she who established the dragon Pytho (or Python) as the oracle's guardian.

As for Gaia's own origins and offspring, Hesiod's *Theogony*, which describes the birth of the universe, offers the earliest account: in the beginning Chaos, a great Void, was first to come into being, followed by Gaia, the Earth; Tartarus, the Earth's deepest recess; and Eros, Desire. Thereafter, the Darkness of Erebus and Night arose from the elemental Chaos, and Night produced Aether, the bright upper atmosphere, and Day, both of whom she conceived with Erebus. Gaia, for her part, first bore Uranus (or Ouranos), the Heavens, to surround and protect her, and then she produced the mountains (Ourea) and Pontus, the sea, that "shaped" her physically. Gaia and Uranus together became the parents of the twelve Titan gods, among whom were Oceanus, Coeus, Hyperion, Iapetus, Rhea, Themis, Mnemosyne, Phoebe, Tethys, and Cronus, the youngest of these. Gaia's next children by Uranus were two sets of monsters. The first of these were the Cyclopes, giants who each had a single eye on their foreheads. They were named Brontes ("Thunderer"), Steropes ("Lightning"), and Arges ("Brightness") and, when Zeus later became king of the gods, they crafted lightning bolts and thunder for him. The second set of monster-brothers were the three Hecatoncheires ("Hundred-handers"), each having one hundred arms and fifty heads. They were Cottus, Briareos, and Gyes, all three being arrogant, violent, and terribly strong. These six monsters were so hateful to their father, Uranus, that he thrust them back inside their mother after their birth, causing her great pain—pain she would not bear. Gaia made a sickle and asked her Titan children to avenge her for the violence she had suffered. Only the youngest, Cronus, came forward. Armed with the sickle, he waited until his father came to lie with Gaia at night and, ambushing Uranus, castrated him. Drops of blood fell on the earth, and from them were born the Erinyes, spirits of vengeance; the Giants, fully armed; and the Meliae nymphs. From the foam that arose where Uranus's severed genitalia fell into the sea was born Aphrodite, goddess of sexuality and desire. His father now emasculated, Cronus became king of the gods, a station he enjoyed until he himself was later overthrown by his son Zeus.

(*See also* Aphrodite, Apollo, Chaos, Cronus, Cyclopes [the], Delphi, Erebus, Erinyes [the], Eros, Giants [the], Hecatoncheires [the], Hyperion, Iapetus, Mnemosyne, Oceanus, Olympia, Phoebe, Python, Rhea, Tartarus, Tellus, Tethys, Themis, Titans [the], Uranus, *and* Zeus.)

GALATEA
The sea nymph Galatea was one of the Nereids, the fifty daughters of the Oceanid Doris and the sea god Nereus. The principal story associated

with her involves the Cyclops Polyphemus, who fell desperately in love with her and wooed her with melodies that he played on a reed pipe large enough to fit into his rough, ungainly giant's hands. He promised her a wealth of rustic delights: his cave; a flock of sheep; and ample harvests of golden apples, berries, and grapes. Her father-in-law, he proudly sang, would be Poseidon. All this did not move Galatea, who was as enamored of young Acis, a son of the rustic god Faunus, as she was revolted by the Cyclops. In a jealous rage at the lovers' dalliance, Polyphemus struck and killed the youth with a rock torn from a mountain. As the poet Ovid writes, in answer to Galatea's prayers, where Acis fell the earth split open to reveal him reborn as river god, larger now than in his previous life, with horns newly grown upon his head and his body blue-green in hue.

The nymph Galatea is to be distinguished from the "animate" statue of the same name sculpted by Pygmalion.

(*See also* Acis, Cyclopes [the], Doris, Faunus, Nereids [the], Nereus, Oceanids [the], Polyphemus, Poseidon, *and* Pygmalion.)

GE Ge is another commonly used name for the Greek earth goddess Gaia.

(*See also* Gaia.)

GEMINI Gemini is the name of the constellation into which the Divine Twins or Dioscuri, Castor and Pollux, were transformed. Castor and Pollux were the brothers of Helen of Troy and of the faithless Clytemnestra.

(*See also* Clytemnestra, Dioscuri [the], Helen, *and* Troy.)

GLAUCUS Glaucus had been a mortal and a fisherman until he ate a bit of grass that caused his transformation into a sea deity with a fish's tail in place of legs. As a god, he was a patron of sailors. He pursued Scylla, and it was he who inadvertently caused her transformation into a monster by the sorceress Circe.

(*See also* Circe *and* Scylla [monster].)

GRACES, THE The Graces, or Charites as they were known in Greece, were goddesses embodying beauty, joy, and grace. According to the Greek poet Hesiod, they were born of Zeus and the lovely Eurynome, a daughter of Oceanus (and thus an Oceanid), and their names were Aglaia ("The Resplendent One"), Euphrosyne ("Good Cheer"), and Thalia ("Blooming One"). Thalia the Grace was distinct from the Muse of the same name. Love and beauty, Hesiod reports, streamed from their eyes. We also learn from Hesiod that they lived with Himerus ("Desire") beside the Muses on Mount Olympus, and they took part in the creation of the first mortal woman, Pandora. In the works of later authors, they are sometimes more numerous, one of their number being called Charis ("Grace"), and their parents are variously said to be Zeus and Eunomia ("goddess of good order"), the sun god Helios and the Naiad nymph Aigle, Hera and Dionysus.

The Graces are best known as attendants of other female goddesses, especially Aphrodite, whom they were said to have clothed with branches of myrtle when she first stepped ashore after her birth from the sea's foam.

(*See also* Aphrodite, Dionysus, Helios, Hera, Muses [the], Naiads [the], Oceanus, Oceanids [the], Olympus [Mount], Pandora, Thalia, *and* Zeus.)

HADES Hades was the god of the Underworld, Lord of the Dead, the god of death, and even death personified. The Underworld was sometimes called the House of Hades, but the god's very name also became synonymous with the Underworld and was accordingly used as a toponym. Though encountering Hades was unavoidable, even calling upon him by name was a frightening prospect. For this reason it was avoided by resorting to circumlocutions such as "Cthonian Zeus" or "Lord of Underworld." The etymology of the name Hades is disputed, but it may mean the "Invisible One." Called by Homer "hateful" and "implacable," Hades was not prayed to or worshipped in cult. He did, however, also have a more benign side, and as such was known as Pluto, "Wealthy One," who was a source of all good things that rise from the earth. As Pluto, he was worshipped alongside his wife, Persephone, queen of the dead, and her mother, the goddess Demeter.

In mythology, Hades was the son of the Titan gods Cronus and Rhea. His siblings were Zeus, Poseidon, Hestia, Hera, and Demeter. When Cronus's children overpowered him, it had not yet been determined what part of the world each of the gods would take control of. In order to establish this, the brothers drew lots from a helmet, and it was in this way that Hades was awarded the Underworld as his realm of influence. Given the nature of this god and his kingdom, it is not surprising that he took his bride, Persephone, by force, abducting her as she was picking flowers in a meadow. As Demeter was despondent over the loss of her daughter, Hades did eventually concede to allowing Persephone to return to the world above, but for a limited time; he obliged Persephone to return for a portion of every year by tricking her into eating the seeds of a pomegranate. The abduction of his bride is his best-known myth.

As a deity who was feared, depictions of him in art were few. In a fresco painting from a Macedonian royal tomb, he is represented as a mature male with a full beard and driving a chariot, a wailing, gesticulating Persephone in his arms. Hades/Pluto could also be depicted holding a cornucopia, a pomegranate, or a scepter.

(*See also* Cronus, Demeter, Hades [place], Hera, Hestia, Persephone, Pluto, Poseidon, Rhea, Titans [the], Underworld [the], *and* Zeus.)

HAMADRYADS, THE Hamadryads were particular tree nymphs whose lives were intertwined with the lives of the trees that they inhabited. While they appear to be a subset of Dryads, who were tree nymphs of all varieties, they were sometimes indistinguishable from them.

(*See also* Dryads [the] *and* Nymphs [the].)

HARMONIA Harmonia, the personification of harmony, was generally said to be a daughter of Aphrodite and Ares, with whom Aphrodite, Hephaestus's wife, was having an affair. It was Zeus's wish that Harmonia should wed the hero Cadmus, and the historian Diodorus Siculus writes that the wedding of Harmonia to Cadmus, who would become the founder of the city of Thebes, was the first for which the gods provided a marriage feast. At this feast, the Muses sang, and Apollo played the lyre. Cadmus's gifts to his bride were a splendid robe and a necklace made by Hephaestus, and though lovely, the necklace, created by Hephaestus in anger over his wife, Aphrodite's, infidelity, would be a source of woe for Cadmus's family. Harmonia and Cadmus became parents to a son, Polydorus, and four daughters, Ino, Autonoe, Semele, and Agave, all of whom gained notoriety. As for the necklace, Oedipus's son Polyneices, who had inherited it, offered it to Eriphyle as a bribe so that she might persuade her husband, Amphiaraus, to join him in marching against his brother Eteocles, the current regent of Thebes; Eteocles had refused to honor the terms of what was to be a joint, alternating regency. Both Eteocles and Polyneices were killed in the battle that ensued, as was Amphiaraus and five of the others who had accompanied Polyneices (the Seven Against Thebes). The necklace (or by some accounts, the robe) was again brought into play when Eriphyle was bribed by Polyneices's son to persuade her son Alcmaeon to lead the sons of Polyneices's cohort against Thebes in order to avenge the deaths of their fathers. Alcmaeon was instructed by the oracle at Delphi to kill his mother for causing his father's death, which he did and, consequently, was visited by madness as a matricide. To complicate his life even further, Alcmaeon married Arsinoe (or Alphesiboeia), daughter of the king of Psophis, to whom he gave Harmonia's necklace as a wedding present. Later, Alcmaeon married Callirrhoe, daughter of Achelous, who wanted the necklace. Alcmaeon attempted to retrieve the necklace from his first wife by employing a ruse but was discovered and killed. Alcmaeon's sons by Callirrhoe avenged his death by killing their father's murderers and dedicated the necklace at Delphi.

PLATE II
Dionysus: God of wine, born of Zeus's thigh

Harmonia and Cadmus, for their part, left Thebes for Illyria as a consequence of the tragedies that had befallen their children. According to the playwright Euripides, both would be transformed into serpents, lead armies of barbarians, and, at the end of their lives, go to live in the Lands of the Blessed.

Alternate versions of the tale, of which there are many, record Zeus and Electra, a daughter of the second-generation Titan god Atlas, as Harmonia's parents and assert that the fateful necklace was a gift from Athena or Aphrodite.

(*See also* Agave, Alcmaeon, Amphiaraus, Aphrodite, Ares, Arsinoe, Athena, Atlas, Autonoe, Cadmus, Delphi, Electra [nymph], Eriphyle, Eteocles, Hephaestus, Ino, Oedipus, Polyneices, Semele, Seven Against Thebes [the], Thebes, Titans [the], *and* Zeus.)

HARPIES, THE

The Harpies, whose name means "Snatchers" or "Grabbers," were two or (according to some sources) three monstrous female *daímones*, or spirits—technically deities—that personified the demonic, unpredictable, grasping forces of storm winds. Early sources do not describe them physically, but they came to be represented as hybrid monsters having the heads of women and the bodies of birds.

(*See* Harpies [monsters].)

HEBE

Hebe, whose name means "youth," was the personification of youthful beauty and vigor. She is described by the Greek poet Hesiod as a daughter of Zeus and Hera and, according to Homer, she was an attendant of the Olympian gods, whose tasks included filling their cups with nectar, bathing and dressing Ares, and yoking Hera's horses to her chariot. Hebe was said to have been married to Hercules after he joined the ranks of the gods. She was also a companion of the various deities associated with weddings: Hera, Aphrodite, the Charites ("Graces"), and Harmonia ("Harmony").

The Romans to some degree identified their goddess of youth, Juventus, with Hebe.

(*See also* Aphrodite, Ares, Graces [the], Harmonia, Hera, Hercules, Juventus, *and* Zeus.)

HECATE

Hecate (or Hekate) was the daughter of the second-generation Titan gods Asteria and Perses. She was known to the poet Hesiod as a beneficent goddess whom Zeus honored above all others, giving her wide-ranging authority on earth and sea as well as in the heavens: she was responsible for wealth and good fortune, victory in battle and in athletic competition, bountiful fishermen's catches, fertility of flocks, the growth and health of the young, kings' well-reasoned judgments, and sound deliberations in the assembly. As a consequence, she was involved with virtually every facet of family and political life. In spite of all this, Hecate is generally remembered for her links with magic, necromancy, and the witching hour, her darker aspects having been emphasized by later Classical authors. She was also the goddess of crossroads and of transitions. In her various guises, Hecate was associated with Artemis, Demeter, Hermes, Selene, and Persephone, whose abduction by Hades she was said to have witnessed, and in the Roman world, she could be known as Trivia, "Goddess of the Three Ways," a reference to Hecate as goddess of the crossroads. She is often represented in art holding torches, with a dog, and even having three bodies.

In mythology, this goddess played a critical role in the expedition of Jason, who succeeded in his quest for the Golden Fleece only through assistance he received from Medea, a priestess of the goddess. Medea had received instruction from Hecate in witchcraft and in the handling of magic herbs; with these herbs she could extinguish fire and change the course of rivers as well as of the stars and moon. Medea supplied Jason with an ointment that made him invulnerable to sword and fire; it was derived from the root of a saffron-colored plant that had sprung from blood dropped by the eagle eating the continuously regenerating heart of Promethus. In order successfully to harvest this plant, Medea needed to cut its root at night and only after cleansing herself ritually.

(*See also* Artemis, Demeter, Hades, Hermes, Jason, Medea, Persephone, Prometheus, *and* Selene.)

HELIADES, THE

The Heliades were nymphs and daughters of the son god Helios with the second-generation Titan goddess Clymene. Their fate is well known from Ovid's *Metamorphoses*: in grief over the death of their young brother Phaethon, who had borrowed Helios's chariot with tragic results, the Heliades were transformed into poplar trees along the Eridanus River (possibly the Po). Their tears, falling eternally, ooze from the trees' boughs and, hardening in the sun, become amber.

(*See also* Clymene, Eridanus River [the], Helios, Phaethon, *and* Titans [the].)

HELIOS

Helios (or Helius) was the Greek sun god who, along with Selene ("the Moon") and Eos ("the Dawn"), was born of the Titans Hyperion and Theia. His own children were numerous and resulted from liaisons with several different consorts. For example, with Perse, a daughter of Oceanus, he became parent to Aeetes, the sorceress Medea's father; Circe, the enchantress goddess who changed Odysseus's men to swine; and Pasiphae, King Minos of Crete's wife, who, as a result of her union with a bull, gave birth to the dread Minotaur. The Heliades were Helios's daughters with Clymene, mother also of the tragic figure Phaethon, who imperiled the universe when he took the reins of his father's chariot; upon the death of Phaethon, his sisters, in their grief, became miraculously transformed. Less important mythologically were the seven sons who resulted from Helios's union with Rhode, a daughter of Poseidon and namesake of the island of Rhodes; descendants of these sons would become rulers of the island and construct the statue of Helios known as the Colossus of Rhodes, one of the Seven Wonders of the Ancient World.

As for Helios's appearance and agency, one of the earliest descriptions of these appears in the so-called *Homeric Hymn to Helios*. There the god rides in a chariot pulled by a team of four splendid stallions. He shines both upon humans and the deathless gods, bright rays beaming dazzlingly from him. His all-seeing eyes flash like fire, and his golden locks stream gracefully around his face. He wears a golden helmet and a rich, finely spun garment that glows and flutters in the wind. Later sources provide additional details. From a lake or bog of Oceanus in the east—or, according Ovid and other poets, from an ornate, golden palace—Helios would drive his chariot up into the heavens, reaching the highest point at noon, and then descend in an arc to the west. In the night, he made his journey on the tides of Oceanus from the west back to the east in a golden skiff or "cup" fashioned for him by Hephaestus.

Since, in the course of his journey through the heavens, he could see everything that transpired on earth, he bore witness to a number of events, whose course he could, by virtue of his knowledge, influence. He saw Ares and Aphrodite lying together and informed Hephaestus, Aphrodite's husband, of the scandalous affair. Helios also witnessed the abduction of Persephone by Hades. Those who felt his wrath included Odysseus, whose men feasted on Helios's 350 sacred cattle when they came ashore the island of Trinacria, and those whom he assisted included Hercules, in spite of the fact that the hero had taken aim at him with his arrows when plagued by excessive heat.

Helios was confused or conflated with his father Hyperion as well as with Apollo in his role as Sun god even in antiquity. His Roman equivalent was Sol, "Sun" in Latin.

(*See also* Aeetes, Aphrodite, Ares, Circe, Clymene, Crete, Eos, Hades, Heliades [the], Hephaestus, Hyperion, Medea, Minos, Oceanus [place], Odysseus, Pasiphae, Persephone, Phaethon, Poseidon, Selene, Titans [the], *and* Trinacria.)

HEPHAESTUS
Hephaestus was the Greek god of volcanic fire as well as of the forge, and thus the patron of blacksmiths and artisans more generally, especially sculptors and potters who relied on the use of fire in the production of their crafts. He was one of the twelve Olympian gods and, as Homer writes, Hephaestus was the son of Zeus and Hera. While being one of the chief gods, he was unlike the rest of them insofar as he engaged in physical labor, at which

he sweated, and, more notably, he was crippled. In Homer's *Iliad*, he is accordingly described as "the god of dragging footsteps," and it was for this infirmity that Hera cast him from the heavens. Hephaestus fell into the waters of Oceanus, where he was rescued by the sea goddesses Thetis and Eurynome, with whom he stayed for a full nine years creating pins, necklaces, cups, and other things of beauty for them at his forge. After being restored to Mount Olympus, he was again thrown from the heavens, this time by Zeus in anger over his assistance to Hera when she and Zeus had quarreled. Hephaestus now landed on the island of Lemnos, where the island's inhabitants cared for him until such time as Dionysus brought him back to Olympus. In the *Iliad*, Hephaestus was married to Charis, one of the Graces. In the *Odyssey*, however, it was Aphrodite to whom he was wed, though she engaged in an infamous affair with Ares, and, to the amusement of all the gods, the lovers were caught in a snare devised by her skilled and crafty husband. Hephaestus, for his part, made unwelcome advances on Athena, his spilled semen giving rise to Erichthonius, who was born from the earth.

Among Hephaestus's wondrous creations were the palaces of all the gods on Mount Olympus: his own was made of bronze and decorated with elaborate bronze tripods, all the work of his hands. He fashioned Pandora, the first woman, at the behest of Zeus, and at the request of Thetis, forged divine armor for Achilles. The palace of the Phaeacian king Alcinous, beloved of the gods, was guarded by golden dogs of his creation, and he made the splendid but cursed necklace that was given by the Theban king Cadmus to his new wife, Harmonia. According to some authors, the workshop in which these splendors were created was on Mount Olympus, but according to others, his workshop was under the earth.

In the Roman world, Hephaestus became identified with the Italian god Vulcan, who assumed Hephaestus's physical traits and mythology. In the works of Roman authors, it is also the case that the workshop of Hephaestus is represented not on Mount Olympus but beneath a volcanic island called Volcania, where he is assisted in his work by the Cyclopes.

As regards the representation of Hephaestus in works of art, he was shown as bearded, wearing a cap, holding a smithy's tongs and hammer, and sometimes with misshapen feet.

(*See also* Achilles, Alcinous, Aphrodite, Ares, Athena, Cadmus, Cyclopes [the], Dionysus, Erechthonius, Graces [the], Harmonia, Hera, Lemnos, Oceanus [place], Olympus [Mount], Pandora, Phaeacians [the], Thebes, Thetis, Vulcan, *and* Zeus.)

HERA
Hera was the queen of the gods and wife of Zeus, their king. Hera, along with Zeus, Poseidon, Hades, Hestia, and Demeter, was a child of the primeval Titan gods Cronus and Rhea, and like all of her siblings, apart from

Zeus, was swallowed upon birth by her father and later disgorged. While she had wide-ranging spheres of influence, she had particular responsibility as the protectress of women as wives and mothers, thus having close ties with wedding ceremonies, marriage, and childbirth. As such, her marriage to Zeus was the divine prototype for marriage between humans. However, Hera was also the protectress of cities, settlements, and their inhabitants. While her precise origins and the meaning of her name are unclear, she likely evolved from a prototypical Aegean earth-mother goddess, and she was associated with Zeus as early as the Bronze Age, which endured from roughly 3000 to 1150 BCE. Hera's sanctuaries are among the oldest in Greece, and while she was worshipped throughout the Greek world, the most important centers of her worship were at Argos and on the island of Samos, at Perachora and Olympia, and at Paestum, Metapontum, and Croton, which were Greek colonial cities in Southern Italy. Both Argos and Samos claimed to be the site of her birth or, more properly, of her emergence from the belly of Cronus. She and Poseidon were said to have competed for control of Argos, and it was Hera who prevailed.

As for her marriage with Zeus, the travel writer Pausanias reports that this took place subsequent to Zeus's seduction of her in the form of a tame cuckoo that she caught and placed in her lap. As a wedding present, the goddess Gaia ("Earth") gave Hera a tree bearing golden apples that later was planted at the ends of the earth and tended by the Hesperides in their garden. Hera's children by Zeus were the gods Hebe ("Youth"); Eileithyia, goddess of childbirth; Ares, god of war; and Hephaestus, god of the forge, though there was an alternate tradition according to which Hera produced Hephaestus alone, with no father, by way of showing up Zeus for his giving birth to the goddess Athena from his head. Hera was always troubled by her husband's numerous love affairs with goddesses, nymphs, and mortals alike, and many of the myths relating to her describe her persecution of Zeus's lovers. Among these was the goddess Leto, whose pregnancy she cruelly extended; the nymph Echo, who with her chattering had diverted Hera's attention at opportune moments; Callisto, whom she transformed into a bear; Semele, mother of Dionysus, whom she tricked into causing her own fiery death; and Io, a maiden in heifer's form, whom she sent a gadfly to chase and sting. Hera's persecution of Hercules extended through his life, from the cradle to the funeral pyre; it was she who engineered the circumstances precipitating his famous Labors, doing so because Zeus had lain with his mother, Alcmena. The Trojans, too, were subject to torment on Hera's part, as she did not forgive the Trojan prince Paris for failing to award her with the golden apple marked "for the fairest," and giving it to Aphrodite instead. The goddess did, however, also exhibit fierce devotion to her favorites, like the Greek warriors fighting at Troy. And for the hero Jason's kindness to her when, disguised as an old woman, he offered aid, she watched over him in the course of his quest for the Golden Fleece, ensuring, among other things, that the sorceress Medea fell in love with him.

Regarding the goddess's attributes, these included both animals and plants that were sacred to her. Her famous ivory-and-gold cult statue at her sanctuary (Heraion) in Argos, as described by Pausanias, depicted the goddess holding a scepter topped by a cuckoo, the bird signifying her seduction by Zeus, in one hand and, in the other, a pomegranate, a many-seeded fruit symbolizing fertility. Other plants sacred to her included myrtle, a symbol of marriage; the poppy, another many-seeded plant; and the fragrant white madonna lily, which was said to have arisen from the milk of her breast—all of these plants being sacred to the goddess of love, Aphrodite, as well. In addition to the cuckoo, Hera's sacred animals included peacocks, horses, and cattle.

The Romans identified Hera with the Italian goddess Juno, who assumed her mythology.

(*See also* Alcmena, Aphrodite, Ares, Argos, Callisto, Cronus, Demeter, Dionysus, Echo, Eileithyia, Gaia, Hades, Hebe, Hephaestus, Hercules, Hestia, Io, Jason, Juno, Leto, Medea, Olympia, Paris, Poseidon, Rhea, Semele, Titans [the], Troy, *and* Zeus.)

HERMES
Hermes, known as Mercury to the Romans, was a messenger god who mediated between heaven and earth as he delivered communications from the gods to humans. Importantly, this god, who was known in Greece as early as the Bronze Age (circa 3000–1150 BCE), had a wide range of powers and spheres of influence, and although he had special ties with Arcadia, Hermes was worshipped throughout Greece. He was the god of herdsmen, whom he protected, and of their flocks, whose fertility he ensured. Hermes was also the protector of travelers, merchants, heralds, and thieves. As Psychopompus ("Leader of Souls"), he guided the souls of the dead from the earth to the Underworld. He was a god of boundaries, embodied in the Herms (pillars topped with his bust) that marked city limits, the borders of private property, and the entrances to houses. As a bringer of culture, he was seen as the inventor of fire and of the lyre, but he was also a mischievous trickster, many of these aspects being reflected in the so-called *Homeric Hymn* in his honor. According to the hymn, Hermes was born in an Arcadian cave to Zeus and the nymph Maia. On the very day of his birth, he sprang up from his cradle, and venturing from the cave, came upon a turtle, which he quickly hollowed and strung, creating from it a lyre, which he began to play. On the same day, he set off to Pieria, where he stole five of the cattle of his half brother Apollo and drove them off sideways and backward so that they could not easily be tracked. Covering a great distance with the cattle, he invented san-

dals as protection for his feet and also discovered how to make fire. When, at long last, he was compelled to return the cattle, Apollo made him keeper of his flocks in exchange for the lyre, which then became his instrument. As a messenger of the gods and intermediary between them and humans, he is inevitably involved in a host of tales, among them the following. He led the goddesses Hera, Athena, and Aphrodite to the Trojan prince Paris, who would make a fatal judgment of the greatest beauty among them, and he accompanied Zeus when he visited the humble home of the generous peasants Baucis and Philemon. As messenger of Zeus, he traveled to the island of Calypso in order to convince her to let Odysseus return home, and he provided the hero with the herb moly, by means of which he was able to withstand the witchcraft of the goddess Circe. Hercules and Persephone were both guided by him out of the Underworld. Hermes was also the famed Argeiphontes, slayer of the monstrous Argus who guarded Zeus's beloved Io when she was transformed into a cow, and he provided the hero Perseus with the sickle whereby to sever the head of the Gorgon Medusa.

As for his attributes, Hermes was distinguished by the caduceus or *kerykeion* (herald's staff) that he carried, his wide-brimmed traveler's hat, and winged sandals, which enabled speedy travel.

(*See also* Aphrodite, Apollo, Arcadia, Argus, Athena, Baucis, Calypso, Circe, Gorgons [the], Hercules, Hermes, Ida [Mount], Io, Maia, Medusa, Mercury, Odysseus, Paris, Persephone, Perseus, Pieria, Underworld [the], *and* Zeus.)

HESPER
Hesper, or Hesperus, was the personified evening star, which was the planet Venus at night. As such, he was the counterpart of the morning star, Lucifer, the planet Venus in the morning. Hesper was called father of the Hesperides and of King Ceyx, transformed after his death into a sea bird.

(*See also* Ceyx, Hesperides [the], *and* Lucifer.)

HESPERIDES, THE
The Hesperides were nymphs entrusted with tending the trees that yielded the golden apples so famous in classical mythology. The Hesperides' trees were guarded by the hundred-headed serpent or dragon, Ladon.

The Hesperides were between four and seven in number, and their names are variously given as Aegle, Erytheia, Hestia, Arethusa, Hespere, Hesperusa, and Hespereia. Accounts of their birth and the location of their garden, the Garden of the Hesperides, are also various. The poet Hesiod, an early source, names the elemental deities Nyx ("Night") and Erebus ("Darkness") as their parents, but later accounts state that their parents were either the sea god Phorcys and his sister Ceto; or Zeus, king of the Olympian gods, and Themis, the personification of justice; or the second-generation Titan god Atlas, who supported the heavens on his shoulders, and Hesperis, daughter of Hesper, the evening star. The location of the Hesperides' garden, equally difficult to pin down, was said to be in Libya (in antiquity, North Africa) near the Atlas mountains (modern Morocco); in the westernmost Mediterranean on the shores of the river Oceanus; or in the lands of the Hyperboreans, in the far east or to the far north, all of these locations being at the "ends of the earth" as it was then conceived.

As for the golden apples, the trees that produced them were presents made by the earth goddess Gaia to Hera, queen of the gods, on the occasion of her marriage to Zeus. The apples were sources of immortality, and thus highly prized. One of these apples ostensibly caused the Trojan War: the goddesses Hera, Aphrodite, and Athena all desired a golden apple inscribed with the words "for the fairest." The Trojan prince Paris was selected to decide who the fairest was—an impossible choice to make objectively. He chose Aphrodite, who had also offered him the most desirable bribe. This was Helen, the most beautiful woman in the world. The challenge was that Helen was married to Menelaus, the Spartan king. When Paris absconded with her to Troy, a thousand Greek ships sailed in hostile pursuit. The golden apples that Aphrodite supplied to Hippomenes in order to help him win the hand of Atalanta were also said to be from the Hesperides' trees.

As his eleventh Labor (or the twelfth, according to Diodorus Siculus), Hercules was told by Eurystheus to bring him apples from the Hesperides' garden. Not knowing the garden's location, Hercules first consulted the nymphs of the river Eridanus, who in turn directed him to the sea god Nereus. Hercules seized Nereus, who possessed prophetic powers, while he was asleep and held him fast while the latter repeatedly changed shape; Nereus would only prophesy under compulsion. Directed by Nereus, Hercules commenced his journey and, on the way, came upon the Titan god Prometheus, whom he released from the torment of having his liver eaten away eternally by vultures. From Prometheus Hercules received further advice regarding the accomplishment of his labor: he should ask Atlas, the Hesperides' neighbor, to fetch the apples in his stead. This Hercules did, asking Atlas to bring the apples in exchange for relieving him, temporarily, of the heavens' burden. Not surprisingly, Atlas was not keen to resume the onerous task of supporting the heavens on his shoulders, but Hercules tricked him by asking for a temporary reprieve in order to place a pillow on his shoulders as a cushion. According to a variant of this story, Hercules slew the guardian serpent Ladon and retrieved the apples himself. Eurystheus ultimately returned the sacred apples to Hercules, who in turn gave them to Athena to return to the Hesperides.

The Hesperides also figure in the related tale of another hero: Jason and the Argonauts, his crew on the ship *Argo*. According to the epic poet Apollonius of

Rhodes, the Argonauts, having accomplished their mission to obtain the Golden Fleece—and with Medea in tow—were driven off course to the Libyan shores by a storm. After carrying their ship over the Libyan desert, the Argonauts, desperate with thirst, encountered the Hesperides, who were lamenting Ladon's slaughter and the golden apples' theft. Out of fear of the men, the Hesperides turned themselves to dust, but Orpheus, one of Jason's band, pleaded with them, promising reverence and offerings of thanks. The Hesperides were moved in pity at the men's suffering and, through their divine powers, caused a lush meadow to spring up in which they, three in number, each stood rooted as a tree: a poplar, elm, and willow. Miraculously, the tree "embodying" Aegle spoke and pointed to a spring created by Hercules himself when, parched from his own labors, he kicked the rocky ground near Triton's lake to reveal a source of water. This was a doubly good omen, as Hercules had been among the *Argo*'s sailors.

(*See also* Aphrodite, Argonauts [the], Atalanta, Athena, Atlas, Eridanus River [the], Eurystheus, Gaia, Helen, Hera, Hercules, Hippomenes, Hyperboreans [the], Jason, Ladon, Medea, Menelaus, Nereus, Oceanus [place], Orpheus, Paris, Phorcys, Prometheus, Sparta, Themis, Titans [the], Triton, Troy, *and* Zeus.)

HESTIA Hestia was a personification and goddess of the hearth in the Greek world. Her central importance to Greek civilization and culture is reflected in the story of her birth: in the poet Hesiod's account of the gods' origins, Hestia was the firstborn child of the Titan gods Rhea and Cronus. In Classical sources she is represented as a virgin goddess, although both Poseidon and Apollo pursued her, to no avail, as she refused both of them. Since her decision to choose neither suitor was critical to preserving peace among the gods on Mount Olympus, Zeus awarded her the highest honors: a place at the center of every house and receipt of the richest portion of sacrifices made there. Further, she would receive sacrifices in the temples of all the gods and would be deemed the most important of all goddesses.

For the Greeks, the hearth represented and ensured the physical security and continuity of the family and, by extension, of any "political" union of families. It was life-giving and life-sustaining, a source of heat, cooked food, weaponry, and tools. As a locus of sacrifice, the hearth also served as a necessary link between vulnerable humans and invulnerable, omnipotent deities. The hearth was the symbolic center of the household and of the clusters of families that constituted a town's populace. For this reason a hearth with Hestia's fire was maintained both in private houses and in the *prytaneion*, an official building that constituted the sacred center of Greek towns.

(*See also* Apollo, Cronus, Olympus [Mount], Poseidon, Rhea, *and* Zeus.)

HIMEROS Himeros (or Himerus) was the personification of desire. The Greek poet Hesiod speaks of him, along with Eros, as attending the birth of Aphrodite and proceeding with her to join the assembly of the gods.

(*See also* Aphrodite *and* Eros.)

HYADES, THE The Hyades were seven nymphs who, like their sisters the Pleiades, were transformed into stars forming a cluster that still bears their name. The Hyades' parents are variously reported as Oceanus and his sister Tethys and as Atlas and Pleione or Aethra, both daughters of Oceanus. As in the case of their parentage, divergent tales of their metamorphosis existed. Hyginus reports that the Hyades were transported to the heavens as a result of their grief over the untimely death of their brother Hyas, who had been killed by a wild boar or lion. Brother and sisters became part of the constellation Taurus, the Hyades forming the bull's face. Hyginus and Apollodorus, following the pre-Socratic philosopher Pherecydes, provide another explanation for the Hyades' starry transfiguration as well, this tale being linked to the god Dionysus, who was born of Semele, a Theban princess and a mortal lover of Zeus. As Semele had met a tragic end, being consumed by fire while still pregnant, Zeus rescued the unborn child and sent him to the nymphs who lived at Nysa to be raised so that the infant could avoid the jealous wrath of Zeus's wife, Hera. These Nysaean nymphs were the Hyades, and as a reward for their service to him, Zeus transformed them into stars.

The Hyades' name ("The Rainy Ones") was linked both to that of their brother, Hyas, and to their stellar "marking" of the rainy season.

(*See also* Atlas, Dionysus, Nymphs [the], Nysa, Oceanus [god], Pleiades [the], Semele, Tethys, Thebes, *and* Zeus.)

HYGEA Hygea (or Hygeia) was the daughter of Asclepius and the personification of good health. According to some accounts, however, she was Asclepius's consort. As a personification of health, she was honored with Asclepius in cult, and the travel writer Pausanias notes that statues of the god were often accompanied by statues of this goddess in his sanctuaries.

(*See also* Asclepius.)

HYMEN Hymen (also Hymenaios or Hymenaius) was the god of weddings and, more properly, a personification of the wedding song itself. For the Roman poet Catullus, he is a son of Urania, one of the Muses. In literature he appears wreathed and bearing nuptial torches, and in Classical art, he is often shown with Eros or Erotes (multiple deities of love).

(*See also* Eros *and* Muses [the].)

HYPERION Hyperion ("The One on High" or "He Who Walks Above") was one of the group of twelve Titan gods born to the elemental deities Gaia ("Earth") and Uranus ("Heaven"). His sister Theia, "The One Who Sees" (also called Euryphaessa "Far-Shining"), was his spouse, and together they became parents to Eos ("Dawn"), Helios ("Sun"), and Selene ("Moon"). As for Hyperion's identity and powers, he was a sun god and thus identified with Helios and later also with Apollo in his capacity of sun deity. It may have been the case that Hyperion's original "role" was to determine the cycles of his "children" the sun, moon, and dawn, thereby establishing the cyclical rhythm of days, nights, and months.

(*See also* Apollo, Eos, Gaia, Helios, Selene, Titans [the], *and* Uranus.)

HYPNUS Hypnus (or Hypnos) was the Greek god of Sleep and its personification. For the Greek poet Hesiod, he is a child of Night, and thus one of the oldest gods. Some of the most memorable stories involving Hypnus appear in Homer's *Iliad*. There the goddess Hera bribes Hypnus to help her ensure that Zeus is out of commission long enough to let the fighting in the Trojan War turn in favor of the Greeks. In return for his assistance, she promises him one of the Graces as bride. With his brother Thanatos ("Death"), Hypnus comes to retrieve the corpse of Zeus's son Sarpedon from the battlefield outside the walls of Troy and returns it to his native Lycia. The Roman poet Ovid reports that Hypnus had a thousand sons, among them Morpheus, a god of dreams. Hypnus's Roman counterpart was the god Somnus.

(*See also* Graces [the], Hera, Lycia, Morpheus, Sarpedon, Somnus, Thanatos, Troy, *and* Zeus.)

IACCHUS Even in antiquity, the name Iacchus was used for Dionysus, the god of wine and liquid life, but in origin, Iacchus was a distinct deity. He may have been a personification of the ritual cry "Iacche" that was part of the cultic activities performed in the course of the Eleusinian Mysteries, which centered on worship of the goddesses Demeter and Persephone. Alternatively, he was perhaps an agricultural deity. In the context of the Mysteries, Iacchus came to be viewed as a son of Demeter or Persephone.

(*See also* Demeter, Dionysus, Eleusis, *and* Persephone.)

IAPETUS Iapetus (or Iapetos) was a Titan god who reportedly assisted his brother Cronus in the castration of their father Uranus. Iapetus married Clymene, daughter of his brother Oceanus, and together, according to the Greek poet Hesiod, they bore Prometheus ("Foresight"), the bold benefactor of humankind; foolish Epimetheus, who was given Pandora as wife; Atlas, who held the heavens on his shoulders; and Menoetius, blasted by Zeus with a thunderbolt for participating in the battle between the Titans and the Olympian gods. As a result of his own role in that battle, Iapetus, Menoetius, and Cronus were among the Titans imprisoned by Zeus in Tartarus.

(See also Atlas, Clymene, Cronus, Epimetheus, Oceanus [god], Olympus [Mount], Pandora, Prometheus, Tartarus, Titans [the], Uranus, and Zeus.)

IDA According to the mythographer Apollodorus, the goddess Rhea gave her newborn son Zeus to the Curetes and to the nymphs Adrastea and Ida, daughters of Melisseus, to nurse in a cave at Dicte on the island of Crete. An alternate tradition, as reported by the poets Callimachus and Ovid, suggests that Zeus was raised in a cave on Mount Ida on Crete and solely by the Curetes.

(See also Adrastea, Crete, Curetes [the], Ida [Mount], Rhea, and Zeus.)

ILITHYIA Ilithyia is a variant spelling of Eileithyia, the Greek goddess who assisted women with childbirth.

(See Eileithyia.)

INACHUS Inachus was the god of the chief river in the Argolis—the eastern region of the Peloponnese. He was a child of the Titan gods Tethys and Oceanus, for which reason he was called an Oceanid ("child of Oceanus"). With the nymph Melia, he fathered the lovely Io, who was later pursued by Zeus and, consequently, was transformed into a white heifer by a jealous Hera.

The travel writer Pausanias, among others, writes of Inachus's role in a contest between the gods Poseidon and Hera for control of the Argolis. Inachus and two other local river gods, Cephissus and Asterion, were tasked with judging who should win this land. They chose Hera, and, as a consequence, Poseidon dried up their waters, which henceforth flowed only after a rain. Pausanias also reports a variant tradition that viewed Inachus not as a god but rather a king of Argos who named the river after himself.

(See also Argos, Cephissus [god], Hera, Io, Oceanids [the], Oceanus, Poseidon, Tethys, Titans [the], and Zeus.)

INO Ino, also known as Leucothea ("The White Goddess"), was a protector of sailors. She was originally a mortal woman who became divine through the providence of the gods. In myth, she played an important role in preserving the life of the hero Odysseus.

(See also Ino [heroine], Leucothea, and Odysseus.)

IRIS Iris was the goddess of the rainbow and the messenger of the gods, whose job it was to convey communications between mortals on earth and the gods in the heavens. In authors writing after Homer, however, this function is chiefly assumed by Hermes, and the swift-footed Iris, sometimes described as traveling on golden wings, becomes a messenger for the goddess Hera. According to Hesiod, she was the daughter of Thaumas ("Marvel" or "Wonder") and Electra, one of the daughters of Oceanus. She was sister to the birdlike, monstrous Harpies, who flew as swiftly as the wind and whom the heroes Jason and Aeneas encountered. By some accounts Iris bore the goddess Pothos ("Desire") to Zephyr (or Zephyrus), the personified west wind.

Because it flowers in a variety of colors, the goddess gave her name to the iris, which belongs to a genus of some 260–300 species of herbaceous perennial plants.

(*See also* Aeneas, Electra [nymph], Harpies [the], Hermes, Jason, Oceanus [god], *and* Zephyr.)

JANUS Janus (more properly Ianus, as the Romans had no letter "j"), whose name is derived from the Latin word *ianua*, door, was the god of doors and gateways and thus a deity of "passage" and beginnings in a physical, temporal, and metaphoric sense. Ancient sources reveal that offerings were made to him on the occasion of all sacrifices and that the first month of the year was sacred to him. As a deity of passage, looking backward and forward at once (or inward and outward, as the case may be), he was represented with two faces oriented in opposite directions. His most important cult building (place of worship) was a double gate in the Roman Forum, which was converted into a shrine with one door that opened to the east and one to the west, so that the god's statue—dedicated, according to encyclopedist Pliny the Elder, by the legendary early king Numa—could look out in both directions. This Gate of Janus was closed in times of peace and open in times of war.

In terms of myth, there was a tradition that Janus was an early king in Italy who ruled over aboriginal peoples. As king, he welcomed the god Saturn, who brought with him the knowledge of agriculture, and thereby also civilization, to primitive Italy.

(*See also* Numa *and* Saturn.)

JOVE Jove, an anglicized form of Latin Iovis, is an alternate name for Jupiter, supreme deity of the Romans.

(*See also* Jupiter *and* Rome.)

JUNO For the Romans, Juno was the queen of the gods, consort of Jupiter, and daughter of Saturn. Though she became identified with the Greek goddess

Hera and assumed her mythology, Juno was an important and established native Italian goddess in her own right. Similar to the Greek Hera, she was both a civic deity and a protectress of women as wives and mothers. In her role as the goddess of birth, she was called Juno Lucina, and in state cult, Juno Regina ("Queen"). As protectress of young men of military age, she was called Juno Curitis ("Goddess of the Lance"), Sospita ("Safe-Keeper"), and Moneta (the "One Who Warns"). As the Roman counterpart of Hera in myth, Juno had a deep-seated hatred of the Trojans for several reasons: Jupiter's abduction of the handsome Trojan prince Ganymede to serve as his cup bearer and Paris's infamous judgment that Aphrodite was to receive the golden apple marked "for the fairest." Her hatred of the Trojans extended to Aeneas, who fled from Troy to Italy, and whose mission to found a new city she attempted strenuously to derail. She did, however, favor Dido, the noble founder of Carthage, whom Aeneas ignobly loved and left, but Juno could not save her from an awful fate.

(*See also* Aeneas, Carthage, Dido, Hera, Jupiter, Lucina, Paris, Saturn, *and* Troy.)

JUPITER Jupiter (or Juppiter or Jove) was the chief god of the Romans, and like Zeus, he was the god of the sky and atmospheric phenomena as well as the supreme civic and political god, ensuring political and social order. Also, as in the case of Zeus, the name Jupiter ("Celestial or Heavenly Father") is derived from the Indo-European word for "brightness," designating the brightness of the sky; the word for father, *pater*, has in Jupiter's case been appended to "sky." As god of the Roman state, Jupiter was worshipped as Jupiter Optimus Maximus ("Best and Greatest"), his most important temple being located on Rome's Capitoline Hill and shared with Juno and Minerva as the so-called Capitoline Triad of deities.

Although Jupiter was a deity distinct from Zeus, he did assume Zeus's mythology as well as his attributes when represented in artistic media.

(*See also* Capitoline Hill [the], Juno, Minerva, Rome, *and* Zeus.)

JUTURNA Juturna was a Roman water nymph associated with fountains, springs, and other sources of water. According to Virgil's *Aeneid*, she was mistress of pools and rivers who had received the gift of immortality as well as her "realm" from Jupiter as compensation for the loss to him of her virginity. Her name is a combination of the Latin word for helping, *iuvare*, and the name Turnus, the Rutulian hero whose sister (and helper) the poet Virgil presents her as; it was she, at the command of Juno, who caused the truce between the Trojans and Latins to be broken, and she took the place of Turnus's charioteer in an effort to save him, all to no avail. Turnus would be killed by the Trojan Aeneas, whose destiny it was to marry Turnus's beloved princess Lavinia.

There was a pool sacred to Juturna in the Roman Forum close to the Temple of Castor and Pollux, where, as the historian Dionysius of Halicarnassus records, the divine twins appeared to water their horses after helping the Romans in the legendary battle at Lake Regillus (said to have taken place circa 496 BCE) against the Latins.

(*See also* Aeneas, Castor, Juno, Jupiter, Latins [the], Lavinia, Pollux, Rome, Rutulians [the], Troy, *and* Turnus.)

JUVENTUS

Juventus/Iuventus (or Juventas/Iuventas) was a Roman goddess and personification of youth who, while retaining her original Italian cultic associations, over time accrued aspects of Hebe, the Greek goddess of youth. Testimony to her importance in Roman religion, Juventus was worshipped in various prominent places inside the city of Rome, among them the sacred Capitoline Hill, where she had a space inside the Temple of Jupiter, and a temple built in her honor at the Circus Maximus. Her particular sphere or realm of agency was a boy's rite of passage whereby, having reached manhood, he was deemed fit for military service and received the white *toga virilis* ("men's toga").

(*See also* Capitoline Hill [the], Hebe, Jupiter, *and* Rome.)

KORA

Kora (also spelled Cora or Kore), "The Maiden," was a name or epithet used for Persephone, the daughter of Demeter, goddess of the harvest. It was this maiden whom Hades, god of the Underworld, abducted to be his queen.

(*See also* Demeter, Hades, Persephone, *and* Underworld [the].)

KRONUS

Kronus is an alternative spelling of Cronus, a Titan and father of the Olympian gods.

(*See* Cronus, Olympus [Mount], *and* Titans [the].)

LACHESIS

Lachesis, "The Caster of Lots," was one of the three Fates, or Moirae, as the Greeks called them. The Moirae determined the "lot" of every person born by various means, including spinning the thread of their life, singing their fate, or inscribing their determination on a tablet or other medium.

(*See also* Fates [the], *and* Moirae [the].)

LARES, THE

The Lares, whose precise origins are disputed, were native Roman deities that may have evolved from deified ancestors or farmland guardians. Their domain extended from the house to the city and from the private to the public sphere. The Lar *familiaris* ("family Lar") became synonymous with the home that he protected. Roman houses each had a shrine called a *lararium* into which offerings were placed daily and that contained statuettes of the Lar and Penates, another set of protective deities, with whom the Lares could be conflated (consequently being called collectively either Lares or Penates). The public Lares had guardianship over districts of the city, villages, roads and crossroads, and military expeditions. In terms of mythology, the Lares and Penates of the hero Aeneas are best known, as he carried these, along with his aged father Anchises, out of a flame-ensconced Troy and set sail with them to Italy.

(*See also* Aeneas, Anchises, Penates [the], *and* Troy.)

LATONA Latona was the Roman name for the goddess Leto, mother of Apollo and Artemis.

(*See* Leto.)

LETO Leto, or Latona for the Romans, is best known as the mother of Apollo and Artemis. She was a second-generation Titan born of the union between Coeus and Phoebe and became either wife or consort to Zeus, the father of her children. The *Homeric Hymn to Apollo* details the challenges faced by Leto in her pregnancy: when the time of delivery was near, she was forced to wander extensively, from island to island, as none would allow her to stay, fearing as they did a prophecy that she would bear a son of great might. When, at last, she came to Delos, she promised the island that it would become the site most sacred to the son she would bear. Delos (which was also known as Ortygia) then welcomed her, but Leto's birth pains endured for nine days and nights before Eileithyia, goddess of childbirth, came, as she had been detained by a jealous Hera. In the end, Eileithyia had to be bribed by the other goddesses with a beautiful necklace to attend to Leto in her time of need. At last Leto gave birth to Apollo and to Artemis while clutching the trunk of a palm tree, which thereafter was a plant sacred to Apollo. Holding her newborns, Leto made her way to Lycia, where she succumbed to the heat and asked for water from a small lake at whose banks some peasants were at work. When a drink was denied her and her babies, she changed the evildoers into frogs so that they could forever "enjoy" their water. At some later point, Niobe, daughter of the Lydian king Tantalus, boasted that she was superior to Leto because she had more children than the goddess: seven sons and seven daughters. For this prideful boast, Leto enlisted Apollo and Artemis to slay all her children, the so-called Niobids, with their arrows. Other stories associated with Leto were the attempted rape of her at the hands of the giant Tityus, who, for this crime, was punished both with death and with eternal torture in the afterlife: his heart (or liver) was eaten eternally by vultures only continuously to grow back.

(*See also* Apollo, Artemis, Coeus, Delos, Eileithyia, Niobe, Ortygia, Phoebe, Tantalus, Tityus, *and* Zeus.)

LEUCOTHEA Leucothea, whose name means "White Goddess," was widely worshipped in Greece, according to the travel writer Pausanias. What, precisely, she was worshipped *for* is more difficult to determine; she appears to have been associated with coming-of-age rituals, and the mythographer Apollodorus states that she assisted storm-besieged sailors at sea. In myth, Leucothea is perhaps best known for having rescued the hero Odysseus when a massive storm, brought on by a wrathful Poseidon, cast him from the raft that he had built on the island of the goddess Calypso. Leucothea, a sea goddess, emerged from the waves as a sea bird and, as Homer recounts, instructed Odysseus to abandon his raft and to swim, buoyed by her veil, to the island of the kindly Phaeacians.

Leucothea had not always been a goddess. Rather, she was originally a mortal woman who became immortal. She began her existence as Ino, daughter of Cadmus, king of Thebes. Accounts of Ino's dramatic mortal life and metamorphosis are various and, in part, conflicting. In brief, she raised the god Dionysus; participated in the dismemberment of her nephew Pentheus; conspired, out of jealousy, to have her stepchildren, Phrixus and Helle, sacrificed; and escaped the murderous rage of her husband, Athamas, by jumping off a cliff into the sea, at which point she was transformed into a goddess either by Dionysus or Poseidon.

(*See also* Cadmus, Dionysus, Helle, Ino [heroine], Odysseus, Pentheus, Phaeacians [the], Phrixus, Poseidon, *and* Thebes.)

LIBER Liber was an Italian god of nature, fertility, and wine. Liber, whose name may be derived from the word for pouring libations or for freedom—insofar as wine served as a liberator from one's normal inhibitions—became identified with the Greek Dionysus. As a fertility deity, Liber naturally had close links with Ceres, goddess of grain and agriculture.

(*See also* Ceres *and* Dionysus.)

LOTIS Lotis is the name of one of the Naiads, who were nymphs of springs, streams, and fountains. According to the Roman poet Ovid in his *Metamorphoses*, Lotis was pursued by the lusty rustic god Priapus and was transformed into a lotus plant to escape him. Ovid does not describe how this occurred, nor is it clear what plant, exactly, the lotus he writes of was. Ovid's lotus had crimson flowers, produced berries, and is called "aquatic." Scholars have long thought that the jujube tree, *Ziziphus lotus*, could be Lotis's lotus, but it is not aquatic, nor does it have crimson flowers. There is reason to believe that the lotus in question is in fact a lotus (*Nymphaea* spp.), but this identification does not correspond with Ovid's suggestion a bit later that the lotus was a tree. In another work, the *Fasti*, Ovid relates a variant of this tale: a drunken, ribald Priapus pursued Lotis and prepared to rape her in her sleep, but the donkey of the elderly Silenus saw what he was up to and brayed to alert Lotis, who consequently awoke and escaped unscathed, without becoming a plant.

(*See also* Naiads [the], Priapus, *and* Silenus.)

LUCIFER   Lucifer was a personification of the morning star, the planet Venus in the morning, and he was also called Phosphorus ("Light-Bearer") or Eosphorus ("Morning-Light Bearer"). According to the Greek poet Hesiod, Lucifer (Eosphorus) and his brother Hesper were children of Eos, goddess of the dawn, and of the second-generation Titan Astraeus. In Roman mythology, Lucifer was thought of as the star that Julius Caesar became upon his deification, and in Late Antiquity, Lucifer came to be equated with Satan.

(*See also* Eos, Hesper, *and* Titans [the].)

LUCINA   Lucina ("Light-Bringer") was a Roman goddess of childbirth, who, as her name suggests, brought new life from the dark womb into the light of day. She was not an independent deity but rather an aspect primarily of the goddess Juno in her capacity as patron deity of women as wives. The goddess Diana, goddess of the hunt and wild animals, was, however, also called Lucina when offering protection over mothers in labor, whether human or animal. Lucina's Greek counterpart was Eileithyia, who existed as an individual deity in addition to reflecting aspects of the goddesses Hera and Artemis, themselves being counterparts of the Roman Juno and Diana respectively.

Among the myriad births assisted by Lucina were several remarkable ones described by the Roman poet Ovid: the birth to Pierus's wife Euippe of the nine daughters who would later challenge the nine Muses, and the birth of Adonis to Myrrha, who, while pregnant, had become a myrrh tree.

(*See also* Adonis, Artemis, Diana, Eileithyia, Hera, Juno, Muses [the], Myrrha, *and* Pierus.)

LUNA   Luna, "Moon" in Latin, was the Roman equivalent of the Greek moon goddess Selene. Although worship of her likely came to Italy via Greece, there was a local tradition that the early Sabine king Titus Tatius, who served as co-regent of the newly born city of Rome with Romulus, instituted it.

(*See also* Rome, Romulus, Sabines [the], *and* Selene.)

LYAEUS Lyaeus, which means the "Deliverer" or "Releaser," was an epithet or descriptive name for the god Dionysus. One of the blessings that this god offered humanity was a welcome release from care and the hardships of everyday life. He also eradicated "normative" distinctions, all people being equal in his eyes: young and old, male and female, slave and free.

(*See also* Dionysus.)

MAGNA MATER Magna Mater ("Great Mother") was the Latin name for the Phrygian mother- and fertility-goddess Cybele.

(*See* Cybele *and* Phyrgia.)

MAIA The nymph Maia was one of the Pleiades, who were children of the second-generation Titan Atlas and Pleione, a daughter of Oceanus. She is chiefly known as the mother of the god Hermes. The *Homeric Hymn to Hermes* characterizes her as shy and thus given to spending her days in a cave in Arcadia, hidden from god and humans alike. In the course of his nocturnal visits to her, Zeus sired the god Hermes, who was precocious from the moment of his birth: he proved instantly to be shifty, cunning, and thieving, but also musically gifted, becoming inventor of the lyre. Hermes availed himself of all of these attributes in order to steal the cattle of Apollo while still a newborn. To no avail, Maia tried to hide her son's guilt from Apollo by holding up the seemingly helpless baby Hermes for his inspection, her argument being that a mere infant could not be responsible. According to the mythographer Apollodorus, Maia later assisted Zeus in the complicated matter of Callisto, one of the god's mortal lovers who was either transformed into a bear or was killed in consequence of that affair. Her motherless baby, Arcas, was brought to Maia to raise.

In the Roman world, Maia appears to have become conflated with a native Italian fertility deity and identified with the Bona Dea ("Goodly Goddess"). Latin authors note that there was a feast in her honor that was celebrated in the temple of Mercury (the Roman equivalent of Hermes) in the Circus Maximus. This celebration took place annually in May—a month to which, some authors state, she gave her name. Maia had ties in cult with the god Vulcan as well.

(*See also* Apollo, Arcadia, Arcas, Atlas, Bona Dea, Callisto, Hermes, Mercury, Oceanus [god], Pleiades [the], Titans [the], *and* Vulcan.)

MANES, THE In Roman religion and thought, the Manes, or, more properly Di Manes ("Ancestral Spirits"), were deified souls of the dead. The Manes were believed to reside in the Underworld but to have a close relation with the living, whom they protected if they received the reverence and sacrificial offerings—which included wreaths, salt, bread, and fruit—that they were due. The Di Parentes, "Deified Ancestral Souls," were among the Manes. A festival known as the Parentalia, a festival of public mourning, was celebrated annually in February, on which occasion the Romans commemorated their deceased parents and other relatives, as was also done privately on the anniversary of their deaths. According to the Roman poets Virgil and Ovid, the hero Aeneas provided the model for the Parentalia when he commemorated the anniversary of the death of his father, Anchises, with offerings.

(*See also* Aeneas, Anchises, *and* Underworld [the].)

MARS
Mars was one of the oldest and, with Jupiter, most important gods in the Roman world. As the god of war and a warrior god, he was a fitting representative of Roman military might and endeavors, but he appears to have been a god of agriculture as well, called upon as the protector of fields and flocks. Among other rituals, a series of festivals were celebrated in his honor at the beginning of the military campaign season in March, the month named after him. For example, prior to leaving the city of Rome, commanders laid hands on the Spear of Mars, which was kept in a building called the Regia, by way of waking the god. Roman emperors also invoked the god on the heels of military victory, when realized or imminent.

In mythology, Mars became identified with the Greek war god Ares, and as such, his consort was the Roman equivalent of Aphrodite, Venus. But Mars had his own distinct mythology as well. In particular, he was known as the father of Romulus and Remus, the sons of the Vestal Virgin Rhea Silvia, and thus the legendary ancestor of the Roman people. Like Ares, Mars was represented as armed, wearing a helmet, and wielding weapons.

(*See also* Aphrodite, Ares, Rhea Silvia, Remus, Rome, Romulus, Venus, *and* Vesta.)

MEGAERA
Megaera, "The Envious One or Grudging One," was one of the fearsome, snake-haired spirits of vengeance, who were known as the Erinyes in the Greek world and as Furies among the Romans. Her sisters were Alecto and Tisiphone.

(*See also* Alecto, Erinyes [the], Furies [the], *and* Tisiphone.)

MELPOMENE
Melpomene, "The Singer," was one of the Muses. She became known as the patron deity of tragedy and is accordingly often shown holding a tragic mask. For the mythographer Apollodorus, she was the mother of the Sirens.

(*See also* Muses [the] *and* Sirens [the].)

MERCURY   Mercury was a Roman god whose origins are disputed. Prior to his identification with the Greek god Hermes, Mercury was established as a deity with important commercial functions, being closely tied with shopkeepers and those who transported goods. By the second century BCE, however, Mercury increasingly assumed the persona and mythology of Hermes, the messenger god whose many services included protection of travelers and guiding the souls of the dead to the Underworld.

(*See also* Hermes *and* Underworld [the].)

MEROPE   The nymph Merope was one of the seven daughters of the second-generation Titan god Atlas and Pleione, a daughter of Oceanus. Collectively, the seven sisters were called Pleiades. Merope, who is to be distinguished from several human legendary heroines of the same name, became the wife of Sisyphus, who attempted to cheat Death and was consigned to eternal torture in the afterlife, being tasked with pushing a stone uphill only to have it, time and again, roll back down. This Merope was the grandmother of the hero Bellerophon, famed for taming the winged horse Pegasus and slaying the hybrid monster known as the Chimaera.

(*See also* Atlas, Bellerophon, Chimaera [the], Merope [heroine], Oceanus, Pegasus, Pleiades [the], Sisyphus, *and* Titans [the].)

METIS   Metis, whose name means "wisdom" or "cunning," was a second-generation Titan goddess and one of the Oceanids, daughters of Oceanus and his sister Tethys. According to the mythographer Apollodorus, the god Zeus pursued Metis, and she tried to avoid his embrace by taking on many shapes. Nonetheless, she did become pregnant. When Zeus later learned from Gaia that his child would be more powerful than he, the solution that he opted for was to swallow Metis with the unborn child still in her womb. However, after a period of gestation, Zeus developed a terrible headache and asked the god Hephaestus (or by another account Prometheus) to relieve him of the pain. This Hephaestus did by striking the god's head with an axe, and from the cloven head sprang the goddess Athena, fully grown and fully armed. The birth of Athena was vividly depicted on the eastern pediment of the Parthenon in Athens. A less-known story about Metis is also reported by Apollodorus: it was she, in her cleverness, who supplied Zeus with a tonic that caused Cronus to disgorge Zeus's siblings.

(*See also* Athena, Athens, Cronus, Gaia, Hephaestus, Oceanids [the], Oceanus, Parthenon [the], Prometheus, Tethys, *and* Zeus.)

MINERVA Minerva was an Italian goddess of art and crafts who, very early on, took on the functions of war goddess and protectress of the state through a fusion of Italian and Greek traditions. As a result, she became a Roman equivalent of the Greek goddess Athena, with whom she was identified. Minerva's origins remain disputed: she may have been a native Italian deity or an import from Greece via Etruria. In the city of Rome itself, Minerva shared a temple—the most important temple of the Roman state religion—with Jupiter and Juno on the Capitoline Hill, and as such was established as one of Rome's major deities.

In terms of mythology, physical appearance, and attributes, she became conflated with Athena.

(*See also* Athena, Capitoline Hill [the], Juno, Jupiter, *and* Rome.)

MNEMOSYNE Mnemosyne, whose name means "memory," was a personification and goddess of memory. She was a daughter of the elemental gods Gaia ("Earth") and Uranus ("Heaven") and was one of the older generation of deities collectively called the Titans. Mnemosyne was said to have borne the nine Muses, patron goddesses of the arts, to Zeus, with whom she lay for nine nights in Pieria.

(*See* Gaia, Muses [the], Pieria, Uranus, *and* Zeus.)

MOIRAE, THE The Moirae (or Moirai) were Greek goddesses of fate. The Moirae and their Roman equivalents, the Parcae, are all referred to as Fates. According to the Greek poet Hesiod, the Moirae, whose name means "Portions" or "Shares" of life, were children of Night and were goddesses of great antiquity. Their names were Clotho, Lachesis, and Atropos, Hesiod writes, and they were responsible for assigning people with portions of good and evil at their birth. Elsewhere, contradicting this statement, Hesiod calls the Moirae daughters of Zeus and the Titan goddess Themis. The individual names of the Moirae are all related to how the allotment of fate was conceived as functioning: Clotho was "The Spinner," in reference to spinning the "thread of life" that the sisters subsequently measured and cut to a determined length; Lachesis, "The Caster of Lots," cast lots that determined a person's fate; and Atropos, "The Unturnable One," saw to it that a person's fate could not be altered. As goddesses associated with death, they had close ties with the Erinyes, spirits of vengeance, and Keres, spirits of death.

It was often, but not always, possible for the gods to influence the Moirae, but humans could not. Some instances of their workings include their determination of the length and course of the hero Meleager's life. According to the mythographer Hyginus, they sang the newborn Meleager's fate as follows: Clotho said that he would be noble, Lachesis that he would be brave, but Atropos, spotting a log burning on the hearth, said, "He will live only as long as this log keeps burning." Hearing this, his mother hastened to the fire, snatched out the log, and kept it hidden to preserve her son's life. Yet it was ultimately she, in a fit of anger, who retrieved the fatal log. In this instance, the Moirae could not be thwarted. By contrast, the god Apollo intervened on noble Admetus's behalf, making it possible for him to find someone to die in his place. Sadly for him, it was his wife, Alcestis, who volunteered.

(*See also* Admetus, Alcestis, Erinyes [the], Meleager, Parcae [the], Themis, Titans [the], *and* Zeus.)

MORPHEUS Morpheus, a personification of dreams, was believed to be one of the thousand sons of Hypnus (Roman Somnus), the god of sleep. Morpheus was associated with a particular type of dream, namely that in human form, since he was best at imitating people's gait, speech, and gestures. According to the Roman poet Ovid, his brother Phobetor (or Icelos), by contrast, assumed the form of animals, and Phantasos took on the shape of rocks, trees, water, and all other inanimate things. Among Morpheus's notable appearances in myth is that in the tale of Ceyx and Alcyone, devoted husband and wife. When Ceyx, a king of the city Trachis, met his death at sea, the goddess Hera, wishing to put an end to Alcyone's ceaseless prayers for her husband's safety, caused Morpheus to appear to her in Ceyx's form to tell her of his death. Recognizing the truth of the dream, a despondent Alcyone ran to the seashore and flung herself into the waves when she caught sight of her husband's corpse floating there. In pity for her the gods transformed her, and also the dead Ceyx, into sea birds so that they could spend the rest of their days together in this new incarnation.

(*See also* Alcyone, Ceyx, Hera, Hypnus, *and* Somnus.)

MORS Mors was the Roman god of death and represented the state of lifelessness as well as the force that causes death. He was the equivalent of the Greek god Thanatos.

(*See also* Thanatos.)

MUSES, THE The Muses inspired human artistic activity and, accordingly, were patron goddesses of literature and the arts. They were generally said to be nine in number and to be the daughters of Zeus and the Titan goddess Mnemosyne ("Memory"). In his account of the origins of the gods, Hesiod establishes their names as follows: Clio (or Cleio), "Praiser," Euterpe, "Bringer of Delight," Thalia (or Thaleia, a deity distinct from the Grace of the same name), "Bounteous One," Melpomene, "Songstress," Terpsichore, "Enjoying the Dance," Erato, "The Lovely," Polyhymnia, "Many-Hymned," Urania (or Ourania), "Celestial One," and Calliope, "Beautiful-Voiced." They were collectively described as Pierian (or Pierides) and Heliconian in reference to their haunts Pieria, at the foot of Mount Olympus, and Mount Helicon in Boeotia, and they were convened or "led" by the god Apollo in his role as god of music and poetry.

While the Muses were not originally assigned to specific spheres of influence, each of them came to be associated with a distinct art form over time as follows: Clio, history; Euterpe, flute playing; Thalia, comedy; Melpomene, tragedy; Terpsichore, dancing; Erato, lyric and love poetry; Polyhymnia, sacred song; Urania, astronomy; and Calliope, epic poetry.

As regards myths that involve the Muses as protagonists, these are relatively few in number and center on various characters' challenging them, always with tragic results. Thamyris, a skilled Thracian bard, foolishly boasted that he could outperform the Muses. For his pridefulness the Muses struck him blind and caused him to forget his art. Similarly, the nine daughters of Pierus, who were called Pierides after their father (and thus could be confused with the Muses), claimed that they could outsing the heavenly sisters. For their affront they were transformed into chattering magpies. Even the Sirens, according the travel writer Pausanias, competed in singing with the Muses, having been persuaded to do this by Hera. As always, the Muses won, and they proceeded to pluck out the Sirens' feathers, using them to make crowns for themselves. And, according to the mythographer Hyginus, the Muses judged the terrible flute contest between the Satyr Marsyas and Apollo.

Some of the Muses also had individual mythologies to the extent that they were pursued by various male deities or heroes and bore them children: Clio bore Hyacinth to King Oebalus (or Pierus); Calliope bore the musicians Orpheus and Linus to Apollo; either Calliope or Euterpe bore Rhesus, who would become a king of Thrace, to the river god Strymon; and Melpomene or Terpsichore bore the Sirens to the river god Achelous.

(*See also* Achelous [god and place], Apollo, Calliope, Clio, Erato, Euterpe, Helicon [Mount], Hyacinth, Linus, Marysas, Melpomene, Mnemosyne, Oebalus, Olympus [Mount], Orpheus, Pieria, Pierides [the], Pierus, Polyhymnia, Rhesus, Sirens [the], Terpsichore, Thalia, Thamyris, Urania, *and* Zeus.)

NAIADS, THE
The Naiads were nymphs, specifically water spirits who inhabited springs, fountains, rivers, lakes, and brooks. While the Naiads were not usually named individually in mythology, instead featuring as a group, there were certainly notable exceptions, among them Lotis, who was pursued by the rustic

god Priapus, and Syrinx, who was pursued by Pan; both were ultimately transformed into plants as a means of escaping their pursuers.

(*See also* Lotis, Nymphs [the], Pan, Priapus, *and* Syrinx.)

NEMESIS   Nemesis was the goddess of retribution, and for the poet Hesiod, she was a daughter of Night, her siblings including Moros ("Doom"), black Ker ("Violent Death"), Thanatos ("Death"), Hypnus ("Sleep"), Oneiroi ("Dreams"), Momos ("Blame"), Oizys ("Misery"), the Moirae ("Fates"), Apate ("Deceit"), and Eris ("Strife"). Nemesis was conceived of as functioning in various capacities. She was an agent of retribution for hubris (not knowing one's limits as a human being) and an inhibitor of actions that would earn retribution, thus being a counterpart to Aidos (reverence or shame). Nemesis appears often in Classical literature, which is filled with tales involving hubris, but plays a leading role in one particular myth, the story of the Trojan War. According to the mythographers Hyginus and Apollodorus, as well as fragments of a lost epic poem entitled the *Cypria*, Nemesis was pursued by Zeus, who forced himself upon her in the guise of a swan. The results of this union were the divine twins, Castor and Pollux, and an egg that, after being given to Leda, hatched the beautiful Helen. As an allegory of Nemesis, Helen would become the cause of the Trojan War, which Zeus initiated so as to free the earth from overpopulation and to punish humans for their lack of piety.

(*See also* Castor, Eris, Helen, Hypnus, Leda, Moirae [the], Pollux, Thanatos, Troy, *and* Zeus.)

NEPHELE   Nephele, whose name means "cloud," was literally a cloud to which Zeus gave the shape of his wife, Hera. It was for a specific purpose that Zeus did this: to verify Hera's claim that Ixion, a Thessalian king, was trying to seduce her. Zeus thus created Nephele in the likeness of his wife. Ixion slept with her, begetting the monstrous Centaurs, hybrid creatures that had the torsos of men and the bodies of horses, or, as the poet Pindar states, Centaurus, who sired the Centaurs. Ixion, for his part, was punished by being fastened to the spokes of a flaming wheel that would turn for eternity.

There was confusion among Classical authors about whether this Nephele was the same Nephele who became the first wife of Athamas, a king of Boeotia. If so, she would become mother to Phrixus and Helle, whose death Athamas's second wife, Ino, would plot but whom Nephele was able to save from sacrifice by placing them on the back of a winged, golden-fleeced ram.

(*See also* Athamas, Boeotia, Centaurs [the], Dionysus, Helle, Hera, Ino, Ixion, Leucothea, Nephele [heroine], Phrixus, Thessaly, *and* Zeus.)

NEPTUNE Neptune was an ancient Italian water deity who became associated and conflated with the Greek sea god Poseidon, assuming the latter's mythology.

(*See* Poseidon.)

NEREIDS, THE The Nereids were sea nymphs and fifty in number. They were born of the sea god Nereus and Doris, a daughter of Oceanus. Among their notable deeds were guiding Jason's ship the *Argo* through the Clashing Rocks on the hero's return from his quest to obtain the Golden Fleece. In this endeavor, one among them, Thetis, took the lead, according to Apollonius of Rhodes. Apollodorus reports a less happy story. Andromeda's mother, Cassiopeia, queen of Ethiopia, had claimed to be more beautiful than the Nereids and, consequently, Poseidon, taking up their cause, sent a flood and sea monster to wreak havoc on the land in vengeance for the queen's insult. Jupiter Ammon prophesied that the monster could be appeased only if Andromeda were left for it as a sacrifice, and thus it was that the hero Perseus found the princess bound in fetters to a crag and, Gorgon's head in hand, came to her rescue. Some of the Nereids accrued individual myths. Thetis, for example, is best known as the mother of Achilles. Galatea, meanwhile, won the heart of the Cyclops Polyphemus, and Amphitrite became mother to the sea deity Triton by the god Poseidon.

(*See also* Achilles, Ammon, Amphitrite, Andromeda, Argonauts [the], Cassiopeia, Clashing Rocks [the], Cyclopes [the], Ethiopia, Galatea, Gorgons [the], Jason, Medusa, Perseus, Polyphemus, Poseidon, Thetis, *and* Triton.)

NEREUS Nereus was an ancient sea god often characterized, like his brother Phorcys, as an "old man of the sea" capable of changing his shape and possessing prophetic powers. The parents of Nereus and Phorcys were said to be Pontus ("Sea") and Gaia ("Earth"). As Hesiod recounts, with Doris, a daughter of Oceanus, Nereus himself fathered fifty daughters, known collectively as the Nereids.

Nereus played a role in Hercules's completion of his eleventh Labor, obtaining the golden apples of the Hesperides. It was Nereus who, when constrained by Hercules, revealed the location of the Hesperides' garden.

(*See also* Doris, Gaia, Hercules, Hesperides [the], Nereids [the], Oceanus, Phorcys, *and* Pontus.)

NIKE Nike was the personification of victory. She was represented as winged and holding a palm branch, garland, or other symbols of victory. In his account of the origin of the gods, Hesiod writes that Styx, a daughter of Oceanus, mated with the Titan god Pallas and gave birth to the slender-ankled Nike as well as a group of other personified qualities that, generally speaking, would be required for victory: Zelus ("Emulation"), Cratos ("Strength"), and Bia ("Force"). Their place of dwelling, Hesiod adds, is always with Zeus. Nike is certainly also well known as a companion to Athena, judging from the monuments of the Athenian acropolis, especially the temple of Athena Nike, which is in close proximity to the Parthenon, and the small winged Nike that the Parthenon's massive cult statue of Athena held in her hand.

(*See also* Acropolis [the], Athena, Athens, Oceanus [god], Styx [the River], Titans [the], *and* Zeus.)

NOTUS Notus (or Notos) was the personified south wind, and there is not much mythology associated with him. Along with the wind gods Boreas and Zephyr, he was said by the Greek poet Hesiod to be a son of the goddess Eos and her consort Astraeus. According to Virgil, he, Boreas, Zephyr, Eurus (the easterly wind), and Africus (the southwest wind) were subject to control by Aeolus, Lord of the Winds. In a meteorological sense, Notus was described as bringing rain and storms in late fall and winter.

(*See also* Aeolus, Boreas, Eos, Eurus, *and* Zephyr.)

NYMPHS, THE Nymphs were a class of minor deity or spirit that inhabited features of and places in the natural world. Nymphs were envisioned as young women, the word "nymph" being used in Greek to designate human maidens as well as these spirits. There were several varieties of nymph, among them being Naiads, who were nymphs of springs, rivers, and other freshwater sources; Oreads, who were mountain nymphs; Dryads, who were tree nymphs; and Hamadryads, tree nymphs whose lives were very closely bound to those of the trees they inhabited. The Oceanids, daughters of the deified river Oceanus, and Nereids, daughters of the sea deity Nereus, feature prominently in mythology. Notably, while nymphs were minor deities, they were not immortal.

(*See also* Dryads [the], Hamadryads [the], Naiads [the], Nereids [the], Nereus, Oceanids [the], Oceanus, *and* Oreads [the].)

NYSAEAN NYMPHS, THE The Nysaean Nymphs, nymphs residing in the mythical place called Nysa, were seven sisters also known as the Hyades who nursed the infant Dionysus after his miraculous second "birth" from the thigh of Zeus.

(*See also* Dionysus, Hyades [the], Nysa, *and* Zeus.)

OCEANIDS, THE The Oceanids were sea nymphs and the daughters—as many as 3,000 in number—of the Titan god Oceanus and his sister Tethys. Of these, only a few had personal mythologies: Doris, who with Nereus became mother to the fifty Nereid nymphs; Amphitrite, who by some accounts became wife to the god Poseidon; and Metis, who with Zeus became mother to the goddess Athena.

(*See also* Amphitrite, Athena, Doris, Metis, Nereids [the], Nereus, Oceanus [god], Poseidon, Tethys, Titan, *and* Zeus.)

OCEANUS Like his parents Gaia ("Earth") and Uranus ("Sky"), the Titan Oceanus was an elemental deity who was conceived of both as a geographic feature, the river Oceanus, and as a personification of that feature, having parents, a wife, and children. With his sister Tethys he became father to the Oceanid nymphs, as many as 3,000 in number, the most notable of whom were Doris, Amphitrite, and Metis. Oceanus and Tethys also produced all the rivers in the world, which apart from the river Styx, were male. Oceanus is variously depicted as a bearded, mature man, sometimes with horns and a fish tail.

From an elemental perspective, Oceanus was early on envisioned as a river that encircled, and thus was the outer boundary of, the flat, disk-shaped world. This, for example, is how Oceanus is depicted on the Shield of Achilles in Homer's *Iliad*. Oceanus was believed to be the source of all rivers. Helios ("Sun") and Eos ("Dawn") were thought to rise from Oceanus's eastern banks and then, having completed their daily journey, to sink back into the river in the west. For Homer, the Elysian Fields and Hades lay beyond Oceanus and thus beyond the limits of the world. Since Oceanus was, in a sense, liminal and a place of transition between known and unknown, real and unreal, a host of monsters and "exotic" human tribes were said to live in proximity to it. These include the Hesperides, the Gorgons, Geryon, the Hecatoncheires, and the Ethiopians.

As geographic exploration and speculation progressed in the course of time, the conception of Oceanus as a river was questioned, and it was increasingly thought of as a great sea beyond the Straits of Gibraltar or as a "world sea" that encompassed all oceanic waters interconnected.

(*See also* Amphitrite, Elysian Fields [the], Eos, Ethiopia, Gaia, Geryon, Gorgons, Hades, Hecatoncheires [the], Helios, Hesperides [the], Metis, Oceanids [the], Oceanus [place], Tethys, Titans [the], *and* Uranus.)

OPS Ops, whose name means "help" or "resource," was a Roman goddess of the harvest and abundance who, in addition to ensuring the fertility of the earth, assisted in military efforts and in childbirth. Ops had a close ritual connection with Consus, god of the granary, and was known also as the consort of Saturn, perhaps originally a god of seed-sowing but identified by the Romans with the primeval deity Cronus, father of the Olympian gods. As Saturn's consort, Ops logically was sometimes identified with the Greek goddess Rhea, the wife of Cronus.

(*See also* Cronus, Olympus [Mount], Rhea, *and* Saturn.)

ORCUS Orcus was a god of death and, at the same time, a lord of the realm of the dead. He was the Roman counterpart of the Greek gods Thanatos ("Death") and Hades ("King of the Dead"), who was also called Pluto. Like Hades, Orcus's name could be used to designate the Underworld itself.

(*See also* Hades [god], Pluto, Thanatos, *and* Underworld [the].)

OREADS, THE Oreads were mountain nymphs, their name being derived from the Greek word for mountain (*oros*) and the related adjective *oreios, -a, -on* ("mountain-dwelling").

(*See also* Nymphs [the].)

OURANOS Ouranos is the Greek name of the god of the Heavens. His Latinized name is Uranus. Ouranos was the consort of the earth goddess Gaia, and with her produced the Cyclopes, Hecatoncheires, and the Titans, the youngest of whom, Cronus, castrated him in vengeance for grievous wrong done to Gaia.

(*See also* Cyclopes [the], Gaia, Hecatoncheires [the], Titans [the], *and* Uranus.)

PALES Pales was a Roman deity who protected shepherds and sheep, ensuring their fertility. The god was sometimes referred to as female and sometimes male, and was associated with the rustic deities Pan and Faunus. While there is much uncertainty about the nature of Pales and his/her worship, it appears that the shepherds' festival Palilia (or Parilia), which was celebrated on April 21 both in the countryside and in the city of Rome, was dedicated to this deity.

(*See also* Faunus *and* Pan.)

PALLAS Pallas was a name for Athena that was used either alone or as an epithet: in other words, Athena could be called "Pallas" or "Pallas Athena." Relatedly, the ancient wooden statue of Athena that was housed in her Trojan temple and stolen by Odysseus and Diomedes was called the Palladium. The origins of the name Pallas are uncertain, though there are possible etymological links with words designating a young person (in Greek) or female ruler (Semitic). The mythographer Apollodorus mentions two different sources for the name: a playmate of Athena's whom the goddess accidentally killed while they were practicing their fighting skills, or a giant by that name whom she killed deliberately.

The goddess Pallas is to be distinguished from the young hero of the same name, who was an ally of Aeneas and son of the Arcadian king Evander.

(*See also* Aeneas, Arcadia, Athena, Diomedes, Evander, Odysseus, Pallas [hero], *and* Troy.)

PAN Pan was a god of goatherds and shepherds, and his home was said to have been the mountainous regions, forests, and pastures of Arcadia. His name was derived from the root *pa-*, designating guardianship of flocks, a root that is evident also in the Latin word *pastor*, shepherd. Originally an Arcadian deity, his worship spread to other parts of Greece, cult sites sacred to him having been found at Delphi and Athens, for example. Accounts of his parentage were various. This rustic god was called a son of the god Hermes with Dryope, and of Zeus with Penelope, the wife of Odysseus, among others. Pan was represented as being of hybrid appearance, having the body and arms of a human but the head, legs, and tail of a goat. In the so-called *Homeric Hymn* in his honor, in which he is a son of Dryope and Hermes, he is described as being a wonder to behold, having cloven hooves and horns, as well as being noisy and prone to laughter. When his mother saw his face and beard, she reputedly ran away in fear, so Hermes brought him to Mount Olympus, wrapped in rabbit skins, and all the gods, especially Dionysus, were delighted, thereafter calling him "Pan," which is here falsely linked to the word for "everyone" (*pantes*). In his rural haunts, Pan kept the company of nymphs and satyrs, who were hybrid creatures like himself, thus being himself absorbed into the entourage of the god Dionysus. Pan's instrument of choice was the reed pipe, which the Roman poet Ovid describes as his invention: Pan became enamored of a nymph called Syrinx, and when, in order to escape his advances, she became a clump of reeds, he fashioned a pipe from them. When, pipes in hand, he later challenged the god Apollo to a music contest, the Phrygian king Midas declared him the winner and was punished by Apollo for his choice by growing an ass's ears.

(*See also* Apollo, Arcadia, Athens, Delphi, Dionysus, Hermes, Midas, Nymphs [the], Odysseus, Olympus [Mount], Penelope, Satyrs [the], Syrinx, *and* Zeus.)

PARCAE, THE The Parcae, also called Fates (*Fata* in Latin), were the three Roman goddesses of fate or prophetic destiny and, as such, were equivalents of the Greek Moirae. Their names were given as Nona ("Ninth"), Decima ("Tenth"), and Parca ("Midwife"), all being names that point strongly to an origin as deities of childbirth who, by extension, determined the course of the newborn's life. As far as how they operated, the Parcae were variously represented as spinning the threads of fate, reciting or singing a song of fate, and inscribing a person's fate on a tablet. Their attributes were the spindle and scroll.

(*See also* Fates [the] *and* Moirae [the].)

PARTHENOS
Parthenos, "Maiden," was an epithet or descriptor used particularly with reference to Athena but also to other virgin goddesses, in particular Hestia and Artemis.

(*See also* Artemis, Athena, Athens, *and* Hestia.)

PENATES, THE
The Penates were Roman deities who protected the home and homeland. Like the Lares, with whom they were linked, the Penates could function in both the private and the public realm. In the domestic sphere, the Penates' particular responsibility was the interior of the home, its provisions, and its storerooms. Functioning in a public capacity, they protected the Roman state.

(*See also* Lares [the].)

PENEUS
Peneus (also Peneius or Peneios) was the god of the Peneus River that flows through the Vale of Tempe in the region of northern Greece known as Thessaly. He was himself a child of the elemental Titan gods Oceanus and Tethys. He is best known in mythology for being father to the lovely maiden Daphne, who was relentlessly pursued by the god Apollo although she wished ardently to remain a virgin huntress. Exhausted from running to escape the god's advances, Daphne begged her father to save her. Her prayer was granted, and before Apollo's very eyes, she became a laurel tree.

(*See also* Apollo, Daphne, Oceanus [god], Peneus River [the], Tempe [Vale of], Tethys, Thessaly, *and* Titans [the].)

PERSEPHONE
Persephone, also known as Cora ("Maiden"), was the wife of Hades and queen of the Underworld. She was the daughter of Zeus and Demeter, goddess of grain and the harvest. As recounted in the so-called *Homeric Hymn to Demeter*, Hades fell in love with the lovely Persephone and wished to marry her. In accordance with a plan contrived by Zeus and executed with the help of Gaia ("Earth"), Hades took his bride by force: Gaia caused a meadow in the valley of Nysa to bloom irresistibly with roses, crocus, violets, iris, hyacinth, and narcissus, and as Persephone lingered there picking flowers, Hades seized her into his chariot, later plunging into the depths of the earth. A despondent Demeter wandered the earth and ceased to concern herself with planting and

the harvest. Consequently, seeds did not sprout, people starved, and the gods did not receive their habitual sacrifices. Zeus and all the gods attempted to console Demeter, offering her all manner of wonderful gifts in order to convince her to return to Mount Olympus. But she was inconsolable and insisted on the return of her daughter. To this Hades eventually agreed, but first he tricked Persephone into eating some pomegranate seeds, which compelled her to spend a portion of the year—one third (or by some accounts, one half)—with him. The months during which Persephone stayed in Hades were months of mourning for Demeter, corresponding to the late autumn and winter months when seed lay dormant in the soil. When Persephone re-emerged in spring, her mother rejoiced, and planted seeds could sprout.

Persephone was worshipped in conjunction with her mother, Demeter, as a fertility and culture-sustaining deity as well as guarantor of a felicitous afterlife. Their most important festivals were the Thesmophoria and the Eleusinian Mysteries, both of which required secrecy on the part of the celebrants.

In art, Persephone, who was called Proserpina by the Romans, was represented as a young woman bearing torches or stalks of grain.

(*See also* Demeter, Eleusis, Gaia, Hades [god and place], Nysa, Olympus [Mount], Underworld [the], *and* Zeus.)

PHOEBE The Titan goddess Phoebe, "Shining One" or "Prophetic One," was known primarily as spouse of her brother Coeus and mother to the second-generation Titan goddesses Asteria and Leto. Phoebe's grandchildren were the deities Hecate, Apollo, and Artemis. As a deity with prophetic powers, Phoebe was said by the Greek playwright Aeschylus to have been in control of the famous oracle at Delphi after her mother, Gaia, and her sister Themis. Phoebe would later give the oracle to her grandson Apollo.

(*See also* Apollo, Artemis, Coeus, Delphi, Gaia, Hecate, Leto, *and* Themis.)

PHOEBUS Phoebus was a name for Apollo, being used alone or as a forename for the god: Phoebus or Phoebus Apollo. The name has been taken to mean "Bright One," but it remains unclear whether it was assigned to Apollo as a reference to his appearance, his divinity, his purity, or his association with the sun.

(*See* Apollo.)

PHORCYS The sea god Phorcys was born of the primeval deities Pontus ("Sea") and Gaia ("Earth"). In Homer's *Odyssey*, he is known as the Old Man of the Sea, and there is a safe harbor on the island of Ithaca named after him.

PLATE III
Poseidon: God of the sea, punisher of Odysseus

It is the harbor of Phorcys, with its olive tree and sacred grotto, that welcomes home a war- and travel-weary Odysseus after a twenty-year absence. With his sister, Ceto, Phorcys became father to the monstrous Graiae and Gorgons. By some accounts, the two also produced the serpent-maiden Echidna and Ladon, the snake that guarded the Hesperides' golden apples. He was also said to have been the grandfather of the Cyclops Polyphemus and to have sired the Sirens and Scylla, all of them monsters.

(*See also* Cyclopes [the], Echidna, Gaia, Gorgons [the], Graiae [the], Hesperides [the], Ithaca, Ladon, Odysseus, Polyphemus, Scylla, *and* Sirens [the].)

PIERIDES, THE

The Muses, goddesses who embodied artistic inspiration, were sometimes called Pierides (as well as Pierian) after their birthplace Pieria at the foot of Mount Olympus. Strictly speaking, Pierides is a patronymic, and means "children of Pierus." As there was a tradition, recorded by the travel writer Pausanias, that Pierus, a king of Macedon, established the worship of the Muses, they could, in a metaphorical sense, be viewed as his daughters. According to the Roman poet Ovid, Pierus happened himself to have nine daughters who had lovely singing voices. His daughters made the fatal mistake of challenging the Muses to a singing contest and, upon their inevitable loss, were changed into chattering magpies.

(*See also* Macedon, Muses [the], Olympus [Mount], Pieria, *and* Pierus.)

PLEIADES, THE

The Pleiades, or Seven Sisters, were nymphs and children of Atlas and Pleione, a daughter of Oceanus. Their siblings were the Hyades, who were also nymphs, and Hyas, their only brother. The Pleiades' names are given as Alycone, Celaeno, Electra, Maia, Merope, Sterope (or Asterope), and Taygete. Almost all of them had children by various gods. The most important of them are as follows: Oenomaus was born to Sterope/Asterope by Ares; Dardanus to Electra, and Hermes to Maia by Zeus. Merope, however, was impregnated by the mortal Sisyphus and, consequently, bore Glaucus (the hero, not the god of this name). The Pleiades became a star cluster, placed in the heavens by Zeus, either because the giant Orion pursued them, and Zeus raised them to the heavens to save them, or as compensation for their grief over the death of their sisters the Hyades. Of the seven, only six are visible. It was said that one of the sisters hid in shame or grief. If this was a grieving Electra, her sorrow resulted from the fall of Troy, which her son Laomedon had founded. If, on the other hand, this was Merope, she was ashamed at having borne a child to a mortal.

The name "Pleiades" is variously explained as derived from the Greek word for sailing and that for weeping. Whatever the case, the rising of the Pleiades corresponded with the beginning of sailing season and with spring sowing. Their setting, in turn, coincided with the harvest.

(*See also* Atlas, Dardanus, Electra [nymph], Glaucus [hero], Hyades [the], Laomedon, Maia, Merope [nymph], Oceanus, *and* Orion.)

PLUTO

Pluto was another name for Hades, god of the Underworld. Derived from the Greek word for wealth, *ploutos*, this incarnation of the god emphasized a different aspect of his association with the Underworld, namely the depths of the earth as a source of bounty.

(*See also* Hades *and* Underworld [the].)

POLLUX

Pollux, known in Greek as Polydeuces, was one of the divine twins, the Dioscuri, who ultimately became the constellation Gemini. Pollux and his brother, Castor, were sons of the Spartan queen Leda, and their sisters were Helen of Troy and Clytemnestra, the faithless wife of king Agamemnon of Mycenae. Though both brothers were represented as horsemen, Pollux's particular skill was boxing, in which art he distinguished himself while particpating in Jason's quest for the Golden Fleece.

(*See also* Agamemnon, Clytemnestra, Dioscuri [the], Gemini, Helen, Jason, Leda, Mycenae, Sparta, *and* Troy.)

POLYHYMNIA

"Many-Hymned" Polyhymnia, goddess of many songs and/or of songs performed by many voices, was one of the Muses. Her spheres of influence included choral song and pantomime and extended to historiography and rhetoric, thus overlapping with Clio. There were obscure legends according to which she was the mother of the hero Triptolemus; the singer Orpheus, who was known also as the son of the Muse Calliope; and even, according to Plato, Eros.

(*See also* Calliope, Clio, Eros, Muses [the], *and* Triptolemus.)

POMONA

Pomona was the Roman goddess of fruit (Latin *pomum*). According to the Roman poet Ovid, the beautiful Pomona had been devoted to gardens and orchards, which she tended with care, watering and pruning the plants. She had no interest in the world outside her garden, nor did she have an interest in love, though she had many suitors, particularly among the rustic deities and spirits: Priapus, Silenus, and Satyrs. When the god Vertumnus saw her, he was instantly smitten and tried to approach her in many guises: as a reaper, a herdsman, a vintner, an apple picker, a fisherman, and a soldier. At last, he disguised himself as an elderly woman and gestured toward an elm around which twined a burgeoning grapevine. He pointed out how the vine would decline if separated from the tree. Like the vine, he argued, she should not be alone. He told her the story of Iphis and Anaxarete, too—a story of tragic love. In the end, he won her heart, and she became his consort.

(*See also* Anaxarete, Iphis, Priapus, Satyrs [the], Silenus, *and* Vertumnus.)

POSEIDON
Poseidon was the Greek god of the sea and thus necessarily the patron deity of navigation and maritime battles; as he had the ability to calm and stir up the seas, he was both savior and potential nemesis of sailors and fishermen. Poseidon was also the god of earthquakes, described by Homer as the "Earthshaker" who caused the earth to tremble when he struck it with his trident. Further, he was the god of horses, which he was believed to have created, and he was closely associated with horse breeding and racing. While the meaning of his name is uncertain, Poseidon was a god of great antiquity in Greece, notations of his name dating to the Bronze Age, a period extending from roughly 3000 to 1050 BCE. Given Poseidon's realm of influence, a great many temples and sanctuaries sacred to him were located on coastal sites, as at Sunion in the territory of Athens and on the Isthmus of Corinth, site of the Pan-Hellenic Isthmian Games that were celebrated in his honor; however, sites sacred to him could also be found inland at places where there were clefts in the earth or springs.

In terms of his mythology, Poseidon was a son of the Titan gods Cronus and Rhea. His siblings were Zeus, Hades, Hestia, Demeter, and Hera, all of whom apart from Zeus were swallowed by their father upon their birth and later disgorged. When Cronus's children prevailed over him and the older Titan gods, seizing rulership of the world from them, it was not a given that Zeus would be king of the gods, nor was it predetermined which part of the world each of the brothers would control. Hades, Poseidon, and Zeus accordingly drew lots from a helmet. Hades became lord of the Underworld, Zeus the lord of the heavens, and Poseidon lord of the sea, with an underwater palace near Aegae on the island of Euboea. Poseidon later became involved in a series of disputes with other Olympian gods over territories in Greece. With Athena he vied for patronage of Athens, engaging with her in a contest in order to win this land; Athena caused an olive tree to grow, and Poseidon, smiting the rock of the Acropolis with his trident, produced a saltwater spring, a symbol of naval power. Athena's gift was deemed more valuable, and she became the patron deity of Athens. As a result of a dispute with the god Helios over Corinth, Poseidon was assigned the Isthmus, while Helios was given the height of Acrocorinth. Poseidon lost his bid for Argos to the goddess Hera.

While the sea goddess Amphitrite was called his consort, as well as mother by him of Triton, Poseidon had numerous extramarital amorous encounters. Among the best known of these was his pursuit of a grief-stricken Demeter, whom he pursued while she searched for her daughter, Persephone; in order to escape him, Demeter transformed herself into a mare, but Poseidon could not be deceived and, in turn, became a stallion, in this way fathering the immortal horse Arion, which would eventually pass to the ownership of Hercules and, later, to the hero Adrastus. Poseidon saved the lovely Danaid Amymone from assault by a Satyr, chasing it off with his trident, but in the process, he fell in love with her and, taking her by force, became father to her son Nauplius. Poseidon also impregnated Medusa with Pegasus and Chrysaor, both of whom were born from her neck when Bellerophon decapitated her. And on the same night that Aegeus slept with Aethra, Poseidon slept with her as well, in this way becoming a second father of the Athenian hero Theseus. With the nymph Thoosa, a daughter of the sea deity Phorcys, he became father to the Cyclops Polyphemus.

Among those who felt Poseidon's wrath were the Trojans and Odysseus. The god's hatred of the former stemmed from the period of his servitude to the Trojan king Laomedon, who refused to pay him and Apollo for building the city's wall. As for Odysseus, he incurred Poseidon's anger by blinding the monstrous Polyphemus, and as a consequence, the god ensured that Odysseus's journey home from Troy would be both long and difficult, filled with perils from the sea. Minos, king of Crete, also incurred the god's displeasure after asking Poseidon to ratify his claim to the throne by producing a bull from the sea. Poseidon obliged him, but Minos subsequently broke his promise to sacrifice the animal to the god. As a result, Poseidon caused Minos's wife, Pasiphae, to develop a passion for the bull, an infatuation that resulted in the birth of the Minotaur.

As for Poseidon's attributes and distinguishing characteristics, he was represented as a mature, bearded male holding a trident. Animals sacred to him included bulls, horses, and dolphins. As regards plants, he had a special connection with pine, which was particularly well suited for the production of ships' masts.

The Romans identified their sea god Neptune with Poseidon.

(*See also* Adrastus, Aethra, Amymone, Apollo, Argos, Athena, Athens, Chrysaor, Corinth, Crete, Cronus, Danaids [the], Demeter, Hades, Helios, Hera, Hercules, Hestia,

Laomedon, Medusa, Minos, Minotaur [the], Neptune, Odysseus, Pasiphae, Pegasus, Persephone, Phorcys, Polyphemus, Rhea, Satyrs [the], Theseus, Titans [the], Troy, *and* Zeus.)

PRIAPUS

Priapus was a fertility god of Phrygian origin and thus an import from northwestern Asia Minor, where he remained more popular than in Greece and Italy. He was responsible for promoting the fertility of animals and plants along with that of humans and, for this reason, was important to the enterprises of animal husbandry and farming. As a fertility deity, he was also a guarantor of good fortune. His statues were believed to promote a bountiful harvest and, at the same time, protect sheep, goats, bees, vines, and garden produce from thieves as well as from the envious evil eye.

This lusty god was distinguished physically by an oversize erect phallus, and he was part of the entourage of the god Dionysus, along with Nymphs, Satyrs, and Silens. Reflecting his "nature," Priapus's parents were generally said to be the goddess Aphrodite and Dionysus, though the gods Hermes, Zeus, and Pan are also mentioned as his father and a nymph as his mother.

(*See also* Aphrodite, Dionysus, Hermes, Nymphs [the], Pan, Phrygia, Satyrs [the], Silens [the], *and* Zeus.)

PROMETHEUS

Prometheus was a second-generation Titan god from a patrilinear perspective. According to the Greek poet Hesiod, he was the son of the Titan Iapetus and Clymene, daughter of Iapetus's brother Oceanus, and his siblings were Atlas, who would be compelled to carry the heavens; the short-lived sinner Menoetius; and the thoughtless Epimetheus. Prometheus, whose name means "forethought," was known both for his cunning and for his kindliness toward humans. On an occasion when the gods and mortals were at odds, Prometheus prepared a joint meal for them, asking Zeus to choose his own portion. The portion that Prometheus rightly suspected Zeus would choose consisted of an animal's bones wrapped in glistening fat, which looked larger and richer than the portion consisting solely of meat. In anger that he had been outwitted and that humans had benefited from his choice of the less nutritious portion, Zeus decided to withhold fire from humans. In this instance, too, Prometheus outwitted him and stole fire for them, hiding some flames in a hollow fennel stalk. For this infraction, Zeus contrived a more lasting punishment: he instructed Hephaestus to create a woman, the first of her gender, as a gift not for Prometheus, who would guess that the gift was a hidden danger, but for Prometheus's brother Epimetheus. The woman was Pandora, who brought with her blessings of all kinds but also every kind of evil. As for Prometheus, Zeus placed him in shackles and drove a shaft through his body so as to anchor him to a rocky crag while an eagle (or vulture) ate perpetually of his eternally regenerating liver. Prometheus was eventually released from this torture by Zeus and Hercules. The latter consulted Prometheus, whom he found in the Caucasus Mountains, when seeking the Garden of the Hesperides, and as compensation for the guidance offered, Hercules killed the eagle that had been tormenting him. Zeus, for his part, released Prometheus from his shackles in exchange for advising him not to pursue the goddess Thetis, for it had been prophesied that a son born to her would be more powerful than her father. As the mythographer Hyginus reports, Zeus compelled Prometheus to wear a finger ring of iron fitted with a piece of the stone to which he had been chained as a reminder of his earlier presumption.

Given the importance of fire to the advancement of human civilization and culture, it is not surprising that Prometheus was not only presented as a bene-factor of humankind but also as a culture hero credited, according to the trage-dian Aeschylus, with introducing the arts of shelter-building, agriculture, mathematics, writing, animal domestication, and navigation. There was also a tradition that it was Prometheus who actually created humans, fashioning them out of earth and water.

(*See also* Atlas, Caucasus Mountains [the], Clymene, Epimetheus, Hephaestus, Hercules, Hesperides [the], Iapetus, Oceanus [god], Pandora, Titans [the], *and* Zeus.)

PROSERPINA
Proserpina was the Roman name for Persephone, who, to the horror of her mother, Demeter, was abducted by Hades, King of the Dead, to become his queen.

(*See also* Hades [god], Persephone, *and* Underworld [the].)

PROTEUS
Proteus was a sea deity who, logically, had close ties with the sea god Poseidon: he was said to be the herdsman of Poseidon's flock of seals, and the mythographer Apollodorus reports that the god Poseidon was his father. Proteus was characterized as elderly and could change his shape as well as foretell the future, attributes that he had in common with the sea gods Nereus and Phorcys. Persons wishing to hear him foretell the future were required to seize him and retain their grip while he assumed every possible shape in order to escape the necessity of prophesying; if steadily held, he resumed his normal appearance and told the truth. Those who consulted Proteus successfully included the Spartan king Menelaus who, after arriving at the island of Pharos on his way home from Troy, followed guidance offered by Proteus's daughter Eidothea:

Menelaus, with the help of three companions all disguised as seals, was to seize the god at midday while he was napping in a cave with his seal flock. Proteus changed from a lion to a serpent, leopard, boar, water, and an enormous tree, but the men held fast. The god then revealed to Menelaus that he would need to make an offering of a hundred head of cattle to the gods so they would grant him safe passage home, and he disclosed the fate of Menelaus's former companions at Troy, among them his brother Agamemnon and Odysseus. Another hero who consulted Proteus was the beekeeper Aristaeus, who availed himself of the god to learn why his bees had died.

There was also an Egyptian king named Proteus who appears in mythology and who may have become confused with the god and, as a result, called by the same name. King Proteus is chiefly known for having given sanctuary to Helen when the god Hermes, according to a variant of Helen's Trojan adventures, brought her to him during the Trojan War.

(*See also* Agamemnon, Aristaeus, Helen, Hermes, Menelaus, Nereus, Odysseus, Phorcys, Poseidon, Sparta, *and* Troy.)

PSYCHOPOMPUS
The name or epithet Psychopompus ("Leader of Souls") was applied to the god Hermes when he served in this capacity. It was Hermes who led the souls of the dead to the Underworld.

(*See also* Hermes *and* Underworld [the].)

PYTHIAN
Pythian was an epithet for Apollo, the god of prophecy, music, archery, healing, and light. According to the so-called *Homeric Hymn to Apollo*, this descriptor was directly linked with the god's slaying of the massive serpent, the Python, that once resided at Delphi and the slaying of which allowed Apollo to take control of the oracle there. Apollo's priestess at Delphi, who served as mouthpiece of the god when he was consulted by those seeking prophecies, was called the Pythia, and Pytho was another name for Delphi.

(*See* Apollo, Delphi, *and* Python.)

QUIRINUS
Quirinus was a Roman god who became identified with the deified Romulus, the legendary founder of Rome. He may originally have been a Sabine war god and, when integrated into Roman state religion, represented the Roman citizen body as their protector.

(*See also* Rome, Romulus, *and* Sabines [the].)

RHEA
In mythology, Rhea was a Titan goddess and a daughter of Gaia ("Earth") and Uranus ("Heaven"). Her brother Cronus was her consort, and,

according to the Greek poet Hesiod, she bore to him Hestia, Demeter, Hera, Hades, Poseidon, and Zeus. Having learned from his parents that he was destined to be overpowered by his own son, Cronus swallowed each of his children as they emerged from their mother's womb, apart from Zeus. For, by that time, Rhea had asked her parents what she could do to outwit Cronus and save her youngest child. On their advice, she went to Crete, where she hid her newborn child in a cave, and to Cronus she gave a stone wrapped in swaddling clothes, which he swallowed, not guessing that he had been tricked. When grown, Zeus, with the help of Rhea (or, by some accounts, his first wife Metis), would trick Cronus into vomiting up both the stone and his siblings and then successfully wage war against him and the other Titan gods. The mythographer Apollodorus supplies additional detail to the story of Zeus's birth to Rhea: it was in the cave of Dicte that Rhea hid Zeus, and she gave him to the Curetes and to the nymphs Adrastea and Ida to nurse. In that cave the nymphs fed the child with the milk of a goat called Amalthea, and the Curetes danced about clashing their spears against their shields so that Cronus might not hear the baby crying.

In Greek religion and culture more broadly, Rhea was an earth-mother goddess, of whom Hera, Demeter, and Aphrodite were also at least to some degree incarnations or refractions. As a Great Mother, Rhea was inherently a goddess of life and fertility who was associated, at the same time, with death. As her mythology suggests, she appears to have enjoyed particular prominence on the island of Crete, and her assimilation with the Phrygian fertility goddess Cybele, whose worship was orgiastic and ecstatic in nature, underscores the notion of a common Anatolian (western-Asian) origin of the two. In Roman religion, Rhea was identified with the goddess Ops.

(See also Adrastea, Aphrodite, Crete, Cronus, Curetes [the], Cybele, Demeter, Gaia, Hades, Hera, Hestia, Ida [nymph], Metis, Ops, Phrygia, Poseidon, Titans [the], Uranus, and Zeus.)

SATURN Saturn was an Italian fertility god, possibly of Etruscan or Sabine origin. As his name, which Roman authors derived from the word *sator* ("one who sows"), indicates, his particular realm was the fertility of the fields and, thus, agriculture. At the same time, he was viewed as a culture hero who established both planting practices and other mainstays of good social order, such as laws, writing, and coinage. Consequently, the temple built at the foot of Rome's Capitoline Hill in his honor served as an archive for laws as well as the seat of the Roman treasury.

Saturn was identified with the Greek god Cronus, father of Zeus and the other Olympian gods. As an equivalent of Cronus, his consort was Ops ("Wealth" or "Resource"), who was herself viewed as the Roman equivalent of the Greek mother-goddess Rhea. Saturn was thought to have established himself as a ruler among the Italians when, partly on the succession model of Cronus and Zeus, he was driven from the heavens by his son. His rule constituted a Golden Age of peace and plenty. Saturn's son, according to the Roman poet Virgil, was Picus, grandfather of the Laurentine king Latinus, whose daughter Lavinia the Trojan hero Aeneas wed.

The originally seven-day December festival of the Saturnalia celebrated in this god's honor marked the wintertime end of work in the fields and served as a model for aspects of the Christian observation of Christmas.

(*See also* Capitoline Hill [the], Cronus, Latinus, Lavinia, Olympus [Mount], Ops, Picus, Rhea, *and* Zeus.)

SATYRS, THE Satyrs were woodland spirits who were originally conceived of as part horse and part human. Over time, they assumed the features of a goat.

(*See* Satyrs [Hybrid Creatures].)

SELENE Selene, goddess of the Moon and the moon's personification, was said by the Greek poet Hesiod to be a daughter of the Titan Hyperion, a sun deity, her sisters being Helios ("Sun") and Eos ("Dawn"). According to the mythographer Apollodorus, she fell in love with the handsome Endymion, the son of Aethlius, founder of Elis, or of Zeus. The gods granted Endymion a wish, and what he chose was to sleep forever, remaining both deathless and ageless.

(*See also* Endymion, Helios, Hyperion, Titans [the], *and* Zeus.)

SOL Sol, "sun" in Latin, was the Roman counterpart of the Greek sun god Helios. In the religious and broader cultural thought of the Roman world, Sol was a judge and champion of law, but also a deity of sun, fire, and light as well as a rainmaker responsible for promoting the growth of plants.

(*See also* Apollo *and* Helios.)

SOMNUS Somnus was a personification and the Roman god of sleep. He was identified with the Greek god Hypnus.

(*See* Hypnus.)

STEROPE Sterope was one of the Pleiades, seven nymphs born of Atlas and Pleione, a daughter of Oceanus. The mythographer Apollodorus records that she became mother to the bird-women known as the Sirens and, by the war god Ares, of Oenomaus, a king of Pisa, who became enamored of his own daughter and found a way to kill all of her suitors but Pelops, the last.

(*See also* Ares, Atlas, Oceanus [god], Oenomaus, Pelops, Pleiades [the], *and* Sirens [the].)

SYLVANUS

Sylvanus (or Silvanus) was an Italian spirit of the woods but also a god of agriculture, cultivated fields, and flocks who straddled and negotiated the divide between nature and culture. His origins are debated, and he has been variously called a particular manifestation of the god Mars, in the guise of a deity of fields and farming, or of Faunus, as well as an outright reflection of the derivation of his name: *silva* in Latin is the word for "forest." He was sometimes identified with the rustic god Pan, and ancient images depict him as an elderly, bearded male wearing an animal skin and holding pine cones, fruit, pine branches, or a sickle.

(*See also* Faunus, Mars, *and* Pan.)

SYRINX

The Naiad (water nymph) Syrinx was the origin of, and gave her name to, the reed pipe played by the nature god Pan. According to the Roman poet Ovid, Syrinx, who lived in the mountains of Arcadia, was spotted one day by Pan, who desired her. Syrinx, wishing to remain a virgin like the goddess Artemis, fled the god's advance and, upon coming to the river Ladon, asked the water nymphs, her sisters, to help her. Her wish was granted. The moment that the god laid hands on her, she became a handful of reeds. As the god breathed upon them, the reeds rustled sweetly in response. Captivated by the sound and wishing in this way to continue communicating with her, Pan bound reeds of graduated lengths, fastening them with wax. The result was the Pan pipe, *syrinx* in Greek.

(*See also* Arcadia, Artemis, Naiads [the], *and* Pan.)

TARTARUS

Tartarus was the name given to the darkest, gloomiest depths of the earth, and was the part the Underworld reserved for sinners. While Tartarus was known primarily as a "place," he is (at least to some degree) a personified primordial deity in the poet Hesiod's account of the origins of the world and its gods. According to Hesiod, Tartarus and Gaia ("Earth") were the first components of the world to come into being from Chaos ("Void"). With Gaia, a personified Tartarus became the father of the monstrous Typhon and Echidna. According to later authors, he was also the father of Zeus's sacred eagle as well as of Thanatos ("Death") and even the sorceress-goddess Hecate.

(*See also* Chaos, Echidna, Gaia, Hecate, Thanatos, Typhon, Underworld [the], *and* Zeus.)

TERMINUS Terminus was a personification of boundary markers (whether stones or buried logs) and the tenacious Roman deity of property boundaries, which were established and safeguarded not only by law but also by this god. According to Roman lore, Terminus would not yield his place on the Capitoline Hill in Rome even for the god Jupiter when Jupiter's temple was being built, this being the reason that the temple enclosed Terminus's sacred boundary stone. The legendary Roman king Numa (or Titus Tatius) was credited with having established the worship of Terminus, whose festival, the Terminalia, was celebrated on February 23.

(*See also* Capitoline Hill [the], Jupiter, Numa, *and* Rome.)

TERPSICHORE Terpsichore, "She Who Delights in the Choral Dance," was one of the nine Muses. She became viewed specifically as the patron goddess of choruses, groups that sang and danced, and of choral song, her attributes being the flute and lyre. Like her sisters Calliope, Euterpe, and Urania, she was named as a mother of the famed bard Linus, and both she and Urania were identified as mothers of the marriage god Hymen. Either she or her sister Melpomene was said to have given birth to the Sirens.

(*See also* Calliope, Euterpe, Hymen, Linus, Melpomene, Muses [the], Sirens [the], *and* Urania.)

TETHYS Tethys was one of the Titan gods, the first set of children born to Gaia and Uranus. To her brother Oceanus, Tethys bore the 3,000 Oceanid nymphs, as well as the river gods, all of them male. She is sometimes described as a sea goddess but was also known as the source of Oceanus's sweet waters. She and her consort, Oceanus, took the goddess Hera into their care when Zeus was at war with his father, Cronus.

(*See also* Cronus, Gaia, Hera, Oceanids [the], Oceanus [god], Tethys, Titan, Uranus, *and* Zeus.)

THALIA There were several deities called Thalia (or Thaleia), "Blooming One." The most prominent of these was the Muse of that name who became the patron deity of comedy and other light literary genres (versus tragedy and epic, for example). The comic mask was her attribute.

The other Thalias were a Nereid nymph, one of the three Graces, and a nymph who bore the Sicilian gods called the Palici.

(*See also* Graces [the], Muses [the], *and* Nereids [the].)

THANATOS Thanatos was the personification of death in Greek mythology. He was the son of Nyx ("Night") and the brother of Hypnus ("Sleep"). He was early on depicted as a winged youth but, over time, was thought of as a grizzled elderly man.

(*See also* Hypnus.)

THEMIS Themis, whose name means "custom" or "sacred law," was, logically, a personification of custom and law as established by nature or the gods versus human law created through legal proceedings. She was one of the Titan gods who were offspring of Gaia ("Earth") and Uranus ("Heaven"). According to the Greek poet Hesiod, Themis became Zeus's second wife after Metis, and she bore to him the Horae ("Seasons"), Eunomia ("Good Order"), Dike ("Justice"), Eirene ("Peace"), and the Moirae ("Fates"), who determine what good things and what misfortunes will come to humans in the course of their lives. All of these children reflect principles or mechanisms that ensure an orderly existence. According to the tragic poet Aeschylus, Themis was given control of the famous oracle at Delphi by Gaia, its original owner; Themis would pass it on to Phoebe, who in turn would pass it on to Apollo. Themis had close ties with Zeus in his role as guarantor of righteousness and good governance; as the poet Pindar writes, she sat on a throne next to him. Themis also had very close ties with her mother, Gaia, as a result of which she was regarded as an earth or fertility goddess and also as a deity having prophetic powers. Among those mythological characters that she helped in her capacity as a prophetic deity were Deucalion and Pyrrha, the sole survivors of the Great Flood; Atlas, who was forewarned of a future attempt to steal the apples of the Hesperides; and Zeus, who ceased to pursue Thetis when he learned that her child would be more powerful than its father. With her Titan brother Iapetus, Themis was also said to be mother to the second-generation Titan Prometheus, the benefactor of humankind.

(*See also* Atlas, Delphi, Deucalion, Dike, Gaia, Hesperides [the], Metis, Moirae [the], Phoebe, Prometheus, Pyrrha, Thetis, Titans [the], Uranus, *and* Zeus.)

TISIPHONE Tisiphone, whose name means "Avenger of Murder," was one of the Erinyes (or Furies, in Latin), who were fearsome, snake-haired spirits of vengeance. Her sisters were Megaera ("Envious One") and Alecto ("Implacable One"). For the Roman poet Virgil, Tisiphone was guardian of the gates to Tartarus, a region in the Underworld reserved for sinners, and she, together with her sisters, was tasked with executing punishments allotted by the Underworld's judge Rhadamanthus.

(*See also* Alecto, Erinyes [the], Furies [the], Rhadamanthus, Tartarus, *and* Underworld [the].)

TITANS, THE As the universe and its gods were born, Gaia ("Earth") produced Uranus ("Heaven") to cover her on every side, and with this elemental male deity, she produced several groups of children, among them the three one-eyed Cyclopes, the Hecatoncheires ("Hundred-Handers"), and the twelve Titans, six male and six female: the brothers Oceanus, Coeus, Crius, Hyperion, Iapetus, and Cronus; and the sisters Theia, Rhea, Themis, Mnemosyne, Phoebe, and Tethys. The best known of the Titans, some of whom are elemental and/or personifications, are the world-river Oceanus; Rhea, who married her brother Cronus and gave birth to Zeus and his siblings; Themis ("Divine Law"); Mnemosyne ("Memory"), who became the mother of the Muses; Tethys, who married Oceanus and bore the Oceanids; and Iapetus, who became father to Atlas, Prometheus, and Epimetheus.

The origins and power struggles of the Titans were described in some detail by the Greek poet Hesiod. Uranus detested the Hecatoncheires and Cyclopes at first sight, and pressed the newborn monsters back inside their mother, Gaia, causing her enormous distress. Gaia called upon the Titans to help her, and only one was bold enough to volunteer. This was Cronus, the youngest of the group, who lay in hiding until Uranus came to lie with Gaia at night and castrated his father. This act resulted not only in the birth of Aphrodite and the fearsome Erinyes but also in Cronus's becoming the king of the gods. Cronus then married his sister Rhea and with her produced Zeus and his siblings, who would become known as the Olympian gods. Having heard that one of his sons was destined to overpower him, Cronus swallowed each of his children as they were born, with exception of Zeus, whom Rhea saved by handing Cronus a stone wrapped in swaddling clothes. A ten-year power struggle between the Titans and the Olympian gods, which was called the Titanomachy (and was even in antiquity confused with the Gigantomachy, "battle between the gods and Giants"), ensued. So intense was the fight that heaven, earth, and sea were shaken. Zeus enlisted the aid of the Hecatoncheires and prevailed over the Titans, whom he imprisoned in Tartarus, with the Hecatoncheires as guards. Later sources specify that not all the Titans were involved in the Titanomachy and, as a result, not all were imprisoned.

The children and grandchildren of the Titans are also often called "Titans," though they are technically a second or, in some cases, third generation of this group of deities.

(See also Aphrodite, Atlas, Coeus, Cronus, Cyclopes [the], Epimetheus, Erinyes, Gaia, Giants [the], Hecatoncheires [the], Hyperion, Iapetus, Mnemosyne, Muses [the], Oceanids [the], Oceanus, Olympus [Mount], Phoebe, Prometheus, Rhea, Tethys, Themis, Uranus, and Zeus.)

TRITON The sea god Triton was the son of the god Poseidon by the Oceanid Amphitrite and resided in the depths of the sea. He was also known to spend time in Lake Tritonis (hence the lake's name) in Libya, where Jason and the Argonauts encountered him. Triton was hybrid in form, having the torso of a human and the tail of a fish. The Roman poet Ovid describes the bearded Triton has being blue-green in color, having barnacle-clad shoulders, and possessing a shell on which he blew to cause the Great Flood's waters to recede when the world had, due to humanity's evil, become one great ocean.

The travel writer Pausanias mentions not one but several Tritons and recounts two strange tales that he heard in Boeotia. A Triton was said to have stolen cattle and to have attacked small ships in the region until the local populace plied him with wine and, when he was asleep, beheaded him. This beheaded Triton, Pausanias opines, appears to have inspired a local headless statue of the creature, who clearly was no longer considered immortal. The second story involves local women who wished to purify themselves in the sea to prepare for worshipping Dionysus. A Triton attacked them, and the creature was driven off by Dionysus himself when the women called for help. In Rome, Pausanias adds, he saw a Triton that had green, matted hair, with the appearance of marsh frogs. His body, ending in a dolphin's tail, was covered with scales like a fish, and he had gills beneath the ears, but he had a human nose. His mouth was broad and bestial; his eyes blue; his hands, fingers, and fingernails like murex shells.

(*See also* Amphitrite, Argonauts [the], Boeotia, Dionysus, Jason, Oceanids [the], Poseidon, *and* Rome.)

URANIA Urania (or Ourania), "The Heavenly One," was one of the Muses, deities who inspired artistic expression. She became identified as the patroness of astronomy and astrology and, as a result, was associated with the natural sciences and philosophy. She was described as the mother both of the famed singer Linus (as, incidentally, was her sister Calliope) and of Hymen, the personification of marriage hymns.

There were several other Uranias in Classical mythology. One was an Oceanid nymph, a daughter of Oceanus and Tethys. The goddesses Hera, Hecate, Hebe, Artemis, and Nemesis were also referred to as Urania in the sense that they were "heavenly" and resided on Mount Olympus. Urania as a cult title of Aphrodite appears to be a reference to her role as a fertility goddess and offspring of Uranus.

(*See also* Aphrodite, Artemis, Hebe, Hecate, Hera, Nemesis, Oceanids [the], Oceanus [god], Olympus [Mount], Tethys, *and* Uranus.)

URANUS Uranus, known in Greek as Ouranos, was a personification of the Heavens or sky as well as the sky itself. According to the poet Hesiod's account of the origin of the gods and the universe, Gaia, the elemental goddess Earth, produced Uranus to cover her on all sides and to be a place of residence for the gods (who were not yet born). Together Gaia and Uranus had several groups of children: the twelve Titan gods, the three one-eyed Cyclopes, and the three Hecatoncheires ("Hundred-Handers"). The six newborn monsters were so distasteful to Uranus that he pressed them back inside their mother, causing her terrible pain. For this outrage she sought vengeance, and she persuaded Cronus, the youngest of the Titans, to carry out her plot. When Uranus next came to lie with her at night, Cronus crept out of his place of hiding and castrated his father, whereby Uranus ceased also to be the most powerful male deity. Uranus's severed genitalia fell into the sea, and from the foam arising around them was born Aphrodite. From the blood that fell on the earth sprang the Giants and the Erinyes, spirits of vengeance. Cronus would, in turn, be overpowered by his own son Zeus, who ultimately became king of all the gods. This succession myth (Uranus-Cronus-Zeus) has Near Eastern parallels that point strongly to a common origin of these stories.

(*See also* Aphrodite, Cronus, Cyclopes [the], Erinyes [the], Gaia, Giants [the], Hecatoncheires [the], Titans [the], *and* Zeus.)

VESTA Vesta was the Roman counterpart of the Greek Hestia, goddess of the hearth. There is no mythology associated with Vesta per se. In the Roman world, Vesta presided over both the family hearth and also the central hearth of the city and state, thus being the symbolic heart of the family and collaborative groups of families. In the city of Rome, the six priestesses of Vesta tended her sacred fire, which resided unextinguished in a circular temple in the Roman forum. These priestesses, six in number, were appointed between the ages of six and ten and served the goddess for a period of thirty years, at which point they were free to marry. Vestals who were discovered to have broken their vows of chastity, a rare occurrence, were buried alive.

(*See also* Hestia *and* Rome.)

VULCAN Vulcan (or Volcanus) was a Roman god of fire, especially of its destructive aspects. He was called upon as Mulciber ("Mitigator"), Quietus ("Peaceful One"), and Mitis ("Gentle One") in his capacity to control conflagrations and their outbreak. Vulcan was a god of great antiquity in Rome, but his origins are unknown; it has been posited that he was originally an Etruscan deity who arrived in Italy via the eastern Mediterranean. His consort was a goddess named Maia, who was distinct from the daughter of Atlas and mother of Hermes. Being a deity of importance to the Romans, Vulcan had a shrine, the Volcanal, at the base of the Capitoline Hill in the Roman Forum and a temple in the Campus Martius that was constructed later. The Volcanalia, a festival celebrated annually in his honor on August 23, involved the sacrifice of live fish from the Tiber that were thrown on the god's flames.

Vulcan was identified with Hephaestus, the Greek god of the forge as well as of volcanoes and subterranean fires, as early as the fourth century BCE and, accordingly, assumed the latter's characteristics and mythology. As an equivalent of Hephaestus, the god Vulcan could be represented wearing a workman's cap and equipped with a smithy's tongs, anvil, and hammer.

(See also Atlas, Capitoline Hill [the], Hephaestus, Hermes, Maia, Rome, and Tiber River [the].)

ZEPHYR Zephyr, also known as Zephyrus or Zephyros, was a personification and god of the west wind, which was both warm and gentle, harbinger of welcome spring and the rebirth of vegetation. The Romans identified him with Favonius. Along with the winds Boreas and Notus, he is described by the Greek poet Hesiod as being a child of Eos, goddess of the dawn, and her consort Astraeus.

We learn from Homer that Zephyr mated with stormy Podarge, "She of the Swift Feet," as she was grazing along the river Oceanus. Their union resulted in the birth to Podarge of Achilles's immortal horses, Xanthos and Balios. Podarge, it should be noted, is known from other sources as one of the Harpies, bird-women who appear, at least originally, to have personified the sudden, grasping nature of wind blasts. Winds were sometimes represented as horses, and it would make sense that she and Zephyr, both in horse form, would produce swift, immortal horses.

A different tale involving Zephyr is preserved by the mythographer Apollodorus: Zephyr and Apollo both vied for the affection of the handsome Spartan youth Hyacinth. Sensing Hyacinth's preference for Apollo, a jealous Zephyr caused a discus thrown by his rival to hit Hyacinth's head, killing him. As a memorial to him a hyacinth flower, with words of mourning inscribed on its petals, sprang from the ground where he had fallen. Another related story of flowers was Zephyr's pursuit of the nymph Chloris ("Greenery"), whom he married and appointed the goddess of flowers, known thereafter as Flora. It was Flora, according to the poet Ovid in his *Fasti,* who actually created the hyacinth.

(See also Achilles, Apollo, Boreas, Favonius, Flora, Hyacinth, Notus, Oceanus [place], and Sparta.)

ZEUS Zeus was the supreme god of the Greeks in both religion and myth, having precedence over the gods who lived with him on Mount Olympus and all others as well. He was "Hypatos" (the "Highest"), and as Homer describes him, he was the omnipotent "father of gods and men." Zeus's origins are indisputably Indo-European, his name being derived from the root *dieu* "to gleam." He was, first and foremost, the bright god of the sky and of atmospheric phenomena, including rain, thunder, and lightning. As mountains are the geologic features of Earth closest to the sky, mountains were sacred to him, particularly the lofty Mount Olympus. Importantly, Zeus was also a civic god, deeply concerned with the establishment and maintenance of the city as an ordered community as well as with the order of individual households and their members. As the deity sustaining interpersonal relationships, he was the protector of suppliants, guarantor of oaths, and sponsor of hospitality. As a reflection of his many functions, he possessed many epithets and *epíkleseis* (names by which he was called upon in prayer and cult), among them Ombrios ("Rainmaker"), Nephelegeretes ("Cloud-Gatherer"), Keraunios ("Thunderer"), Olympios ("of Mount Olympus"), Agoraios ("God of the Assembly"), Xenios ("God of Hospitality"), Hikesios ("God of Suppliants"), and Horkios ("God of Oaths"). Zeus was worshipped throughout Greece and protected all cities equally; for this reason, he was not the patron deity of any particular city. His most important cultic festival, complete with Panhellenic games, was held at Olympia in the Peloponnese, and it was the temple built there in his honor that contained his best-known cult statue, the colossal gold-and-ivory creation of the famed sculptor Phidias. In addition to being the supreme weather and civic god, Zeus possessed prophetic powers, his oldest and most prominent oracle being located at Dodona in Epirus, where his utterances were believed to have been conveyed through the fluttering of his sacred oak's leaves and through the flight or calls of doves settling in this tree.

In mythology, Zeus was the son of the Titan gods Cronus and Rhea, and his siblings were Poseidon, Hades, Hestia, Hera, and Demeter. Having learned that he would be dethroned by one of his children, Cronus swallowed each of them as they were born, apart from Zeus, whom Rhea saved by giving Cronus a stone wrapped in swaddling clothes to swallow in Zeus's place. The infant Zeus, for his part, was taken to Mount Ida (or Dicte) on the island of Crete, where he was nursed by the nymphs Adrastea and Ida while the Curetes hid his cries by clashing their weapons. When Zeus reached maturity, a decade-long battle between the older-generation Titan gods and Zeus and his siblings, the so-called Olympian gods, raged until Zeus, with the aid of the Cyclopes and Hecatoncheires, prevailed. The Titans were now imprisoned in Tartarus, and it was left to Zeus and his brothers to divide the world between them. To this end, they drew lots, Zeus in this way becoming lord of the heavens, Hades lord of the Underworld, and Poseidon lord of the sea.

Zeus married his sister, Hera, and with her became father to Ares, god of war; Eileithyia, goddess of childbirth; and Hebe, goddess of youth. Zeus also had a great many other consorts and lovers, divine and mortal, among them the goddess Metis, whom he swallowed while she was pregnant and with whom he became the father of Athena. The twin gods Apollo and Artemis were his children with the second-generation Titan goddess Leto; Hermes with the nymph Maia; Dionysus with the Theban princess Semele; Persephone with Demeter; and the nine Muses with Mnemosyne. By some accounts, he was the father of Aphrodite with Dione. His best-known mortal child was Hercules, whom he co-fathered with Amphitryon, both god and mortal having slept with Alcmena, Hercules's mother, on the same night. In two spectacular instances, Zeus himself gave birth to the children he had fathered: Athena, who sprang from his head; and Dionysus, whose pregnant mother, Semele, Zeus had killed with a thunderbolt and who, after a period of gestation, emerged from his thigh.

Zeus was known to resort to unorthodox means of seduction, notably transforming himself into a shower of golden rain in order to gain access to an imprisoned Danae, who by him became mother of Perseus. He abducted the Tyrian princess Europa in the form of a lovely, tame white bull, and assumed the appearance of the goddess Artemis in order to approach Callisto, that goddess's chaste devotee. In order to seduce Leda, who would bear to him Helen of Troy, Zeus disguised himself as a swan. However, it was the god's sacred eagle, and not the god himself, that carried off the handsome Trojan prince Ganymede.

Those who incurred his wrath included the second-generation Titan Prometheus, Lycaon, and the entire human Race of Iron, as the current, wicked race of mortals was known. Zeus felt that Prometheus was too great a benefactor of humankind and for that reason he was placed in chains, his liver eternally eaten by vultures. The evil king Lycaon was transformed into a wolf as a consequence of his bestial behavior, and humankind, which Zeus had determined to be utterly evil, was extinguished by a great flood apart from the devout Deucalion and Pyrrha.

Zeus's distinguishing characteristics and attributes were his scepter, lightning bolts, and his sacred bird, the eagle. Among plants, it was the regal oak that was most sacred to him.

The Romans identified their supreme god Jupiter with Zeus.

(*See also* Alcmena, Amphitryon, Aphrodite, Apollo, Ares, Artemis, Athena, Callisto, Crete, Cronus, Curetes [the], Cyclopes [the], Danae, Demeter, Deucalion, Dione, Dionysus, Dodona, Eileithyia, Europa, Ganymede, Hades, Hebe, Hecatoncheires [the], Helen, Hera, Hercules, Hermes, Hestia, Ida [Mount], Jupiter, Leda, Leto, Lycaon, Maia, Metis, Mnemosyne, Muses [the], Olympia, Olympus [Mount], Persephone, Perseus, Poseidon, Prometheus, Pyrrha, Rhea, Rome, Semele, Titans [the], Troy, *and* Underworld [the].)

PART

II

HEROES

HEROINES

AND

PEOPLES

HOUSE OF
ATREUS

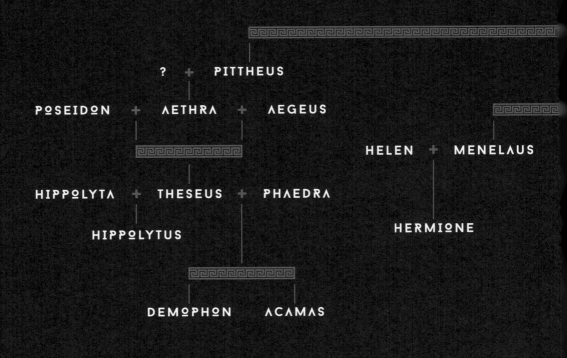

? + PITTHEUS

POSEIDON + AETHRA + AEGEUS

HELEN + MENELAUS

HIPPOLYTA + THESEUS + PHAEDRA

HERMIONE

HIPPOLYTUS

DEMOPHON   ACAMAS

1. Pelopia was Theyestes's own daughter.

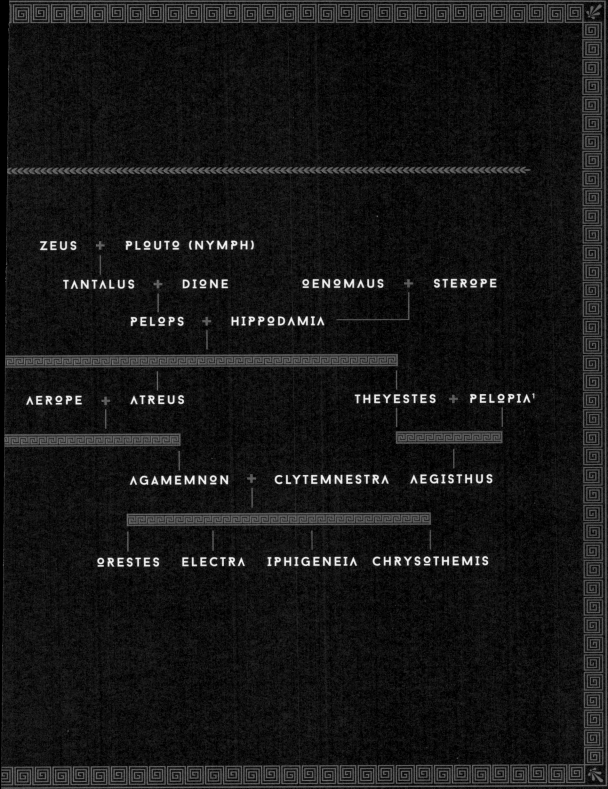

ZEUS + PLOUTO (NYMPH)

TANTALUS + DIONE   OENOMAUS + STEROPE

PELOPS + HIPPODAMIA

AEROPE + ATREUS   THEYESTES + PELOPIA¹

AGAMEMNON + CLYTEMNESTRA   AEGISTHUS

ORESTES   ELECTRA   IPHIGENEIA   CHRYSOTHEMIS

ABAS Abas was a king of Argos and father of future kings of that city and its territory. According to the mythographer Apollodorus, Abas was the son of the King Lynceus and his wife Hypermnestra, one of the Danaids. Abas, in turn, had twin sons, Acrisius and Proetus, by Aglaia, daughter of Mantineus. The twins reputedly quarreled with each other even while still in the womb, and later waged war for their father's kingdom, in the course of which conflict they became the inventors of shields. Acrisius gained the upper hand and drove Proetus from Argos. The latter went to the court of the Lycian king Iobates, whose daughter Anteia (or Stheneboea) he married. With the support of Iobates, Proetus returned to Argos, and the brothers divided the whole of the city's territory between them, Acrisius reigning over Argos and Proetus over Tiryns, which city he founded.

(*See also* Acrisius, Aglaia [heroine], Argos, Danaids [the], Hypermnestra, Lycia, Lynceus, Proetus, *and* Tiryns.)

ACESTES Acestes (or Aegestus) was king in the Sicilian town of Eryx. Acestes himself was of Trojan ancestry; according to the Roman poet Virgil, he was the son of the local Sicilian river god Crinisus and a Trojan mother, though an alternate tradition named his mother as a Trojan nymph named Egesta. Acestes welcomed Aeneas and his band of Trojan refugees when they stopped in Sicily on their way to Italy after the fall of Troy. Aeneas ultimately left those who were weary of travel to live with Acestes in Sicily.

(*See also* Aeneas, Nymphs [the], Sicily, *and* Troy.)

ACETES Acetes (or Acoetes) was captain of a Tyrrhenian ship whose crew, according to the Roman poet Ovid, had taken a sleepy child Dionysus captive; the young god had, apparently, asked the sailors for conveyance to the island of Naxos, and they pretended to grant this request. As the youth had a princely appearance, the sailors entertained high hopes for ransom or other gain. Only the ship's captain, Acetes, sensed immediately that he was in the presence of divinity, uttered a prayer, and did all he could to prevent his crew from setting sail with the young god. Suddenly the ship was stayed in its course, becoming immovable and covered with branches of twining ivy. At the god's feet lay tigers, lynxes, and panthers, all of them phantoms. The ship's crew were terrified and leaped overboard into the sea, where they were transformed into dolphins. Dionysus urged Acetes not to be afraid, however. He thus delivered the god to Naxos, which had been his destination, and became both his follower and his priest.

(*See also* Dionysus *and* Naxos.)

ACHAEANS, THE

The Greek poet Homer refers to all of the Greeks as Achaeans (from Achaea), Hellenes (from Hellas), or Argives (from Argos). Technically, Achaea was only the northern coast of the Peloponnese, and the Achaeans were descended from Xuthus, a son of Hellen, and Creusa, daughter of the Athenian king Erechtheus. There were several branches of Achaeans descended from Xuthus: one in Thessaly, where Achaeus, Xuthus's son, became king, and another in the Peloponnese, since Achaeus's sons emigrated to Argos and ultimately settled in the northern Peloponnese, naming it Achaea.

(*See also* Argos, Athens, Creusa, Erechtheus, Hellen, *and* Xuthus.)

ACHATES

Achates appears in the Roman poet Virgil's epic the *Aeneid* as the most loyal companion of Aeneas in the course of his travels from Troy to Italy.

(*See also* Aeneas *and* Troy.)

ACHILLES

Achilles, the best warrior among the Greeks at the time of the Trojan War, was a son of Peleus, King of Phthia in Thessaly, and the sea goddess Thetis. While Achilles was still an infant, Thetis took measures to make him immortal, an effort in which she did not succeed. Thetis was said to have placed him in the embers of a fire at night and to have anointed him with ambrosia at day, in the course of which Peleus, fearing for his son, interrupted her. According to an alternate tradition, she dipped him in the waters of the river Styx while holding him by the ankles, as a result of which he was vulnerable only at his "Achilles heel." While a young child, Achilles was raised and received tutelage from the wise Centaur Chiron, and later, back at Phthia, Patroclus, who would be his most cherished companion, became his squire. When his mother learned that Achilles was destined to meet his end at Troy, she, hoping in this way to avoid his recruitment for the war effort, sent him away to the court of King Lycomedes on the island of Scyros, where he remained hidden among Lycomedes's daughters, disguised as one of them. With one of their number, Deidamia, Achilles became father to a son, Neoptolemus, who like his father, would ultimately join the fighting at Troy. Achilles was ultimately discovered on Scyros by Odysseus, who had been sent by the Greeks to find him. The clever Odysseus relied on a trick to get Achilles to reveal himself: he laid out presents for the

girls, jewels and other feminine adornments, but also a sword and shield. When a trumpet sounded, this being the usual signal of attack, Achilles leaped for the weapons, thus revealing himself. According to Homer's *Iliad,* after arriving at Troy, Achilles, leader of the Myrmidons, and the other Greeks engaged in a number of forays in the vicinity of Troy. In the course of these, Achilles took captive Briseis, whose husband, brothers, and parents he had slain and who became his concubine. As Briseis was a war prize and a symbol of his bravery, Achilles withdrew from the war effort when Agamemnon, leader of the combined Greek forces, took her for himself. As a consequence of this grievous slight to Achilles's honor, the Greek forces suffered at the hands of the Trojans; indeed, this was the outcome that Achilles had requested of his mother. The Greeks attempted to persuade Achilles to return to the fighting, and Agamemnon offered a wealth of gifts to tempt him, but he remained steadfast in his resolve. It was only when his beloved comrade Patroclus was killed by the Trojan hero Hector that Achilles rejoined the war effort. His motivation was vengeance, not the victory of the Greeks. Achilles did succeed in killing Hector, whereupon he stripped him of his armor, and the surrounding Greeks all brutally stabbed the corpse. Possessed by an inhuman rage, Achilles fastened the body of Hector to his chariot and dragged it around the city of Troy for twelve days until the gods intervened. Thetis was summoned to persuade Achilles to allow King Priam to ransom the body of his son Hector, and this Priam did, bravely entering the tent of fierce Achilles. Face to face with Priam, Achilles thought of his own father, and the two joined in grief, Achilles's humanity now having been restored.

After the death of Hector, Achilles battled at Troy with the Amazon queen Penthesileia, and, tragically, at the moment when he had mortally wounded her, they fell in love. Achilles himself died at Troy. He was slain by Helen's abductor, the Trojan prince Paris, whose arrows struck him at the only point where he was vulnerable, his heel. Achilles's corpse was retrieved by the greater of the two Ajaxes, who then engaged with Odysseus in a contest for the fallen hero's coveted armor, which had been made for him by the god Hephaestus. Odysseus prevailed, and Ajax committed suicide. After Achilles's burial, his ghost appeared above his tomb and demanded the sacrifice of the Trojan princess Polyxena.

(*See also* Agamemnon, Ajax [the Great], Amazons [the], Briseis, Centaurs [the], Chiron, Deidamia, Hector, Helen, Hephaestus, Lycomedes, Myrmidons [the], Neoptolemus, Odysseus, Paris, Patroclus, Peleus, Penthesileia, Polyxena, Priam, Scyros, Styx [the River], Thessaly, Thetis, Troy, *and* Zeus.)

ACIS Acis, a handsome son of the woodland deity Faunus and an otherwise unknown sea nymph Symaethis, was pursued by the Nereid nymph Galatea when he was just sixteen years of age. At the same time, Galatea was herself being pursued by the Cyclops Polyphemus, whom she detested as much as she was enamored of Acis. In a jealous rage, Polyphemus crushed Acis with a massive rock. In answer to Galatea's prayer that Acis be saved, the earth split open to reveal Acis, larger now than he had been, reincarnated as a blue-green river god whose waters still bear his name.

(*See also* Cyclopes [the], Faunus, Galatea, Nereids [the], *and* Polyphemus.)

ACRISIUS Acrisius and Proetus were twin sons born of Aglaia to Abas, king of Argos and possessor of a fear-inspiring shield that deterred all potential foes. Acrisius and his twin were great-grandsons of Danaus, father of the Danaids, who were notorious for the murder of their husbands.

Relations between the twins were contentious, reputedly even in the womb. Their father had wished that his sons would rule alternately after his passing, but Acrisius refused. A battle ensued. Subsequently, Acrisius ruled Argos, and Proetus nearby Tiryns, which he had founded.

With Eurydice (or Aganippe), Acrisius fathered Danae, whom he confined in an impenetrable room (or, by some accounts, a tower) so as to prevent the fruition of an oracle that had foreseen his death at the hands of his grandson. These measures were no deterrent to Zeus, who visited Danae as a shower of gold, fathering Perseus. Wishing to avoid the pollution of blood guilt, Acrisius set mother and child adrift at sea in a chest. Saved by a fisherman on the island of Seriphus, whom Danae later married, Perseus grew to manhood and, after accomplishing the task given him to behead the Gorgon Medusa, returned to Argos. Acrisius, however, had left the kingdom for the city of Larissa in Thessaly, having heard that his grandson was alive and still fearing the oracle. In Larissa, Perseus, who was participating in the local regent's funeral games, caused Acrisius's accidental death with an ill-aimed discus.

(*See also* Aglaia, Argos, Danae, Danaids [the], Danaus, Eurydice [heroine], Gorgons, Larissa, Medusa, Perseus, Seriphus, Thessaly, Tiryns, *and* Zeus.)

ACTAEON The hero Actaeon was a son of Autonoe, a daughter of the Theban king Cadmus, and Aristaeus, who was skilled in husbandry and was himself a child of the god Apollo. Actaeon was cousin to the god Dionysus and Pentheus, who would become regent of Thebes and prove hostile to Dionysus's worship. Actaeon himself was a hunter, having been instructed in this art by the wise Centaur Chiron. The Roman poet Ovid vividly describes his gruesome death. While out hunting with his dogs and seeking respite from midday's heat, Actaeon came upon a pool in which Diana (the Roman equivalent of Artemis) and her companion nymphs were bathing. Though his discovery of them in their nakedness was accidental, Diana, in a rage, splashed water on him, thus transforming him from a man into a stag. His dogs, stirred into a frenzy, no longer recognized their master and bit him to death, whereby Diana's anger was satisfied. A less usual explanation for his punishment is recorded by mythographer Apollodorus, according to whom Zeus could have been to blame, jealous over Actaeon's attention to Semele, who would become mother to Dionysus by Zeus.

(*See also* Apollo, Aristaeus, Artemis, Autonoe, Cadmus, Chiron, Diana, Dionysus, Pentheus, Semele, Thebes, *and* Zeus.)

ADMETA

Admeta (or Admete) was a daughter of Eurystheus, the king of Argos (and/or Mycenae and Tiryns) for whom Hercules performed his twelve Labors. Among those labors was bringing Admeta the belt of the Amazon queen Hippolyta.

(*See also* Amazons [the], Argos, Eurystheus, Hercules, *and* Hippolyta.)

ADMETUS

Admetus was a son of Pheres, king and founder of Pherae in Thessaly, and Periclymene, a daughter of Minyas, eponymous ancestor of the people known as the Minyans. When Admetus succeeded his father as regent, Zeus sent Apollo to him as a servant by way of punishing Apollo for killing the Cyclopes, itself an act of vengeance for Zeus's killing of his son Asclepius. Admetus was so kind a master that Apollo came to his aid repeatedly. According to the mythographer Apollodorus, when Admetus sought the hand of Alcestis, daughter of King Pelias of Iolcos, the latter would only concede to give his daughter to that man who could yoke a lion and boar to a chariot. Apollo completed this task on Admetus's behalf, and Admetus thus won Alcestis as bride. The god also obtained a special favor for Admetus from the Fates: if Admetus should be faced with death, another person would be allowed to volunteer to be a surrogate. When, while still a young man, Admetus fell gravely ill, he asked both his parents if they would save him, but they would not. His devoted wife, Alcestis, however, did volunteer, and when Thanatos ("Death") came to fetch her, Admetus was despondent. Fortunately, it so happened that Hercules passed through Pherae at this point and repaid Admetus for his hospitality by wrestling Thanatos for Alcestis, whom he was able to restore to her husband. The story of Admetus and his wife Alcestis is the subject of the tragedian Euripides's *Alcestis*.

(*See also* Alcestis, Apollo, Asclepius, Fates [the], Hercules, Iolcos, Minyans [the], Minyas, Pelias, Pherae, Thanatos, Thessaly, *and* Zeus.)

ADONIS The mythology and cult of the Greek hero Adonis was inextricably linked with Aphrodite, who loved him, and like the goddess, he appears to have had Near Eastern origins. In particular, Adonis is thought to be a Greek adaptation of an eastern nature deity who was the consort of an earth goddess and embodied the cycle of seasonal growth, wilting, and death or dormancy in the plant world. According to the mythographer Apollodorus, Adonis was the son of Smyrna, the beautiful daughter of Assyria's king Theias. Smyrna had refused all of her many suitors, thus dishonoring Aphrodite, and for this she paid a heavy price: the goddess caused Smyrna to fall in love with her own father. The Roman poet Ovid also tells this story, but calls Smyrna "Myrrha," making her a princess of Cyprus. In this version, it is not Aphrodite but one of the Fates who inflames the girl with passion for her father, King Cinyras. Not knowing that it was his daughter who came to share his bed, Cinyras impregnated Myrrha, who fled the kingdom—and her father's murderous rage—in shame once her sin was discovered. Believing herself to be a source of pollution for the dead and the living alike, she asked the gods for salvation. In answer to her prayers, she was transformed into a myrrh tree that eternally sheds resinous tears, the source of precious myrrh. With the help of the goddess Lucina, Myrrha would bear the child Adonis from her bark-clad belly.

Of Aphrodite's attraction to Adonis there are various accounts. Whether regretting that she had punished Myrrha too harshly or immediately enamored of Adonis at his birth, Aphrodite brought the baby to Persephone, queen of the Underworld, to safeguard. Yet Persephone, too, was smitten with Adonis and, when asked to do so, refused to give him up. Zeus or the Muse Calliope ultimately settled the goddess's custody dispute, judging that Adonis should spend a third of his time with each goddess and a third on his own. Ovid's well-known version is different: grazed by one of Cupid's arrows, Aphrodite became so enamored of the grown youth that she abandoned her accustomed comforts and, like the huntress Artemis, followed him into the wilderness where he went to hunt. To no avail she warned him of hunting's dangers. He was gored by a boar that he himself had wounded.

The Adonis myth provides the basis for tales regarding the origins of several plants and flowers. These include not only myrrh but also the red rose and the poppy anemone. Originally white, roses were dyed red by blood from Aphrodite's thorn-grazed foot as she ran to a wounded Adonis. Thereafter, in her grief, the goddess sprinkled his blood with divine perfumed nectar, and from it grew a blood red poppy anemone, a flower with a lovely but short-lived bloom. From her tears, too, there sprang red roses.

Although, according to myth, Adonis was a mortal, the Greeks venerated him as a god and celebrated him at a midsummer festival called the Adoneia.

In the course of the festivities, small images of Adonis were carried in procession and small pots or baskets were planted with the seeds of quick-sprouting grain, lettuces, and herbs. These so-called "Adonis gardens" were carried to rooftops and terraces where the seedlings quickly sprouted and just as quickly wilted, occasioning a renewal of ritualized grief.

(*See also* Aphrodite, Artemis, Calliope, Cinyras, Cupid, Cyprus, Lucina, Muses [the], Myrrha, Persephone, Underworld [the], *and* Zeus.)

ADRASTUS

Adrastus was a king of Argos who became a pivotal figure in the fate of the city of Thebes. Polyneices, son of Oedipus, and Tydeus, son of Oeneus, had both gone in exile to Argos and, when there, began to fight one another. Adrastus came upon them and, remembering the words of a prophet who had instructed him to yoke his daughters in marriage to a boar and a lion, he offered them his two daughters as brides; this he did because he saw that the shield of one of the youths bore a boar as emblem and the other's a lion. Adrastus then promised that he would restore to them the lands from which they had come. In order to help Polyneices take the Theban throne from his brother Eteocles, who was to have relinquished it after a year, Adrastus organized the contingent of seven captains, the so-called Seven Against Thebes, to march on that city. This he did in spite of the fact that the seer Amphiaraus had foretold a disastrous outcome. Among these Seven, Adrastus alone survived, and when the sons of the fallen Seven later attacked Thebes to avenge the death of their fathers, his son was the only one of the leaders of that campaign to die.

(*See also* Amphiaraus, Argos, Eteocles, Oedipus, Polyneices, Thebes, *and* Tydeus.)

AEACIDES, (THE)

Aeacides is a patronymic meaning "descendant(s) of Aeacus." The name was applied to the Greek hero Peleus as well as his son Achilles and grandson Neoptolemus.

(*See also* Achilles, Aeacus, Neoptolemus, *and* Peleus.)

AEACUS

Aeacus was the son of Aegina, daughter of the river god Asopus, and Zeus, who had abducted Aegina and brought her to the island of Oenone, which was then renamed Aegina. There Aegina gave birth to Aeacus. According to the Roman poet Ovid, the goddess Juno, in anger over Zeus's infidelity to her with Aegina, decimated the island's population with a terrible plague. Consequently, Aeacus prayed to Zeus for help by way of acknowledging his paternity; he asked that he should either himself die alongside his countrymen or that Zeus repopulate the island with as many men as there were ants climbing up a nearby oak. The tree quivered, and the ants were transformed into people, who then declared Aeacus their king. These people were called Myrmidons after the Greek word for ant, *myrmex*, and they were as frugal and industrious as the ants from which they originated.

With Endeis, sometimes called a daughter of Chiron, Aeacus became the father of Telamon, later the father of Ajax the Great, and of Peleus, later the father of Achilles.

(*See also* Achilles, Aegina [goddess and place], Ajax [the Great], Asopus, Chiron, Juno, Peleus, Telamon, *and* Zeus.)

AEETES Aeetes was regent of the kingdom of Colchis on the eastern coast of the Black Sea, and he ruled from the city of Aea, where the god Hephaestus had reputedly built him a palace. Aeetes was the son of the sun god Helios and Perse, one of the Oceanids. His siblings were the sorceress Circe and Pasiphae, mother of the Minotaur, and his best-known children were his son Apsyrtus and his daughter Medea. It was to Colchis that the hero Jason traveled in his quest for the Golden Fleece. After the miraculous golden-fleeced ram bearing Phrixus had arrived in Colchis, Aeetes sacrificed the ram, hung its fleece on a tree in a grove sacred to Ares, and ensured that it was closely guarded by a dragon. He allowed Phrixus, a refugee from Boeotia, to stay in Colchis and gave him his daughter Chalciope in marriage. As for Jason, this hero was less hospitably received by Aeetes, who, according to the Greek poet Apollonius of Rhodes, responded to Jason's request for the Fleece by stating that he would first have to harness a pair of fire-breathing bulls, plow a field, sow dragon's teeth, and kill the armed men who would spring from the sown teeth. Aeetes's expectation was that Jason could not survive this task, but Jason received help from Medea. When Jason made off with both the Fleece and Medea, Aeetes sent his son Apsyrtus in pursuit, but Medea engineered the latter's murder.

(*See also* Apsyrtus, Ares, Circe, Colchis, Helios, Hephaestus, Jason, Medea, Minotaur [the], Oceanids [the], Pasiphae, *and* Phrixus.)

AEGEUS Aegeus was a legendary king of Athens and a son (or adopted son) of the king Pandion. Aegeus remained childless, although he married repeatedly, and went to consult the oracle of Apollo at Delphi regarding this situation. The oracle advised that he should not loosen his wineskin (goatskin container for wine) until he returned home. Aegeus shared the oracle's response with his friend King Pittheus of Troezen, who immediately understood the real meaning of the oracle and arranged for his daughter, Aethra, to sleep with a drunken Aegeus. Before departing Troezen, Aegeus told Aethra that, should she become the mother of a son by him, she should send him to Athens once he was strong enough to retrieve the sword and sandals that he had placed under a boulder. Aethra's child was Theseus, who, after his arrival in Athens, survived attempted poisoning by Aegeus's new wife, Medea, and volunteered (or was sent) to travel to Crete in order to slay the Minotaur. Concerned that his son would be killed while attempting to accomplish this feat, Aegeus instructed him to raise a white sail upon his return to signal his safe return. But Theseus forgot to do what his father had asked, and, in his grief, the old king threw himself from the Acropolis where he had been standing watch.

(*See also* Acropolis [the], Aethra, Apollo, Athens, Crete, Delphi, Medea, Minotaur [the], Pittheus, *and* Theseus.)

AEGISTHUS

Aegisthus was the son of Thyestes by his own daughter Pelopia and was the grandson of Pelops, all of whose descendants were cursed. In Homer's *Odyssey*, Aegisthus is presented as having seduced Clytemnestra, King Agamemnon's wife, and having plotted Agamemnon's murder while the best of the Greeks were away fighting at Troy. At a feast, he, with the help of Clytemnestra, killed Agamemnon like an ox at the manger. According to the tragedian Aeschylus, however, it was Clytemnestra alone who slew her husband, a version of Agamemnon's death adopted by later authors. Aegisthus, for his part, was portrayed as cowardly. After growing to maturity, Agamemnon's son Orestes wrought vengeance upon his mother and Aegisthus, killing them both.

(*See also* Agamemnon, Clytemnestra, Orestes, Pelops, *and* Theyestes.)

AEGYPTUS

Aegyptus and his twin brother, Danaus, were sons of the Egyptian king Belus, who gave Aegyptus Arabia and Danaus Libya to rule. Aegyptus fathered fifty sons and sought to wed them to Danaus's fifty daughters. As Danaus suspected that this was a ploy on his brother's part to absorb more territory, he refused this alliance but later was compelled to accept it. However, Danaus instructed his daughters to kill their husbands on their wedding night. All of Aegyptus's sons were killed but one: Lynceus, who was spared by his bride Hypermnestra. Aegyptus ended his days in the Peloponnese, where he was also buried.

(*See also* Belus, Danaids [the], Danaus, Hypermnestra, *and* Lynceus.)

AENEAS

Along with Romulus, Aeneas was the most important of Rome's heroes. He was the son of the goddess Aphrodite and Anchises, who became a king of Dardania and was a member of the royal family of Troy. Aeneas was born on Mount Ida, where he was raised by the resident nymphs, and later fought valiantly in the Trojan War. When the Trojans were defeated by the Greeks and the city was in flames, Aeneas—at the urging of the Trojan Hector's ghost and Aphrodite, followed by an omen of harmless flames appearing above his young son's head—left Troy with his aged father, Anchises, on his shoulders, his son by the hand, and his wife, Creusa, walking close behind. Creusa soon was lost, prompting Aeneas to turn back, but her ghost appeared to him urging him to carry on, as he was destined for greater things. What he was destined for was to lead a group of Trojan refugees to Italy, there to found a new city and, in the process, become the ancestor of the Roman people. Importantly, it was not clear to Aeneas when he set sail that Italy was his goal: he knew only that he was to seek the ancient homeland of the Trojans. The journey was a long and perilous one, not unlike Odysseus's journey home from Troy and in this sense being a Roman odyssey. The Trojans came first to Thrace, mistaking this as the prophesied site of their new city, but soon departed, having been warned of Thrace's dangers by the ghost of the Trojan prince Polydorus. Aeneas and his followers next came to Delos and then to Crete, where they attempted to settle and experienced a devastating famine. Aeneas's household gods appeared to him in a vision instructing him again to set sail. Along the way, the Trojans were attacked by the Harpies and then came to Sicily, where Anchises died and where Aeneas later left those too feeble to continue with the local king, his kinsman Acestes. Among those who welcomed the Trojans was Dido, founder and queen of Carthage, who, through the machinations of the goddess Aphrodite, fell in love with Aeneas. Tragically for Dido, who ultimately committed suicide, Aeneas left her in order to fulfill his destiny. It was at Cumae, home of the Sibyl, a prophetic priestess of Apollo, that Aeneas first touched on Italian shores. With the Sibyl as his guide, Aeneas next journeyed into the Underworld, past Tartarus to Elysium, where his father, Anchises, now resided. There Anchises revealed to him the glorious future of the Romans and warned him of wars to come. Conflict soon ensued when Aeneas arrived in Latium, where the king Latinus welcomed him and, in fulfillment of a prophecy, offered Aeneas his daughter Lavinia in marriage. This angered Latinus's queen Amata as well as Turnus, the Rutulian prince to whom Lavinia had been promised. Through the goddess Juno's intervention, the Italian (Latin) tribes rallied around Turnus against Aeneas, who in essence had become a second Achilles. Aeneas sought an alliance with king Evander, whose settlement lay on the future site of Rome, and eventually prevailed over the Latins, slaying Turnus. Aeneas would then make peace with the Latins, marry Lavinia, and found the city of Lavinium in Latium. Aeneas's son, Ascanius (also known as Iulus, ancestor of the Julian family and Julius Caesar), would establish Alba Longa, which became the most powerful city in Latium until the founding of Rome by Romulus and Remus.

(*See also* Acestes, Achilles, Alba Longa, Amata, Anchises, Aphrodite, Apollo, Ascanius, Carthage, Creusa, Cumae, Dardania, Dido, Elysium, Harpies [the], Hector, Ida [Mount], Iulus, Juno, Latinus, Latium, Lavinia, Nymphs [the], Odysseus, Polydorus, Sibyl of Cumae [the], Sicily, Tartarus, Thrace, Trojans [the], Troy, Turnus, *and* Underworld [the].)

AEOLUS

Aeolus was the "Lord of the Winds." In Homer's *Odyssey*, Aeolus was the son of Hippotas and lived on a floating island called Aeolia, which was encircled by a rampart of bronze. Aeolus, who was a favorite of the gods, had six daughters and six sons, who were married to each other. Aeolus offered Odysseus and his companions hospitality on their return voyage from Troy and entertained them for an entire month. When Odysseus set sail, Aeolus gave him a precious gift: a bag containing winds to convey him rapidly home. However, as Odysseus's ship approached Ithaca, his companions, thinking that the bag contained gold and silver, opened it, only to have the ship driven greatly off course by the emerging winds and back to Aeolus's island. Upon their return, Aeolus refused to help the Greeks on the grounds that they must be hated by the gods. In the case of the Trojan Aeneas, who was making his way to Italy, Aeolus, having been bribed by Juno, released the winds that he kept imprisoned in a cave so that they would destroy Aeneas's ships: these winds were Eurus, Notus, Zephyr, and Africus.

Aeolus, who became known as a wind god, also became confused and conflated with another Aeolus, a son of Hellen and the nymph Orseis. Aeolus had been assigned Thessaly when Hellen divided Greece between him and his two brothers, Dorus and Xuthus. This Aeolus was the eponymous ancestor (namesake) of the Aeolians, and his children included Athamas, Salmoneus, Sisyphus, Canace, and Alcyone.

(*See also* Aeneas, Alcyone, Canace, Dorus, Eurus, Hellen, Ithaca, Juno, Notus, Odysseus, Salmoneus, Sisyphus, Thessaly, Troy, Xuthus, *and* Zephyr.)

AEPYTUS

Aepytus was a son of King Cresphontes of Messenia, and Merope, and was one of the numerous descendants of Hercules. When Messenia was threatened by a rebellion in which her husband and her two older sons were killed, Merope sent her infant son Aepytus away to Arcadia, where he was raised by his maternal grandfather Cypselus, or, by another account, to Aetolia. When he had grown to manhood, Aepytus returned to Messenia in order to avenge himself on Polyphontes, the man who had killed his father, married his mother, and assumed the kingship. The mythographer Hyginus reports that Polyphontes had offered a reward to anyone who should kill Aepytus (whom Hyginus calls Telephontes). When Aepytus returned to the palace, he went unrecognized, which fact he used to his advantage, claiming that he was the one who had killed Aepytus and had come to collect the reward. A distraught Merope would have killed him, had he not been recognized at the last minute. Mother and son then plotted the murder of Polyphontes, which they accomplished while the latter was making sacrifice. With the usurper dead, Aepytus reclaimed his father's kingdom and became regent.

(*See also* Arcadia, Cypselus, Hercules, Merope [heroine], Messenia, *and* Polyphontes.)

AERO Merope, the daughter of Oenopion, king of Corinth, and his wife, Helice, was known primarily as Merope but also as Aero. Merope is chiefly known for the hunter Orion's pursuit of her in marriage, as a result of which he was blinded.

(*See also* Corinth, Merope [heroine], *and* Orion.)

AEROPE Aerope was daughter of the Cretan king Catreus, who had heard a prophecy to the effect that he was destined to be killed by her child or, according to a variant of the story, by one of his own children, Aerope or her sister. Catreus consequently sent Aerope away to Nauplius, king of Nauplia, to be killed or sold. Escaping both slavery and death, she married Atreus, king of Mycenae, to whom she bore the heroes Agamemnon and Menelaus.

(*See also* Agamemnon, Atreus, Crete, Menelaus, *and* Mycenae.)

AETHRA Aethra was the daughter of Pittheus, a son of Pelops and king of Troezen, a city in the northeastern Peloponnese. Her father arranged for her to sleep with the Athenian king Aegeus when he arrived at his kingdom; Aegeus, who was childless and concerned about the fate of his kingdom, had gone to Delphi to consult the oracle about this problem. The oracle responded that he should not unloose his wineskin (goatskin used as a container for wine) until he reached Athens. Aegeus did not understand the oracle, but Pittheus did, and plied Aegeus with wine. In this state of intoxication, Aegeus impregnated Aethra, who was visited the same night by the god Poseidon. Before departing for Athens, Aegeus told Aethra that, if she gave birth to a son, she should raise the boy without revealing his paternity and send him to Athens when he was strong enough to retrieve a sword and sandals that he had left under a heavy rock. Her son was Theseus, who became Aegeus's heir. Aethra was later taken captive by Castor and Pollux, who conveyed her to Troy. When that city had fallen, she was taken back to Greece, where she died.

(*See also* Aegeus, Athens, Castor, Delphi, Dioscuri [the], Pelops, Pittheus, Pollux, Poseidon, Theseus, Troy, *and* Zeus.)

AETOLUS Aetolus was variously known as a descendant of Deucalion, who with his wife, Pyrrha, survived the Great Flood, or the son of Endymion, a king of Elis whom the goddess Selene loved. Aetolus accidentally killed a man while competing in funeral games and, as a consequence of his guilt, went in exile to the land by the Achelous River and named it Aetolia after himself.

(*See also* Achelous [River, the], Deucalion, Endymion, Pyrrha, *and* Selene.)

AGAMEMNON Agamemnon, son of Atreus, was the king of Mycenae at the time of the Trojan War. Since he ruled the most populous and presumably most powerful kingdom in Greece, he served as commander-in-chief of the Greek kings and their armies who sailed to Troy, their numbers so great that it took 1,000 ships to carry them. Importantly, Agamemnon was also the brother of the Spartan king Menelaus, the husband of Helen, whom the Trojan prince Paris had abducted, which was the cause of hostilities. It was the case, too, that, as a descendant of Pelops, son of Tantalus, Agamemnon could not escape the family curse.

It is Agamemnon's role in the Trojan War and its aftermath for which he is principally known. When the Greeks were gathering at the port of Aulis, Agamemnon unknowingly killed a deer sacred to the goddess Artemis, a sin for which the Greeks and Agamemnon himself paid dearly. In anger, Artemis caused the winds to be unfavorable for sailing, and the assembled Greeks became restless and hungry. Advice was sought from the prophet Calchas, and the prescribed remedy was the sacrifice of Agamemnon's daughter Iphigeneia to the goddess. Agamemnon was torn, but, placing country above family, tricked his wife, Clytemnestra, into sending Iphigeneia to Aulis on the pretext that she would there wed the young Achilles. The terrible deed was accomplished, and the Greeks set sail. But Clytemnestra would never forgive Agamemnon and, in the course of his long years of absence, took a lover, her husband's cousin Aegisthus, with whom she plotted her revenge. Meanwhile, in the tenth year of the Trojan War, Agamemnon occasioned the withdrawal of Achilles from battle by insisting on taking the latter's war prize and concubine Briseis as compensation for the loss of his own concubine Chryseis; returning Chryseis to her father had been the only way to end the plague that Apollo had sent upon the Greeks. Agamemnon's slight to Achilles was the cause of much suffering for the Greeks and the cause of much loss of life. Among the casualties were Achilles's beloved friend Patroclus, and it was the loss of his friend alone that prompted Achilles to fight once more, now motivated by the desire for vengeance. After the fall of Troy, in which the hero Odysseus and his ruse of the Trojan Horse were instrumental, Agamemnon returned home, only to be stabbed to death in the bath by his wife, Clytemnestra, who was still angry about the killing of her daughter and angry, too, about Agamemnon's appearance in Mycenae with a concubine from Troy, the priestess Cassandra, whose death Clytemnestra also engineered. Agamemnon's death would later be avenged by his son, Orestes.

(*See also* Achilles, Aegisthus, Artemis, Atreus, Aulis, Briseis, Calchas, Cassandra, Chryseis, Clytemnestra, Helen, Iphigeneia, Menelaus, Mycenae, Odysseus, Orestes, Patroclus, Paris, Sparta, *and* Troy.)

AGAVE
Agave was one of the daughters of Cadmus, founder of Thebes, and his wife, Harmonia. She was married to Echion, one of the warriors who sprang from the dragon's teeth that Cadmus had sown, and became mother to Pentheus, who as regent of Thebes made the fatal mistake of failing to acknowledge Dionysus as a god. Since Agave, together with her sisters Ino and Autonoe, had maligned their sister Semele when she became pregnant with Dionysus, Zeus's child, they were punished by Dionysus, who made them complicit in Pentheus's death: in a Bacchic trance that affected all of them, they tore him to bits. Not knowing what she had done, Agave, in the belief that it was a lion cub that she had killed, brought the head of Pentheus to show Cadmus. For this crime she and her sisters were exiled.

(*See also* Autonoe, Cadmus, Dionysus, Echion, Harmonia, Ino, Pentheus, Semele, Thebes, *and* Zeus.)

AGENOR
According to the mythographer Apollodorus, Agenor was a son of the god Poseidon and Libya, daughter of Memphis and Nile. His twin brother was Belus, who became a king of Egypt, while Agenor became king either of Sidon or Tyre in Phoenicia. With Telephassa, Agenor became father to a daughter, Europa, and three sons, Phoenix, Cilix, and Cadmus, the future founder of Thebes. When Europa was abducted by Zeus, Agenor sent his sons in search of her, instructing them not to return empty-handed. None of them found her, so all eventually settled elsewhere.

(*See also* Belus, Cadmus, Europa, Poseidon, Sidon, *and* Zeus.)

AGLAIA
The heroine Aglaia was a daughter of Mantineus and the wife of King Abas of Argos, to whom she bore twin sons, Acrisius and Proetus. Acrisius would become the father of Danae, whose prison Zeus breached by taking the form of a golden shower. As for Proetus, his wife, Stheneboea, developed a fatal attraction to the hero Bellerophon.

(*See also* Abas, Acrisius, Argos, Bellerophon, Danae, Proetus, *and* Zeus.)

AGLAUROS Aglauros was a daughter of Cecrops, a snake-man and the first king of Attica (the territory of Athens). According to the mythographer Hyginus, when the miraculous infant Erichthonius was born from the earth, Minerva placed him in a chest that she entrusted to Aglauros and her sisters Pandrosus and Herse to guard, instructing them under no circumstances to open the chest. Their curiosity got the better of them and, as punishment for this, Minerva consequently drove them mad. In this altered state they threw themselves into the sea.

(*See also* Athens, Attica, Cecrops, Erichthonius, *and* Minerva.)

AJAX THE GREAT Ajax, or Aias (also called Ajax the Great or Telamonian Ajax), was the son of King Telamon of Salamis and Periboea (or Eeriboea). Ajax was named after the eagle (*aíetos* in Greek) that, according to the mythographer Apollodorus, appeared as a sign when Hercules prayed Telamon would be blessed with a son as a reward for helping him in his assault on the Trojan king Laomedon. Having been one of the suitors of Helen, Ajax was oath-bound to lead a contingent of twelve ships from Salamis to Troy. After Achilles, he was the best fighter among the Greeks at Troy, and he was the tallest. In Homer's *Iliad*, Ajax, a skilled defensive warrior equipped with a "tower" shield, is represented as fighting valiantly, often next to the Lesser Ajax, son of Oileus. In the course of that war, he met Hector in single combat and wounded him, but the two parted at nightfall, calling a truce and exchanging gifts of friendship, as had been the gods' wish. It was later Ajax who protected the body of Achilles's companion Patroclus from depredation by the Trojans and, later still, carried the body of his great friend Achilles from the battlefield. As the best surviving warriors among the Greeks, both Ajax and Odysseus were well positioned to receive the armor of Achilles. Odysseus prevailed, whether by drawing lots or by being selected as the person who contributed most to the defeat of the Trojans. As a consequence of this loss, and driven mad by Athena, Ajax set upon the livestock taken as booty from Troy thinking that the animals were Greeks. When his sanity was subsequently restored, his shame was so great that he threw himself upon his sword.

(*See also* Achilles, Ajax [the Lesser], Athena, Hector, Helen, Hercules, Laomedon, Odysseus, Patroclus, Salamis, *and* Troy.)

AJAX THE LESSER The so-called Lesser Ajax (or Aias) fought valiantly at Troy alongside Ajax, son of Telamon, in Homer's *Iliad*, together being known as the Ajaxes (or Aiantes). The Lesser Ajax was a son of Oileus, a king of Locris in Central Greece, and had come to Troy leading a contingent of Locrians. He is perhaps better known in mythology for his misdeeds and consequent punishment than for his heroism. When, upon the fall of Troy, King Priam's daughter Cassandra had taken refuge in Athena's temple, Ajax dragged her out, thus committing sacrilege by violating the rights of suppliants to the gods. There are varying accounts of his punishment. According to the tragedian Euripides's *Trojan Women*, at Athena's request, Zeus and Poseidon caused the near-complete destruction of the Greek contingent at sea, preventing most of the men from returning to their homeland; the whole army accordingly suffered on account of Ajax's sin. Homer adds that Poseidon drove Ajax and his ship against some rocks but saved the hero from drowning. He would have escaped with his life had he not bragged of his survival in the face of the gods' anger. In a rage at this further affront, Poseidon smote the great rock upon which Ajax stood with his trident, causing its top to fall into the sea, Ajax with it.

(*See also* Ajax [the Great], Athena, Cassandra, Poseidon, Priam, Telamon, Troy, *and* Zeus.)

ALCAEUS Alcaeus was a son of the hero Perseus and the princess Andromeda, whom Perseus had rescued from a sea monster. Alcaeus's wife was Astydameia, a daughter of Pelops. Among his children was Amphitryon, who married Alcmena, the mother of Hercules by Zeus.

(*See also* Alcmena, Amphitryon, Andromeda, Hercules, Pelops, Perseus, *and* Zeus.)

ALCESTIS Alcestis was the eldest daughter of King Pelias of Iolcos in Thessaly and became the wife of Admetus, a king of Pherae. Admetus was required by her father to accomplish what he believed to be an impossible task to win her hand in marriage, but Admetus, with the help of Apollo, succeeded. When Admetus was later faced with early death, the faithful Alcestis alone volunteered to die in his place; the possibility of finding a surrogate for his death was another favor that Apollo had secured for Admetus. Alcestis did die, much to the horror of Admetus, but Hercules was able to wrestle with Thanatos in order to restore her to Admetus.

(*See also* Admetus, Apollo, Hercules, Iolcos, Pelias, Pherae, Thanatos, *and* Thessaly.)

ALCIDES The patronymic Alcides means "son" or "descendant" of Alcaeus and is generally used as a name for Hercules, who was son of Amphitryon and grandson of Alcaeus.

(*See also* Alcaeus, Amphitryon, *and* Hercules.)

ALCINOUS Alcinous was king of the Phaeacians, a people loved by the gods, and he ruled on the mythical island of Scheria; technically, according to

PLATE IV
Andromeda: Princess and daughter of Cassiopeia and Cepheus

Homer's *Odyssey*, he was one of thirteen kings on the island. Alcinous was the son of Nausithous, who had brought the Phaeacians to Scheria from their home in Hypereia since that land lay close to that of Cyclopes, who were a constant source of torment. As his name, which means "strength of mind," implies, Alcinous was both wise and generous. He hospitably received Odysseus when the latter appeared at his palace alone, having lost all of his companions in the course of his journey from Troy. And he allowed Odysseus both the time and opportunity that he needed to fully disclose who he was and what he had suffered up to that point. Alcinous's generosity extended to sending a ship to convey Odysseus home to Ithaca even though he had long been aware of a prophecy to the effect that the god Poseidon would punish the Phaeacians for offering conveyance to all who needed it: one day, the god would stun a returning ship, transfixing it, and pile a mountain over Alcinous's city. When the ship that had carried Odysseus returned to harbor, the prophecy came true, for Poseidon turned it to stone.

Alcinous's well-ordered kingdom was clearly a utopia that contrasted markedly with the other settlements that Odysseus had encountered previously: those of the lawless Cyclopes, the cannibalistic Laestrygons, the cave-dwelling earth goddess Calypso, the amnesic Lotus Eaters, and the sorceress Circe among others.

(*See also* Arete, Calypso, Circe, Cyclopes [the], Ithaca, Laestrygons [the], Lotus Eaters [the], Nausicaa, Odysseus, Poseidon, *and* Scheria.)

ALCMAEON

Alcmaeon was a son of the seer Amphiaraus and Eriphyle, sister of King Adrastus of Argos. Adrastus would lead a major campaign against Thebes to instate Polyneices, son of Oedipus, as that city's regent. Using the infamous necklace of his great-great-great-grandmother Harmonia, Polyneices had bribed Eriphyle to intervene when Amphiaraus, foreseeing his own death, refused to join the cohort against Thebes. Amphiaraus was bound by a promise to obey her wish but instructed Alcmaeon and his brother to kill their mother for her treachery. This they did not do, and Eriphyle was bribed a second time, now to urge her sons to join a band of warriors marching against Thebes in order to exact vengeance for the deaths of their fathers in the previous war. Alcmaeon went to fight at Thebes, by some accounts killing the young Theban king Laodamas. At this stage Alcmaeon did kill his mother after consulting the oracle at Delphi and was driven mad by the Erinyes, who then pursued him. Coming to Phegeia, he married Arsinoe, to whom he presented Harmonia's necklace. Later, again on the oracle's advice, he went to the Achelous River in Aetolia to be purified of murder. While in Aetolia, Alcmaeon took Callirrhoe, the river god Achelous's daughter, as a second wife. Regrettably, Callirrhoe found out about Harmonia's necklace, and Alcmaeon returned to Phegeia in order to retrieve it for her, lying that he intended to dedicate it at Delphi. When his ruse was revealed, he was killed by the Phegeian king's sons.

(*See also* Achelous [god and place], Adrastus, Amphiaraus, Arsinoe, Delphi, Erinyes [the], Eriphyle, Harmonia, Oedipus, Polyneices, *and* Thebes.)

ALCMENA

Alcmena (or Alcmene) was a daughter of Electryon, a son of the Gorgon-slayer Perseus and Andromeda. Alcmena became betrothed to her cousin Amphitryon, and, while Amphitryon was away, Zeus, disguised as Amphitryon, spent the night with her. Amphitryon soon returned and also spent the night with her. As a consequence, Alcmena was impregnated both by Zeus and Amphitryon, and the result was twins: Hercules, whose father was Zeus, and Iphicles, whose father was Amphitryon. The goddess Hera was angered over the fact that Zeus had yet again been unfaithful to her, and she had heard that a son, descended from Zeus, would soon be born and become king of Mycenae and Tiryns. For these reasons, Hera caused Eileithyia, the goddess of childbirth, to protract Alcmena's labor for a painful seven days, allowing Eurystheus, whose father was Perseus's son Sthenelaus (thus also being descended from Zeus), to be born earlier than Hercules and his twin, Iphicles. Eurystheus would later become Electryon's successor and assign Hercules his twelve Labors. Alcmena survived her famous son and was driven out of Tiryns by Eurystheus, consequently ending her days in Thebes, where she married the Cretan prince Rhadamanthus.

(*See also* Amphitryon, Andromeda, Crete, Eileithyia, Electryon, Eurystheus, Hera, Hercules, Iphicles, Mycenae, Perseus, Rhadamanthus, Tiryns, *and* Zeus.)

ALCYONE

Alcyone was a daughter of Aeolus, Lord of the Winds, and she was married to Ceyx, king of the city of Trachis. When Ceyx departed on a sea journey to the oracle at Claros in Ionia, she prayed fervently to Hera for his safe return, continuing to do so even after Ceyx, unbeknownst to her, had already died at sea. The goddess sent Morpheus, the god of dreams, to appear to Alcyone as Ceyx and reveal the truth of her husband's tragic end. When Alcyone ran to the sea and found her husband's floating corpse, the gods transformed them both into kingfishers and saw to it that their seven days of nesting in winter, the so-called Halcyon Days, would be marked by calm seas.

(*See also* Aeolus, Ceyx, *and* Hera.)

ALEXANDER

Alexander (or Alexandros) was another name for Paris, a son of King Priam of Troy and his wife, Hecuba. It was he who abducted the beautiful Helen from Sparta, thus causing the Trojan War.

(*See also* Hecuba, Helen, Paris, Priam, Sparta, *and* Troy.)

ALOEUS Aloeus, son of the god Poseidon and Canace, a daughter of Aeolus, Lord of the Winds, is best known as the father or, more properly, stepfather of the giants Otus and Ephialtes who, among their outrageous acts, attempted an assault on the gods.

(*See also* Aeolus, Canace, *and* Otus.)

ALTHEA Althea (or Althaea) was the wife of Oeneus, king of Calydon, who brought the wrath of Artemis upon himself and his kingdom. Her most notable children were Meleager and Deianeira, both of them tragic figures. Deianeira was married to Hercules and unwittingly caused his death. Althea herself caused the death of Meleager.

(*See also* Artemis, Calydon, Deianeira, Hercules, Meleager, *and* Oeneus.)

AMATA Amata was the wife of Latinus, who was king of Latium in Italy when Aeneas and his band of Trojan refugees arrived there. Amata, who favored the Rutulian prince Turnus as a son-in-law, opposed her daughter Lavinia's proposed marriage to Aeneas, although omens suggested that a Trojan union was Lavinia's destiny. Since Amata was already ill-disposed toward Aeneas, she became a perfect vehicle for Juno to stir up war between the Italians and the newcomers. This Juno did by setting upon her the Fury Alecto, whose weapon was a snake that wound its way over Amata's body, spreading its poison and inflaming her already seething hatred. Amata consequently raged about the city maddened like a Bacchante and calling upon the women of Laurentum, Latinus's capital city, to join her cause. Later, in the course of the conflict between the Trojans and Latins, Amata killed herself when she believed that her favorite, Turnus, had been slain.

(*See also* Aeneas, Alecto, Bacchantes [the], Furies [the], Latinus, Latium, Lavinia, Rutulians [the], *and* Turnus.)

AMAZONS, THE The Amazons were a legendary tribe of female warriors who were expert at archery and horsemanship. Their name was explained as being derived from the word *a-mazos*, missing a breast, for they were said to have removed their right breasts in order to eliminate interference with the use of the bow and arrow. Since theirs was a counterculture to that of the male-dominated society of the Greeks, they were believed to have resided in the Caucasus region on the fringes of the civilized world, but the historian Diodorus Siculus mentions Amazons from Libya as well. A number of formidable Greek heroes had encounters with them, including Bellerophon, Hercules, Theseus, and Achilles. Among their notable queens were Hippolyta, Penthesileia, and Antiope.

Penthesileia had come to Troy in order to support Priam and the Trojans. She was slain by Achilles, who fell in love with her at the moment of her death. Hercules was sent to fetch the belt of Hippolyta and killed her in the process. According to the tragedian Euripides, she became the mother of Hippolytus by the Athenian king Theseus, who had accompanied Hercules, but some sources name Antiope, Hippolyta's sister, as Hippolytus's mother. It was because Theseus had abducted either Antiope or Hippolyta that the Amazons attacked Athens, a battle that was depicted on the sculptural decoration of the Parthenon.

(*See also* Achilles, Antiope, Athens, Bellerophon, Caucasus Mountains [the], Hercules, Hippolyta, Hippolytus, Parthenon [the], Penthesileia, *and* Theseus.)

AMPHIARAUS   The hero Amphiaraus possessed the gift of prophecy and was a descendant of the seer Melampus. His father was variously known as Oicles, a king of Arcadia, or the god Apollo. Amphiaraus was married to Eriphyle, sister of King Adrastus of Argos. Amphiaraus, Adrastus, and Eriphyle would all become fatally entangled with affairs in the city of Thebes. It so happened that Eteocles and Polyneices, the sons of Oedipus, had agreed to share the kingdom of Thebes, each ruling alternately for a year. Eteocles, who assumed the kingship first, refused to step down. Consequently, Polyneices set out to raise an army to claim Thebes for himself. Amphiaraus knew that his brother-in-law, Adrastus, alone would survive if they joined Oedipus's son Polyneices, and for this reason, Amphiaraus refused. However, Polyneices successfully bribed Amphiaraus's wife, Eriphyle, to persuade her husband and brother to join the march against Thebes. Both Eteocles and Polyneices were killed in the battle that ensued, as were Amphiaraus and five of the others who had accompanied Polyneices (the so-called Seven Against Thebes). Polyneices's son later bribed Eriphyle, this time to persuade her son Alcmaeon to join a cohort that intended to avenge the deaths of their fathers.

(*See also* Adrastus, Alcmaeon, Apollo, Arcadia, Argos, Eriphyle, Eteocles, Harmonia, Oedipus, Polyneices, Seven Against Thebes [the], *and* Thebes.)

AMPHION   Amphion and his twin brother, Zethus, were children of the Theban princess Antiope, whom Zeus had impregnated. To hide her shame, Antiope fled—or, by some accounts, was brought by force—to Sicyon, whose regent Epopeus she wed. Antiope's father, Nycteus, killed himself and appointed his brother Lycus his successor, instructing him to punish both Epopeus and Antiope. Lycus slew the former and imprisoned Antiope, who, on her way to Thebes, had given birth to Amphion and Zethus. Lycus exposed the youths in the expectation that they would meet their end in the wild, but they survived, having been rescued and raised by a kindly herdsman. When Antiope later escaped, she was reunited with her sons, who wrought vengeance upon Lycus and his wife, Dirce. For her ill treatment of Antiope, Dirce was tied to the horns of a bull that dragged her to her death, and Lycus was driven from his throne. Amphion and Zethus now became joint regents of Thebes.

Amphion was said to have been an expert musician, having been taught how to play the lyre by the god Hermes. The poet Hesiod reports that it was by enchanting stones with his music that Amphion constructed the walls of Thebes. He was also said to have married the hapless Niobe, daughter of the Lydian king Tantalus. When Niobe boasted that she was more fortunate than the goddess Leto, Niobe and Amphion's fourteen children were slain by Leto's children, Apollo and Artemis. Amphion then either killed himself or was driven mad and, when attacking Apollo's temple, was killed by the god for this affront.

(*See also* Antiope, Apollo, Artemis, Dirce, Hermes, Leto, Lycus, Lydia, Niobe, Tantalus, Thebes, Zethus, *and* Zeus.)

AMPHITRYON Amphitryon was a son of Alcaeus and grandson of the hero Perseus. Sources do not agree on the identity of Amphitryon's mother, who, according to the mythographer Apollodorus, was either Astydamia, daughter of Pelops; Laonome, daughter of Guneus; Hipponome, daughter of Menoeceus; or Lysidice, another daughter of Pelops. Amphitryon's wife was Alcmena, daughter of his uncle Electryon, a king of Mycenae. Electryon entrusted both Alcmena and his kingdom to Amphitryon in the course of a matter involving the theft of his cattle. Amphitryon was able to ransom and return the cattle to Electryon but accidentally killed him with a club that he had thrown at a charging bull. Amphitryon was subsequently purified of murder, and Alcmena agreed to marry him if he avenged the death of her brothers, who had lost their lives to the cattle thieves. So Amphitryon set off and, after a series of conquests, returned to Thebes. But before Amphitryon reached Thebes, Zeus, in the guise of Amphitryon, visited Alcmena and slept with her. When Amphitryon himself later arrived and was not greeted enthusiastically by his wife, he asked why this was so; much to his confusion, she responded that he had come to her on the previous night. Amphitryon then learned from the seer Teiresias that it was a disguised Zeus who had visited her. Alcmena bore twin boys: Hercules, who was older by one night and was the son of Zeus, and Iphicles, the son of Amphitryon.

(*See also* Alcaeus, Alcmena, Andromeda, Electryon, Hercules, Iphicles, Mycenae, Pelops, Perseus, Teiresias, Thebes, *and* Zeus.)

AMYMONE Amymone was one of the fifty infamous, husband-murdering daughters of Danaus, a Libyan king who had fled his homeland to

Argos, which the reigning king surrendered to his authority. At that time, the land of Argos was suffering from drought, since the god Poseidon, angered that Hera and not he had been named the city's patron deity, had caused all the springs to run dry. Danaus accordingly sent his daughters to find water. While searching for water, Amymone pursued a deer and, taking aim at it with her spear, accidentally hit a sleeping Satyr. The startled but ever lusty Satyr immediately gave chase, but Poseidon came to the rescue, driving off the Satyr with a throw of his trident. Amymone then lay with Poseidon, who demonstrated his gratitude by pulling his trident from the earth, thus producing the spring or river subsequently called "Amymone." This river was known also as the spring of Lerna, where the dread Hydra would later reside. From her union with Poseidon, Amymone bore Nauplius, who would establish the city of Nauplia in the Peloponnese.

(*See also* Argos, Danaids [the], Danaus, Hera, Hydra of Lerna [the], Lerna, Poseidon, *and* Satyrs [the].)

ANAXARETE

Anaxarete was a princess descended from Teucer. According to the Roman poet Ovid, Anaxarete repeatedly spurned the overtures of Iphis, a young man of humble origins. Her rejection of him caused him to hang himself at her very door. The poor youth's mother cried out in despair asking the gods for vengeance. Consequently, Anaxarete was turned to stone as she craned out her window to watch Iphis's funeral procession.

(*See also* Iphis.)

ANCAEUS

Ancaeus was a son of Lycurgus, a king of Arcadia. He joined Jason in his quest for the Golden Fleece in spite of the fact that his concerned grandfather had hidden his armor in hopes of preventing this. He also participated in the hunt for the boar that was ravaging Calydon. It was in the course of that hunt that Ancaeus lost his life, having been gored by the boar.

(*See also* Arcadia, Calydon, *and* Jason.)

ANCHISES

Anchises was a son of Capys, an early Trojan ruler descended from Tros. His mother was variously known as Hieromnene, daughter of the river god Simoeis, or Themiste, daughter of King Ilus of Troy and sister of Laomedon, a future Trojan king. Anchises was thus descended from the very founders of Troy. According to the *Homeric Hymn to Aphrodite*, the goddess fell in love with the young and handsome Anchises as he was tending cattle on Mount Ida; falling in love with a human was Zeus's retribution for her ridiculing him and the other gods for their amorous involvement with mortals.

Aphrodite approached Anchises in disguise, claiming that she was the daughter of the Phrygian king Otreus and that she had been brought to Anchises as his bride by the god Hermes. Although Aphrodite's great beauty caused him to fear that she was one of the immortals, this story satisfied him, and he received the goddess into his bed happily. The next morning, however, Aphrodite revealed herself to Anchises in her full divinity and disclosed that she was with child. She explained that their son, Aeneas, would be raised by mountain nymphs and that she herself would deliver him to Anchises. Aeneas, she said, was destined to be a king. Anchises was to bring him to Troy but never disclose the identity of his mother. The mythographer Hyginus records that Anchises did, in a drunken state, reveal this information and that he was consequently struck dead by Zeus's thunderbolt. This account of his death does not, however, correspond to the better-known story found in Virgil's *Aeneid*: when Troy was aflame, having been vanquished at long last by the Greeks, Aeneas persuaded his father only with difficulty to leave the city with him. Aeneas placed his aged father, who was holding statues of the household gods, on his shoulders, took his son by his hand, and left the city. His wife, Creusa, followed. In so doing, Aeneas became an icon of filial piety. With Anchises and other Trojan refugees, Aeneas set sail for the Trojans' ancestral land, which was Italy. In the course of this journey Anchises died, succumbing to old age in Sicily. Even in death, however, Anchises remained a guiding force for Aeneas: he appeared to his son in a dream, convincing him to leave behind those of his followers too feeble to continue to Italy. Aeneas famously later descended into the Underworld with the guidance of Cumae's Sibyl to visit Anchises in Elysium. There Anchises revealed to him the full spectrum of his descendants and the glory that would be Rome's.

(*See also* Aeneas, Aphrodite, Creusa, Cumae, Elysium, Hermes, Ida [Mount], Phrygia, Sibyl of Cumae [the], Sicily, Trojans [the], Tros, Troy, Underworld [the], *and* Zeus.)

ANDROGEUS Androgeus was a son of Minos, king of Crete, and his wife, Pasiphae. He was a skilled athlete who defeated all of his competitors in the Athenian Panathenaic Games (athletic contests in honor of Athena). According to the mythographer Apollodorus, he met his end at the hands of one of the men he had bested, but the travel writer Pausanias suggests that the Athenians caused Androgeus to go hunt the dread Bull of Marathon, which killed all who came upon it, including Androgeus. Whatever the cause of his death, Minos held the Athenians responsible, attacked them, and exacted a tribute of seven youths and seven maidens to be fed to the Minotaur every nine years.

(*See also* Athens, Crete, Minos, Minotaur [the], *and* Pasiphae.)

ANDROMACHE Andromache was the daughter of Eetion, king of the city of Thebe (or Thebes) near Troy. She was married to the Trojan prince Hector and bore him a son, Astyanax. Since Achilles had killed her father and her seven brothers, Hector was her only remaining family, and she begged him not to risk his life fighting the Greeks on behalf of Helen and Hector's faithless brother Paris. After Hector's death, the fall of Troy, and the murder of Astyanax, Andromache was taken captive and given as a concubine to Achilles's son Neoptolemus, to whom she bore three sons. According to the tragedian Euripides, Neoptolemus's wife, Hermione, was jealous of her and unsuccessfully plotted against her life. Andromache was subsequently given to Hector's brother Helenus in marriage and returned to Asia Minor.

(*See also* Achilles, Astyanax, Hector, Helenus, Hermione, Neoptolemus, *and* Troy.)

ANDROMEDA The princess Andromeda was the daughter of Cassiopeia and Cepheus, a king of Ethiopia. According to the mythographer Apollodorus, Andromeda was shackled to the coast's jagged cliffs as a consequence of her mother's boasting to be more lovely than the Nereid nymphs. Alternatively, as the poet Ovid and Hyginus note, it was Andromeda's beauty that Cassiopeia bragged of. Taking action at this affront to the Nereid nymphs, Poseidon sent a sea monster to ravage the land of Ethiopia. Consequently, King Cepheus consulted the oracle of Ammon and was instructed to sacrifice his own daughter, Andromeda, to the monster. Reluctantly, Cepheus left Andromeda at the sea's edge for the monster.

Andromeda had been betrothed to her father's brother, Phineus, but he was unable to save her. However, by a stroke of luck, the hero Perseus, Medusa's severed head in hand, happened to be flying overhead and caught sight of her. Falling instantly in love, Perseus offered to rid Cepheus and his kingdom of the monster in exchange for Andromeda's hand. A bargain struck, Perseus slew the monster and claimed Andromeda as his bride. Phineus then launched an attack on Perseus to prevent the wedding, but the hero, holding up the head of Medusa, turned his adversaries to stone. Andromeda accompanied her new husband to Greece, where she bore him three sons and three daughters. Upon her death, the goddess Athena placed her among the stars as the constellation that bears her name.

(*See also* Ammon, Athena, Cassiopeia, Cepheus, Ethiopia, Medusa, Nereids [the], Perseus, *and* Phineus.)

ANTEIA Anteia (or Antea) was the name by which Homer knew Stheneboea, wife of Proetus, a king of Tiryns. When a young Bellerophon came to Tiryns, Anteia became enamored of him, but he spurned her overtures. Embarrassed and seeking vengeance, she accused Bellerophon of making improper advances upon her and demanded that her husband punish the youth. Proetus consequently sent Bellerophon away for punishment to Iobates, the king of Lycia, who in turn sent him on a quest for the head of the Gorgon Medusa.

(*See also* Bellerophon, Gorgons [the], Lycia, Medusa, *and* Tiryns.)

ANTIGONE
Antigone was a daughter of Oedipus and his wife, Jocasta. Her sister was Ismene, and her brothers Eteocles and Polyneices. Antigone's story is well known from Greek tragedy. Upon discovering that he had unwittingly married his mother and killed his father, Oedipus blinded himself and left the city of Thebes as a polluted exile. Accompanied by Antigone, Oedipus subsequently journeyed through Greece. When the two arrived at the sacred site of Colonus in Attica, the territory of Athens, Oedipus was welcomed by the Athenian king Theseus and found his final resting place there at Colonus. Antigone now returned to Thebes. With Oedipus gone, her brothers had decided to share the Theban kingdom, each ruling in turn for a year. Eteocles was first to assume the throne but refused to relinquish it. This caused Polyneices to enlist the help of Adrastus, king of Argos, who came with any army led by seven captains, the so-called Seven Against Thebes. The invaders were defeated, and both Polyneices and Eteocles lost their lives in the combat. Queen Jocasta's brother, Creon, then became regent, and decreed that Polyneices, whom he considered an enemy of the state, should not be buried. Eteocles, on the other hand, would receive burial rites as a defender of the city. Antigone defied Creon's decree, even when threatened with public stoning, as she felt it her duty to honor divine law (*nomos*), which dictated that the dead should be buried, or their souls could never come to rest. When caught red-handed sprinkling the body of Polyneices with soil in a ritual burial, Antigone was imprisoned in a cave, a fate that Creon's son Haemon, to whom she was betrothed, was unable to prevent. While captive, Antigone hanged herself, and Haemon, finding her dead, thrust himself upon his sword. News of the tragedy reached Creon's wife, Eurydice, who then took her own life, and as a consequence of his imprudent intransigence, Creon was left a broken man.

(*See also* Adrastus, Argos, Athens, Colonus, Creon, Eurydice [heroine], Haemon, Ismene, Jocasta, Oedipus, Polyneices, Seven Against Thebes [the], Thebes, *and* Theseus.)

ANTILOCHUS
According to Homer's *Iliad* and *Odyssey*, Antilochus was the oldest son of the wise king Nestor of Pylos. Antilochus accompanied his father to Troy, where he fought bravely. It was he who brought Achilles the terrible news of his beloved friend Patroclus's death. In the latter's funeral games, he resorted to trickery in order to win second prize, but later apologized and

offered to return his prize. Antilochus lost his life while defending his father and was buried with Achilles and Patroclus.

(*See also* Achilles, Nestor, Patroclus, Pylos, *and* Troy.)

ANTINOUS

Antinous, whose name is roughly translated as the "thoughtless one," was one of the most vocal and heinous of the men who aspired to win the hand of Penelope, Ithaca's queen, when they thought Odysseus had died at Troy. As the suitors waited for Penelope to make her selection, a thing that she did everything in her power to avoid, they proceeded to eat Penelope and her son, Telemachus, out of house and home. Antinous took the lead in plotting the death of Telemachus, threw a footstool at Odysseus when he returned to his palace in the guise of a beggar, and, deservedly, was the first of the suitors to be killed by Odysseus.

(*See also* Ithaca, Odysseus, Penelope, Telemachus, *and* Troy.)

ANTIOPE

There were two mythical Antiopes of note. One was a daughter of the Theban king Nycteus. By some accounts, this Antiope caught the roving eye of Zeus, who impregnated her in the guise of a Satyr. In order to hide her shame from her father, Antiope fled to Sicyon, whose king Epopeus she married. According to an alternate tradition, Epopeus kidnapped and impregnated Antiope, for which he incurred the wrath of her father. In any event, Nycteus enjoined his brother Lycus, who succeeded him as regent of Thebes, to avenge the insult done to him by exacting punishment from both Epopeus and Antiope. Lycus killed Epopeus and took Antiope captive. As the mythographer Apollodorus writes, Antiope gave birth to twin boys, Zethus and Amphion, on the way to Thebes, and Lycus exposed them in the wilds of Mount Cithaeron, where they were later found and raised by a herdsman. In Thebes, Antiope was then imprisoned and mistreated by Lycus's wife, Dirce. When, in the passage of time, Antiope managed to escape, she made her way to the mountain and the herdsman's hut. There she found Zethus and Amphion, to whom the herdsman revealed that this was their mother. The youths now killed Lycus (or drove him from the kingdom) and devised a terrible punishment for Dirce: they tied her to a bull that dragged her to her death.

The other Antiope was a queen of the Amazons. Antiope (or Hippolyta, as she is known in some sources) was abducted by the Athenian hero Theseus and taken by him to Athens. She became the mother of Hippolytus, for whom Phaedra, another of Theseus's wives, developed a tragic lust.

(*See also* Amazons [the], Amphion, Athens, Cithaeron [Mount], Dirce, Hippolyta, Hippolytus, Phaedra, Satyrs [the], Thebes, Theseus, Zethus, *and* Zeus.)

APSYRTUS Apsyrtus was a son of Aeetes, king of Colchis, and brother (or half brother) of Medea. Tales surrounding him focus on his death, which is variously recounted. According to Apollonius of Rhodes, Apsyrtus spearheaded the Colchian pursuit of Jason and the Argonauts when, with Medea and the Golden Fleece in tow, they were making their way back to Thessaly. Medea and Jason concocted a ruse whereby to entrap and kill Apsyrtus. Medea asked to meet him in secret at a temple of Artemis and sent him a false message stating that she intended to steal the fleece and return with him to Colchis. Apsyrtus appeared at the temple, where he was ambushed and killed by Jason, who then hid his body. The mythographer Hyginus, however, writes that Aeetes pursued Jason and Medea, and when Medea saw her father's ship draw near, she herself murdered Apsyrtus, cutting him limb from limb and throwing the pieces into the sea. This put an end to Aeetes's pursuit, as he stopped to retrieve all of his son's remains and then turned back to bury them.

(See also Aeetes, Argonauts [the], Artemis, Colchis, Jason, Medea, and Thessaly.)

ARACHNE Arachne is described by the Roman poet Ovid as having been a young woman of common birth, but of uncommon skill as a weaver. She lived in the village of Hypaepa in Lydia. Her father was a humble wool dyer, and her mother was deceased. Despite her lowly rank, Arachne became famous throughout the towns of Lydia for her expert ability to spin and weave wool. Even the local nymphs came to marvel at her. Though spinning and weaving were specifically Minerva's arts, Arachne would not admit that the goddess had been her teacher. Instead, she made it known that she would gladly challenge the goddess to a weaving contest. Minerva could not bear this insult and, appearing to her in the guise of an old woman, cautioned Arachne not to dishonor the gods with such arrogance. Arachne still would not relent, so Minerva revealed herself to the girl in her full divinity. The contest thus commenced. Minerva wove into her design the contest in which she had prevailed over Neptune to win the stewardship of the city of Athens by producing an olive tree. As a clear warning to Arachne, she also depicted a host of mortals who had challenged the gods and been punished terribly. Arachne, for her part, wove vignettes depicting misdeeds of the gods, a twofold affront to the goddess. There appeared Jupiter taking on the shape of a bull to seduce Europa, of a swan to make advances on Leda, of her own husband to lie with Alcmena, of a golden shower to penetrate the cell of Danae, and of a flame to approach Aegina. Neptune, too, was shown. He assumed the shape of a dolphin in pursuit of Melantho, of a bird to approach Medusa, and of a ram, river, and stallion to make advances on other maidens still. Apollo, Bacchus, and Saturn, all behaving ignobly, also found a place in Arachne's design. Arachne's work was perfection, flawless even in Minerva's eyes. So great was the goddess's anger that she tore apart Arachne's weaving and struck Arachne on the head until, unable to bear this assault, she hanged herself. Arachne did, however, live on, now as a spider, misshapen but spinning for all time.

(*See also* Aegina, Alcmena, Apollo, Athens, Bacchus, Danae, Leda, Lydia, Medusa, Minerva, Neptune, *and* Jupiter.)

ARCAS

Arcas was a son of Zeus and Callisto, daughter of the Arcadian king Lycaon. Arcas was raised by the god Hermes's mother, Maia, after his own mother was transformed into a bear by a jealous Hera. After Arcas was returned to his grandfather's court, Lycaon cut him into pieces, using them to cook a stew that he served to Zeus, who was visiting Arcadia in disguise. Lycaon was punished for his barbarism by being transformed into a wolf, but Arcas was reassembled and restored to life. The travel writer Pausanias records that when Arcas succeeded to the throne of Arcadia, he introduced the cultivation of crops, which he had learned from the culture hero (bringer of civilization and culture) Triptolemus, and taught his subjects how to make bread and weave clothes. It was in honor of Arcas that his kingdom came to be known as Arcadia instead of Pelasgia and its inhabitants Arcadians instead of Pelasgians. When, at a later time, Arcas was on the verge of accidentally killing his own mother while hunting, Zeus came to the rescue and transformed them both into the constellations Arctophylax ("Guardian of the Bear") and the Great Bear.

(*See also* Arcadia, Callisto, Hera, Hermes, Lycaon, Maia, Pelasgus, Triptolemus, *and* Zeus.)

ARETE

Arete, whose name means "virtue," was the queen of the goodly Phaeacians and wife of Alcinous. Her daughter was Nausicaa, who assisted the shipwrecked Odysseus when he came ashore the Phaeacians' island of Scheria, showing him the way to his parents' palace. Nausicaa also advised Odysseus that, upon arriving at the palace, he should address Arete before her husband Alcinous, a clear indicator of her influence. In an unrelated myth, Arete advocated the Phaeacians' protection of Jason and Medea when, with the Golden Fleece in tow, they arrived at Scheria pursued by the Colchians.

(*See also* Alcinous, Colchis, Jason, Medea, Nausicaa, Odysseus, Phaeacians [the], *and* Scheria.)

ARGONAUTS, THE

The Argonauts ("Argo-Sailors") were the crew of heroes who accompanied Jason on his quest for the Golden Fleece. Their ship was the *Argo*, which, by some accounts, was the first ship and, by others, the largest and most miraculous because it had the ability to speak. According to Apollonius of Rhodes in his *Argonautica* (*Voyage of the Argo*), the Argonauts included Orpheus, Telamon, Admetus, Peleus, Hercules, Hylas, Castor and Pollux, Meleager, and Zetes and Calais, among others.

(*See also* Admetus, Castor, Hercules, Hylas, Jason, Meleager, Orpheus, Telamon, *and* Zetes.)

ARIADNE

Ariadne was a daughter of Minos, king of Crete, and his wife, Pasiphae. Ariadne fell in love with the Athenian prince Theseus when he arrived on the island as one of the fourteen youths and maidens to be fed to her monstrous half brother, the Minotaur. Theseus intended to attempt to kill the Minotaur, who was kept captive in a labyrinth. Ariadne, wishing to do what she could to help the object of her affections, gave him a ball of string to unroll as he entered the labyrinth. Theseus was able both to slay the Minotaur and retrace his steps out of the labyrinth by following the thread he had earlier unwound. For her assistance, Theseus agreed to take Ariadne with him to Greece, though this did not occur. By some accounts, Theseus abandoned Ariadne on the island of Dia (modern Naxos), where she was found by the god Dionysus, who made her his bride; according to Diodorus Siculus, by contrast, she was abducted by the god when Theseus put her on the island. Upon her death, the god transferred her to the heavens as the constellation Corona Borealis.

In his biography of Theseus, Plutarch relates that there were, in fact, many divergent tales about the fate of Ariadne, among them the following: she hanged herself because she had been abandoned by Theseus; she was brought to Naxos by sailors and settled there with a priest of Dionysus; she was abandoned by Theseus because he loved another woman; and she had several sons by Theseus. Ariadne was worshipped in cult on the islands of Naxos and Cyprus, where one tradition places her burial.

(*See also* Athens, Crete, Cyprus, Dionysus, Minos, Minotaur [the], Naxos, Pasiphae, *and* Theseus.)

ARIMASPI, THE

The Arimaspi were a mythical group of one-eyed people who, according to the Greek historian Herodotus, lived in the extreme north, beyond the Issedones (a Central Asian people) and near the land of the Griffins, whose gold they repeatedly attempted to steal.

(*See also* Griffins [the].)

ARION The noted poet Arion of Lesbos was a historical personage, part of whose life story became mythologized. The Greek historian Herodotus credits Arion (late seventh century BCE) with having been the first person to compose a dithyramb (a hymn to the god Dionysus), give it a name, and perform it at Corinth. Since the dithyramb, according to Aristotle, was a plausible forerunner to dramatic performances, Arion's work was significant to the development of the theater. In any event, Herodotus also reports that he spent most of his life at the court of the tyrant Periander of Corinth, but at some point traveled to Italy and Sicily, where he made a great deal of money through his performances. Having most faith in Corinthian sailors, Arion decided to return home on a Corinthian vessel. The crew, however, had become aware of the riches that he carried and ordered him either to kill himself or to jump overboard. Arion dressed to perform one last song and, lute in hand, leaped into the sea, where a dolphin came to his rescue and carried him safely to land. Arion related this adventure to Periander, who put the ship's crew to death. The mythographer Hyginus adds that, because of Arion's skill at playing the cithara, Apollo placed him and the dolphin among the stars.

(*See also* Apollo, Corinth, *and* Dionysus.)

ARSINOE Arsinoe, a daughter of Leucippus, was named in some sources as mother of the healing god Asclepius by Apollo. Most sources, however, claim that Asclepius was born of Coronis.

(*See also* Apollo, Asclepius, Coronis, *and* Leucippus.)

ARUNS Aruns (or Arruns) was an Etruscan warrior who appeared in Virgil's epic *Aeneid*. He was responsible for the untimely death of Camilla, a noble and skilled huntress. Camilla had formed part of the Italians' armed resistance to the Trojan Aeneas's arrival in Italy and his proposed marriage to Lavinia, princess of Latium.

(*See also* Aeneas, Camilla, Etruria, Latium, Lavinia, *and* Troy.)

ASCANIUS Ascanius was the son of Aeneas by his Trojan wife, Creusa. In Virgil's *Aeneid*, he was known as Ilus, after Ilium (another name for Troy), as long as Troy remained undefeated. Subsequent to Troy's fall, he was known as Iulus, a name that highlighted his role as founder of the Julian family, which would yield Julius Caesar and the emperor Augustus. Ascanius accompanied his father in the journey from Troy to Italy. While in Italy he became responsible for the outbreak of hostilities between the Latins and the recently arrived Trojans by virtue of shooting the pet stag of Silvia, daughter of Tyrrhus, chief herdsman for King Latinus. Ascanius was destined, after the conflict's subsidence, to rule in Lavinium for thirty years and then to establish Alba Longa as capital, where his descendants would rule for three hundred years until the founding of Rome by Romulus and Remus.

(*See also* Aeneas, Creusa, Ilium, Iulus, Latinus, Latium, Remus, Rome, Romulus, *and* Troy.)

ASCLEPIUS Asclepius (or Aesculapius) was a son of Apollo and healing hero who became divinized, thus being known more generally as god of healing and medicine.

(*See also* Apollo *and* Asclepius [god].)

ASTYANAX Astyanax, whose name means "Lord of the City," was the son of Hector, Troy's brave defender, and his wife, Andromache. Hector called him Scamandrius after the Trojan river Scamander. In Homer's *Iliad*, Astyanax was only a baby, and Andromache was justifiably concerned about his fate should Hector die while fighting. Later authors describe Astyanax's death at the hands of the Greeks. The usual story is that Astyanax was thrown from the walls of Troy, either by Odysseus or some other Greek, in order to prevent the survival of any of Priam's descendants.

(*See also* Andromache, Hector, Odysseus, Priam, Scamander River [the], *and* Troy.)

ATALANTA Atalanta was an expert huntress and exceedingly fleet of foot. Her father was variously said to be the Boeotian king Schoeneus (as in the works of Ovid, Statius, Pausanias, and Theocritus) or Iasus, an Arcadian king, whose wife was Clymene, daughter of Minyas, ancestor of the Minyans (as in Callimachus, Propertius, and Apollodorus). Upon her birth, Atalanta was taken to the wilderness and abandoned, since her father did not want a daughter. By the providence of the goddess Artemis, a kindly she-bear came upon her and raised her until she was taken in by some local hunters. Artemis, for her part, provided Atalanta with instruction in hunting. The poet Apollonius of Rhodes reports that, when grown, Atalanta aspired to join Jason on his dangerous quest for the Golden Fleece, but that he prevented her from doing so on the grounds of his affection for her. Atalanta, did, however join Meleager, son of the Calydonian king Oeneus and Althea, in hunting the terrible boar that the goddess Artemis had sent to ravage the countryside; the goddess was angered that Oeneus, while a pious man, had somehow overlooked her when making sacrifice to the gods in thanks for the first fruits of harvest. All the strongest and bravest men gathered for the hunt, but it was the maiden Atalanta who inflicted the first wound, allowing Meleager to complete the task of killing it. In recognition of this fact, Meleager presented her with the boar's head as a trophy, an action that drew the resentment of his mother's brothers. A fierce battle, and fulfilment of a prophecy foretelling Meleager's untimely death, then ensued.

Atalanta wished to remain a huntress, unmarried and a virgin like the goddess Artemis, but numerous men pursued her. Conceding to her father's entreaties that she consider marriage, she agreed to marry whoever could outrun her. Many unsuccessfully attempted to win her hand and paid the penalty for loss with their lives. Still, one, undaunted, prevailed. Ovid calls him Hippomenes, a great-grandson of Poseidon, although for Pausanias and others he is Melanion. This youth called upon the goddess Aphrodite for aid, and she responded, bringing him three golden apples from her sanctuary on the isle of Cyprus. The race commenced, and Meleager threw one apple after another out to the side of the racecourse. Atalanta could not resist the apples, retrieving each of them in turn. Atalanta's dash after the last apple allowed the youth to win the race and so win her as bride. Atalanta developed affection for her new mate, but the couple's joy did not last, for in his excitement over his victory, Hippomenes had forgotten to thank Aphrodite. The angry goddess drove him wild with passion, and consequently, they defiled a temple of the goddess Cybele with their lovemaking. For this Cybele punished them by transforming them into lions, which she then fastened to the yoke of her carriage.

(See also Althea, Aphrodite, Arcadia, Artemis, Boeotia, Calydon, Clymene, Cybele, Cyprus, Hippomenes, Jason, Melanion, Meleager, Minyas, Oeneus, Poseidon, and Schoeneus.)

ATHAMAS Athamas was a king of Orchomenus in Boeotia. His wives were, in succession, Nephele, the Theban king Cadmus's daughter Ino, and the Thessalian king Hypseus's daughter Themisto. Athamas's numerous troubles began with his marriage to Ino, who was jealous of Phrixus and Helle, his children by his first wife, Nephele. Ino devised a stratagem whereby to have the children killed, but they escaped her clutches by spectacular means: a golden-fleeced ram that ultimately bore one of them, Phrixus, to safety. Zeus later brought the infant Dionysus to Athamas and Ino to raise, but an angry Hera saw to it that both were driven mad. Athamas accidentally killed his son Learchus, believing him to be a deer (or a lion), and Ino threw her son Melicertes into a boiling cauldron or, by some accounts, leaped with him in her arms into the Saronic Gulf, where they perished, only to be transformed into the sea deities Leucothea and Palaemon.

(See also Boeotia, Dionysus, Helle, Hera, Ino, Leucothea, Nephele, Phrixus, Thessaly, and Zeus.)

ATREUS Atreus was a son of Pelops, king of Pisa, and Hippodamia. He, his siblings, and his descendants all suffered the consequences of a curse uttered upon Pelops for his treachery. At his mother's request, Atreus and his brother Theyestes killed their half brother Chrysippus, and for this they were exiled from Pisa. Atreus wed Aerope, a Cretan princess, and with her became father to Agamemnon and Menelaus, the future kings of Mycenae and Sparta respectively. His wife, Aerope, either developed a passion for Theyestes or else was seduced by him. In any event, she betrayed Atreus when the throne of Mycenae became available. According to the mythographer Apollodorus, Atreus was in possession of a golden-fleeced lamb that he should have sacrificed to Artemis but kept for himself instead. With the help of Aerope, Theyestes obtained the lamb, killed it, stripped its fleece, and suggested that the kingship of Mycenae should be awarded on the basis of its possession. Atreus agreed and was surprised to discover that he no longer had the lamb or the fleece. Crying foul, Atreus caused this decision to be revisited and was awarded the kingship on the basis of being able to reverse the course of the sun, which he did with the help of Zeus. Atreus now contrived a means to punish Theyestes for taking up with his wife and, after serving him his own children in a stew, drove him from the land. While away, Theyestes impregnated his own daughter Pelopia, as he had learned from an oracle that it was by this means that he could best avenge himself upon his brother, and Aegisthus, the product of this union did, when grown to manhood, indeed kill Atreus. Atreus was succeeded briefly by Theyestes, but the latter was driven from Mycenae by Atreus's sons Agamemnon and Menelaus. It was Agamemnon, the elder of the two, who became king of Mycenae, until he, too, was murdered, as the curse against Pelops had dictated.

(*See also* Aerope, Agamemnon, Artemis, Hippodamia, Menelaus, Mycenae, Pelops, Theyestes, *and* Zeus.)

AUGEAS Augeas (or Augeias) was a king of Elis in the Peloponnese whose father was variously recorded as the god Helios or Poseidon, among others. His claim to fame was his enormous herd of cattle and the even greater mess that they made. As his fifth Labor, Hercules was sent to clean Augeas's stables, a seemingly impossible task, and to do so in the course of one day. This Hercules accomplished by diverting the rivers Alpheus and Peneus through the stables. Augeas then withheld the payment for which Hercules had negotiated, a tenth of the cattle, and drove him from his kingdom. Hercules would later return with an army in order to exact vengeance for the wrong done to him by sacking the city of Elis. By some accounts, Hercules killed Augeas in the conflict.

(*See also* Alpheus River [the], Helios, Hercules, Peneus River [the], *and* Poseidon.)

AUTONOE Autonoe was one of the daughters of Harmonia and Cadmus, founder of the city of Thebes. Her sisters, all of them tragic figures in their own right, were Ino, Agave, and Semele. With the agricultural culture hero Aristaeus, Autonoe became mother to Actaeon, who, as punishment for catching sight of the goddess Artemis unclothed, was killed by his own hunting dogs. Autonoe, Ino, and Agave later participated in the gruesome dismemberment of Agave's son Pentheus.

(*See also* Actaeon, Aristaeus, Cadmus, Harmonia, Ino, Pentheus, Semele, *and* Thebes.)

BACCHANTES Bacchantes (or Bacchants and Bacchae) were the female worshippers of the wine god Bacchus, who was also called Dionysus. The Bacchantes were also known as Maenads after the *mania* ("madness" in Greek) that overcame them while they were possessed by the god.

(*See also* Bacchus, Dionysus, *and* Maenads [the].)

BATTUS Battus was a poor herdsman and the servant of a wealthy man. According to the Roman poet Ovid, he witnessed Mercury's theft of Apollo's cattle, and, for a bribe, promised not to reveal what he had seen. Mercury, however, disguised himself in order to make trial of Battus and offered him a still greater reward for information. Battus did not hesitate to accept his new offer and was instantly changed by the god into a stone. This was the origin of the "touchstone," a measure or criterion for judgment.

(*See also* Apollo *and* Mercury.)

BAUCIS The Roman poet Ovid tells the story of Baucis, "Tender One," and her husband, Philemon, "Friendly One," elderly peasants living in Phrygia. It happened that Jupiter and Mercury visited their village disguised as mortals. Weary from travel, the gods knocked on a thousand doors in hopes of being offered respite and refreshment. All the doors were shut on them but one, that of Baucis and Philemon, who provided all they could by way of hospitality in spite of their humble circumstances: a rustic bench with a homespun cover; the remnants of a fire; a bit of long-saved bacon; a grass-stuffed mattress; plates of olives, cherries, cheese, apples, and grapes; and wine. Miraculously, the wine bowl filled each time it was drained, a blessing from the gods. When the peasants even offered their only goose, the gods intervened to spare the bird and revealed themselves in their divinity. Baucis and Philemon were told to retreat to a nearby hilltop, and the surrounding village and its inhabitants were flooded in retribution for their wickedness. Baucis and Philemon's hut, meanwhile, remained untouched by the waters and was transformed into a temple. When asked what they would most wish for, the couple responded that they would like to spend the rest of their days as priests and guardians of the temple. They also asked that neither should outlive the other. And so it came to pass. They served the gods faithfully through their lives, and when they reached an advanced age, they became an oak tree and a linden that stood adjacent to each other.

(*See also* Jupiter, Mercury, *and* Phrygia.)

BELLEROPHON

The hero Bellerophon is best known for taming the winged horse Pegasus and slaying the Chimaera, a triple-headed monster with the forequarters of a lion, the tail of a dragon, and at its midsection, the fire-spewing head of a goat. The story of Bellerophon's life is one of rise and ignoble fall. He was the "stepson" of Sisyphus's son Glaucus, a king of Corinth, and son of a woman named either Eurymede or Eurynome; his actual father was reputedly Poseidon. By accident, Bellerophon had caused the death of another man. By some accounts, this was his own brother. By others, it was a Corinthian tyrant called Bellerus, after whose death Bellerophon, previously called Hipponous, reputedly was renamed killer (-*phontes*) of Bellerus. With blood on his hands, Bellerophon fled Corinth and took refuge with Proetus, king of Tiryns. While in Tiryns, the king's wife Stheneboea (or Anteia) became enamored of him, and Bellerophon rejected her advances. In retribution for this slight, Stheneboea accused him of having propositioned her and demanded that he be duly punished. Not wishing to violate the bond between guest and host by punishing the youth directly, Proetus sent Bellerophon to Lycia, where he was to deliver a letter to King Iobates, Stheneboea's father. Unbeknownst to Bellerophon, the letter revealed his alleged violation of Stheneboea and contained a request that the youth be killed. Iobates, too, wanted to avoid the stain of blood guilt and sent Bellerophon to complete a task sure to prove fatal: slaying the Chimaera, which was devastating the Lycian countryside. With the aid of Minerva, Bellerophon was able to tame the winged horse Pegasus and, borne aloft, to slay the Chimaera with his arrows. According to the mythographer Apollodorus, a surprised Iobates next ordered him to defeat the exceedingly warlike Solymi. Once Bellerophon had completed that task, Iobates next commanded him to attack the Amazons as well. When Bellerophon had prevailed in all these conflicts, Iobates set the bravest of his own men to ambush and kill him, but they did not succeed. Now deeply impressed by Bellerophon's bravery and prowess, Iobates gave him his other daughter, Philonoe, in marriage and declared him heir to his own throne. At this news an anguished Stheneboea killed herself—or, according to a variant tradition, Bellerophon pushed her from Pegasus's back to fall to her death. Of

Bellerophon's own end there are several different accounts. In Homer's *Iliad*, he is said to have become hated by the gods. This may have been because, as the poet Pindar reveals, Bellerophon aspired to exceed human limits. Spurring Pegasus on to reach the heavenly abode of Zeus, Bellerophon was thrown so as to fall back to earth, being consigned, thenceforth, to wander as an outcast, alone.

Bellerophon was worshipped both in Lycia and at the city of Corinth, where travel writer Pausanias saw a grove of cypresses called Craneum, the location of a precinct sacred to Bellerophon and a temple of Aphrodite.

(*See also* Amazons [the], Anteia, Aphrodite, Chimaera [the], Corinth, Glaucus [hero], Iobates, Lycia, Minerva, Pegasus, Poseidon, Proetus, Sisyphus, Solymi [the], Tiryns, *and* Zeus.)

BELUS Belus was a legendary king of Egypt. According to the mythographer Apollodorus, Belus was the child of the god Poseidon with Libya, daughter of Epaphus and Memphis. His twin brother was Agenor, who became a king of Phoenicia. Belus, remaining in Egypt, became regent of that country and married Anchinoe, daughter of the Nile, by whom he, too, had twin sons, Aegyptus and Danaus. Belus gave regency of Libya to Danaus and that of Arabia to Aegyptus. Aegyptus became father to fifty sons and Danaus to fifty daughters. When Aegyptus proposed that his sons should wed Danaus's daughters, Danaus fled, suspecting that his brother wished to annex his kingdom. Eventually, Danaus agreed to the union but had instructed his daughters to kill their husbands on their wedding night. His daughters, the Danaids, consequently became infamous denizens of the Underworld.

The Carthaginian queen Dido as well as the kings of Persia were said to have been descended from Belus.

(*See also* Aegyptus, Carthage, Danaids [the], Danaus, Dido, Epaphus, *and* Poseidon.]

BITON Biton and his brother Cleobis were strong and virtuous youths whose act of selfless heroism in honor of their mother and the goddess Hera earned them the highest honor that could be bestowed on a mortal: death upon accomplishing his noblest achievement.

(*See* Cleobis *and* Hera.)

BRISEIS Briseis was the wife of Mynes, king of the city of Lyrnessus, near Troy. The hero Achilles sacked this city and killed Briseis's husband as well as her three brothers during the ten-year period that the Greeks were fighting at Troy. Briseis was consequently seized as a war captive and became Achilles's concubine. When, in the tenth year of the Trojan War, Agamemnon was compelled to return his own concubine, Chryseis, to her father, Chryses, a priest of Apollo, he demanded that Achilles give him Briseis to replace his loss. Since Briseis constituted a measure of his valor, Achilles was justifiably angered at this outrage. When Briseis was taken from him, he withdrew from the fighting and asked his divine mother, Thetis, to convince Zeus to let the Trojans prevail so that Agamemnon would quickly see the results of his prideful folly. When Agamemnon did, eventually, return Briseis, many Greeks had died, among them Patroclus, Achilles's closest friend.

(*See also* Achilles, Agamemnon, Apollo, Chryseis, Patroclus, Thetis, Troy, *and* Zeus.)

CADMUS Cadmus was a son of the Tyrian (or Sidonian) king Agenor.

When his daughter Europa was abducted by Zeus, Agenor sent his sons in search of her. The brothers dispersed, each eventually establishing a colony wherever he gave up his quest. Cadmus made his way to Boeotia and thence to Delphi, where he sought the oracle's advice. The oracle urged him to abandon the search and to settle where a cow came to rest. At this place he founded the city of Cadmeia, later known as Thebes. According to the mythographer Apollodorus, who preserves a wealth of detail about the city's founding, Cadmus wanted to sacrifice this cow to the gods in thanks and sent some of his men to fetch water for the ritual. When the men did not return from the spring, Cadmus went to investigate and found a dragon guarding the water's source, which was sacred to the god Ares. Cadmus slew this dragon and, with instruction from the goddess Athena, sowed a portion of the dragon's teeth. From them grew men, the so-called Sparti, "Sown Ones," fully grown and armed. Cadmus threw rocks into their midst, and they, in confusion, turned upon each other, all but five perishing in the fray. Zeus later gave Cadmus Harmonia, daughter of Aphrodite and Ares, as a bride, and all the gods celebrated their union. As wedding gifts, Cadmus gave Harmonia a fine robe and a wondrous necklace created by Hephaestus; both gifts would become central to conflict among their descendants. Cadmus and Harmonia had a son, Polydorus, and four daughters, Autonoe, Ino, Semele, and Agave, all of whom would become tragic characters. Ino was married to Athamas, Autonoe to Aristaeus, and Agave to Echion. Semele was impregnated by Zeus and became the mother of the god Dionysus. Agave, for her part, was the mother of Pentheus, who became regent of Thebes when Cadmus relinquished the throne to him. Pentheus met a horrific end at the hands of his mother and his aunts, all of them in a Bacchic trance, because he had refused to recognize his cousin Dionysus (also called Bacchus) as a god. Autonoe's son Actaeon also met a terrible end, having been torn to bits by his hunting dogs. In a bizarre turn of events, Cadmus and Harmonia were banished to Illyria, a remote land in the western Balkan Peninsula, where they led a barbarian horde in battle and were turned into snakes, perhaps in retribution for Cadmus's slaying of Ares's dragon. Cadmus and Harmonia were ultimately sent by Zeus to live in the Elysian Fields.

(*See also* Actaeon, Agave, Agenor, Aphrodite, Ares, Aristaeus, Autonoe, Boeotia, Delphi, Dionysus, Elysian Fields [the], Europa, Harmonia, Ino, Pentheus, Polydorus, Semele, Thebes, *and* Zeus.)

CALAIS

Calais and his twin brother Zetes were swift, winged sons of Boreas, the north wind, and, being children of Boreas, were called "Boreads." The two are best known for their assistance to the king Phineus, who had been endlessly tortured by the Harpies' snatching away his food.

(*See also* Boreas, Harpies [the], Phineus, *and* Zetes.)

CALCHAS

Calchas was the prophet or seer regularly consulted by the Greeks in the course of the Trojan War. His many pivotal predictions included disclosing to Agamemnon and the assembled Greek forces that it was due to the wrath of Artemis that the winds had fallen and their ships were unable to set sail from Aulis to Troy; the remedy that he disclosed was the sacrifice to Artemis of Agamemnon's daughter Iphigeneia. Agamemnon's wife, Clytemnestra, never forgave Agamemnon for the death of their daughter, a fact that led directly to her vengeful killing of him. Calchas also revealed to the Greeks that the plague that they were suffering while encamped outside the walls of Troy could be dispelled if Agamemnon returned his concubine, Chryseis, to her father, the priest Chryses. This, too, Agamemnon did, only to take Achilles's concubine Briseis from him, an affront that Achilles could not bear. Calchas is also credited by sources including Apollodorus, Quintus of Smyrna, and Seneca with predicting that Troy would not fall to the Greeks without the help of Achilles's son Neoptolemus and Philoctetes. He further proclaimed that the Greeks could not return home before sacrificing Hector's infant son Astyanax and the Trojan princess Polyxena.

(*See also* Achilles, Agamemnon, Artemis, Astyanax, Aulis, Briseis, Chryseis, Clytemnestra, Hector, Hercules, Iphigeneia, Neoptolemus, Philoctetes, Polyxena, *and* Troy.)

CALLISTO

Callisto was a beautiful maiden, or nymph, who lived in the wilds of Arcadia as a companion of the virgin goddess Diana. Most sources claim that Callisto's father was the Arcadian king Lycaon, a savage tyrant who, for his outrageous acts, was, fittingly, transformed by Jupiter into a savage wolf. The Roman poet Ovid tells the best-known version of her fate. Like so many lovely women, nymphs, and goddesses, Callisto did not escape the roving eye of Jupiter, who happened upon her while she was bathing. The god used an especially loathsome ruse to get close to her: he disguised himself as the goddess Diana, and for this reason, Callisto was not alarmed at his approach. The result was rape, and Callisto became pregnant. She bore her shame as long as possible, but one day, when Diana, hot and weary from hunting, urged all her companions to join her for a refreshing plunge in a shaded stream, Callisto held back. The others stripped her bare, and the shame of her growing belly exposed, Callisto was banished by the goddess. Jupiter's wife, Juno, too, was angered when she bore a son, young Arcas, and in a rage at her husband's infidelity, transformed Callisto into a bear. When, in the passage of time, Arcas was old enough to hunt, he encountered his bear-mother and was only just prevented by Jupiter from killing her with a cast of his spear. The god lifted mother and son into the heavens where they became the constellations Arctos, "Bear" (Ursa Major, "Great Bear" in Latin, also called Bootes), and Arctophylax (literally, "guardian of the bear" in Greek and Ursa Minor, "Lesser Bear," in Latin). Her rage unabated, Juno devised one last punishment: neither constellation would be permitted to rest by setting in the river Oceanus, and as a result, neither slips below the horizon. The mythographer Apollodorus, writing in Greek and using the characters' Greek names, provides other versions of the tale: either Hera persuaded Artemis to shoot Callisto, or Artemis shot her of her own accord since Callisto had not kept her vow of chastity. When Callisto perished, Zeus quickly seized the baby, named it Arcas, and gave it to the nymph Maia to raise.

(*See also* Arcadia, Arcas, Diana, Hera, Juno, Jupiter, Lycaon, Maia, Oceanus [place], *and* Zeus.)

CAMILLA
Camilla's father, Metabus, a tyrannical king of the Volscians, had fled his homeland when she was just an infant. Arriving at the river Amisenus, he tied Camilla to an ash spear, pledging that he would dedicate her to the goddess Diana if the spear could carry her safely across the river. His wish was granted, and he subsequently kept his promise to the goddess: Camilla grew up a virgin huntress in the forest. She would later join forces with the Rutulian prince Turnus against Aeneas and his band of Trojans, whose appearance in Italy occasioned a grievous war. In the course of this conflict, Camilla was ignobly slain by a warrior named Aruns, and her death caused widespread expressions of grief among the Latins.

(*See also* Aeneas, Aruns, Diana, Latins [the], Rutulians [the], Troy, *and* Turnus.)

CANACE
According to the mythographer Apollodorus, Canace was one of the twelve children of Aeolus, Lord of the Winds. With the god Poseidon,

she became mother to five sons, who included Aloeus, later the stepfather of the giants Otus and Ephialtes. The Roman poet Ovid records the dramatic events surrounding Canace's death. As a result of an incestuous relationship with her brother Macareus, she became pregnant and, although she and her nurse attempted to abort the child, a son by her brother was born to her. An enraged Aeolus ordered the newborn child to be thrown to the dogs and birds of prey, and he supplied Canace with a sword whereby to take her own life.

(*See also* Aeolus, Aloeus, Otus, *and* Poseidon.)

CAPANEUS
Capaneus was a prime exemplar of hubris (excessive pride) and its consequences. He was one of the seven commanders who joined forces with Oedipus's son Polyneices to march on the city of Thebes. Polyneices organized this campaign when, contrary to prior agreement, his brother Eteocles refused to step down as Thebes's regent. According to the tragedian Aeschylus, Capaneus boasted that he would destroy Thebes with or without the support of Zeus; he even claimed that conflict with the god himself would be no deterrent, Zeus's thunderbolts being no more harmful than midday heat. For all his bravado, this blasphemer did not escape the wrath of Zeus, who smote him with his divine fire as he scaled the walls of Thebes.

(*See also* Eteocles, Oedipus, Polyneices, Thebes, *and* Zeus.)

CASSANDRA
Cassandra was a daughter of the Trojan king Priam and his wife, Hecuba. According to Homer, Cassandra was extraordinarily beautiful, comparable in this regard even to Aphrodite. Her beauty, however, was more curse than blessing. She attracted the attention of Apollo, who gave her the gift of prophecy in the expectation that she would yield to his advances. Yet she resisted him, and for this insult, Apollo made it so that although she could foretell the future, nobody would believe her. Thus, when she prophesied that her brother Paris would bring ruin upon Troy, Priam nonetheless equipped him with a fleet to go fetch Helen from Sparta, which then became the direct cause of the Trojan War. She also told the Trojans to be wary of the Trojan Horse, knowing that it was filled with Greeks and was not, as had been thought, an offering to Athena. Among the outrages that Cassandra suffered was rape at the hands of the Greek hero Ajax, son of Oileus (or the Lesser Ajax), though she had taken refuge at Athena's altar in Troy. For this sacrilege and affront to the goddess, Ajax and the remaining Greeks were punished by Athena, Zeus, and Poseidon. Ajax's ship was wrecked on the return voyage from Troy, and he was struck by lightning or, by some accounts, drowned at sea. As for Cassandra, she was given to King Agamemnon of Mycenae, commander of the combined Greek

forces, as a concubine. When Agamemnon brought Cassandra back home with him to Mycenae, her presence further angered an already irate Queen Clytemnestra, who killed them both. Cassandra's death and her foreknowledge of it are vividly described in the tragedian Aeschylus's play *Agamemnon*.

In an alternate tradition, Cassandra and her twin brother, Helenus, both received the gift of prophecy as babies by virtue of having their ears licked by snakes in a temple of Apollo.

(*See also* Agamemnon, Ajax [the Lesser], Aphrodite, Apollo, Athena, Clytemnestra, Hecuba, Helen, Helenus, Mycenae, Paris, Poseidon, Priam, Sparta, Troy, *and* Zeus.)

CASSIOPEIA
Cassiopeia was the wife of the Ethiopian king Cepheus and mother of the lovely Andromeda. As a consequence of her prideful boast that she—or by some accounts, her daughter—was more beautiful than the Nereid nymphs, Poseidon sent a sea monster to ravage Ethiopia, and the only remedy was the sacrifice of her daughter. Fortunately, Andromeda was rescued by the hero Perseus, fresh from his encounter with Medusa. Upon her death, Poseidon transformed Cassiopeia into a constellation, her body arranged in an undignified position: on her back, feet in the air.

(*See also* Andromeda, Cepheus, Ethiopia, Medusa, Nereids [the], *and* Poseidon.)

CECROPS
Cecrops was known as the first king of Athens and its territory, Attica, which in his time was called Cecropia. He was reputedly autochthonous—literally being born from the earth—and hybrid in form, his lower body being that of a snake. As the first king, he was also regarded as a culture hero responsible for acknowledging Zeus as the supreme deity, instituting monogamy and funeral rites, ending human sacrifice, introducing the alphabet, and uniting the region's communities as a city. When the gods each decided to take possession of a city, Athena and Poseidon both famously laid claim to Athens. By some accounts, Zeus appointed Cecrops as judge in the contest between the two gods, but by others, it was all the Olympian gods or even Cecrops's short-lived son Erysichthon who made the decision. Poseidon struck the rock of the Acropolis with his trident, producing a salt spring, symbol of what would be the city's power at sea. Athena, for her part, caused an olive tree to grow. It was the olive that was judged the most valuable gift, and the olive indeed became a mainstay of the Athenian economy. As a result of her victory over Poseidon, Athena became patron deity of the city and named it Athens after herself.

(*See also* Acropolis [the], Athena, Athens, Attica, Olympus [Mount], Poseidon, *and* Zeus.)

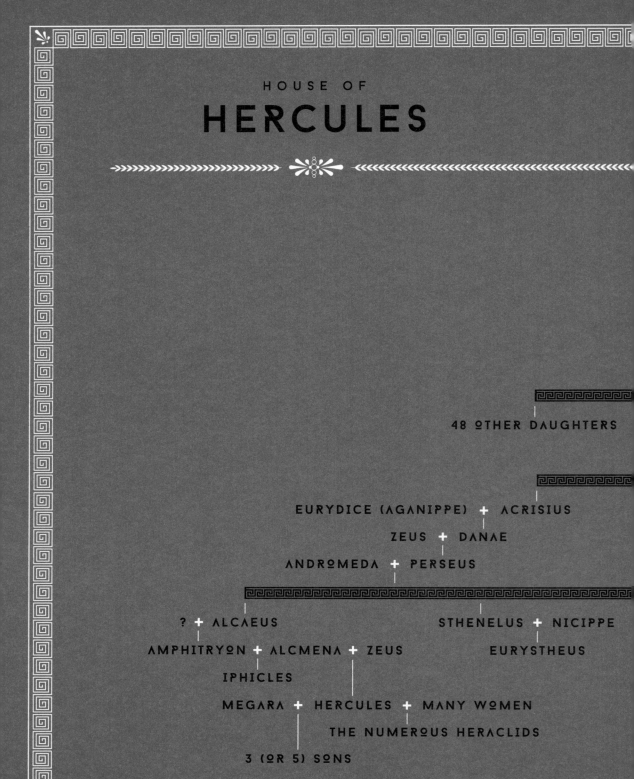

HOUSE OF
HERCULES

48 OTHER DAUGHTERS

EURYDICE (AGANIPPE) **+** ACRISIUS

ZEUS **+** DANAE

ANDROMEDA **+** PERSEUS

? **+** ALCAEUS

STHENELUS **+** NICIPPE

AMPHITRYON **+** ALCMENA **+** ZEUS

EURYSTHEUS

IPHICLES

MEGARA **+** HERCULES **+** MANY WOMEN

THE NUMEROUS HERACLIDS

3 (OR 5) SONS

IO + ZEUS

EPAPHUS + MEMPHIS

LIBYA + POSEIDON

LELEX   AGENOR   BELUS + ANCHINOE

DANAUS + MANY WIVES   AEGYPTUS + MANY WIVES

POSEIDON + AMYMONE   HYPERMNESTRA + LYNCEUS   49 OTHER SONS

NAUPLIUS   ABAS + AGLAIA

PROETUS + STHENEBOEA (ANTEIA)

3 OTHER CHILDREN

CELEUS Celeus (or Keleos) was a legendary king of Eleusis who was greatly rewarded for the hospitality that, upon the urging of his daughters, he offered to the goddess Demeter as she, in the guise of an old woman, wandered the earth in search of her daughter, Persephone. While in Celeus's palace, Demeter became nurse to the king's infant son, Demophoon, whom she attempted to make immortal by anointing him with ambrosia and placing him in the embers of a fire. Celeus's wife, Metaneira, saw her child in the flames and cried out, afraid for the life of her son. Demeter then revealed herself as a goddess and instructed the Eleusinians to build her a temple at Eleusis; she herself would then instruct the populace in the rituals to perform there. Celeus wisely acquiesced, thus becoming founder of the Eleusinian Mysteries.

(*See also* Demeter, Demophoon, Eleusis, *and* Persephone.)

CEPHALUS Cephalus was the husband of Procris, an Athenian princess, and was himself the son of Deion, a king of Phocis. Cephalus was abducted by Aurora, goddess of the dawn, but as he was clearly miserable being separated from his wife, Aurora released him. Tragedy ensued since Cephalus, prompted by Aurora, had become jealous of his bride and made trial of her faithfulness. He found her deficient, she fled, they were reconciled, and he later killed her by accident.

(*See also* Aurora *and* Procris.)

CEPHEUS There were several heroes by the name of Cepheus in Classical mythology. The best known of these appears to have been the father of the princess Andromeda, whom the hero Perseus rescued from sacrifice to a sea monster. This Cepheus was married to Cassiopeia, whose offense against the Nereids nearly cost the life of her daughter. Although he was generally known as a king of Ethiopia, he was also reported to have been a Persian, a Babylonian, or a Phoenician, according to Herodotus, Hellanicus, and Pausanias, respectively. Cepheus named Andromeda and Perseus's son Perses his heir. After their deaths, Cepheus, his wife, Cassiopeia, and his daughter, Andromeda, all became constellations.

The lesser-known Cepheus was a king of Tegea, the most important city in Arcadia. This Cepheus joined Jason and the Argonauts in their quest for the Golden Fleece, and participated with the hero Meleager in the hunt for the Calydonian boar. As the mythographer Apollodorus reports, the hero Hercules asked Cepheus to join him in his vengeful march against Sparta. Cepheus initially declined, fearing an attack on Tegea in his absence, but Hercules gave Cepheus's daughter Sterope a lock of Medusa's hair as a safeguard for the city. Although the city remained safe, Cepheus himself perished in the Spartan conflict.

(*See also* Andromeda, Arcadia, Argonauts [the], Babylon, Calydon, Cassiopeia, Ethiopia, Hercules, Jason, Medusa, Meleager, Nereids [the], Perseus, *and* Sparta.)

CEYX

Ceyx was a son of Hesper, the evening star (or of Lucifer, the morning star), and became king in Trachis, a Thessalian city in the Spercheius Valley. Ceyx was known for having granted asylum to Hercules, who had accidentally killed a kinsman of the Calydonian king Oeneus, his host, and had departed Calydon in self-imposed exile. It was on their way to Trachis that Hercules and his wife, Deianeira, had their fateful encounter with the Centaur Nessus, an encounter that would lead to Hercules's death by suicide soon thereafter. As for Ceyx, his own life was filled with tragedy. His son Hippasus participated in Hercules's campaign against Oechalia and was killed in battle. His brother's daughter Chione was raped by Hermes and Apollo in succession and, having been impregnated by both gods, bore twins: Autolycus, a dishonest schemer like his father, Hermes, and Philammon, expert at singing and playing the lyre like his father, Apollo. Chione, swollen with pride over her divine offspring, boasted that she was more beautiful than the goddess Diana, for which sin Diana shot an arrow through her tongue, causing a wound that extinguished her voice and life alike. In despair, her father flung himself from the cliffs of Parnassus, though mid-flight, the gods transformed him into a hawk. As the Roman poet Ovid recounts, troubled over his brother's mysterious fate, Ceyx resolved to travel by sea to consult an oracle at Claros in Ionia for illumination, but he lost his own life in stormy seas. His wife, Alcyone, had begged him not to go and prayed endlessly to Hera for his safe return, not knowing what had happened. Hera sent Morpheus, the god of dreams, to appear to Alcyone as Ceyx and reveal the truth of her husband's tragic end. When Alcyone ran to the sea and found her husband's floating corpse, the gods transformed them both into kingfishers, seeing to it that their seven days of nesting in winter, the so-called Halcyon Days, would be marked by calm seas.

(*See also* Alcyone, Apollo, Calydon, Centaurs [the], Deianeira, Diana, Hera, Hercules, Hesper, Morpheus, Nessus, Oeneus, Parnassus [Mount], *and* Thessaly.)

CHRYSEIS

Chryseis played a pivotal role in the course of the Trojan War and the fate of Achilles. She was the daughter of Chryses, a priest of Apollo. Having been taken captive by the Greeks, she was given to King Agamemnon, king of Mycenae, as war prize and concubine. When her father later came to the encampment of the Greeks offering generous ransom for her return, Agamemnon refused on the grounds that he preferred her to his own wife, Clytemnestra. Chryses prayed to Apollo for assistance, and the god answered his prayers by sending a deadly plague to decimate the Greeks. The seer Calchas was consulted, and he responded that the remedy was Chryseis's return. A grievous quarrel between Agamemnon and Achilles ensued, for Agamemnon insisted that if he was compelled to give up Chryseis, he would take Achilles's prize Briseis as compensation. Agamemnon did take Briseis, causing Achilles, the Greeks' best warrior, to withdraw from the fighting, at least for a time.

(See also Achilles, Aegisthus, Agamemnon, Apollo, Briseis, Calchas, Clytemnestra, Mycenae, and Troy.)

CHRYSOTHEMIS

Chrysothemis was one of the children of Agamemnon, king of Mycenae, and his wife, Clytemnestra. Chrysothemis's sister Iphigeneia was sacrificed by Agamemnon to the goddess Artemis when the ships of the Greeks were unable to set sail for Troy from Aulis. Her other siblings, Orestes and Electra, avenged their father's murder at the hands of Clytemnestra and her lover, Aegisthus. In the tragedian Sophocles's play *Electra*, Chrysothemis is sympathetic to her sister Electra's keen desire for revenge but is unwilling to help execute a plot for vengeance on the grounds that she and her sister are merely women and thus inherently too weak.

(See also Agamemnon, Aulis, Clytemnestra, Electra [heroine], Mycenae, Orestes, and Troy.)

CINYRAS

Cinyras was a legendary king of Cyprus. In mythology he had strong ties with Aphrodite, whose temple he was said to have built on the island of Cyprus and whose worship he reputedly established there. He was also known as founder of the Cypriot city of Paphos. Accounts of his origins are conflicting. According to the Roman poet Ovid, he was a son of Paphos, the daughter of Pygmalion and his statue-wife, Galatea. Other authors, however, claim that he hailed from Assyria or Cilicia, among other places, with Eos ("Dawn") and Tithonus being his ancestors. Unbeknownst to him, Cinyras became the father of Adonis, and to his horror, the mother was his own daughter Myrrha (or Smyrna, according to some sources). Myrrha had many suitors, but she refused them all, since none was as noble as her father. Though she tried to fight it, her passion for Cinyras grew stronger daily. The only way to escape this base love, she thought, was to hang herself. Myrrha's nurse prevented her from committing suicide, however, and helped to sneak her into her father's bed. When Cinyras, at last, discovered the crime in which he had been complicit, he drew his sword, and Myrrha fled. For nine months she traveled through Arabia to the distant land of the Sabaeans, and with her baby due, she fell into despair, calling upon the gods to help her in some way. She asked to be transformed, as she was a source of pollution both to the living and to the dead. Her prayers were answered, and she became a precious myrrh tree. Her endlessly streaming tears became myrrh's fragrant resin, and from her bark emerged the beautiful baby Adonis, with whom Aphrodite would fall in love.

(*See also* Adonis, Aphrodite, Cyprus, Eos, Galatea, Myrrha, Paphos, Pygmalion, *and* Tithonus.)

CLEOBIS

CLEOBIS The Greek historian Herodotus records the miraculous tale of the brothers Cleobis and Biton. The story is preserved in an account of the Athenian statesman Solon's visit to the fabulously wealthy Croesus, king of Lydia. Croesus was surprised when he asked Solon whom he considered the most fortunate of men and the answer was not "you, Croesus." Solon responded that this distinction fell to a certain Tellus, a man of adequate means who had fathered fine children, witnessed the birth of grandchildren to all his children, and met a glorious death in the service of his city. Solon deemed Cleobis and Biton, two brothers from the city of Argos, to be the second most fortunate. These brothers were not only strong but noble. On the occasion of a festival in honor of the goddess Hera, their mother, Cydippe, a priestess of that goddess, needed to be conveyed to the goddess's temple in a timely manner. When her oxen could not be found, her sons yoked themselves to her heavy cart and pulled it a great distance (45 stadia, approximately 4.5 miles, or 7,000 meters) to the temple. To the rejoicing of the populace, she arrived in time and prayed before the statue of Hera that, in compensation for their pious act, her sons receive the greatest possible reward. When the youths thereafter fell asleep on the temple's floor, they did not wake again, having met their end at the moment of their greatest glory. Consequently, the people of Argos dedicated statues of them at Delphi as being the best of men. Solon concluded his moralizing tale with the summary remark to Croesus that no man could be counted happy or fortunate until one knew how he met his end.

(*See also* Argos, Delphi, Hera, *and* Lydia.)

CLYTEMNESTRA

CLYTEMNESTRA Clytemnestra (variously spelled also as Clytaemnestra or Clytaeaestra) was a daughter of the Spartan king Tyndareus and Leda. Her siblings were the beautiful Helen of Troy (and Sparta) and the Dioscuri, Castor and Pollux. Agamemnon, king of Mycenae, murdered her first husband, Tantalus, son of Thyestes, subsequently taking her as bride. Motherhood marked the beginning of Clytemnestra's tragedy. To Agamemnon, Clytemnestra bore Iphigeneia (also called Iphianassa), Electra (also called Laodice), Chrysothemis, and Orestes. When the assembled Greek forces were unable to set sail for Troy, being stayed by adverse winds, the Greeks, beset by hunger and disease, consulted the seer Calchas in search of a remedy, and he revealed that the goddess Artemis was responsible: the goddess was angered by Agamemnon's accidental killing of a deer that had been sacred to her. The terrible remedy for the Greeks' predicament, Calchas pronounced, was the sacrifice of Iphigeneia to Artemis. Agamemnon sent for Iphigeneia, doing so by resorting to a ruse: he made it known to Clytemnestra that Iphigeneia was to wed Achilles at Aulis. For his treachery as well as for this dreadful deed, Clytemnestra never forgave Agamemnon, and upon his return from Troy, she stabbed him to death in the bath. Clytemnestra also murdered Cassandra, Agamemnon's concubine, whose presence in the palace offended her, underscoring as it did the faithlessness of her husband. Clytemnestra and her lover Aegisthus were, in turn, slain by Orestes, who had been prompted by the god Apollo to avenge the death of his father. In Aeschylus's tragedy the *Eumenides*, it is Athena who ultimately absolves Orestes of matricide.

(*See also* Achilles, Aegisthus, Agamemnon, Apollo, Artemis, Aulis, Calchas, Cassandra, Chrysothemis, Electra, Eumenides [the], Iphigeneia, Leda, Mycenae, Orestes, Tantalus, Theyestes, Troy, *and* Zeus.)

CLYTIE The maiden Clytie had been one of the sun god Helios's lovers. When the god turned his attentions to Leucothoe, daughter of the Persian king Orchamus, she was heartbroken and revealed the affair to Orchamus. In anger at his daughter's indiscretion, Orchamus buried Leucothoe alive. As the Roman poet Ovid writes, Helios attempted to disinter and revive her, but was too late. The grief-stricken god then sprinkled nectar on her body and the ground, and a precious shrub of frankincense grew from the place where her body had been. As for Clytie, who had hoped that Helios would again direct his attentions toward her, she waited in vain, watching the course of the sun for nine days and nights under an open sky without eating or sleeping. She became rooted to the ground, her body transformed into a flower, a heliotrope, that would continue always to turn her face toward the sun.

(*See also* Apollo *and* Helios.)

CORONIS There were several heroines by the name of Coronis and various stories about each of them. The best-known Coronis was a daughter of the Thessalian king Phlegyas, and became the mother of the healing god Asclepius. The travel writer Pausanias preserves two versions of her story. The first of these explains why Epidaurus was especially sacred to Asclepius. King Phlegyas, as it happened, was a warlike king who made frequent forays into neighboring lands to steal others' crops and cattle. When, on one occasion, he traveled to the Peloponnese in order to learn whether that region's inhabitants, too, were warlike, he brought Coronis with him. Unbeknownst to her father, Coronis was pregnant by the god Apollo, and when they arrived at Epidaurus, she bore a son (Asclepius), and exposed him on a mountain. Asclepius, however, was nursed by goats that ranged the mountain and was guarded by a herdsman's dog. Eventually the herdsman himself came upon the baby but did not move him, recognizing, when lightning flashed from the child, that he was in the presence of divinity. According to the second version of Asclepius's birth, Coronis, while pregnant with Apollo's child, was unfaithful to the god with a young man named Ischys, with whom she had fallen in love. For infidelity to her brother, Apollo, the goddess Artemis shot Coronis with her arrows, but Hermes snatched the unborn child from Coronis's body as it burned on the funeral pyre.

(*See also* Apollo, Artemis, Asclepius, Hermes, *and* Thessaly.)

CREON

The name Creon means "Ruler," and there were two significant rulers of this name in Classical mythology. One was a regent of Thebes and brother of Jocasta, wife of Oedipus. Creon's wife was Eurydice, and his children included Haemon, the betrothed of Antigone; Megara, the ill-fated wife of Hercules; and Menoeceus, who was named after his grandfather (Creon's father) and sacrificed himself for Thebes. Creon repeatedly served as ruler of Thebes. He became that city's regent after the death of Laius; again when Oedipus departed from Thebes and his sons, Eteocles and Polyneices, were still too young to rule; and yet again upon the death of Eteocles and Polyneices at each other's hands. In the tragedian Sophocles's plays *Antigone* and *Oedipus at Colonus*, Creon is depicted as a dark character. When, after Oedipus's departure from Thebes, Eteocles and Polyneices turned against each other, Creon attempted to keep power for himself by seeking Oedipus, who had wandered to Attica as an exile accompanied by Antigone; it had been prophesied that retention of power depended on possession of Oedipus, so both Creon and Polyneices went in search of him. Creon resorted to subterfuge and force to accomplish his end, but was prevented from seizing Oedipus by the Athenian king Theseus. After both Polyneices and Eteocles had died, Creon proclaimed a sentence of death for anyone attempting to bury his nephew Polyneices. When it was revealed that his own niece Antigone had attempted this, he refused to relent, even when faced with a good argument: divine law dicatated that family members must bury their dead. As a result, he lost both Antigone and his son, Haemon, both of whom committed suicide.

Another Creon was ruler of Corinth. He is known primarily for having welcomed Jason and Medea to his city once the pair had wrought their deadly vengeance on Pelias, king of Iolcos. Creon offered his daughter Creusa (or Glauce, as some sources call her) to Jason in marriage, a fact that Medea could not stomach. Medea gave her children a poisoned robe and headdress to give to Creusa as wedding gifts. When Creusa tried these on, she burst into flame, and Creon, too, perished, becoming stuck to her poisoned garments, when he attempted to help her.

(*See also* Antigone, Athens, Attica, Corinth, Creusa, Eteocles, Eurydice [heroine], Haemon, Hercules, Iolcos, Megara [heroine], Menoeceus, Oedipus, Pelias, Polyneices, Thebes, *and* Theseus.)

CRESPHONTES

Cresphontes was a third-generation descendant of Hercules. When Cresphontes, his brother Temenus, and the sons of their dead brother Aristodemus, Procles and Eurysthenes, were faced with dividing control of the Peloponnese between them, the decision was made by drawing lots. Cresphontes favored Messenia and secured his first choice by resorting to a ruse: three lots designating the territories of Argos, Sparta, and Messenia were put in a pitcher of water. Two of the lots, those for Argos and Sparta, were made of fired clay, while the third, for Messenia, was unfired and dissolved in the water. Cresphontes asked to draw his lot last, thus ensuring that the lots for Sparta and Argos, which were not dissolved, were necessarily drawn before it came time for his turn. Cresphontes's rule was short-lived, however, as he and his two eldest sons were killed in a revolt led by a man called Polyphontes, who subsequently married Cresphontes's wife, Merope, and made himself king. Cresphontes's youngest son, Aepytus, ultimately avenged his father's death with help from his mother and thus gained control of the kingdom.

(*See also* Aepytus, Argos, Hercules, Merope [heroine], Messenia [place], *and* Sparta.)

CREUSA

There were several characters by the name of Creusa. One was a daughter of Praxithea and Erechtheus, a king of Athens. This Creusa was pursued and impregnated by Apollo. After bearing the god's son, Ion, she hid the baby in a cave under the Acropolis. At Apollo's instruction, the god Hermes brought the infant Ion to Delphi, where he became a priest. As for Creusa, she later wed Xuthus, a son of Hellen. Since they remained childless, Xuthus traveled to Apollo's oracle at Delphi seeking a remedy. There Xuthus was told that he could claim as his son the first person he should meet upon leaving the sanctuary. That person happened to be Ion. Not knowing Ion's true identity, a jealous Creusa nearly succeeded in poisoning him, but recognition between mother and son took place in time.

Another Creusa, who is called Glauce in some sources, was the daughter of King Creon of Corinth. She became betrothed to Jason, and a jealous Medea engineered her gruesome death.

A third Creusa was the Trojan wife of Aeneas, who became separated from Aeneas, their son Ascanius, and her father-in-law, Anchises, when they were fleeing Troy as a family. When Aeneas realized that she was gone, he turned to rush back into the burning city, but the ghost of Creusa appeared to him and urged him to carry on to Italy, where he was destined to become a king and find a new wife.

(*See also* Acropolis [the], Aeneas, Anchises, Apollo, Ascanius, Athens, Corinth, Creon, Delphi, Erechtheus, Hellen, Ion, Jason, Medea, Troy, *and* Xuthus.)

CYCNUS There were several heroes by the name of Cycnus in Classical mythology. One of them was a son of the war god Ares. Cycnus made a career of robbing pilgrims on their way to Delphi by challenging them to a chariot race that he would always win. He beheaded the losers and decorated his father's temple with their skulls. The hero Hercules would prove to be the undoing of Cycnus. With the help of his chariot driver Iolaus and of Athena, Hercules won the race and slew Cycnus. According to the mythographer Hyginus, Hercules consequently came to blows with Ares himself, and the two had to be separated by a lightning bolt hurled by Zeus.

Another Cycnus was a distant cousin of Phaethon's, according to the Roman poet Ovid. When Phaethon, while driving Helios's chariot, was killed by Zeus, Cycnus, a king of Liguria, wandered through the woods and along rivers, lamenting until his voice was nothing but a shrill strain and he himself had become a swan.

A third Cycnus was a son of the god Poseidon and the nymph Calyce. He ruled as king in Colonae, a city in the vicinity of Troy. In the Roman poet Ovid's *Metamorphoses*, the invincible Cycnus, an ally of the Trojans, is savagely struck on the head repeatedly and strangled by Achilles, frustrated at his numerous unsuccessful attempts to kill his adversary. When Achilles, thinking Cycnus dead, attempts to strip his armor from him, he finds the armor empty save for a swan.

(*See also* Achilles, Ares, Athena, Delphi, Helios, Hercules, Phaethon, Poseidon, Troy, *and* Zeus.

CYDIPPE Cydippe was a priestess of the goddess Hera and proud mother of Cleobis and Biton, who would be remembered as among the most fortunate of all men. After her sons had accomplished a deed not only virtuous but requiring enormous strength, Cydippe prayed to Hera that they should receive the greatest possible reward. Consequently, when Cleobis and Biton fell asleep in Hera's temple, they did not wake again.

(*See* Cleobis *and* Hera.)

CYRENE According to the historian Diodorus Siculus, Cyrene was the daughter of Hypseus, a son of the river god Peneus. Apollo caught sight of her in the wilds of Mount Pelion and took her away to Libya, where he founded a city named after her. At that place, Cyrene gave birth to the culture hero Aristaeus, who taught humans the arts of beekeeping and agriculture.

(*See also* Apollo, Aristaeus, Cyrene [place], Pelion [Mount], *and* Peneus [god and place].)

DAEDALUS Daedalus was a skilled sculptor and inventor—by some accounts, he was the first of these. His parents are variously recorded as Eupalamus (or Palamon), son of Metion, with Alcippe or as Metion, son of Erechtheus, with Iphinoe, in all cases indicating Daedalus's direct descent from the Athenian king Erechtheus. According to the mythographer Apollodorus, Daedalus fled from Athens to Crete as he had been found guilty of murdering his sister Perdix's son Talus. While on the island of Crete, Daedalus constructed a hollow wooden cow into which Pasiphae, King Minos's wife, could crawl in order to satisfy her passion for a bull that Poseidon sent to Crete by way of punishing Minos. Daedalus subsequently constructed the labyrinthine lair that housed Pasiphae's child by the bull, the human-eating Minotaur. Minos later held Daedalus and his son Icarus captive, and so as to engineer their escape, Daedalus constructed wings made of feathers and wax. Icarus, however, flew too close to the sun, and he fell to his death in the sea. Daedalus, for his part, made his way safely to Sicily. Minos came to Sicily in pursuit of Daedalus, and flushed him out by means of a stratagem: he offered the Sicilian king Cocalus a prize for passing a thread through a spiraling shell, a near-impossible task that only someone with Daedalus's ingenuity could accomplish. When Cocalus succeeded, Minos knew that Daedalus was behind it. Minos now demanded Daedalus's surrender, but, in defense of Daedalus, Cocalus's daughters killed the Cretan king.

(*See also* Athens, Crete, Erechtheus, Icarus, Minos, Minotaur [the], Pasiphae, *and* Sicily.)

DANAE Danae was the daughter of Acrisius, king of Argos, and Eurydice (or Aganippe). When she reached childbearing age, her father, Acrisius, confined her in an impenetrable structure—according to some accounts in an underground chamber and according to others, a tower. This Acrisius did in hopes of avoiding the fulfillment of a prophecy that his grandson would kill him. However, the god Zeus was able to penetrate the enclosure in the form of a stream of gold and impregnated Danae, who later gave birth to a son, Perseus. Wishing to rid himself of the child without bloodshed, Acrisius ordered his daughter and her baby to be placed in a chest and cast out to sea. The chest and its precious contents arrived safely on the island of Seriphus, where it was discovered by a kindly fisherman named Dictys. This fisherman's brother, Polydectes, king of the island, wished to marry Danae, and contrived to rid himself of Perseus, now a youth, by sending him to fetch the head of the Gorgon Medusa. Perseus accomplished his task, turned Polydectes to stone by exposing him to Medusa's severed head, and designated Danae and Dictys regents of the island. According to the Roman poet Virgil, Danae eventually left Seriphus and returned to Argos, only later to immigrate to Italy, where she founded Ardea. The Trojan Aeneas's great rival, Turnus, king of the Rutulians, was descended from her and had Ardea as the seat of his kingdom.

(*See also* Acrisius, Aeneas, Argos, Dictys, Eurydice [heroine], Gorgons [the], Medusa, Perseus, Polydectes, Rutulians [the], Seriphus, Troy, Turnus, *and* Zeus.)

DANAIDS, THE

The Danaids were the fifty daughters of Danaus, a king of Libya who, later in life, became king of Argos in Greece, to which place he had fled with his family. The Danaids are collectively best known for having murdered their husbands on their wedding nights at their father's behest. In the afterlife, the Danaids were compelled to collect water with perforated containers, their labor being an eternal punishment. Two of the Danaids were particularly notable: Hypermnestra, the only one of the sisters to refuse to kill her husband, and Amymone, who was pursued and impregnated by the god Poseidon.

(*See also* Amymone, Argos, Danaus, Hypermnestra, *and* Poseidon.)

DANAUS

The Egyptian king Belus was the father of twin sons, Danaus and Aegyptus, by Anchinoe, a daughter of the Nile. To Danaus he entrusted the rule of Libya, and to Aegyptus, Arabia. Upon Belus's death, the brothers quarreled over division of their father's kingdom, and when Aegyptus proposed that his fifty sons should marry Danaus's fifty daughters, the so-called Danaids, in order to consolidate their power, Danaus suspected ulterior motives. His daughters in tow, Danaus fled to Argos in the Peloponnese. By some accounts, Danaus subsequently became king of Argos, displacing the sitting king, doing so because a wolf's killing of the community's prize bull was interpreted as an omen in his favor. Whatever the reason, Danaus ultimately agreed to the marriage of his daughters to his brother's sons, but he instructed the brides to kill their husbands on their wedding nights. All but one of them obeyed, this being Hypermnestra, who spared her husband for his respectful treatment of her. The Danaids buried their husband's heads on the acropolis of Argos and their bodies at Lerna, and, according to the mythographer Apollodorus, they were purified of blood guilt by the gods Hermes and Athena. Danaus later took measures to marry off his daughters again, instituting a race in which a competitor's performance would dictate choice of bride: the winner would have first choice, the runner-up second, and so on. In spite of reputedly having been absolved of guilt in this life, the Danaids were punished in the afterlife, being compelled eternally to fetch water in containers that drained as quickly as they filled.

(See also Aegyptus, Argos, Athena, Belus, Danaids [the], Hermes, Hypermnestra, *and* Lerna.)

DAPHNE
Daphne, whose name means "laurel," was the daughter of Peneus, god of the river Peneus in Thessaly. Exceedingly lovely, Daphne had many suitors, but preferred to spend her days a virgin huntress like the goddess Artemis. Among her suitors, however, was the god Apollo, who would not be denied. The Roman poet Ovid vividly tells of their encounter. Apollo, filled with pride over slaying Python, the dragon that guarded the oracle at Delphi, mocked the god Cupid, saying that his arrows were merely a child's toys. To prove Apollo wrong, Cupid turned his arrows on Apollo and Daphne: Apollo was struck by an arrow that inflamed him with passion, and Daphne with one that inspired flight. Catching sight of the maiden, Apollo set off in hot pursuit, pleading his case by recounting his divine parentage, his powers, and his real estate. But the faster Apollo pursued, the faster Daphne fled until, exhausted, she begged her father, Peneus, to save her from the god. Thus, when Apollo finally reached her, she was transformed into the tree that bears still her name: she became rooted in place, her body enclosed in bark. Her hair now leaves and her arms graceful branches, the god loved her still and made her his sacred tree. From that day forward, Apollo would wear a wreath of bay laurel, and the laurel would become a potent symbol of prophecy, purity, poetry, music, healing, and victory, as such having great importance in the daily lives of the Greeks and Romans.

A less known version of the story is told by the poet Parthenius and travel writer Pausanias, according to whom Cupid played no part. Instead, Daphne's transformation occurred as a result of Apollo's jealousy over her having become close with Leucippus, a son of Oenomaus, king of Pisa. Leucippus, enamored of Daphne but knowing that she wanted nothing to do with men, had disguised himself as a maiden so as to gain her confidence. His ruse was exposed, when Daphne and her other maiden friends went to swim, all but Leucippus taking off their clothes voluntarily. The maidens then viciously attacked Leucippus, and Apollo set off in pursuit of Daphne.

(*See also* Apollo, Artemis, Cupid, Delphi, Leucippus, Oenomaus, Peneus [god and place], Python, *and* Thessaly.)

DAPHNIS

Daphnis was a legendary Sicilian herdsman who, according to the historian Diodorus Siculus, was the inventor of bucolic or pastoral poetry and song. He was a son of Hermes and a nymph who bore him (or, by some accounts, exposed him) in a dense grove of sweet bay laurel (*daphne*) from which he derived his name. The Greek poet Parthenius writes that a particular nymph fell in love with him, and told him always to remain faithful to her or he would lose his vision. He resisted temptation for a long time but eventually fell victim to desire for a princess who had offered him too much wine. As a consequence, he was blinded. The Roman author Aelian adds that it was for this princess that Daphnis sang the first pastoral song. In the *Idylls* of Theocritus, however, Daphnis dies of love at a young age, and is widely lamented.

(*See also* Hermes *and* Sicily.)

DARDANUS

Dardanus was an ancestor of the Trojans, who are sometimes referred to as Dardanians as an indicator of their heritage. According to the mythographer Apollodorus, Dardanus was a son of Zeus and Electra, a daughter of Atlas. His parentage is known differently to Homer, however, who writes that he was the most beloved son of Zeus by a mortal woman. Dardanus was variously said to have arrived in the territory by Mount Ida from Arcadia via Samothrace or from Italy. When he arrived, that territory was ruled by Teucer, son of the river Scamander and of a nymph Idaea, and its inhabitants were called Teucrians after their king. Teucer welcomed Dardanus and offered him both a part of his lands and the hand of his daughter, Batia (or Bateia). On his newly acquired land he built a city at the foot of Mount Ida, and upon Teucer's death, he called the whole country Dardania. With Batia he became father to Ilus and Erichthonius, later father of Tros (after whom Troy was named).

(*See also* Arcadia, Atlas, Electra [nymph], Erichthonius, Ida [Mount], Ilus, Scamander River [the], Teucer, Tros, Troy, *and* Zeus.)

DEIANEIRA

The princess Deianeira was the daughter of King Oeneus of Calydon and his wife, Althea. The god Dionysus, however, is also cited as her father. Her brothers were Tydeus and Meleager, both tragic figures in their own right. Deianeira, for her part, unwittingly lived up to her name, which means "husband-killer." Hercules successfully wrestled the river god Achelous to win her hand, thus fulfilling a promise that he had made to the ghost of Deianeira's brother Meleager, which he had encountered while fetching Cerberus from the Underworld. Since Hercules later killed one of his father-in-law's kinsmen by accident, he and Deianeira departed Calydon in voluntary exile and, in the course of their journey, came to the Evenus River. There they found the Centaur Nessus, who offered to carry Deianeira across the river's strong currents, but while Hercules was making the crossing, Nessus attempted to rape Deianeira. Hercules felled the Centaur with one of his lethal arrows, which had been dipped in the monstrous Hydra's toxic venom. Before he breathed his last, Nessus convinced Deianeira to take a vial containing a sample of his blood, which, he claimed, could be used as a love potion to ensure that she would never lose Hercules's love. When, after a successful military campaign against King Eurytus of Oechalia, Hercules sent home the king's daughter Iole to be his concubine, a jealous Deianeira doused a tunic for Hercules with the Centaur's blood. This tunic burned Hercules's flesh, causing him to end his life with the help of the hero Philoctetes, and Deianeira, in horror at the unintended outcome of her actions, killed herself as well.

(See also Althea, Calydon, Centaurs [the], Cerberus, Dionysus, Eurytus, Hercules, Hydra of Lerna [the], Iole, Meleager, Nessus, Oeneus, Philoctetes, Tydeus, and Underworld [the].)

DEIDAMIA Deidamia was one of the seven daughters of King Lycomedes of Scyros. While Achilles was in hiding at Scyros among the princesses, Deidamia became pregnant by him. After Achilles left for Troy, she gave birth to a son, Neoptolemus, who would later follow his father to join the Greek forces at the end of the Trojan War. After the death of Achilles and upon his return to Greece, Neoptolemus gave Deidamia to the Trojan seer Helenus as bride.

(See also Achilles, Helenus, Lycomedes, Neoptolemus, Scyros, and Troy.)

DEMOPHOON Demophoon was the son of Celeus, king of Eleusis, and his wife, Metaneira. In the course of her wanderings in search of Persephone, the goddess Demeter—disguised as a mortal—came to the palace of Celeus. Demeter was welcomed into the household and employed as nurse for the king's infant son, Demophoon. The goddess anointed Demophoon with ambrosia and, at night, placed him in the embers of a fire in an effort to make him immortal. When Metaneira observed this, she cried out in fright, and the angered goddess let the child fall. The goddess then revealed her full divinity and ceased to act

PLATE V
Daphne: Daughter of Peneus, god of the river Peneus

as Demophoon's nurse. While he did not become immortal, he grew to have a godlike appearance.

(*See also* Celeus, Demeter, Eleusis, *and* Persephone.)

DEUCALION
Deucalion was a son of the second-generation Titan god Prometheus, and his wife, Pyrrha, was a daughter of Prometheus's brother Epimetheus and Pandora. The Roman poet Ovid tells the best-known tale of their adventures. When Zeus, horrified at the depravity that he had witnessed among humans, decided to flood the earth to erase all traces of humanity, Deucalion and Pyrrha alone survived, doing so by chance or, as mythographer Apollodorus suggests, because Prometheus had helped them. In any event, the boat that carried them came to rest on the peak of Mount Parnassus, which protruded from the vast sea that now covered the surface of the earth. The pious couple, grateful to be safe, sacrificed to the local nymphs and to Themis, whose oracle was nearby. Zeus was moved by the sight of them alone, two innocent people known for kindliness and fairness, and caused the flood waters to recede. The couple then prayed to Themis to help them in their dire circumstances. The goddess's oracle responded that they should throw their mother's bones over their shoulders. Pyrrha refused, as this would be a sacrilege, but Deucalion knew that Themis would not ask a taboo of them. He reasoned correctly that Gaia, the Earth herself, was their mother, and that her bones were the stones lying on the ground. The two cast stones over their shoulders, and from the stones sprang the current race of people, durable like the stones from which they originated. The stones thrown by Pyrrha became women, and those by Deucalion, men.

(*See also* Epimetheus, Gaia, Pandora, Parnassus [Mount], Prometheus, Pyrrha, Themis, Titans [the], *and* Zeus.)

DICTYS
Dictys was a fisherman and the twin brother of Polydectes, a king of the island of Seriphus. The two were the offspring of Aeolus, god of the winds, and a water nymph. It was the kind-hearted Dictys who rescued the princess Danae and her baby son Perseus when, having been cast into the sea in a chest, they washed ashore on Seriphus. Dictys was said to have protected mother and child, raising the latter as a fisherman. Polydectes, meanwhile, had taken an interest in Danae and attempted to force her to marry him. Once Perseus had slain the Gorgon Medusa, he took vengeance on Polydectes by using the Gorgon's severed head to turn the king into stone. With Polydectes dead, Dictys became regent of Seriphus.

(*See also* Aeolus, Danae, Gorgons [the], Medusa, Perseus, Polydectes, *and* Seriphus.)

DIDO Dido, also called Elissa, was the legendary founder of the city of Carthage. Her dramatic story is told by the Roman poet Virgil in his epic the *Aeneid*. Dido's husband, Sychaeus, had been murdered for his riches by her brother, Pygmalion, the king of Tyre in Phoenicia. For this reason, Dido fled, taking with her a group of people who, like her, loathed or feared Pygmalion. When they arrived on the Libyan coast, Dido purchased land on which to build the city of Carthage, which was actively under construction when Aeneas arrived on the same shores. Up to this point, Dido had remained faithful to her beloved, deceased husband, having refused a marriage proposal from the African king Iarbas. Now, however, Dido became the victim of the goddess Venus's stratagems, and Cupid was sent to inflame her with passion for Aeneas. Dido welcomed Aeneas and his band of Trojans into the city and became romantically involved with Aeneas, under the misapprehension that their relationship was a marriage. When Aeneas, without a word of warning, made preparations to leave, a distraught Dido—now fully aware of the cost to her reputation and her city, which had ceased to grow and thrive—confronted him. However, Aeneas, having received a reminder from the gods that it was his destiny to carry on to Italy, remained steadfast in his intent to leave. As the Trojan ships set sail, Dido instructed her sister Anna to build a pyre for the purposes of burning Aeneas's armor and the bed upon which she had lain with him. This act, she said, would release her from the clutches of this desperate love. What Anna did not guess, was that Dido would climb onto the burning pyre herself and plunge a sword into her breast. Before the spirit left her, Dido uttered a curse upon Aeneas and the future Romans, his descendants; the Carthaginian Hannibal, Dido's avenger, would later fulfill that curse and march upon Italy. As the funeral pyre blazed, the goddess Juno, who had loved Dido, ordered Iris to cut a lock of hair from the queen's head, thus releasing her soul to travel to the Underworld.

(*See also* Aeneas, Carthage, Cupid, Iris, Juno, Pygmalion, Rome, Sychaeus, Troy, Underworld [the], *and* Venus.)

DIOMEDES There were two significant heroes by the name of Diomedes. One was the son of Tydeus, son of the Calydonian king Oeneus, and Deipyle, a daughter of Adrastus. This Diomedes participated in the Epigoni's war of vengeance against Thebes, in his case wishing to avenge the death of his father, Tydeus, who had joined the Seven Against Thebes. Diomedes later fought at Troy, being one of the bravest there of the Greeks. In the course of the Trojan War, he wounded Aphrodite when she tried to save her son Aeneas. In that war, Diomedes also wounded the god Ares, exchanged armor with the Lycian Glaucus on the basis of family ties, accompanied Odysseus on a spying mission, was wounded by

Paris, assisted Odysseus both in fetching Philoctetes from Lemnos and stealing the sacred statue of Athena called the Palladium, and joined Odysseus and others in concealing themselves in the belly of the Trojan Horse. Unlike Odysseus and others, Diomedes's return voyage from Troy to Greece was uneventful.

Another Diomedes was king of the Bistones, a warlike people of Thrace. As his eighth Labor, Hercules was sent by Eurystheus to bring him Diomedes's infamous mares: Diomedes fed them human flesh. After killing Diomedes himself, Hercules fed the king to his horses, who then were cured of their taste for such unnatural food. According to the mythographer Hyginus, Eurystheus released the mares when Hercules brought them to him, and they subsequently perished on the slopes of Mount Olympus, where they were eaten by wild beasts.

(*See also* Adrastus, Aeneas, Aphrodite, Ares, Athena, Calydon, Epigoni [the], Eurystheus, Glaucus, Hercules, Lemnos, Lycia, Odysseus, Oeneus, Olympus [Mount], Paris, Philoctetes, Seven Against Thebes [the], Thebes, Thrace, Troy, *and* Tydeus.)

DIRCE

Dirce, wife of Lycus, regent of Thebes, was most famous for the punishment that she underwent for mistreating her husband's niece Antiope while Lycus kept her imprisoned. When Antiope later escaped, she was fortuitously reunited with her sons, Zethus and Amphion, whom she had believed dead. The stalwart youths killed Lycus (or drove him from the kingdom) and fastened Dirce to a bull that dragged her to her death. The mythographer Apollodorus reports that Dirce's body was cast into the spring that thereafter bore her name.

(*See also* Amphion, Antiope, Lycus, Thebes, *and* Zethus.)

DORUS

Dorus was a son of the nymph Orseis and Hellen, eponymous ancestor of all the Greeks, according to the mythographer Apollodorus. Dorus's brothers were Xuthus and Aeolus. When Hellen divided Greece among his sons, Xuthus received the Peloponnese; Dorus received the land opposite the Peloponnese (by Mount Parnassus), calling the settlers Dorians after himself; and Aeolus received Thessaly, subsequently naming the inhabitants Aeolians. The Dorians, with the help of the descendants of Hercules (the Heraclids), ultimately invaded the Peloponnese and took control of Argos, Sparta, Messenia, Megara, and Corinth.

(*See also* Aeolus, Argos, Corinth, Hellen, Hercules, Megara [place], Messenia, Parnassus [Mount], Thessaly, *and* Xuthus.)

DRYOPE

Dryope was a daughter of Eurytus, king of Oechalia, in Thessaly. Famed for her beauty, Dryope was pursued and impregnated by the god Apollo and, subsequently, was married to Andraemon. According to the Roman poet Ovid, Dryope brought her baby Amphissus with her when picking flowers to make garlands for the nymphs. While at a particular lake surrounded with myrtle thickets, she picked a handful of crimson lotus flowers to give to her son. But the lotus bled, for it had only recently been the Naiad nymph Lotis. In fear over her accidental transgression, Dryope prayed and made an offering to the nymphs—too late, for she became rooted to the ground, her body was enclosed in bark, and her once lovely hair was only leaves. She too was now a lotus. Ovid's lotus is deeply problematic to identify botanically, though scholars have speculated that it was the jujube or *Ziziphus lotus*, which neither is aquatic nor does it have red or even prominent flowers.

A different, later variant of Dryope's story is preserved by the mythographer Antoninus Liberalis. His Dryope was a daughter of Dryops ("Man of Oak"), and she was loved by Apollo, who, in order to gain access to her, changed himself into a tortoise that she found and put into her lap. The tortoise became a serpent, and in this form, Apollo impregnated her. Dryope subsequently gave birth to Amphissus, but she was later abducted by the Hamadryad (tree) nymphs with whom she had once kept company. At the place of her abduction the nymphs caused a black poplar and a spring to appear. As for Dryope, they made her a nymph.

(*See also* Apollo, Eurytus, Hamadryads [the], Lotis, Naiads [the], *and* Thessaly.)

ELECTRA Electra was a daughter of King Agamemnon of Mycenae and his wife, Clytemnestra. Her siblings were Orestes, Iphigeneia, and Chrysothemis. Electra is best known from the tragedies of Aeschylus, Sophocles, and Euripides. While Electra was still a child, her sister, Iphigeneia, was sacrificed by Agamemnon in order to appease the goddess Artemis, who was preventing the Greeks from sailing to Troy. For this act Clytemnestra would never forgive her husband and, having taken up with Aegisthus in Agamemnon's absence, plotted her revenge: upon Agamemnon's return, Clytemnestra killed him while he was in the bath. In the meantime, Electra (or someone else) had sent away the infant Orestes for his own safety. Electra, for her part, was either kept prisoner in the palace or, according to Euripides, had been given to a peasant farmer in marriage. Grown to manhood, Orestes returned to Mycenae and, effecting a reunion with his sister, avenged himself on Clytemnestra and Aegisthus, killing them. In Euripides's version of the tale, a bloodthirsty Electra played an active part in the killing of her mother, and she ultimately wed Orestes's trusty companion Pylades.

The mortal Electra is to be distinguished from the Electra who was a daughter of Oceanus and another who was one of the Pleiades.

(*See also* Aegisthus, Agamemnon, Artemis, Chrysothemis, Clytemnestra, Electra [nymph], Iphigeneia, Mycenae, Oceanus [god], Orestes, Pleiades [the], Pylades, *and* Troy.)

ELECTRYON Electryon was a king of Mycenae and son of the hero Perseus and the Ethiopian princess Andromeda. He himself was the father of Alcmena and, consequently, the grandfather of Hercules, Alcmena's son by Zeus. Electryon was accidentally (or in the course of a quarrel) slain by his son-in-law Amphitryon.

(*See also* Alcmena, Amphitryon, Andromeda, Ethiopia, Hercules, Perseus, *and* Zeus.)

ENDYMION The mythographer Apollodorus recounts two versions of Endymion's parentage: he was a son of Zeus's son Aethlius and Calyce, a daughter of Aeolus, or he was a son of Zeus himself. Endymion became a king of Elis in the Peloponnese, and by some accounts was that city's founder. As Endymion was extraordinarily handsome, the moon goddess Selene fell in love with him and, over time, bore him fifty children. Selene approached Zeus, asking him to allow Endymion to choose his fate, and what Endymion chose was to fall into an eternal slumber, remaining both ageless and deathless. Among the variants of this story is one told by the Greek poet Hesiod: as a favorite of Zeus, Endymion was allowed to select the manner of his own death, but when he made advances on the goddess Hera, he was consigned to Hades.

(*See also* Aeolus, Hades [place], Hera, Selene, *and* Zeus.)

EPAPHUS Epaphus was the son of Zeus and Io, daughter of the river god Inachus. When Io, in the form of a cow, was forced to wander far and wide, she came to the banks of the Nile in Egypt, where Zeus, by a touch of his hand, restored her to human form. There, according to the tragedian Aeschylus, she bore a son named Epaphus, who would rule the fertile land of Egypt. The mythographer Apollodorus adds that Hera instructed the Curetes to make off with him but that when Zeus heard this, he killed the Curetes. Io, for her part, went looking for Epaphus and found him at the court of the king of Byblos in Syria, where he was being nursed by the queen. Epaphus eventually married Memphis, daughter of the river god Nile, and named the city of Memphis, which he had founded, after her. With Memphis, Epaphus became father to a daughter, Libya, after whom the country of Libya was named. Among Epaphus's descendants was Danaus, whose fifty daughters killed the fifty sons of his brother Aegyptus.

(*See also* Aegyptus, Curetes [the], Danaus, Hera, Inachus, Io, Libya, *and* Zeus.)

EPEUS Epeus (or Epeios and Epius) was named by the Roman poet Virgil as creator of the Trojan Horse, and he was among the Greek warriors who hid in its belly.

(*See also* Troy.)

EPIGONI, THE

The Epigoni ("Descendants") were the sons of the Seven Against Thebes, the seven captains and their followers who marched against the city of Thebes in order to back Oedipus's son Polyneices's claim to the throne. All of the seven captains died in that disastrous effort apart from Adrastus, the expedition's leader. Later, the seven captains' sons, the Epigoni, banded together to avenge the deaths of their fathers by launching a second expedition against Thebes. The Epigoni's leader was Alcmaeon, whose mother, Eriphyle, had been bribed to convince a reluctant Amphiaraus to join the Seven. The Epigoni were successful in their effort, and Polyneices's son Thersander became regent of Thebes.

(*See also* Adrastus, Alcmaeon, Amphiaraus, Eriphyle, Oedipus, Polyneices, Seven Against Thebes [the], Thebes, *and* Thersander.)

ERECHTHEUS

Erechtheus was the grandson of Erichthonius, with whom he was sometimes confused, and one of the legendary early kings of Athens. According to the tragedian Euripides, Erechtheus was a son of Pandion and brother of Butes. Erechtheus married Praxithea, and with her became father to three sons, whose names were Cecrops, Pandorus, and Metion, and to a number of daughters, the best known of whom were Procris, Orithyia, and Creusa. Erechtheus was victorious in a conflict with Eleusis, securing this victory by sacrificing one of his daughters. In the course of this conflict, Erechtheus killed Poseidon's son Eumolpus, leader of the enemy forces, and as retribution for this, Poseidon struck Erechtheus dead with his trident. Xuthus, one of Erechtheus's sons-in-law, chose Cecrops as Erechtheus's successor to the rule of Athens.

(*See also* Athens, Cecrops, Creusa, Erichthonius, Orithyia, Poseidon, Procris, *and* Xuthus.)

ERICHTHONIUS

Erichthonius, whose name is a combination of the Greek words for wool (*erion*) and earth (*chthon*), was an early king of Athens born of Athena and Hephaestus. The unusual story of his birth is told in detail by the mythographer Apollodorus. When, on one occasion, Athena visited Hephaestus in order to ask him to make her new armor, the god fell in love with her and hobbled in pursuit. When Athena fell, Hephaestus attempted to embrace her, but Athena fought him off and wiped his semen from her thigh onto the ground with her woolen robe. From this semen grew Erichthonius, who was autochthonous, his tale underscoring the Athenians' belief that they themselves were an autochthonous people. Wishing to make the infant Erichthonius immortal, Athena placed him in a chest with a serpent and gave the chest to the daughters of Cecrops for safekeeping, with a strict injunction not to open its lid. Curiosity got the better of them, however, and when they opened the lid, they were shocked to discover a serpent wound around a baby. The snake either killed the daughters of Cecrops, or they went mad at the sight and threw themselves to their death from the Acropolis. Erichthonius was raised on the Acropolis by Athena and ultimately became king of Athens. As regent he instituted the Panathenaia, an Athenian festival in honor of Athena. According to an alternate tradition, Erichthonius himself was half serpent, having a serpent's tail. When the lid of the chest was raised, he took shelter beneath the shield of Athena.

The Athenian Erichthonius is to be distinguished from another hero of that name who was a king of Dardania and an ancestor of the Trojans. He was a son of Dardanus and a daughter of Teucer, both important figures in the early history of Troy. His brother was Ilus, and upon the latter's death, Erichthonius became Dardania's king. Erichthonius would become the father of Tros, who gave his name to the Trojans, and would become extraordinarily wealthy, owning a herd of 3,000 wondrous horses.

(*See also* Acropolis [the], Athena, Athens, Cecrops, Dardanus, Hephaestus, Ilus, Teucer, *and* Troy.)

ERIPHYLE Eriphyle was the wife of the seer Amphiaraus and proved herself to be the epitome of greed and faithlessness. Since Eriphyle had successfully settled a dispute between Amphiaraus and his brother Adrastus, the brothers agreed to abide by all her decisions in the future. It happened that Polyneices, Oedipus's son, later asked Adrastus and Amphiaraus to join the army he was raising to displace his brother Eteocles as regent of Thebes. Amphiaraus was not keen to comply, since he had foreseen the death of all who joined the expedition, apart from Adrastus. Polyneices bribed Eriphyle with the splendid necklace of his great-great-great-grandmother Harmonia, and she prevailed upon her husband to join Polyneices. As he had predicted, Amphiaraus was killed in the conflict. Eriphyle was subsequently approached by Thersander, Polyneices's son, to convince her sons Alcmaeon and Amphilochus to join those marching against Thebes to seek vengeance for the death of their fathers. She again succumbed to a bribe, which this time was Harmonia's robe, and convinced her sons to join this new war effort. When Alcmaeon returned home, he killed his mother, whose spirits (the Erinyes) consequently pursued him.

(*See also* Adrastus, Alcmaeon, Amphiaraus, Erinyes [the], Eteocles, Harmonia, Oedipus, Polyneices, Thebes, *and* Thersander.)

ERYSICHTHON Erysichthon was a king and a godless man. As the Roman poet Ovid writes, Erysichthon scorned the gods and refused to make offerings at their altars. His hubris was so great that he chopped down an ancient oak tree in a grove sacred to the goddess Ceres. In the process, he killed a man who attempted to stop him, lopping off the man's head with his axe. Erysichthon did not stop hacking at the tree, even when a voice emanated from it calling for retribution: the voice belonged to the Dryad nymph who inhabited the tree, her life ebbing from her with every blow. Even this did not stop him, so Ceres summoned the goddess Famine, who took possession of him. Nothing now could sate his limitless hunger. He eventually resorted to selling his daughter to raise money for more food, but as she had the ability to change her shape at will, she repeatedly escaped enslavement. With nothing else left to eat, Erysichthon ate himself.

This Erysichthon is to be distinguished from the son of the Athenian king Cecrops, about whom little is known.

(*See also* Athens, Cecrops, Ceres, *and* Dryads [the].)

ETEOCLES Eteocles was the brother of Polyneices, both of them being sons of Oedipus and his wife, Jocasta. His sisters were Antigone and Ismene. When a blind and disgraced Oedipus left Thebes, Polyneices and Eteocles had agreed to share the kingdom, each of them ruling alternately for a year. Eteocles assumed the kingship first and, after the passage of his first term, refused to step down. This prompted Polyneices to raise an army, led by the so-called Seven Against Thebes, to depose Eteocles. The seven captains were Adrastus, Amphiaraus, Capaneus, Tydeus, Hippomedon, Parthenopaeus, and Polyneices himself. Apart from Adrastus, all met their end in the conflict, Eteocles and Polyneices having died at each other's hands. Thebes's new regent, Creon, allowed Eteocles, as ostensible defender of the city, to be buried, but denied burial to Polyneices. It was Antigone's burial of Polyneices that led to her own death.

(*See also* Adrastus, Amphiaraus, Antigone, Capaneus, Ismene, Jocasta, Oedipus, Parthenopaeus, Polyneices, *and* Thebes.)

EUMAEUS The story of Eumaeus is told in Homer's *Odyssey*. Eumaeus was a prince by birth but had been kidnapped and sold as a slave to Laertes, king of Ithaca, whom he served faithfully as the royal swineherd. Eumaeus later served Laertes's son Odysseus as well. Upon Odysseus's return to Ithaca from Troy after a twenty-year absence, Eumaeus received him hospitably, although he did not initially recognize him. In his kindness and humble generosity, Eumaeus was the polar opposite of the goatherd Melanthios, who had formed an allegiance with the awful men attempting to win the hand of Odysseus's wife, Penelope. In contrast to Eumaeus, Melanthios insulted and kicked Odysseus, believing him only to be a worthless beggar.

(*See also* Ithaca, Laertes, Odysseus, Penelope, *and* Troy.)

EUROPA Europa was the daughter of Agenor, king of Tyre (or Sidon) in Phoenicia, and his wife Telephassa. Her brothers were Phoenix, Cilix, and Cadmus, who would become the founder of Thebes. Zeus developed a passion for her, and, having transformed himself into a gentle, lovely white bull, he approached her at the seashore. Taken with his beauty and unafraid, Europa placed garlands on him and eventually climbed up onto his back. Then the bull-god sped across the sea to Crete, where Europa bore Minos, Sarpedon, and Rhadamanthus. Agenor, meanwhile, had sent Europa's brothers to find her, telling them not to return without her. All ultimately gave up and founded settlements where they ended their search. Europa eventually wed the Cretan prince (or king) Asterius, who brought up her sons as his own.

(*See also* Agenor, Cadmus, Crete, Minos, Rhadamanthus, Sarpedon, Sidon, Thebes, *and* Zeus.)

EURYALUS There were several heroes by the name of Euryalus. In Virgil's epic the *Aeneid*, Euryalus was the young companion of Nisus, both of whom had accompanied Aeneas to Italy from Troy. Euryalus was so young and so precious to his mother that she had made the journey to Italy with him. Euryalus's bravery and youthful indiscretion together led to his tragic death. With Nisus he volunteered to leave the Trojan camp which, at the time, was besieged by Italians, and to go find Aeneas, who had gone to recruit auxiliary forces. Once outside the camp, Nisus and Euryalus became carried away with bloodlust and slaughtered many of the sleeping enemy. Stripping the armor from one of the slain warriors and putting it on was Euryalus's undoing: the plundered helmet, reflecting light from the moon, was spotted by the enemy, and Euryalus was taken captive. Although Nisus risked his own life trying to save his young friend, both were slain.

(*See also* Aeneas, Nisus, *and* Troy.)

EURYCLEIA Eurycleia, whose name means "wide-spreading fame," had been the nurse of Odysseus and had later also become the nurse of Odysseus's son, Telemachus. Even when Odysseus's wife, Penelope, did not do so, Eurycleia recognized Odysseus, who had been away from his kingdom in Ithaca for twenty years, doing so on the basis of a scar that he had received in a boar hunt while a young man. Odysseus urged Eurycleia to keep his identity secret until he could punish Penelope's suitors, who had been consuming all the palace's resources.

(*See also* Ithaca, Odysseus, Penelope, *and* Telemachus.)

EURYDICE There were several mythological characters by the name of Eurydice. One Eurydice was the wife of Creon, who became regent of Thebes after the death of Oedipus. She committed suicide upon the death of her son Haemon, who had taken his life in grief over the suicide of his fiancée, Antigone.

Another Eurydice was the daughter of Lacedaemon, namesake of the territory of Sparta, and mother, by Acrisius, of Danae, whom Zeus impregnated taking the form of a shower of golden rain.

These two mortal Eurydices are to be distinguished from the nymph of the same name who was married to Orpheus and was pursued by him into the Underworld.

(See also Acrisius, Antigone, Creon, Danae, Eurydice [nymph], Haemon, Nymphs [the], Oedipus, Orpheus, Sparta, Thebes, Underworld [the], and Zeus.)

EURYSTHEUS Eurystheus was a mythical king of Argos or, according to variant traditions, of Mycenae and Tiryns. It was in service to Eurystheus that Hercules performed his famous Twelve (or Ten) Labors, a situation that the goddess Hera had engineered. When Alcmena, whom Zeus had impregnated, was on the verge of giving birth to Hercules, Zeus made it known to Hera that a son of his blood would soon be born and would have an expansive kingdom. Hera, jealous of Zeus's dalliance with Alcmena, protracted Alcmena's labor, thereby causing Alcmena's son Hercules to be born after Eurystheus, who happened to be a descendant of Zeus through the hero Perseus. Later, driven mad by Hera, Hercules killed his wife Megara and his children. Hercules then went to consult the oracle at Delphi, which proclaimed that he should go the court of Eurystheus and, over the course of twelve years, perform whatever labors the latter imposed. As a consequence, the oracle continued, Hercules would achieve immortality. Eurystheus's death, which occurred after Hercules had completed the Labors, is variously reported: he was either killed by one of Hercules's sons or executed at Alcmena's wishes.

(See also Alcmena, Argos, Delphi, Hera, Hercules, Megara [heroine], Mycenae, Perseus, Tiryns, and Zeus.)

EURYTUS Eurytus was a king of Oechalia, a place of uncertain location. According to the mythographer Apollodorus, Eurytus, an expert archer, gave instruction to a young Hercules in the art of archery. After completing his Labors, Hercules, wishing to marry, learned that Eurytus was offering his daughter Iole to the man who could defeat him and his sons in an archery contest. Hercules did prevail in this contest, but Eurytus refused to give him Iole, fearing that

Hercules would kill Iole if he married her; as Eurytus was aware, Hercules had killed his first wife and children in a fit of madness. Hercules later brought an army to attack Oechalia, killed Eurytus and his sons, vanquished the city, and took Iole captive. Driven by jealousy of Iole, Hercules's new wife, Deianeira, doused Hercules's cloak with what she thought was a love charm given to her by the Centaur Nessus. But it was not a love charm; rather, it was a poison that burned Hercules's flesh.

In Homer's *Odyssey*, it was the bow of Eurytus with which Odysseus killed the suitors of his wife, Penelope, since, in his absence from Ithaca, they had been eating him out of house and home and had treated his family outrageously. Homer also records a different version of Eurytus's death: he was killed by Apollo in punishment for having challenged the god to a contest in archery.

(*See also* Apollo, Centaurs [the], Deianeira, Hercules, Iole, Ithaca, Nessus, Odysseus, *and* Penelope.)

EVANDER The travel writer Pausanias reports that Evander, who became an important ally to Aeneas and his Trojan comrades when they came to Italy, was the child of a nymph and the god Hermes. Being the wisest man and the best fighter among the Arcadians of Greece, he had been sent to establish a colony in Italy. He founded a city called Pallantium on what would later be called the Palatine Hill, one of the Seven Hills of Rome. The god of the Tiber River appeared to the hero Aeneas in a dream, urging him to seek Evander's aid, which the aged king readily gave: he sent his son, Pallas, and a contingent of men to join the Trojan forces, and Aeneas promised to watch over Pallas as he would his own son. It happened that when Aeneas went to visit Evander, he and his people were celebrating Hercules's victory over the monstrous Cacus.

(*See also* Aeneas, Arcadia, Cacus, Hercules, Hermes, Pallas, Rome, Tiber River [the], *and* Troy.)

EVENUS Evenus was the father of Marpessa. When the hero Idas made off with her, Evenus drove his chariot in pursuit. But when it came clear to him that he could not catch Idas, he killed both himself and his horses.

(*See also* Idas *and* Marpessa.)

GANYMEDE Ganymede was the handsome young son either of the Trojan king Laomedon or of the Trojan king Tros, from whom the city of Troy's name is derived. Ganymede became the cup-bearer of Zeus, having been carried to Olympus by Zeus's eagle, or as the Roman poet Ovid writes, by a love-struck

Zeus himself in the guise of an eagle, his sacred bird. Ganymede's father was despondent over the abduction of his son, and Zeus offered him compensation by way of a special gift. This gift was variously identified in ancient sources as a pair of beautiful mares or a golden grapevine. Ganymede himself was said to have been transformed into the constellation Aquarius after his death.

(*See also* Laomedon, Olympus [Mount], Tros, Troy, *and* Zeus.)

GLAUCUS   There were several heroes by the name of Glaucus. One of these was a king of Corinth and was the son of Sisyphus and the second-generation Titan Atlas's daughter Merope. This Glaucus's wife became pregnant by Poseidon, and the result was the hero Bellerophon, whom Glaucus raised as his own. According to the mythographer Hyginus, Glaucus's own mares devoured him at the funeral games of Pelias, former king of Iolcos, after being defeated by Hercules's comrade Iolaus in a chariot race.

Another Glaucus was a fisherman who became a minor sea deity, having been transformed by grass that he tasted. A third Glaucus was a young son of King Minos of Crete. This third Glaucus had fallen into a large vat of honey while chasing a mouse. According to the mythographer Hyginus, his distraught parents consulted Apollo, who told them that a prodigy had recently appeared and that whoever could explain it would be able to find their son and restore him to life. This prodigy was duly located: it was a newborn bull that changed color three times a day: first white, then red, then black. Only one man could offer an explanation, this being the seer Polyidus, who said that the bull was like a mulberry tree, the fruit of which changes color while ripening from white to red and, finally, to black. The seer located Glaucus by correctly interpreting an omen: he saw an owl (*glaux* in Greek) sitting on a wine vat circled by bees. When Polyidus subsequently declared that he could not revive Glaucus, Minos ordered him to be buried with the boy. A snake appeared in the tomb, and Polyidus killed it. Then another snake appeared seeking its mate, and, finding the other dead, it returned with an herb that revived it. Polyidus used the same herb to revive Glaucus and was amply rewarded for his efforts.

Still another Glaucus fought alongside the Trojans in the Trojan War. With Zeus's son Sarpedon, he was a captain of the Lycians. When he came face-to-face with Diomedes, the two realized that they were bound by ancestral ties of friendship established by their grandfathers, Bellerophon and Oeneus. Honoring this bond, they did not fight each other and instead exchanged armor.

(*See also* Apollo, Atlas, Bellerophon, Corinth, Crete, Diomedes, Glaucus [god], Hercules, Iolcos, Lycia, Merope [nymph], Minos, Oeneus, Pelias, Polyidus, Poseidon, Sarpedon, Sisyphus, Titans [the], Troy, *and* Zeus.)

GORDIUS Gordius (or Gordias) was the legendary founder of the Phrygian state and namesake of its capital, Gordium. Gordius was a poor farmer who had only two oxen to his name, one that pulled his plow and another that pulled his wagon. One day as he was plowing, an eagle settled on the plow's yoke and remained there for the duration of his work. Gordius took this to be an omen and told his story to a girl from a local prophetic tribe. She instructed him to return to the place of the omen's occurrence and there to make sacrifice to Zeus. This girl became Gordius's wife, and together they became the parents of Midas. Later, when the Phrygians were engaged in civil war, Gordius was named their king, for an oracle from Zeus had proclaimed that the first wagon driver to come their way would be their new regent. Gordius then dedicated his wagon in the god's temple, securing it with a segment of cornel bark tied in a manner such that it could not readily be untied (the so-called Gordian Knot). Another oracle foretold that whoever should be able to untie this insoluble knot would rule all of Asia. That person would be Alexander the Great.

(*See also* Midas, Phrygia, *and* Zeus.)

HAEMON Haemon was the son of Creon, who became regent of Thebes after the death of Oedipus. Haemon is best known from the tragedian Sophocles's play *Antigone* as the betrothed of Oedipus's daughter Antigone. In that play, Haemon interceded with his father to prevent Antigone's death by stoning for burying her brother Polyneices, who had been declared an enemy of the city. Being unable to convince his father to spare her, Haemon threw himself on his sword by Antigone's corpse.

A different tradition makes him a casualty of the Sphinx that had been terrorizing Thebes before Oedipus solved its famous riddle.

(*See also* Antigone, Creon, Oedipus, Polyneices, Sphinx of Thebes [the], *and* Thebes.)

HECABE Hecabe is another name for Hecuba, the wife of Priam, who was king of Troy at the time of the Trojan War.

(*See also* Hecuba, Priam, *and* Troy.)

HECTOR Hector was the best of the Trojan warriors and leader of the Trojan forces in the course of the Trojan War. He was a son of Troy's king Priam and the queen Hecuba, and his siblings included Paris, the abductor of Helen; the prophetic twins Helenus and Cassandra; the ill-fated Polyxena; and Troilus, who was ambushed and killed by Achilles. Hector's wife was Andromache, herself a princess from the Asian city Thebes. Andromache and Hector became the parents of Astyanax, who at the end of the Trojan War was flung to his death from the ramparts of Troy by Achilles's son Neoptolemus or Odysseus. Hector's own fate was sealed when he killed Patroclus, the close friend and companion of Achilles: it was the desire for vengeance that drove Achilles, who had withdrawn from the fighting, back into the fray and to seek Hector specifically. Even when Achilles had killed Hector, his rage did not abate. Achilles fastened Hector's corpse to his chariot and dragged it around the walls of Troy for days on end. To this outrage even the gods took exception. Hector's father, Priam, eventually went to the camp of Achilles, terrifying as that undertaking was, and successfully retrieved his son's body. It is with the funeral of Hector that Homer's *Iliad* ends, the hero's blazing funeral pyre presaging the fiery fall of Troy.

(*See also* Achilles, Andromache, Astyanax, Cassandra, Hecuba, Helenus, Neoptolemus, Odysseus, Patroclus, Polyxena, Priam, Troilus, *and* Troy.)

HECUBA Hecuba (or Hecabe) was the wife of King Priam of Troy and the mother of Hector, Paris, Troilus, Helenus, Polydorus, Cassandra, and Polyxena. The Greek poet Pindar writes that while pregnant with Paris, Hecuba dreamed that she had given birth to a fire-wielding Hecatoncheir ("Hundred-Hander")—or a firebrand, according to the mythographer Apollodorus. This dream, coupled with a prophecy uttered by Cassandra, caused her to expose her infant son Paris, who was destined to bring destruction by fire to the city of Troy. In Homer's *Iliad*, she prayed to Athena for help to no avail and attempted to prevent Hector from risking his life in battle with Achilles, again to no avail. In the course of the Trojan War or in its aftermath, she witnessed the death of her husband and a number of her children. She herself was taken captive and given as a war prize to Odysseus. The Roman poet Ovid records that when Hecuba was weeping over the corpse of her daughter Polyxena, she discovered the murdered body of her son Polydorus, who she thought (and hoped) had been safeguarded by King Polymestor of Thrace. Learning that Polymestor had killed Polydorus for his gold, she attacked him, gouging out his eyes. When Polymestor then set upon her in pursuit, she was transformed into a dog and made her escape.

(*See also* Achilles, Athena, Cassandra, Hecatoncheires [the], Hector, Helenus, Odysseus, Paris, Polydorus, Polyxena, Priam, Thrace, Troilus, *and* Troy.)

HELEN Helen, whom the poetess Sappho describes as "the most beautiful of all humankind," was "Helen of Sparta" before becoming "Helen of Troy." There were various accounts of her birth. Her mother, Leda, a daughter of the Aetolian king Thestius, was married to the Spartan king Tyndareus. Helen was variously said to have been born from an egg that Leda produced after being impregnated by Zeus in the guise of a swan or from an egg produced by Nemesis, the goddess of retribution, who, herself having assumed the shape of a goose, was embraced by Zeus in the form of a swan. According to this second version, Leda found (or was given) Nemesis's egg and kept it safe until it hatched. Helen's siblings were Clytemnestra, who would become queen of Mycenae, and the divine twins Castor and Pollux. Clytemnestra, Castor, and Pollux were sometimes said to have emerged from the same egg as Helen, or to have emerged from separate eggs, or even to have been the children of Tyndareus, who lay with Leda on the same night as Zeus did.

When word of Helen's beauty spread, she was kidnapped by the heroes Pirithous and Theseus but was rescued by her brothers, Castor and Pollux. Later, when it was time for her to marry, Tyndareus, realizing that it would be impossible to choose between Helen's numerous suitors, allowed her to make the choice. She selected Menelaus, younger brother of Agamemnon, who through marriage became the regent of Sparta. With Menelaus Helen became mother to Hermione, her only child, and lived happily in Sparta until the arrival of the Trojan prince Paris, who abducted her or, by some accounts, with whom she left willingly. Paris had come to Sparta seeking his prize after the famous judgment in which he was asked to decide who among the goddesses Aphrodite, Hera, and Athena was most beautiful. Aphrodite had successfully bribed him with an offer of the most beautiful woman in the world, which was Helen. In the wake of Helen's departure, Agamemnon assembled the best of Greece's warriors. This he was able to do, since Tyndareus had wisely called upon all of Helen's suitors to swear to abide by her choice and to come to the couple's assistance should the need arise. The Greeks fought with the Trojans for a ten-year period in order to retrieve her. After the death of Paris in the war's tenth year, Helen was given to Paris's brother Deiphobus in marriage, but the latter was brutally murdered by Menelaus, according to the Roman poet Virgil. In Homer's *Odyssey*, Helen ultimately returned to Sparta, where she and Menelaus hospitably received Odysseus's son, Telemachus, who was seeking news of his father. There was a tradition, too, that Helen and Menelaus both had stayed for a time in Egypt on their return voyage from Troy.

According to the Greek poet Stesichorus, Helen never went to Troy but rather was wafted by the gods to Egypt, where Menelaus later found her. In this variant, followed by the playwright Euripides, a phantom of Helen accompanied Paris in her place. Among the accounts of the end of her life are several preserved by the travel writer Pausanias: she was hanged on the island of Rhodes or, upon her death, she joined Achilles as his bride on White Island in the Black Sea.

(*See also* Achilles, Agamemnon, Aphrodite, Athena, Castor, Clytemnestra, Hera, Hermione, Leda, Menelaus, Mycenae, Nemesis, Odysseus, Paris, Pirithous, Pollux, Sparta, Telemachus, Theseus, Troy, Tyndareus, *and* Zeus.)

HELENUS Helenus was a son of King Priam of Troy and his wife, Hecuba, and he was said to be the twin brother of the prophetess Cassandra. Helenus, like Cassandra, was blessed with the gift of prophecy, and Homer calls him "best by far of the augurs." In his capacity as seer, he foretold the disastrous consequences of Paris's sailing off to fetch Helen from Sparta. He later aided the Greeks in their effort finally to defeat Troy by revealing to them the fact that the city would not fall unless the Greeks obtained the ancient statue of Athena called the Palladium and brought both Achilles's son Neoptolemus and the hero Philoctetes, bow of Hercules in hand, to fight with them at Troy. In his epic the *Aeneid*, Virgil writes that Helenus became the successor to Neoptolemus's kingdom and had married Andromache, his deceased brother Hector's wife, who, like he, had been taken captive by the Greeks.

(*See also* Achilles, Andromache, Athena, Cassandra, Hecuba, Helen, Hercules, Neoptolemus, Philoctetes, Priam, Sparta, *and* Troy.)

HELLE Helle was a daughter of Athamas, king of Orchomenus in Boeotia, and Nephele. Ino, Athamas's second wife, devised a plot whereby to do away with Helle and her brother Phrixus, who, having been born earlier than her own children, stood to become her husband's heirs. Ino thus caused the realm's stockpile of grain seed to become corrupted, with the result that when sown, the seed failed to germinate. Athamas then sent messengers to consult the Delphic Oracle regarding a remedy for this catastrophe. Ino, however, compelled the messengers to report falsely that the Oracle recommended the sacrifice of Phrixus and, by some accounts, Helle, too. Nephele was able to save her children at the last minute, sending a golden fleeced and winged ram to carry them away to safety. In the course of the ram's flight, however, Helle lost her balance and fell into the waters below, which, thereafter, were called Hellespont, "Helle's Sea," and now are called the Dardanelles.

(*See also* Athamas, Boeotia, Delphi, Hellespont [the], Ino, Nephele, *and* Phrixus.)

HELLEN According to the Greek poet Hesiod as well as the historians Thucydides and Diodorus Siculus, Hellen was a son of Deucalion and Pyrrha, the sole survivors of the great flood that Zeus sent to wipe out the human race, which he considered utterly wicked. Other sources name Hellen's father as the god Zeus himself. Hellen was considered to be the ancestor of all the Greeks, who were called "Hellenes" after Hellen. The tribes of Greece were said to be descended from his sons and grandsons: Dorus (after whom the Dorians were named), Ion (after whom the Ionians were named), Achaeus (after whom the Achaeans were named) and Aeolus (after whom the Aeolians were named).

(*See also* Achaeans [the], Aeolus [hero], Deucalion, Dorus, Ion, Pyrrha, *and* Zeus.)

HERACLES Heracles is the original Greek name for the hero Hercules. (*See* Hercules.)

HERCULES Hercules was the most important and best known of all the Greek heroes. His original Greek name Heracles means "glory of Hera," being a combination of the Greek word for "glory," *kleos,* and the name of the goddess Hera. Ironically, Hera's persecution of him throughout his life, and his perseverance in the face of extreme adversity, is how he earned his fame. Hercules was the son of Alcmena, daughter of Electryon, a former king of Tiryns. Alcmena was married to Amphitryon, her cousin, but she became pregnant in Amphitryon's absence when Zeus came to her disguised as her husband. Amphitryon returned home shortly thereafter and also slept with her, impregnating her a second time. When nine months had passed, Alcmena was ready to give birth, but Zeus boasted that a descendant of his born on that day would become king with an extensive kingdom. Hera, jealous and angry that Zeus had once again had an affair, protracted Alcmena's labor so that Eurystheus, who happened to be descended from Zeus through his grandfather Perseus, would be born before Hercules. After Eurystheus, who would later become king of Tiryns and Mycenae, was born, Alcmena gave birth to twins in the city of Thebes: Hercules, the child of Zeus, and Iphicles, the son of Amphityron. As Hercules and Iphicles lay in their crib, Hera sent serpents to kill them. Iphicles, being a normal baby, did nothing, but Hercules leaped up and strangled the snakes. As he matured, Hercules gained a reputation for his strength as well as for his skill in archery and wrestling. He apparently had less of an aptitude for music, killing his lyre teacher Linus in an outburst of anger. Hercules was also known for having a voracious appetite both for food and for women, reputedly sleeping with all fifty daughters of Thespius, ruler of a neighboring kingdom, and consequently becoming the father of a great many children. A strict chronology of Hercules's many exploits is difficult to establish not only because he lived a most eventful life but also because his exploits increased in number and in their details as they were narrated over the centuries. At one stage, Hercules became entangled with the Minyans, who had been exacting tribute from Thebes; gathering a group of young warriors, he attacked the Minyan city of Orchomenos, burning the palace. As a reward for ridding Thebes of the Minyan threat, the Theban king Creon gave his daughter Megara to Hercules in marriage. With Megara, Hercules became the father of three (or five) sons. In a fit of madness sent upon him by his eternal enemy Hera, Hercules killed his children, two of his brother's sons, and Megara as well. Hercules left Thebes in horror over what he had done, and although having been expiated of blood guilt, traveled to Delphi in order there to consult the oracle of Apollo. The oracle's pronouncement was that he should volunteer his services to Eurystheus and accomplish whatever tasks he should set for Hercules, this being a means of achieving immortality. This Eurystheus was the aforementioned descendant of Zeus's who, through the interference of Hera, had been born just before Hercules. Hercules now accomplished his famous Twelve Labors, which required him to travel to the far reaches of the world: killing the invincible Nemean Lion; eliminating the multi-headed Hydra of Lerna; capturing the Cerynitian Hind, distinguished by its golden antlers; trapping the vicious Erymanthian Boar; cleaning the enormous stables of Augeas; chasing away the projectile-feathered Stymphalian Birds; capturing the flesh-eating mares of the Thracian Diomedes; fetching the belt of the Amazon queen Hippolyta; claiming the cattle of the triple-bodied Geryon; fetching golden apples from the garden of the Hesperides; and bringing the hell-hound Cerberus up from the Underworld. Hercules's further exploits, some of which took place between individual Labors, included his joining the expedition of Jason and the Argonauts to fetch the Golden Fleece; ridding the future site of Rome of the dread monster Cacus; freeing Prometheus from bondage on the Caucasus Mountains; retrieving Alcestis, wife of Admetus, from the Underworld; rescuing the daughter of the Trojan king Laomedon from a sea monster; attempting to steal the Pythia's tripod from Delphi and wrestling over it with Apollo; serving as a slave to the Lydian queen Omphale at the behest of the Pythia; wrestling the river god Achelous for the hand of Deianeira, who, unknowingly, would cause his death; and killing the Centaur Nessus when the latter attempted to abduct Deianeira. When Hercules later made Iole, princess of Oechalia, his concubine, a jealous Deianeira gave Hercules a robe dipped in the love potion given her by Nessus. This was not a love potion at all but rather a poison that caused Hercules's flesh to burn. In agony, he ascended the Thessalian Mount Oeta and, having instructed his son Hyllus to build a funeral pyre for him, climbed onto it. None would dare to light the pyre but the hero Philoctetes, who bravely put the great hero out of his misery. As a reward, Philoctetes received Hercules's famed bow and arrow, and Hercules himself became divine.

(See also Achelous [god], Admetus, Alcestis, Alcmena, Amazons [the], Amphitryon, Apollo, Argonauts [the], Augeas, Cacus, Caucasus Mountains [the], Centaurs [the], Cerberus, Cerynitian Hind [the], Creon, Deianeira, Delphi, Diomedes, Electryon, Erymanthian Boar [the], Eurystheus, Geryon, Hera, Hesperides [the], Hippolyta, Hydra of Lerna [the], Iole, Iphicles, Jason, Laomedon, Linus, Lydia, Megara [heroine], Minyans [the], Mycenae, Nemean Lion [the], Nessus, Oeta [Mount], Omphale, Philoctetes, Prometheus, Stymphalian Birds [the], Thebes, Thessaly, Thrace, Tiryns, Troy, Underworld [the], and Zeus.)

HERMIONE Hermione was the daughter of Helen and Menelaus, king of Sparta, and according to Homer, she was Helen's only child. When Helen departed with Paris for Troy, she left her nine-year-old daughter in the care of her sister Clytemnestra, wife of Agamemnon. Hermione became betrothed to Clytemnestra's son Orestes, but the marriage did not take place, by some accounts because he was a matricide and was accordingly polluted in religious and ritual terms. Hermione was later betrothed to Achilles's son Neoptolemus by way of bribing him to join the Greek effort against Troy. This marriage did take place, but Hermione remained childless. According to the tragedian Euripides's play *Andromache*, Hermione became envious of Andromache, former wife of the deceased Trojan hero Hector, who, after the fall of Troy, had become Neoptolemus's concubine and had borne him children. Hermione accused Andromache of placing a spell on her and unsuccessfully plotted her death. In the end, Orestes appeared, killed Neoptolemus, and took Hermione away with him.

(*See also* Achilles, Agamemnon, Andromache, Clytemnestra, Hector, Neoptolemus, Orestes, Paris, Sparta, *and* Troy.)

HERO Hero was a young priestess of the goddess Aphrodite and lived on the European side of the Hellespont. She was in love with Leander, a youth who lived in Abydus on the shore just opposite. Leander would visit in secret at night, swimming the Hellespont's treacherous waters to meet her. Aphrodite discovered the lovers, however, and Leander perished while swimming to meet his beloved Hero. She, in consequence, threw herself from her tower, thus ending her own life.

(*See also* Abydus, Aphrodite, Hellespont [the], *and* Leander.)

HESIONE Hesione was a daughter of Laomedon, one of the legendary kings of Troy, and she was rescued from sacrifice to a sea monster by Hercules. When the hero had completed his ninth Labor, fetching the belt of the Amazon queen Hippolyta, he came to Troy. At the time, that land was experiencing a twofold disaster: Apollo had sent a plague, and Poseidon had sent a sea monster that snatched up members of the populace, all of this intended as a punishment for Laomedon. As the mythographer Apollodorus writes, the gods had heard how evil Laomedon was and, disguising themselves as mortal men, made trial of him by offering to build the walls of Troy for wages. When their labor was complete, Laomedon failed to make the requisite payment, and it was for this that he and his land were punished. Learning from an oracle that deliverance from these problems depended on his offering his own daughter to the sea monster, Laomedon tied her to cliffs by the sea. It was there that Hercules saw her and offered to save her life, but for a price: the splendid mares that Zeus had given Laomedon as compensation for the loss of his son Ganymede. Hercules killed the monster and saved Hesione but he, like Apollo and Poseidon before him, did not receive payment. For this reason, Hercules later returned to the city leading a contingent of warriors and conquered it. Hercules took Hesione and gave her as a prize to his friend Telamon. Hesione, for her part, ransomed her brother Priam, who would later become king of Troy.

(*See also* Amazons [the], Apollo, Ganymede, Hercules, Hippolyta, Laomedon, Poseidon, Priam, Telamon, Teucer, Troy, *and* Zeus.)

HIPPODAMIA There were several desirable heroines by the name of Hippodamia, which means "tamer of horses" in Greek. One was the daughter of Oenomaus, king of Pisa, and his queen Sterope. Either because Oenomaus loved his own daughter, or because it had been prophesied that his son-in-law would kill him, Oenomaus took measures to prevent her marriage: he challenged all of her suitors to a chariot race in full confidence that he would win, since his horses, a gift from Ares, were known to be swifter than all others. Those who had unsuccessfully attempted to win Hippodamia's hand were killed, their heads suspended outside the palace as a warning to other aspirants. Pelops, son of Tantalus, was undeterred and resorted to trickery to defeat Oenomaus; he bribed Oenomaus's charioteer Myrtilus with the offer of a night with Hippodamia and half of Oenomaus's kingdom in exchange for removing the linchpin from the king's chariot wheel (or, according to another tradition, replacing it with one of wax). When the race was underway, the compromised wheel came loose, and Oenomaus was thrown to his death. Pelops, for his part, did not honor his promise to Myrtilus and, instead, threw him from a cliff to his death. Before his death, Myrtilus cursed Pelops and his many descendants, thus being the cause of their woes. Among the children whom Hippodamia bore to Pelops were Atreus and Thyestes, both tragic characters, and Pittheus, who would become the grandfather of the Athenian hero Theseus.

Another Hippodamia was the bride of the Lapith king Pirithous, who invited his neighbors, the Centaurs, to his wedding. When the Centaurs became drunk, they attempted to abscond with Hippodamia and the other Lapith women. As a result, a battle broke out between them, and the Centaurs were driven from the land.

(*See also* Ares, Athens, Atreus, Centaurs [the], Lapiths [the], Myrtilus, Oenomaus, Pelops, Pirithous, Pittheus, Sterope, Tantalus, Theseus, *and* Theyestes.)

HIPPOLYTA Hippolyta was a queen of the Amazons, a tribe of warrior women thought to have lived on the Thermodon River in what is now Turkey.

In the mythographer Apollodorus's account of the Labors of Hercules, the great hero was sent to fetch Hippolyta's belt as his ninth Labor. Having once belonged to the god Ares, the precious belt was embroidered with gold, according to the tragedian Euripides, and had been given to Hippolyta as a mark of her preeminence in war. Since Eurystheus's daughter Admeta desired the belt, Hercules was sent to fetch it for her, and he departed for the Amazons' lands with just one ship manned by a group of his comrades. When Hercules and his men arrived, Hippolyta went to inquire what it was that the men were seeking, and when told that it was her belt, promised to give it to Hercules. But the goddess Hera, ever causing trouble for Hercules, disguised herself as an Amazon and spread a rumor that the newcomers intended to make off with their queen. In alarm, the Amazons attacked, and in the fray, Hercules killed Hippolyta. Hercules stripped her belt and returned with it to Greece.

(*See also* Admeta, Amazons [the], Ares, Eurystheus, Hera, *and* Hercules.)

HIPPOLYTUS

Hippolytus is best known from the playwright Euripides's tragedy *Hippolytus*. He was a son of the Athenian king Theseus and the Amazon queen Hippolyta (or, by other accounts, Antiope). Hippolytus was a chaste hunter and a devotee of the goddess Artemis, a fact that angered Aphrodite, who caused Theseus's wife, Phaedra, to fall in love with Hippolytus. Though she tried hard to suppress her inappropriate feelings, Phaedra did eventually reveal them to her nurse, who in turn informed a horrified Hippolytus. Having been scorned, and her reputation beyond repair, Phaedra hanged herself after composing a note falsely accusing Hippolytus of having made advances upon her. Upon reading this note, Theseus prayed to his father, Poseidon, to fulfill a wish, this being the death of his son. Consequently, while Hippolytus was driving his chariot along the seashore, a bull appeared from the waves, terrifying his horses. Hippolytus was thrown and, being dragged, was fatally injured. Before he breathed his last, the goddess Artemis appeared and assured Hippolytus that he would not be forgotten and would be honored by maidens of Troezen in a newly instituted coming-of-age ceremony.

(*See also* Amazons [the], Antiope, Aphrodite, Artemis, Athens, Hippolyta, Phaedra, Poseidon, *and* Theseus.)

HIPPOMENES

Hippomenes was, according to the poet Ovid, a great-grandson of Poseidon and son of Megareus, a Boeotian king. Other sources, however, list Megareus as one of Hippomenes's offspring and call Hippomenes Poseidon's grandson. Regardless of his parentage, Hippomenes became one of the many suitors of the lovely huntress Atalanta. Wishing to remain a virgin like Artemis, the goddess that she most admired, Atalanta resisted marriage for as long as possible but at last agreed to wed whoever could outrun her. Many young men attempted this, and all paid with their lives. Hippomenes, however, was undeterred by this perilous challenge and prayed to the goddess Aphrodite for help. The goddess gave him three golden apples, which, in the course of the race, he threw one by one. Each of these Atalanta sprinted to retrieve, and fetching the last of these cost her the race. Hippomenes thus won his bride but in his elation forgot to thank Aphrodite for her aid. As punishment for this, he was driven by lust to sleep with his new bride in a temple of the goddess Cybele, violating it. Cybele, in turn, changed the lovers into lions that henceforth would draw her carriage.

In some traditions, it was not Hippomenes but the Arcadian youth Melanion of whom this tale is told.

(*See also* Aphrodite, Arcadia, Atalanta, Boeotia, Cybele, Melanion, *and* Poseidon.)

HYACINTH Hyacinth (also Hyacinthos or Hyacinthus) was most often said to be the son of the Spartan king Amyclas and Diomede, a daughter of Lapithus, ancestor of the Thessalian Lapiths. Others who are called his parents include the Muse Clio and the Spartan king Oebalus, father of Tyndareus. Hyacinth was a youth of such beauty that he was pursued by the god Apollo, the west wind Zephyr, and Thamyris, a bard of extraordinary skill who was said to be the first mortal man ever to desire another male. The Roman poet Ovid's version of Hyacinth's tragic end is the best known: Apollo and Hyacinth were enjoying a respite from the hunt and began to throw the discus. Apollo threw his discus first, and as Hyacinth bent to retrieve it, the discus bounced against his head with force enough to kill him. The travel writer Pausanias reports that it was a jealous Zephyr who, with a gust of wind, caused this accident. Ironically, Apollo, the god of healing, was unable to save him. Stricken with grief, Apollo caused a flower, the hyacinth, its petals bearing marks that spelled out the cry of mourning, to grow from the place where Hyacinth had fallen.

Hyacinth would be worshipped as a culture hero in the Hyacinthia, a festival celebrated in his honor. From sources such as the historian Herodotus and Pausanias, we learn that the Hyacinthia comprised ritualized mourning for Hyacinth as well as musical performances and athletic contents engaged in by boys and young men, a banquet and dance, a procession of maidens, and the gift of a robe to Apollo. Hyacinth's tomb and cult, meanwhile, were located in Amyclae near Sparta.

(*See also* Apollo, Clio, Lapiths [the], Muses [the], Sparta, Thamyris, Thessaly, Tyndareus, *and* Zephyr.)

HOUSE OF
OEDIPUS

ARES + APHRODITE

HARMONIA + CADMUS

ECHION + AGAVE   ARISTAEUS + AUTONOE   ATHAMAS + INO

PENTHEUS   ACTAEON   LEARCHUS   MELICERTES

AMPHIARAUS + ERIPHYLE

AMPHILOCHUS   ALCMAEON   DEMONASSA + THERSANDER

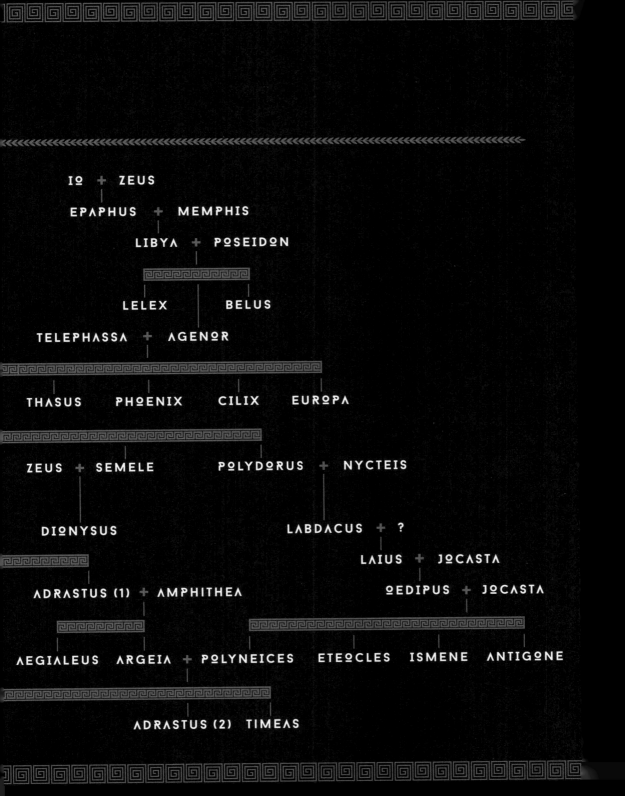

HYLAS Hylas was the son of Theiodamas, king of a people called the Dryopes, and the nymph Menodice, a daughter of Orion. According to Apollonius of Rhodes, Hercules raised Hylas, whose father, Theiodamas, Hercules had killed in anger over his refusal, while plowing, to relinquish his ox. Young Hylas would become Hercules's lover as well as his companion on the *Argo* when Hercules joined Jason in the quest for the Golden Fleece. When the Argonauts (sailors on the *Argo*) reached the country of Mysia, Hylas went in search of water. Just then a water nymph, or Naiad, spotted him, instantly smitten with his beauty. Losing all control, she pulled him with her beneath the water's surface to make him her husband. A distraught Hercules went searching for the youth, and ultimately was left behind by the Argonauts. According to the poet Theocritus, it was not one but several nymphs that pulled a pitcher-bearing Hylas into the water.

(*See also* Argonauts [the], Hercules, Jason, Naiads [the], *and* Orion.)

HYPERBOREANS, THE The Hyperboreans, those "beyond the north wind (Boreas)," were a mythical people believed to live in the extreme north, at the fringes of the known world: the Caucasus Mountains or just beyond. The Hyperboreans' existence was a felicitous, paradisiacal one, and they enjoyed proximity to the gods, especially Apollo, who spent a portion of each year in their land. According to the Greek poet Pindar, the Hyperboreans could be reached neither by ship nor on foot, the hero Perseus arriving among them borne on winged sandals. The poet writes also that the Hyperboreans were celebrants of the Muses, dancing and playing the flute and lyre in the goddesses' honor; wore wreaths of golden laurel, the plant most sacred to Apollo; and were not subject to illness or old age.

(*See also* Apollo, Boreas, Caucasus Mountains [the], Muses [the], *and* Perseus.)

HYPERMNESTRA Hypermnestra was one of the fifty daughters of King Danaus, who were collectively known as the Danaids. What distinguished Hypermnestra from her infamous sisters is the fact that she alone refused her father's order to kill her husband on her wedding night: her forty-nine sisters, on the other hand, did as their father asked, for their bridegrooms were the sons of Danaus's twin brother Aegyptus, who had designs on the lands that Danaus ruled. Instead of ending his life, Hypermnestra helped her husband, Lynceus, to flee. For her act of disobedience, Hypermnestra was imprisoned by her father but, as the mythographer Apollodorus writes, she was later reunited with her husband. The travel writer Pausanias, on the other hand, records that Hypermnestra was placed on trial but acquitted by the people of Argos. She and Lynceus became the parents of a son by the name of Abas.

The Danaid Hypermnestra is to be distinguished from the daughter of Thestius of the same name, who was said to be the mother of the seer Amphiaraus.

(*See also* Aegyptus, Amphiaraus, Argos, Danaids [the], Danaus, *and* Thestius.)

HYPSIPYLE
Hypsipyle was the daughter of Thoas, a king of the island of Lemnos. When the women of Lemnos killed the island's male population, Hypsipyle spared her father, Thoas, and hid him or, as the mythographer Hyginus writes, secretly placed him on a ship that conveyed him to safety. A year after the men's extermination, Jason and the Argonauts appeared on the island. Hypsipyle, who was acting regent, persuaded the other women to welcome the men and invite them to stay. Though the Argonauts did not stay on, Hypsipyle did become pregnant by Jason and bore him two sons. When the other women later discovered that the former king, Thoas, was still alive, he was put to death, and Hypsipyle was sold into slavery to Lycurgus, king of Nemea, where she served as nurse to the king's young son.

(*See also* Argonauts [the], Jason, Lemnian Women [the], Lemnos, Lycurgus, *and* Thoas.)

IASUS
Iasus, a king of Tegea in Arcadia, is one of the individuals named as father of the fleet-footed huntress Atalanta. In the Roman poet Ovid's well-known version of her story, her father was Schoeneus, a Boeotian king, but for the playwright Euripides, her father was Maenalus.

(*See also* Arcadia, Atalanta, Boeotia, *and* Schoeneus.)

ICARUS
Icarus was the young son of the craftsman Daedalus. It so happened that father and son were held captive on the island of Crete by its king, Minos, and Daedalus wished very much to find a means of escape. However, Daedalus was faced with a particular challenge, since Minos was lord of the seas and land, leaving only the sky as a region that offered clear passage. Daedalus accordingly crafted wings made of feathers held in place with wax for both himself and his son. Although Daedalus had cautioned against it, Icarus, carried away by the wonder of this gift of flight, flew too close to the sun. The wax in his wings melted, and the boy plummeted into the sea that now, after him, is called Icarian. Icarus's first and final flight is described by the Roman poet Ovid in his *Metamorphoses*.

(*See also* Crete, Daedalus, *and* Minos.)

IDAS
Idas was a son of the king of Messenia and participated in both the hunt for the Calydonian boar and Jason's quest for the Golden Fleece. According to the mythographer Apollodorus, Idas claimed his bride by unconventional

means. He abducted Marpessa, daughter of Evenus, in a winged chariot that he had received from Poseidon. Evenus drove his own chariot in pursuit, but, realizing that he could not catch Idas, killed his horses when he came to the river Lycormas and then leaped into the river's current to his death. Marpessa had also been desired by the god Apollo, and the god, too, pursued Idas's chariot. When Idas and Apollo came to blows, Zeus intervened and asked Marpessa to choose between her suitors. Her choice was Idas, a mortal like herself, and together they became parents to Cleopatra, who would later wed Meleager.

(*See also* Apollo, Calydon, Evenus, Jason, Marpessa, Meleager, Messenia, Poseidon, *and* Zeus.)

ILUS Ilus was the namesake of the city of Troy, which was also known as Ilion (or Ilium and Ilios). Ilus was reputedly the city's founder and the son of King Tros, who gave his name to the Trojans, and Callirrhoe ("Beautiful-Flowing"), daughter of the local Trojan river god Scamander.

(*See also* Scamander River [the], Tros, *and* Troy.)

INO Ino was a mortal woman who became divine through the providence of the gods. As a deity, she was known as Leucothea (the "White Goddess") and played an important role in preserving the life of the hero Odysseus in the course of his ten-year journey home from Troy: she provided him with a veil that helped him stay afloat while swimming to the island of the Phaeacians after becoming shipwrecked.

Surviving accounts of Ino's mortal life and metamorphosis are various and, in part, conflicting. In broad sweeps, her story is as follows. Ino was a daughter of Cadmus and Harmonia, a king and queen of the city of Thebes. Her sisters were Agave, Autonoe, and Semele, who was impregnated by Zeus and became mother to the god Dionysus. Upon Semele's tragic death by incineration, Zeus rescued the still unborn baby Dionysus and saw to it that he was delivered to Ino and her husband, the Boeotian king Athamas, to bring up. This fact was discovered by an ever-jealous Hera, who vented her anger on Ino and her husband by causing Athamas, in fit of madness, to kill his own son Learchus. A fearful Ino snatched up her remaining son Melicertes, and with the child in her arms, flung herself from a cliff into the sea below. According to the poet Ovid, it was Aphrodite who pitied Ino and asked Poseidon to save mother and child by making them immortal. For the mythographer Hyginus, it was Dionysus who saved her, moved by the plight of the woman who had raised him.

In the course of her life as a mortal, Ino was central to several other well-known tales. Along with her sisters, she was responsible for the gruesome dismemberment of Pentheus, her sister Agave's son. Pentheus had become regent of Thebes and, when Dionysus (also called Bacchus) arrived there in order to introduce the Bacchic rites and their benefits to the populace, Pentheus resisted. Pentheus's death at the hands of his own mother and her sisters while all were in a Bacchic frenzy was his punishment. Ino was also involved in the saga of the hero Jason's quest for the Golden Fleece, although more indirectly. King Athamas had, as it happened, been married previously (or was married simultaneously) to Nephele ("Cloud"). In the knowledge that Nephele's children and not her own were to inherit the Boeotian throne, Ino contrived a plot whereby the kingdom's store of grain seed was spoiled—by some accounts, by burning—so that, when sown, it would not sprout. When the region's crops inevitably failed, Athamas consulted the Oracle of Delphi regarding a remedy, but Ino persuaded the messengers that had been sent on this errand to bring back a false response: Nephele's children, Phrixus and Helle, must be sacrificed. Although unwillingly, Athamas was prepared to do this, but Nephele was able to save her children by placing them on the back of a winged and golden-fleeced ram that would carry them far from the kingdom. Only Phrixus survived the journey, arriving safely at Colchis on the shores of the Black Sea. The Colchians welcomed him, and the region's king, Aeetes, gave him one of his daughters in marriage. The golden ram, meanwhile, was sacrificed by way of thanksgiving, and its hallowed fleece was guarded by a sleepless dragon. It was this fleece that the hero Jason would be sent to fetch, a task that he accomplished with the help of the sorceress Medea. As for Ino, the poet Nonnus recounts that it was in vengeance for her evil plot against Nephele's children that Athamas set upon her and her children, killing one of them and causing Ino to leap into the sea with the other.

(*See also* Aeetes, Agave, Aphrodite, Athamas, Autonoe, Boeotia, Cadmus, Colchis, Delphi, Dionysus, Harmonia, Helle, Hera, Jason, Leucothea, Medea, Nephele, Odysseus, Pentheus, Phaeacians [the], Phrixus, Poseidon, Semele, Thebes, *and* Zeus.)

IO Io was the daughter of Inachus, god of the river Inachus in Argos, and her mother is sometimes given as one of the Oceanid nymphs. Like so many comely maidens, she caught the attention of Zeus, who pursued her. She fled the god's advances, but he stayed her flight and overpowered her, covering the site of her ravishment with a cloud to conceal his infidelity. Zeus's wife, Hera, however, was not long deceived, suspecting that the god's trickery lay behind the sudden presence of a cloud in an otherwise cloudless sky. At Hera's approach, Zeus transformed Io into a white heifer, but Hera, suspecting the truth, asked that the heifer be given to her, a favor that Zeus, under the circumstances, could not deny her. As the Roman poet Ovid tells it, Hera enlisted the hundred-eyed monster Argus to guard Io at all times. Argus let her graze by the light of day but hobbled her at night. Io's distress at her misfortune was heightened by the fact that neither her sisters nor her father recognized her until, with her hoof, she traced her name in the sand. Finally, Zeus could not bear her suffering any longer and sent Hermes to slay Argus. Still, Hera's persecution of Io continued, for the goddess sent a gadfly after her. In an effort to escape this torment, Io fled from continent to continent and swam the seas. The Ionian Gulf and the Bosphorus "Cow's Passage" (also called Bosphorus "Cow's-Foot"), both of which she crossed, owe their names to her. She eventually made her way to Egypt and the banks of the Nile. In sympathy for her sufferings, the Nile beseeched Zeus to help. Io now resumed her former shape and bore to Zeus a son called Epaphus, who, like his mother (revered now as the Egyptian goddess Isis), became the object of worship in Egypt.

(*See also* Argus, Bosphorus [the], Epaphus, Hera, Hermes, Inachus, Oceanids [the], *and* Zeus.)

IOBATES Iobates was a king of Lycia and father of Stheneboea, wife of Proetus, a king of Argos. It was while the hero Bellerophon was staying at the court of Proetus that Stheneboea conceived a passion for him. When her advances were rebuffed by Bellerophon, she accused him of rape. Proetus accordingly sent Bellerophon to Iobates with a letter instructing the latter to kill him. Iobates dealt with this request by sending Bellerophon to complete an impossible task, slaying the dread Chimaera. When Bellerophon later returned victorious to Iobates's palace, the king offered Bellerophon his other daughter, Philonoe, in marriage.

(*See also* Argos, Bellerophon, Chimaera [the], Lycia, *and* Proetus.)

IOLE Iole was a daughter of King Eurytus of Oechalia. When Eurytus made it known that he would offer his hand in marriage to anyone who could defeat him in a contest of archery, Hercules accepted the challenge and won. But Eurytus did not make good on his promise, and Hercules later returned to Oechalia and took Iole by force, making her his concubine. Iole's presence made Hercules's wife, Deianeira, jealous. Deianeira's subsequent efforts to retain Hercules's affections led to his death.

(*See also* Deianeira, Eurytus, *and* Hercules.)

ION Ion was the eponymous ancestor of the Ionians. Ion was the stepson of the Athenian king Xuthus, according to the playwright Euripides's *Ion*. His mother was Creusa, daughter of Erechtheus, himself one of the legendary kings of Athens. Creusa had been impregnated by the god Apollo and abandoned her newborn son, Ion, at the site of her ravishment, which was a cave. The infant was discovered and brought to the Temple of Apollo at Delphi, where he was raised by priests and joined their number. When Xuthus arrived at Delphi in order to consult the oracle regarding his childlessness, he was told that the first person that he came upon while leaving the precinct would be his son. The first person he saw was Ion, whom he subsequently claimed as kin. While still at Delphi, Creusa attempted to kill Ion, as she had been led to believe that he was Xuthus's son by a concubine, but mutual recognition between mother and son occurred just in time. Ion would become king and have four sons who, in turn, would be the progenitors of the four tribes of Athens.

Ion's half brother was Achaeus, and his paternal uncles were Aeolus and Dorus, all of whom would become the progenitors of the four Greek tribes into which the Hellenes were divided: the Ionians, Achaeans, Aeolians, and Dorians respectively.

(*See also* Aeolus, Apollo, Athens, Creusa, Delphi, Erechtheus, Ionians [the], *and* Xuthus.)

IONIANS, THE
The Ionians were one of the four tribes or groups into which the Greeks divided themselves. The Ionians were said to have been descendants of the Athenian king Ion and to have emigrated from Athens to the territory on the central western coast of Asia Minor that would be called Ionia.

(See Athens, Hellen, Hellenes [the], Ion, *and* Ionia.)

IPHICLES
Iphicles was the twin half brother of Hercules: both he and Hercules were sons of Alcmena, although Hercules's father was Zeus and Iphicles's father was Alcmena's mortal husband, Amphitryon. When Hera sent serpents to kill Hercules in his crib, Iphicles reputedly was terrified, but Hercules, demonstrating bravery and brawn even as a baby, strangled the serpents, thus saving both himself and his brother. Iphicles would later participate in the hunt for the Calydonian Boar and join Hercules in the latter's attack on Troy and the city's king Laomedon. According to the mythographer Apollodorus, Iphicles later joined Hercules in a campaign against Sparta and was killed in that conflict.

(*See also* Alcmena, Amphitryon, Calydon, Hera, Hercules, Laomedon, Sparta, Troy, *and* Zeus.)

IPHIGENEIA
Iphigeneia, whose name means "born for violence," was a daughter of King Agamemnon of Mycenae and his wife Clytemnestra. Her siblings were Orestes, Electra, and Chrysothemis. When the Greeks had assem-

bled at Aulis to sail for Troy in pursuit of the beautiful Helen, they were unable to do so, since the winds were unfavorable. This condition persisted, and the men began to grow weary and starve. When the seer Calchas revealed the cause for the Greeks' suffering, Agamemnon, the Greeks' commander-in-chief, was put in a terrible spot: the cause for the adverse winds was the goddess Artemis, who was angry over Agamemnon's accidental killing of a deer sacred to her, and the only remedy was the sacrifice to Artemis of Iphigeneia. Agamemnon put the interests of the Greeks above those of his family and sent for Iphigeneia, making it falsely known to her and to his wife, Clytemnestra, that Iphigeneia would wed the young Achilles at Aulis. According to the tragedian Aeschylus, Agamemnon sacrificed his daughter although she begged for her life; in Euripides's *Iphigeneia in Tauris*, however, she was rescued at the last minute by Artemis, who substituted a deer for Iphigeneia on the sacrificial altar. The goddess then transported Iphigeneia to the barbarian land of Tauris on the northern coast of the Black Sea. There Iphigeneia became Artemis's priestess, her particular task being to ritually prepare foreigners for human sacrifice at the hands of the Taurians. Later, Iphigeneia's brother Orestes, accompanied by his friend Pylades, appeared at Tauris, seeking a particularly sacred ancient statue of Artemis at Apollo's command. Iphigeneia assisted Orestes in securing the statue and successfully loading it onto a vessel bound for Greece. The goddess Athena appeared and instructed Orestes to take the statue to Halae in Attica and to establish a temple to Artemis there; Iphigeneia, for her part, was to be taken to Brauron, where she would serve as a priestess of Artemis for the rest of her days.

(*See also* Achilles, Agamemnon, Artemis, Athena, Attica, Aulis, Calchas, Clytemnestra, Electra [heroine], Mycenae, Orestes, Pylades, *and* Troy.)

IPHIS Iphis was a young man of humble origins. His increasingly desperate overtures to the princess Anaxarete were repeatedly rejected by her, as a consequence of which he hanged himself at her door. When Anaxarete leaned out her window to watch his funeral procession, the gods who had heeded his mother's prayer for vengeance turned her to stone.

(*See also* Anaxarete.)

ISMENE Ismene was one of the children of Oedipus and Jocasta. Her siblings were Antigone, Polyneices, and Eteocles. She is best known for her role in the playwright Sophocles's tragedy *Antigone*, in which she refuses to join Antigone in resistance to the Theban regent Creon's edict forbidding burial of their brother Polyneices. Ismene's argument is that that the sisters are merely weak women. She is the polar opposite of Antigone, who is brave and stubborn in the extreme, willing to risk her life for what she believes to be right in the eyes of the gods.

(*See also* Antigone, Creon, Eteocles, Jocasta, Oedipus, Polyneices, *and* Thebes.)

IULUS In Virgil's epic the *Aeneid*, Iulus was the son of the Trojan hero Aeneas and his first wife, Creusa. Iulus was also called Ascanius and, in a Trojan context, Ilus. The name Iulus marked him as founder of Rome's Julian family, which included Julius Caesar and the Julian line of emperors.

(*See also* Aeneas, Ascanius, Creusa, Rome, *and* Troy.)

IXION Ixion was known, among other things, as the first murderer or, alternatively, the first to murder a blood relative, for this reason becoming one of those individuals who, after their death, were subject to eternal punishment in the Underworld for their sins. Ixion was said to be either the son of Antion or of the violent Phlegyas, both of whom were kings of the Lapiths, a people who lived in Thessaly and would famously battle the Centaurs. As for the details of Ixion's sins, he became betrothed to Dia, daughter of a certain Eioneus, promising but failing to deliver a generous bride-price. When Eioneus then seized Ixion's prized mares as collateral, the latter agreed to pay his father-in-law in full. Instead of making payment, however, Ixion laid a trap: a fiery pit in which Eioneus perished. According to historian Diodorus Siculus, no person dared to purify Ixion of his blood guilt, but, eventually, Zeus himself did so, going so far as to invite Ixion to Mount Olympus. While enjoying the hospitality of the gods, Ixion conceived a lust for Hera, on whom he made unwanted advances. When Hera made this known to Zeus, the god fashioned a replica of Hera from a cloud to ascertain the truth of his wife's claim. Sure enough, Ixion came to sleep with the counterfeit Hera, a cloud-woman called Nephele, and impregnated her with Centaurus, ancestor of the Centaurs. For this crime Zeus punished Ixion by fastening him to a flaming wheel that, bearing Ixion, would spin eternally in the Underworld.

(*See also* Centaurs [the], Hera, Lapiths [the], Nephele [goddess], Olympus [Mount], Underworld [the], *and* Zeus.)

JASON The hero Jason's father was Aeson, who, as son of the Thessalian king Cretheus, should have become the king of Iolcos. Aeson's half-brother Pelias, however, seized the throne. In fear for Jason, his newborn son, Aeson made it known that the infant was dead and, in secret, brought him to the Centaur Chiron to be raised. When Jason was of age, he set out to claim the throne of Iolcos. On his way he came to a raging river, where he found an old woman who wished to cross but lacked the strength. This woman, unbeknownst to Jason, was the goddess

Hera in disguise, and she rewarded him by becoming his protector. As Jason was carrying her across the river on his shoulders, he lost a sandal in its currents. As it happened, Pelias had been warned by a prophecy that he was destined to lose his kingdom to a stranger who would one day appear wearing just one sandal. Upon laying eyes on the one-sandaled stranger, Pelias was justifiably concerned. Hoping to dispose of the youth by a means other than murder, Pelias sent Jason to fetch the Golden Fleece that was kept in a grove sacred to the god Ares in the barbarian land of Colchis. Pelias's expectation was that Jason could not survive the journey to this distant land even if he managed to lay hands on the Fleece. Jason assembled a crew of the bravest men that Greece had to offer and with them, he set sail on the ship *Argo*, built specially for this voyage; it was after this vessel that Jason and his men were called the Argonauts ("sailors on the *Argo*"). On their way to Colchis, Jason and his Argonauts encountered the Lemnian Women, the Harpies, and the Clashing Rocks (Symplegades), surviving all the challenges these posed and other dangers, too. In Colchis, the region's king Aeetes, being reluctant to release the Fleece, challenged Jason to complete a series of tasks sure to get the best of the young newcomer. However, with the assistance of Aeetes's daughter Medea, a sorceress and priestess of Hecate, Jason completed the tasks: yoking fire breathing oxen, plowing a field and sowing it with dragon's teeth, and then killing the armed warriors who sprang from the sown seed. Jason then seized the Fleece, again with the assistance of Medea, who lulled to sleep the dragon guarding it. Medea in tow, Jason returned to Greece, along the way encountering the Phaeacians, Scylla and Charybdis, and the giant Talus. In Thessaly, Medea engineered the death of Pelias, and thereafter, she and Jason fled to Corinth, where Jason would later seek the hand of the regent's daughter with tragic results: the death of his children, the death of his new bride-to-be, and the death of Creon, king of Corinth. Medea predicted in Euripides's tragedy *Medea* that Jason would die a broken man after being struck by the ship *Argo*'s rotting timber.

(*See also* Aeetes, Aeson, Ares, Argonauts [the], Centaurs [the], Charybdis, Chiron, Colchis, Corinth, Creon, Harpies [the], Hecate, Hera, Iolcos, Lemnian Women [the], Medea, Pelias, Phaeacians [the], Scylla, Symplegades [the], Talus, *and* Thessaly.)

JOCASTA
Jocasta was the daughter of Menoeceus, a Theban noble, and the sister of Creon, who would serve repeatedly as regent of Thebes. Jocasta had been married to the Theban king Laius, with whom she became mother to Oedipus. Since Laius had received a prophecy stating that his son by Jocasta was destined to kill him, their baby, Oedipus, was left to die on the slopes of Mount Cithaeron. Oedipus was soon found, however, and brought to Corinth, where he was adopted by that city's king. After Laius was killed by Oedipus, who was

ignorant of his victim's identity, Oedipus won the throne of Thebes by virtue of solving the Sphinx's riddle. Oedipus thus became the king of Thebes and took Jocasta, his mother, as bride. Importantly, neither Oedipus nor Jocasta was aware of Oedipus's true identity. Jocasta bore Oedipus four children: Eteocles, Polyneices, Antigone, and Ismene. When Jocasta learned the horrible truth of Laius's murder at the hands of her son and of her own incest, she hanged herself.

(*See also* Antigone, Cithaeron [Mount], Corinth, Creon, Eteocles, Ismene, Jocasta, Laius, Oedipus, Polyneices, Sphinx of Thebes [the], *and* Thebes.)

LABDACUS
Labdacus was the father of Laius and grandfather of Oedipus. Labdacus himself was the son of Polydorus, the only son of Harmonia and Cadmus, the founder of Thebes. Since Labdacus was too young to rule when Polydorus died, Lycus, his great-uncle, ruled Thebes in his place. When Labdacus did become king, his rule was short-lived, as he lost his life in a boundary dispute with the Athenians. Lycus now again became regent until being killed (or being expelled from the city) by Zethus and Amphion.

(*See also* Amphion, Athens, Cadmus, Harmonia, Laius, Lycus, Oedipus, Polydorus, Thebes, *and* Zethus.)

LAERTES
Laertes was a king of Ithaca and, with Anticleia, the father of Odysseus. In Homer's *Odyssey*, Laertes, too old to be serving as regent, was living on a farm far outside the city when Odysseus returned to Ithaca after a twenty-year absence, and it was on this farm that he and his son were reunited. After this reunion, the goddess Athena breathed strength into Laertes so that he could fight side-by-side with his son in the battle that ensued between Odysseus and the kinsmen of Penelope's slain suitors.

(*See also* Athena, Ithaca, Odysseus, *and* Penelope.)

LAIUS
Laius was the son of Labdacus, grandson of Polydorus, and great-grandson of Cadmus, all of them kings of Thebes. As Laius was too young to assume the throne upon the death of his father, Labdacus, he was placed under the guardianship of Lycus, who ruled Thebes in his place. When Lycus was killed by Zethus and Amphion for mistreating their mother, Antiope, Laius was expelled from the city but took refuge at the court of Pelops, king of Pisa. While teaching Pelops's son Chrysippus how to drive a chariot, Laius became enamored of him and made off with him to Thebes. There Laius became king, and it was ostensibly in retribution for kidnapping Chrysippus that his real troubles began. When he married Jocasta and bore a son, Oedipus, he exposed the child since it had been prophesied that his own son would kill him. Yet Oedipus was saved, reared in

Corinth, and later killed Laius at a crossroads without knowing his identity. Oedipus consequently became king of Thebes and married his mother, Jocasta, with whom he had four children: Eteocles, Polyneices, Antigone, and Ismene.

(*See also* Amphion, Antigone, Antiope, Cadmus, Corinth, Eteocles, Ismene, Jocasta, Labdacus, Lycus, Oedipus, Pelops, Polyneices, Thebes, *and* Zethus.)

LAOCOON According to the Roman poet Virgil, Laocoon was a priest of Neptune and the only one among the Trojans to suspect that the Trojan Horse was not an offering to the goddess Minerva, as the treacherous Greek Sinon led the Trojans to believe, but rather was a war engine to be used to breach the walls of Troy, or else contained Greek warriors in its belly. He hurled his spear at the horse's belly, but there was no telltale sound. After voicing his concerns, Laocoon proceeded to prepare a sacrifice for Poseidon, but two enormous serpents appeared from the sea and wound themselves around Laocoon's two sons, killing them and their father as well. Their terrible task complete, the serpents then took refuge in Minerva's temple. The horrified Trojans wrongly interpreted the gruesome death of Laocoon and his sons as an omen signifying that Laocoon had been wrong and that the horse was indeed a gift for Minerva. They accordingly proceeded to pull it inside the Trojan citadel.

(*See also* Minerva, Neptune, Sinon, *and* Troy.)

LAOMEDON Laomedon was the son of Ilus, a king of Troy, and the father, among others, of Priam, king of Troy at the time of the Trojan War; Tithonus, beloved of the goddess Eos; Hesione; and, by some accounts, Ganymede, who became Zeus's cup-bearer. Laomedon is primarily known for having cheated the gods Apollo and Poseidon out of the wages he owed them when, either as punishment on Zeus's part for an attempted revolt or, as the mythographer Apollodorus writes, because they wished to see Laomedon's reputed wickedness firsthand, they worked for him for one year. By most accounts, both gods were employed to build the walls of Troy. As punishment for Laomedon's offense, Apollo sent a pestilence and Poseidon a man-eating sea monster to plague the region. Laomedon discovered from an oracle that the remedy for this was to sacrifice his daughter, Hesione, to the sea monster. When Hercules, who was passing by, agreed to save Hesione in exchange for Laomedon's immortal horses—a gift to Laomedon from Zeus as compensation for the loss of Ganymede—Laomedon again refused to make good on his promise. Hercules later returned to attack Troy, kill Laomedon, and take Hesione. At this point Priam became king of Troy.

(*See also* Apollo, Eos, Ganymede, Hercules, Hesione, Ilus, Poseidon, Priam, Tithonus, Troy, *and* Zeus.)

LAPITHS, THE The Lapiths were a legendary tribe of northern Thessaly. They are variously described as being descended from Lapithus, a son of Apollo and a daughter of Peneus, or from Ixion. If descended from Ixion, they would be half brothers of the Centaurs, with whom they famously battled at the wedding of the Lapith king Pirithous. At this wedding, the Centaurs became drunk and attempted to ravage the Lapith women. This violent act precipitated a conflict that ended in the Centaurs' being driven from Thessaly. The Athenians would view the battle between the Lapiths and Centaurs as emblematic of historical battle between the Greeks and Persians in the Persian Wars.

(*See also* Apollo, Athens, Centaurs [the], Ixion, Lapiths [the], Peneus [god], Pirithous, *and* Thessaly.)

LATINS, THE The Latins were an Italian people who lived in the region of Latium. In Virgil's *Aeneid*, their king is Latinus, and the Latin people become united with the immigrant Trojans, led by Aeneas, to become the Romans' ancestors.

(*See also* Aeneas, Latinus, Latium, Rome, *and* Troy.)

LATINUS Latinus was king of the Latin peoples of Latium in west-central Italy. According to the Roman poet Virgil, he was the son of the rustic god Faunus and a nymph, and he was the great-grandson of Saturn. According to variant traditions, he was known also as a son of Odysseus and the sorceress Circe, or of Odysseus's son, Telemachus, and Circe, however. In Virgil's *Aeneid*, his capital is Laurentum, a city taking its name from a sacred laurel tree that Latinus had dedicated to Apollo when he built the citadel. It was to this tree that a swarm of bees flew, indicating that the princess Lavinia should marry a man from overseas. That man would be Aeneas, but the match was one that Latinus's queen, Amata, vehemently opposed. Although Latinus wished for peace with Aeneas and the Trojans who appeared on his shore, the people of Laurentum would be swept into a conflict that he could not prevent. When Lavinia did, eventually, marry Aeneas, Latinus became an ancestor of the future Romans and lent his name to their language, Latin.

(*See also* Aeneas, Amata, Apollo, Circe, Faunus, Latium, Lavinia, Odysseus, Rome, Saturn, *and* Telemachus.)

LAUSUS Lausus was the son of the Etruscan king Mezentius. In the course of the war in Italy between the newly arrived Trojans and the Latins, Mezentius, an ally of the Latins, was gravely wounded by the Trojan hero Aeneas. Lausus bravely and nobly sacrificed himself to ensure his father's safety, protecting him with his shield from further injury. With Mezentius safely off the battlefield, Lausus returned to the fray and was himself slain by Aeneas, who, deeply moved by Lausus's filial devotion, refrained from stripping his armor as a prize. Lausus's death prompted a grief-stricken Mezentius to return to battle where he, too, fell by Aeneas's sword.

(*See also* Aeneas, Etruria, Latins [the], Mezentius, *and* Troy.)

LAVINIA Lavinia was the daughter of Latinus, king of Latium, and his wife, Amata. Prior to the arrival of Aeneas and his cohort of Trojan refugees in Italy, she had many suitors, foremost among them Turnus, king of the Rutulians. It was Turnus whom Lavinia's mother, Amata, favored, but Latinus had received a prophecy from the oracle of his father, Faunus, that would prevent that union: on the basis of a sequence of omens, namely the sudden appearance of a swarm of bees that settled in Laurentum's sacred laurel and Lavinia's hair bursting into flames, Faunus prophesied that strangers would come from abroad who, united with Latinus's family, would give him descendants of great fame. Lavinia herself, Faunus added, would gain glory but bring war upon her people. Soon thereafter war did, indeed, break out between the Trojans and the Latins. When the Trojans prevailed, Aeneas made peace with the Latins, wed Lavinia, and founded the city of Lavinium, which was named after his new bride.

(*See also* Aeneas, Amata, Faunus, Latins [the], Latinus, Latium, Rutulians [the], Troy, *and* Turnus.)

LEANDER Leander was a youth who lived in Abydus, a town on the Asiatic shores of the Hellespont. He was in love with a maiden by the name of Hero, who lived in Sestos, on the Hellespont's opposite shore. However, their love was forbidden, since Hero was a priestess of Aphrodite, her service to the goddess demanding chastity. For this reason, Leander swam the strait's treacherous waters under the cover of night, with only light from Hero's tower to guide him. But the lovers were discovered by the goddess, and Leander consequently drowned while swimming to meet his beloved. Hero, in turn, threw herself into the Hellespont's currents in anguish over Leander's death.

(*See also* Abydus, Aphrodite, Hellespont [the], *and* Hero.)

LEDA Leda was the daughter of Thestius, king of Aetolia, and his wife, Eurythemis, and her sisters were Althea, mother of the Calydonian hero Meleager, and Hypermnestra, mother of the seer Amphiaraus. Leda married the Spartan king Tyndareus, and with him became mother to Clytemnestra, future queen of Mycenae, and the twins Castor and Pollux. She was impregnated by Zeus in the guise of a swan, her child by Zeus being the lovely Helen. By some accounts Castor and Pollux (or only Pollux) were also Zeus's children.

(*See also* Althea, Amphiaraus, Calydon, Castor, Helen, Hypermnestra, Meleager, Mycenae, Pollux, Sparta, Thestius, Tyndareus, *and* Zeus.)

LEMNIAN WOMEN, THE

The story of the island of Lemnos's female inhabitants is vividly told by the Greek poet Apollonius of Rhodes in his account of the hero Jason's quest for the Golden Fleece. These women, as it happened, had killed every male inhabitant of the island (but one) in the year prior to Jason's arrival. The women committed this mass murder in anger that their husbands had forsaken them for their Thracian concubines. This had occurred because the Lemnian women had neglected the rites of the goddess Aphrodite, and as punishment, the goddess had made them distasteful to their husbands. When Jason and his Argonauts appeared, the women's queen, Hypsipyle, argued persuasively that the women should welcome these newcomers so as to rebuild their populace and to help them defend themselves against marauding neighbors. The Argonauts enjoyed the women's hospitality but did not stay. The Lemnian women would later discover that Hypsipyle had spared her father, Thoas, the island's former king, and for this both killed Thoas and sold Hypsipyle into slavery.

(*See also* Aphrodite, Argonauts [the], Hypsipyle, Jason, Thoas, *and* Thrace.)

LEUCIPPUS

Leucippus was a grandson of Perseus. He was the father of Arsinoe, who was sometimes named as mother of the healing god Asclepius, as well as of Phoebe and Hilaira, whose abduction by Castor and Pollux (the Dioscuri) is referred to as the "rape of the Leucippides" ("rape of the daughters of Leucippus").

(*See also* Arsinoe, Asclepius, Castor, Dioscuri [the], Perseus, *and* Pollux.)

LINUS

The famed musician Linus may have originated as personification of the ritual cry of lamentation *ailinon*, and over time, a complicated mythology developed around him. He was called the son of Apollo and one of the Muses, either Urania, Calliope, Terpsichore, or Euterpe, which parentage would make him divine. However, his father was also identified as Amphimarus, a son of Poseidon, or Oeagrus, a Thracian king, and his mother as Psamathe, daughter of Crotopus of Argos, or Aethusa, a daughter of Poseidon.

A version of his story preserved by the travel writer Pausanias serves to explain Linus's connection with lamentation: Linus's mother, Psamathe, had exposed him as an infant in order to avoid her father's anger over her pregnancy by Apollo. While in the wilds, Linus was killed by Crotopus's hunting dogs, for which act Apollo avenged himself upon Argos by causing an outbreak of plague. As a remedy for the plague, the women of Argos instituted a ritualized lament for Linus. According other traditions, Linus was killed by the god Apollo in jealousy over his skill as a musician or, alternatively, he became the lyre teacher of Hercules, who killed him in a fit of rage over being reprimanded. The legendary bards Orpheus and Thamyris were also named as pupils of Linus.

(*See also* Apollo, Argos, Calliope, Euterpe, Hercules, Muses [the], Orpheus, Poseidon, Terpsichore, Thamyris, Thrace, *and* Urania.)

LOTUS EATERS, THE

In the course of their ten-year journey home from Troy, Odysseus and his men came to the mythical land of the Lotus Eaters. Odysseus sent three of his men as scouts to determine what sort of people the inhabitants of this land might be, and they were hospitably received by the Lotus Eaters, who offered them the honey-sweet fruit of the lotus to eat. While kind of them, this act of hospitality was in actual fact a threat, as the lotus made those who ate of it wish to stay with the Lotus Eaters, forgetful of their friends, family, and homecoming. Odysseus himself had to go and forcibly tear his men away. The Greeks then set sail immediately, lest any others be tempted by this seductive fruit.

As was the case with all the places that Odysseus visited, efforts were made even in antiquity to identify the land of the Lotus Eaters. While there was no consensus, the Greek historian Herodotus and others assert that the Lotus Eaters lived on the Libyan coast. An effort was also made to identify the lotus, with the most plausible arguments being made for fruit of the jujube, *Ziziphus lotus*.

(*See also* Odysseus *and* Troy.)

LYCAON

Lycaon was an infamous king of Arcadia. He was a son of Pelasgus, namesake of the legendary aboriginal people of Greece, the Pelasgians. His mother was Meliboea, a daughter of Oceanus, or the mountain nymph Cyllene. By numerous wives, Lycaon was father to fifty sons and two daughters, Dia and Callisto, who was pursued by Jupiter and transformed into a bear. Lycaon's own metamorphosis is dramatically narrated by the Roman poet Ovid. Through his contempt for the gods and wickedness, Lycaon became emblematic of humanity's moral decline. Jupiter came to know Lycaon's depravity firsthand. Having heard how badly humans were behaving, Zeus was determined to see the state of affairs for himself. The god disguised himself as a mortal and came to the palace of Lycaon in Arcadia. When he made it known that a god had arrived, all present offered prayer except Lycaon, who mocked the others for their piety.

In fact, Lycaon planned to kill his divine guest in his sleep in order to determine whether or not he was actually an immortal and, adding worse to bad, he killed one of his hostages, serving the still-warm flesh to Jupiter. At this outrage, the god struck the palace with lightning and turned Lycaon into the beast he already was: a bloodthirsty wolf. On the basis of his encounter with Lycaon, Jupiter later decided to eliminate all humans with a great flood, which Deucalion and Pyrrha would miraculously survive.

(*See also* Arcadia, Callisto, Deucalion, Jupiter, Oceanus [god], Pelasgus, *and* Pyrrha.)

LYCOMEDES
Lycomedes was a king of the Dolopes on the island of Scyros. At the request of the sea goddess Thetis, who wished to prevent her young son Achilles from being taken to fight and die at Troy, Lycomedes hid him among his daughters. One of Lycomedes's daughters, Deidamia, would become pregnant by Achilles and give birth to a son, Neoptolemus. Achilles, for his part, was discovered on Scyros by Odysseus, who tricked him into revealing himself. When the Athenian king Theseus came to Scyros, he was less hospitably treated: according to the biographer Plutarch, Lycomedes became concerned that Theseus might take the kingdom from him and hurled him from a cliff to his death.

(*See also* Achilles, Deidamia, Neoptolemus, Odysseus, Scyros, Theseus, *and* Thetis.)

LYCURGUS
Lycurgus, a son of Dryas (or the god Ares) and king of the Edonians in Thrace, became the epitome of sacrilegious disdain for the gods. According to Homer, when the god Dionysus and his nursemaids arrived in Thrace, Lycurgus set upon them, attempting to drive them away; the god's nurses scattered when Lycurgus struck them with an ox-goad, and a terrified Dionysus took refuge with the goddess Thetis in the sea. For this affront, the gods struck Lycurgus blind. The story is told differently by the mythographer Apollodorus: Dionysus came to Thrace accompanied by female followers, the Bacchantes. The latter, together with the Satyrs who formed part of Dionysus's entourage, were imprisoned by Lycurgus. The god released his imprisoned followers and struck Lycurgus with madness. In his altered mental state, Lycurgus killed his own son, chopping him to bits, believing him to be a grapevine. Now the land of Thrace suffered from infertility, and an oracle declared that Lycurgus should be put to death. The Edonians accordingly shackled their king and took him to Mount Pangaeus, where he was killed by the horses that resided here.

The evil Lycurgus is to be distinguished from several other, less well known legendary personages of the same name, which included the king of Nemea to whom the Lemnian queen Hypsipyle was sold, and the Arcadian king, whose son Ancaeus joined the expedition of Jason and the Argonauts.

(*See also* Ancaeus, Arcadia, Ares, Argonauts [the], Bacchantes [the], Dionysus, Hypsipyle, Jason, Lemnos, Satyrs [the], Thetis, *and* Thrace.)

LYCUS

There were a number of characters by the name of Lycus in Classical mythology, but the most dramatic story centers on Lycus of Boeotia. Lycus's brother Nycteus had been appointed regent of Thebes until the legitimate king, Labdacus, came of age. When Nycteus's daughter Antiope was impregnated by Zeus, she ran away, taking refuge with the king of Sicyon. At his brother's request, Lycus, who now had become king, retrieved and imprisoned her. Meanwhile, Antiope's newborn sons, Zethus and Amphion, were exposed in the wilds of Mount Cithaeron in the expectation that they would perish there. Lycus's wife, Dirce, proceeded to treat Antiope terribly, and when Antiope later was able to escape, both Lycus and Dirce paid for their misdeeds with their lives.

(*See also* Antiope, Boeotia, Cithaeron [Mount], Dirce, Labdacus, Thebes, *and* Zethus.)

LYNCEUS

Lynceus was one of the fifty sons of Aegyptus and grandson of the Egyptian king Belus. Lynceus alone was spared by his wife, Hypermnestra, when her father, Danaus, instructed his fifty daughters to kill their husbands, the fifty sons of Aegyptus, on their wedding night. Lynceus later succeeded Danaus on the throne of Argos and with Hypmermnestra became father to Abas, who in turn succeeded him.

(*See also* Abas, Aegyptus, Argos, Belus, *and* Hypermnestra.)

MAENADS, THE

Female celebrants of the god Dionysus were called Bacchantes but also Maenads after the "mania" that they experienced when possessed by the god. This "mania" (from the Greek word *mania* of the same meaning) went hand in hand with the Maenads' ecstasy, Greek *ek-stasis*, "standing outside oneself." Women in ancient Greece had few opportunities to escape their domestic duties, and the worship of Dionysus provided a welcome release. As is vividly portrayed in the tragedian Euripides's play, *The Bacchae*, the god's female worshippers would leave their looms, families, and houses. Having partaken of wine, an embodiment of the god, these women loosened their hair, donned fawnskins, and holding thyrsi (fennel staffs topped with ivy), made for the mountains in order there to dance and commune with nature. A part of their ritual was the tearing apart (*sparagmos*) of small animals and eating them raw (*omophagia*), this being another way of partaking of the god, since Dionysus was a god of all liquid life and life-sustaining fluids, in this case blood.

(*See also* Bacchantes [the] *and* Dionysus.)

MARPESSA Marpessa was a daughter of Evenus and, through her father, a descendant of the god Ares. When the lovely Marpessa was being courted by the god Apollo, Idas, son of Aphareus, carried her off in a winged chariot that he had received from Poseidon. Evenus leaped into his chariot and went in pursuit. Realizing that he could not catch Idas, Evenus slaughtered his horses when he came to the Lycormas River and drowned himself in the river's current. After this occurrence, the river became known as Evenus. As for Marpessa, when she and Idas arrived at Messene, Apollo attempted to seize the girl. A conflict between her suitors ensued, but Zeus put an end to it, stating that Marpessa should choose which of them to wed. Marpessa chose her mortal suitor, Idas, as she feared that as she grew older, the god might abandon her. With Idas, Marpessa bore Cleopatra, who would become the wife of Meleager.

(*See also* Apollo, Ares, Idas, Meleager, *and* Poseidon.)

MEDEA Medea was a daughter of King Aeetes of Colchis and the Oceanid Eidyia. Her paternal grandfather was the sun god Helios, and her aunt was the sorceress Circe. Medea herself was a priestess of the goddess Hecate and skilled in the use of magic herbs, charms, and incantations. While there are many versions of the dramatic events in her life, the best-known are recounted in the poet Apollonius of Rhodes's *Voyage of the Argo* and the tragedian Euripides's play *Medea*. When the hero Jason arrived at Colchis in search of the Golden Fleece, the goddesses Hera and Aphrodite contrived to make Medea fall in love with Jason so that she would help him complete the seemingly impossible tasks that Aeetes made a requirement for releasing the Golden Fleece: yoking a pair of fire-breathing bulls, plowing a field with the bulls, sowing dragon's teeth, and killing the warriors that would spring from those teeth when sown, all in the space of a single day. Medea did help Jason, who promised to marry her as a sign of his gratitude. Medea supplied him with a salve that would protect him against the bulls' flames, and instructed him how to deal with the dragon-teeth warriors, namely by throwing a rock in their midst causing them to turn against each other. These tasks complete, Medea then lulled to sleep the fearsome dragon that guarded the Fleece in Ares's sacred grove and accompanied the Greeks on their journey back to Greece. When pursued by Medea's brother Apsyrtus, Medea contrived a plan whereby to ambush and kill him. Jason and Medea were wed and purified of pollution from murder on the island of the Phaeacians. When, at last, they arrived in Thessaly, Pelias refused to keep his promise to give Jason the throne, and Medea devised his punishment. She cut up an elderly ram and put the pieces into a cauldron from which the ram emerged not only intact but also rejuventated: this, Medea said to Pelias's daughters, she could do for their elderly father. Pelias's daughters consented, but the cauldron into which his body parts were placed contained no magic potion. With Pelias now dead, Jason and Medea fled Iolcos and took refuge in the city of Corinth. There Jason became engaged to the Corinthian king Creon's daughter Glauce. Meanwhile, Medea, whom the Corinthians considered to be a dangerous sorceress, was to be banished. In anger over this slight, Medea caused the death of Creon, Glauce, and her own children. Glauce was given a poisoned headdress and cloak as wedding presents, and when she put these on, her flesh burst into flames and dissolved. As Creon tried to help Glauce, he became stuck to her gown. As for Medea's children, these she killed with her own hands. Medea herself escaped the gruesome scene in the chariot of Helios and married the Athenian king Aegeus. When in Athens, Medea attempted to poison Theseus, Aegeus's son by the princess Aethra, and when this fact was discovered, she was again banished. Now she returned to Colchis with her son by Aegeus, Medus, namesake of the Asian Medes. By some accounts, Medea became the consort of Achilles in the Isles of the Blessed at the end of her life.

(*See also* Achilles, Aeetes, Aegeus, Aethra, Aphrodite, Apsyrtus, Ares, Argonauts [the], Circe, Colchis, Corinth, Creon, Hecate, Helios, Hera, Iolcos, Jason, Oceanids [the], Pelias, Phaeacians [the], Theseus, *and* Thessaly.)

MEGARA

Megara was the daughter of Creon, ruler of Thebes after the death of Oedipus and his sons. Creon offered her as a wife to Hercules by way of rewarding the hero for releasing Thebes from paying tribute to the Boeotians. There were varying accounts of Megara's demise. Megara bore Hercules three (or five) sons. In a fit of madness induced by the goddess Hera, who persecuted Hercules throughout his life, Hercules killed both Megara and his children using his club and bow after completing his Twelve Labors, according to the tragedian Euripides. By contrast, the mythographer Apollodorus writes that Hercules, in a fit of madness, threw his own children and two of his brother Iphicles's into a fire, as a consequence for which he condemned himself to exile. Hercules traveled to Delphi's oracle to ask where he should go live. The response was that he should go to Tiryns and there serve the king Eurystheus for twelve years and perform labors that Eurystheus would impose on him.

Megara was also the name of a city in Greece at the Isthmus of Corinth.

(*See also* Creon, Delphi, Eurystheus, Hera, Hercules, Iphicles, Megara [place], Oedipus, Thebes, *and* Tiryns.)

MELANION

Some authors name Melanion, and not Hippomenes, as the young man who won the hand of the huntress Atalanta by defeating her in a footrace. This he could do only because he had received some golden apples from Aphrodite, which he strategically used to lure Atalanta off course.

(*See also* Aphrodite, Atalanta, *and* Hippomenes.)

MELEAGER

Meleager was a son of Oeneus, king of Calydon, an Aetolian city, and his niece Althea. According to the mythographer Hyginus, upon Meleager's birth, the Fates foretold his destiny: Clotho said that he would be noble, Lachesis said that he would be brave, but Atropos, spotting a log burning on the hearth, said, "He will live only as long as this log keeps burning." Hearing this, his mother hastened to the fire, snatched out the log, and kept it hidden to preserve her son's life. While Meleager did join Jason and the Argonauts on the quest for the Golden Fleece, he is best known for his role in the hunt for the dread Calydonian Boar. It happened that his father, Oeneus, while a pious man, had somehow overlooked the goddess Artemis when making sacrifice to the gods in thanks for the first fruits of harvest. In anger at him, the goddess sent a boar—the so-called Calydonian Boar—to ravage the land and its orchards. All the strongest and bravest men gathered for the hunt, but it was Meleager who killed the boar. According to Homer in the *Iliad*, a battle broke out between the Aetolians and the neighboring Curetes, all of whom had been party to the hunt. The cause for the conflict was the boar's head and hide, which constituted the prizes of the hunt. In the course of this conflict, one of Althea's brothers died, and in anger at her son, Althea called for his death. Then, aggrieved at his mother's curse, Meleager withdrew from the fighting, and the Curetes gained ground. Meleager's wife, Cleopatra, the city's elders, his own father, his mother, his sisters, and his friends begged him to return to the battlefield and offered gifts to entice him, but to no avail. It was only when the Curetes had set fire to the city that his wife was able to prevail on him to help. Later authors, including the Roman poet Ovid and the mythographer Hyginus, provide additional details. It had been the fleet-footed maiden Atalanta who inflicted the boar's first wound, allowing Meleager to complete the task of killing it. In recognition of this fact, Meleager presented Atalanta with the boar's head as a trophy, an action that drew the resentment of his mother's brothers. A fierce battle ensued, in the course of which Meleager killed his mother's brothers. Meleager was said either to have died in the course of the fighting or to have met his untimely end when Althea, in despair over the loss of her brothers, threw the long-hidden, fatal log on the hearth.

(*See also* Althea, Argonauts [the], Artemis, Atalanta, Calydon, Fates [the], Jason, *and* Oeneus.)

MENELAUS Menelaus was a major figure in the saga of the Trojan War. He was the younger brother of Agamemnon, king of Mycenae, the most powerful Greek ruler at the time. As sons of Atreus, Menelaus and Agamemnon were called "Atreidae" ("Sons of Atreus"), and they were great-grandsons of the ill-fated Tantalus. Menelaus was one of the many suitors of the beautiful Helen and prevailed when her father, Tyndareus, allowed her to make her own selection from among them. By virtue of marriage to Helen, Menelaus became Tyndareus's successor to the throne of Sparta. Menelaus's fortunes turned for the worse when the Trojan prince Paris arrived in Sparta. While Menelaus was briefly away in Crete, Paris made off with Helen to Troy. When this occurred, Agamemnon gathered the best of Greece's warriors to lead them in a military effort to retrieve Helen. In Homer's *Iliad*, Menelaus is said to have met Paris in single combat in order to bring the ten-year war to a close, and he would have slain Paris had not the goddess Aphrodite intervened. According to Homer's *Odyssey*, Menelaus lost a number of his ships on the way home at the conclusion of the war but, after a time in Egypt, did eventually return to Sparta with Helen.

(*See also* Agamemnon, Aphrodite, Atreus, Helen, Mycenae, Paris, Sparta, Tantalus, Troy, *and* Tyndareus.)

MENOECEUS There are two significant heroes by the name of Menoeceus in Classical mythology. The first of these was the father of Creon, regent of Thebes after the death of Oedipus and his sons. This Menoeceus, according to the mythographer Hyginus, was descended from the warriors who sprang from the dragon's teeth that Cadmus sowed at Thebes, the so-called Sparti (or Spartoi). By his wife Eurydice, Creon had a son also named Menoeceus. When, in the course of the conflict between Oedipus's sons, Polyneices and Eteocles, and their respective supporters, Thebes was in dire straits, the seer Teiresias proclaimed that the city could be saved only if this younger Menoeceus were sacrificed to Ares; the god, it was said, was still angered over Cadmus's killing of the dragon from whose teeth the Sparti, Thebes's original inhabitants, had sprung. It was Menoeceus specifically who had to die as he was descended from the Sparti on both his mother's and his father's side. Creon attempted to prevent the sacrifice of his son, but Menoeceus sacrificed himself by leaping to his death from the city's walls.

(*See also* Ares, Cadmus, Creon, Eteocles, Eurydice [heroine], Oedipus, Polyneices, Teiresias, *and* Thebes.)

MEROPE There are several characters named Merope who appear in Classical mythology. One Merope (also known as Aero) was a daughter of Oenopion, king of the island of Chios. When the hunter Orion came to the island, he either pursued the hand of Merope in marriage or, in a variant of the story, violated her out of wedlock. In anger at Orion, Oenopion, according to the mythographer Apollodorus, got him drunk, put out his eyes as he slept, and threw him out onto the beach.

Another Merope was the wife of the Messenian king Cresphontes, a descendant of Hercules. After a short reign, Cresphontes was killed in a revolt by Polyphontes, who then married Merope. Cresphontes's son Aepytus, whom Merope had sent away to keep him safe during the revolt, sought to avenge his father's death and was nearly killed by his mother, who did not recognize him when he returned to the kingdom. Mother and son ultimately collaborated in the killing of Polyphontes, and Aepytus became king.

A third Merope, also called Perioboea, was the wife of the Corinthian king Polybus and foster mother of Oedipus.

All three heroines are to be distinguished from the Pleiad nymph Merope who was a daughter of the second-generation Titan god Atlas, wife of Sisyphus, and mother of Glaucus, father of the hero Bellerophon.

(*See also* Aepytus, Atlas, Bellerophon, Chios, Corinth, Glaucus, Merope [nymph], Oedipus, Orion, Pleiades [the], Polybus, Sisyphus, *and* Titans [the].)

MEZENTIUS

According to Virgil in the *Aeneid*, Mezentius was an Etruscan king of extraordinary cruelty, his atrocities having included chaining living men face-to-face with corpses, ensuring a gruesome death for those being tortured in this way. His subjects rose up in rebellion against him, set fire to the palace, and killed his guards. Mezentius escaped with his life and took refuge with Turnus and the Rutulians, a Latin people. When Turnus and other Latin tribes later engaged in armed conflict with Aeneas and his band of Trojans, the godless Mezentius and his son Lausus faced Aeneas in battle. A wounded Mezentius was conveyed to safety by Lausus, who later fell victim to Aeneas's sword. With his son dead, a grief-stricken Mezentius embraced the idea of engaging again with Aeneas and fought bravely until he also met his end at Aeneas's hands.

(*See also* Aeneas, Etruria, Lausus, Latins [the], Rutulians [the], Troy, *and* Turnus.)

MIDAS

Midas was a historical king of Phrygia around whom a host of legends arose. He was a son of Gordius, whom some sources call the founder of the city of Gordium. Other sources cite Midas as Gordium's founder and claim that Midas named the city after his father. The Roman poet Ovid writes that when old Silenus became separated from Dionysus and his entourage of Satyrs and Maenads, Midas entertained him hospitably for ten days and then restored him to the god. In gratitude, Dionysus granted Midas whatever he desired, and what he wished was that everything he touched would turn to gold. The foolishness of this request soon became apparent, as food and drink, too, became solid gold. When Midas asked the god for forgiveness, this was readily granted, and he was instructed to wash his hands in the river Pactolus, whose streams thereafter turned to gold all the soil that they contacted. Later, when the god Pan, playing his reed pipe, challenged Apollo, with his lyre, to a music contest, Midas proclaimed Pan to be the winner. Exclaiming that Midas could not possibly have human ears, an angry Apollo punished Midas by giving him donkey's ears. Only Midas's barber knew his secret, for Midas now kept his head covered. In the passage of time, however, the barber could no longer contain his secret and, digging a hole in the ground, told it to the hollowed earth. In this way having unburdened himself of keeping the secret, the barber then closed up the hole. In spite of this precaution, Midas's secret emerged when reeds growing from this spot whispered it as they rustled in the wind.

(*See also* Apollo, Dionysus, Gordius, Maenads [the], Pactolus River [the], Pan, Phrygia, Satyrs [the], *and* Silenus.)

MINOS

Minos was a legendary king of Crete whose sea power became wide-ranging. He ruled from a palace at Cnossus, and it was after him that the Bronze Age civilization (circa 3000–1150 BCE) of the island was called Minoan. Minos was a son of Zeus and Europa, the Phoenician princess whom Zeus abducted to Crete, and his siblings were variously known as Rhadamanthus, Aeacus, and Sarpedon. Minos succeeded Europa's mortal husband, Asterius, to the throne of Crete, and, when his right to rule was questioned, he asserted that it had been divinely sanctioned. According to the mythographer Apollodorus, Minos proved his proximity to the divine by stating that the god Poseidon would grant him any request he might make. What he asked for was a bull to be sent to him from the sea; this bull, he said, would subsequently be sacrificed to the god. The bull did indeed appear, but Minos, finding it too handsome to part with, sacrificed another in its stead. For this Poseidon punished Minos by causing the king's wife, Pasiphae, to develop a passion for the bull. So relentless was her desire that she enlisted the aid of the craftsman Daedalus, then resident on the island, to craft a device—a hollow wooden cow—that she could use to approach the bull and satisfy her desire. Pasiphae became pregnant by the bull and bore the monstrous Minotaur ("Bull of Minos"), half human and half bull. Minos, wishing to avoid the pollution that bloodshed would bring, did not kill the monster but instead instructed Daedalus to construct a maze to house the creature. Minos fed the Minotaur humans, specifically the seven youths and seven maidens that he had required the Athenians to send every nine years in compensation for their killing of his son, Androgeus. The third group of Athenian victims included Theseus, the king of Athens's son, who had undertaken to slay the Minotaur. This Theseus did with the help of Minos's daughter Ariadne, who had fallen in love with him but whom Theseus soon abandoned. Presumably suspecting that Daedalus had been in some way complicit in Theseus's victory, Minos imprisoned Daedalus, but the latter escaped on wings made of feathers and wax, though he lost his young son Icarus on their airborne route. Minos pursued Daedalus to Sicily, where he was killed in battle or, by some accounts, was murdered by the daughters of the Sicilian king.

After his death, Minos, like his brother Rhadamanthus, was said to have become a judge of the dead in the Underworld.

(*See also* Aeacus, Androgeus, Ariadne, Athena, Athens, Cnossus, Crete, Daedalus, Europa, Icarus, Minotaur [the], Pasiphae, Poseidon, Rhadamanthus, Sarpedon, Theseus, Underworld [the], *and* Zeus.)

MINYANS, THE

The Minyans were a people or tribe said to have been descended from Minyas, a relatively shadowy figure who was variously described as a son of Zeus, Poseidon, or Ares and as a grandson of Aeolus. The Minyans were based in northern Boeotia, the center of their power being the city of Orchomenos, and were known for their great wealth. As a reward for defeating the hostile Minyans, who had been exacting tribute from Thebes, that city's regent Creon offered Hercules his daughter Megara in marriage.

The band of men who accompanied the hero Jason on his quest for the Golden Fleece, the so-called Argonauts, were called Minyans, though it would appear that only Jason himself was, strictly speaking, a descendant of Minyas.

(*See also* Aeolus [hero], Ares, Argonauts [the], Boeotia, Creon, Hercules, Jason, Megara [heroine], Poseidon, Thebes, *and* Zeus.)

MYRMIDONS, THE

The Myrmidons, "Ant People," were said to have been ants who, at the request of Aeacus, king of Aegina, were transformed into people. Aeacus made this request of his father, Zeus, when the island's populace had been decimated by a plague. The Myrmidons emigrated to Thessaly, and in the Trojan War, the Myrmidon warriors were led by Achilles.

(*See also* Achilles, Aegina [island], Thessaly, Troy, *and* Zeus.)

MYRRHA

Myrrha, who is called Smyrna in some sources, was the daughter of the Cinyras, king of Cyprus. She refused to marry any of the many young men who pursued her, falling prey, instead, to a forbidden love, love of her own father. By some accounts, this occurred as a result of some affront to Aphrodite on her part or on the part of her mother. Myrrha attempted suicide, but was saved by her nurse, who contrived a plan whereby Myrrha could spend the night with her father under cover of night and unbeknownst to him. The queen, as it happened, was away celebrating a festival of Hera, and Myrrha came to Cinyras on several nights. When Cinyras discovered the horrible truth of what has transpired, he lunged at a pregnant Myrrha with his sword. She fled and, when ready to give birth, asked the gods to help her in some way, as she was fit to be among neither the living nor the dead. She then became the precious tree that still bears her name, and her flowing tears are myrrh's fragrant resin. When, after nine months, the tree's bark parted, it was the baby Adonis who emerged.

(See also Adonis, Aphrodite, Cinyras, Hera, and Cyprus.)

MYRTILUS Myrtilus was a son of Hermes and was charioteer to Oenomaus, a king of Pisa, who challenged all of his daughter Hippodamia's suitors to a chariot race that he would inevitably win. Losers in the challenge were beheaded. Undeterred, Pelops, son of Tantalus, found a way to beat Oenomaus: he bribed Myrtilus with the promise of a night with the bride and half the kingdom. Myrtilus accepted, and removed the linchpin from the wheel of Oenomaus's chariot. Thus, when the race was in full swing, the wheel came loose, and Oenomaus, having been thrown, was mortally injured. After his victory, Pelops both failed to honor his promise and cast Myrtilus into the sea to his death. Before dying, however, Myrtilus was able to utter a curse on Pelops and all of his descendants with his last breath.

(See also Hermes, Hippodamia, Oenomaus, Pelops, and Tantalus.)

NARCISSUS Narcissus was a handsome youth born to a Naiad nymph named Liriope and the god of the river Cephissus, who had overpowered her. According to the Roman poet Ovid, Liriope consulted the seer Teiresias regarding the span of her child's life, and he replied that Narcissus would live until he came to know himself. This self-knowledge came at the age of sixteen, when he was adored by maidens and youths alike but ignored everyone's advances, including those of the nymph Echo, who pined away in lovesickness to become nothing but a disembodied, echoing voice. As punishment for his arrogant slight of all who desired him, the goddess Nemesis caused him to fall in love with himself, which occurred when he caught sight of his reflection in a pool. Not knowing it was his own face that he saw reflected, he tried vainly to touch and kiss the apparition, but to no avail. Like Echo, he too pined away, leaving no trace of his former self but the flower that thereafter bore his name.

(See also Cephissus [god and place], Echo, Naiads [the], Nemesis, and Teiresias.)

NAUSICAA Nausicaa was the daughter of the Phaeacian king Alcinous and his queen, Arete. When Odysseus was swept up on the shores of Scheria, Nausicaa happened to be there as well, since the goddess Athena, who did what she could to help Odysseus, had inspired her to go to the seashore at just that moment. Nausicaa, who clearly viewed Odysseus as a potential suitor, directed Odysseus to her father's palace, where he was hospitably received. Alcinous did offer Nausicaa's hand in marriage to Odysseus, who deftly sidestepped the issue without causing offense by revealing that he was already married.

(*See also* Alcinous, Arete, Athena, Nausicaa, Odysseus, Phaeacians [the], *and* Scheria.)

NELEUS Neleus was a son of Tyro and Poseidon. Neleus and his brother Pelias, who had been abandoned by their mother as infants, were later reunited with her and killed their evil stepmother. Later, as a result of a disagreement between him and his brother, Neleus left Thessaly and made for the Peloponnese, where he became the king of Pylos, a city that, according to the mythographer Apollodorus, he founded. Neleus wed Chloris, daughter of Amphion, and together they had one daughter and twelve sons, among them Nestor, who would become Pylos's most famous legendary king. In the course of time, Neleus became involved with Hercules, when the latter came to him in hopes of being purified of the murder of Iphitus, brother of Iole, whose hand in marriage Hercules had unsuccessfully sought. Hercules killed Neleus and eleven of his sons, leaving Nestor to inherit the throne of Pylos.

(*See also* Amphion, Hercules, Iole, Nestor, Pelias, Poseidon, Pylos, Thessaly, Troy, *and* Tyro.)

NEOPTOLEMUS Neoptolemus ("Young Fighter") was the son of the Greek hero Achilles and Deidamia, a daughter of Lycomedes, king of the island of Scyros. Neoptolemus was conceived while Achilles was in hiding on the island of Scyros among the king's daughters, as his mother, Thetis, wanted to prevent his being sent to fight at Troy. The war at Troy was in its tenth year and, with Achilles dead, the Greeks' chances of taking the city were decreasing. The Trojan prophet Helenus revealed that Troy would only fall if the Greeks went to fetch Neoptolemus and Philoctetes, who had been abandoned on the island of Lemnos. According to the tragedian Sophocles, it was Neoptolemus and Odysseus who were sent to persuade Philoctetes to join the Greeks. Neoptolemus fought bravely at Troy but was also ruthless and cruel. He was one of the Greeks who hid inside the belly of the Trojan Horse and, once inside the city of Troy, set fire to the city. According to the Roman poet Virgil, he also killed King Priam when the latter had taken refuge at an altar of Zeus, which was an act of sacrilege, and it was either he or Odysseus who sacrificed Priam's daughter Polyxena to the ghost of Achilles. It was also he, or Odysseus, who was said to have thrown the Trojan prince Hector's young son, Astyanax, from the walls of Troy to his death. Hector's wife, Andromache, meanwhile, was awarded to Neoptolemus as a concubine. By some accounts Neoptolemus gave Andromache to the Trojan seer Helenus after he married Hermione, daughter of the Spartan king Menelaus and Helen. In an account of the end of his life, the tragedian Euripides writes that it was the Mycenaean king Agamemnon's son, Orestes, who had Neoptolemus killed while the latter was at Delphi, doing so since he had also been promised Hermione's hand in marriage.

(*See also* Achilles, Agamemnon, Andromache, Astyanax, Deidamia, Delphi, Hector, Helen, Helenus, Hermione, Lemnos, Lycomedes, Menelaus, Mycenae, Odysseus, Orestes, Philoctetes, Polyxena, Priam, Scyros, Sparta, Troy, *and* Zeus.)

NEPHELE Nephele was the first wife of Athamas, a king of Boeotia, and mother to two children, Phrixus and Helle. Athamas's second wife, Ino, resented Nephele's children, as it was they, and not her own children, who would be Athamas's heirs. Ino accordingly contrived a plot whereby to convince Athamas to kill Nephele's children. Nephele was, however, able to rescue her children by sending a winged, golden-fleeced ram to carry them to safety. Phrixus was ultimately carried to Colchis on the Black Sea, but Helle fell to her death.

The heroine Nephele is conflated by some ancient authors with the cloud goddess Nephele whom Zeus created to trick the sinner Ixion.

(*See also* Athamas, Boeotia, Colchis, Helle, Ixion, Nephele [goddess], Phrixus, *and* Zeus.)

NESTOR Nestor was one of the twelve sons of Neleus, a king of Pylos, and Chloris, daughter of Amphion. Nestor succeeded his father on the throne of Pylos and ruled for three generations. In his youth, he was a skilled warrior, having encountered foes as diverse as Hercules and the Centaurs. As an old man, he led a contingent of ninety ships to Troy, where he was a source of sound advice for the Greeks. Nestor survived the Trojan War and hospitably received Odysseus's son Telemachus when he traveled to Pylos while gathering information about his father.

(*See also* Amphion, Centaurs [the], Hercules, Neleus, Odysseus, Pylos, Telemachus, *and* Troy.)

NIOBE Niobe was a daughter of Tantalus, king of Lydia, and the wife of the Theban king Amphion, co-regent with his brother Zethus. Having been blessed not only with a distinguished ancestry, social status, and beauty, she had a wealth of children: according to Homer there were twelve, and according to Ovid fourteen, half of them being sons and half daughters. This richness of blessings caused her to proclaim publicly that she was worthier of worship than Leto, mother of the divine twins Artemis and Apollo, as that goddess merely had two children. At this insult, an aggrieved Leto (the Roman Latona) called upon her children for help. Coming equipped with their bow and arrow, they slew all of Niobe's children. Amphion, in grief, took his own life, and Niobe, in the extremity of her grief, turned to stone, becoming the "eternally weeping rock" on Mount Sipylus in Lydia.

(*See also* Amphion, Apollo, Artemis, Leto, Lydia, Tantalus, Thebes, *and* Zethus.)

NISUS One mythological Nisus was the son of Pandion, a legendary king of Athens who, while in exile from Athens at Megara, begat Nisus. Pandion eventually became regent of Megara, and Nisus succeeded him. Whether it was because King Minos of Crete had his sights set on Athens, which was ruled by Nisus's brother Aegeus, or for some other reason, Minos's forces attacked Megara. Scylla, Nisus's daughter, watched the conflict and, catching sight of Minos, the enemy commander, fell instantly in love. She planned to win Minos's heart by presenting him with her father's lock of purple hair, which, if severed from his head, would end the invincibility of his kingdom. Under cover of night, Scylla cut Nisus's purple lock and offered it to Minos, who was horrified at her deed and wanted nothing to do with her. When Scylla plunged into the sea in pursuit of Minos's ship, she was prevented from climbing aboard by Nisus, who had become an osprey (or sea eagle) and dove at her menacingly. Scylla's fate is variously described as drowning or as transformation into a sea bird or fish.

Another Nisus appears in Virgil's *Aeneid* as the devoted friend of the handsome young warrior Euryalus. According to Virgil, this Nisus was a son of Hyrtacus and the nymph Ida. He had accompanied Aeneas in the flight from Troy, and during the war between the forces of Aeneas and the Rutulians, he and Euryalus volunteered to venture forth from the besieged Trojan camp at night in search of Aeneas. As they made their way, they slaughtered a number of the enemy, and Euryalus made a fatal, youthful mistake: he stripped the armor of an enemy captain, and the helmet's gleam gave him away. Euryalus was taken captive, and although Nisus sacrificed his life to save him, both were slain.

(*See also* Aegeus, Aeneas, Athens, Crete, Euryalus, Megara [place], Minos, Pandion, Rutulians [the], Scylla [heroine], *and* Troy.)

NUMA Numa Pompilius, known more commonly simply as Numa, was the second of the seven legendary kings of Rome and the successor of Romulus. Details of his life and his accomplishments were recorded by the historian Livy and the biographer Plutarch. According to tradition, Numa was born in the city of Cures in the territory of the Sabines in Italy. His birthday, it was said, coincided with the date of the foundation of Rome: April 21 in the year 753 BCE. Numa married Tatia, daughter of Titus Tatius, king of the Sabines, and he enjoyed a reputation for being deeply versed, even at a young age, in both divine and human law. The senators of Rome thus invited him to become regent, an honor he accepted only after, at his request, an omen from Jupiter himself had been secured. Numa was remembered not only for the era of peace that he brought to Rome but also, critically, for his establishment of Roman sacred law and state cult. Recognizing that his institution of religious practices, priesthoods, festivals, and other observances might meet with resistance from those disinclined or unable to see their value, he invented a story indicating that he had been instructed in his efforts by the gods themselves: he made it known that he had met after nightfall with the goddess Egeria, who herself had guided him in the establishment of rites and priesthoods most appropriate to each of the gods. After a reign of forty-three years, Numa was buried on the Janiculum, one of Rome's seven hills.

(*See also* Egeria, Rome, Romulus, *and* Sabines [the].)

ODYSSEUS Odysseus (or Ulysses) was the son of the Ithacan king Laertes and his wife, Anticleia. He succeeded Laertes on the throne of Ithaca when the latter stepped aside in his old age. Odysseus's wife was Penelope, a daughter of Icarius, and with her he became the father of Telemachus. Odysseus, who had been one of the suitors of Helen, was bound by oath to join the massive Greek contingent that set sail for Troy in pursuit of Helen, and he brought twelve shiploads of men. Odysseus played a significant role in the ten-year Trojan War. Among other things, he attempted to broker peace between the Greeks and Trojans; joined an embassy that tried to convince Achilles to return to the fighting after he, in response to grievous insult, had withdrawn; went to spy on the Trojans and their allies; and, in addition to going on a killing spree, took captive a Trojan spy. After Achilles, who had eventually resumed fighting, was killed by the Trojan prince Paris, Odysseus and Telamonian Ajax retrieved his body. When the two subsequently competed for Achilles's armor, Odysseus prevailed. Famous for his cleverness, Odysseus was credited with devising the stratagem of the Trojan Horse as a means to gain access to Troy and with capturing the Trojan seer Helenus, who revealed that Troy would not fall if the Greeks did not go get the hero Philoctetes from the island of Lemnos, bring Achilles's son Neoptolemus to Troy, and gain possession of the sacred wooden statue of Athena (the Palladium) housed in a Trojan temple. Diomedes joined Odysseus in the theft of the Palladium, and it was due to the goddess's anger over this that so many Greeks died on their way home from Greece. After setting sail from Troy, where Odysseus (or Neoptolemus) sacrificed the Trojan princess Polyxena to the ghost of Achilles, Odysseus spent another ten years trying to get home. His journey, as recounted in Homer's *Odyssey*, took him to distant lands, where he faced a host of challenges, all of which he overcame due to his adaptability, ingenuity, and ability to persevere. In the course of his travels he negotiated perils arising from encounters with the Cicones, whose town his men sacked; the overly hospitable Lotus Eaters; the Cyclops Polyphemus; the island of Aeolus, Lord of the Winds; the cannibalistic Laestrygons; the sorceress Circe; the land of the dead; the deadly but euphonious Sirens; the dread monster Scylla and the whirlpool Charybdis; the cattle of Helios; and the seductive earth goddess Calypso. By the time he came to the island of Calypso, Odysseus was alone, all of his companions having perished. With the help of Calypso and the goddess Ino, Odysseus made it safely to the island of the kindly Phaeacians, who brought him home to Ithaca. There he faced still more challenges, as in his long absence, a group of ill-behaved young men had settled in his palace, each of them wanting to win the hand of Penelope, and his servants, with the notable exception of the swineherd Eumaeus and the nurse Eurycleia, had switched their allegiance to the suitors. With the help of Eumaeus and his son, Telemachus, with whom he was reunited, Odysseus slew the suitors, the worst of whom, Antinous, died first. Only then did Odysseus reveal himself to Penelope and his father, the latter joining him in battle against the townsfolk angered at the slaying of their sons. When, with the help of Athena, order was reestablished, Odysseus again ruled Ithaca. It had been prophesied in the *Odyssey* that Odysseus would end his days at sea after first wandering on land and making sacrifice to Poseidon, but another tradition told of his death at the hands of Telegonus, his son by the sorceress Circe.

While a positive, heroic character in the Homeric tradition, Odysseus came to be presented in a less flattering light by later authors, for whom his cleverness became a vehicle for treachery, and it was in such contexts, as in Sophocles's play *Philoctetes*, that he was called a son not of Laertes but of Sisyphus.

(*See also* Achilles, Aeolus, Antinous, Ajax [the Great], Athena, Calypso, Charybdis, Circe, Cyclopes [the], Diomedes, Eumaeus, Eurycleia, Helen, Helenus, Helios, Ino, Ithaca, Laertes, Laestrygons [the], Lotus Eaters [the], Neoptolemus, Penelope, Phaeacians [the], Philoctetes, Polyphemus, Polyxena, Poseidon, Scylla, Sirens [the], Sisyphus, Telamon, Telemachus, *and* Troy.)

THE RULING HOUSE OF
TROY

SCAMANDER RIVER ✛ IDAEA

TEUCER

BATEIA ✛ DARDANUS

ILUS (1)

EURYDICE ✛ ILUS (2)

PLACIA (?) ✛ LAOMEDON

TITHONUS   OTHER SONS   PRIAM ✛ HECUBA

MANY OTHERS   HELENUS   ANDROMACHE ✛ HECTOR   PARIS

ASTYANAX
*[Last of the Trojan
royal line (Ilium)]*

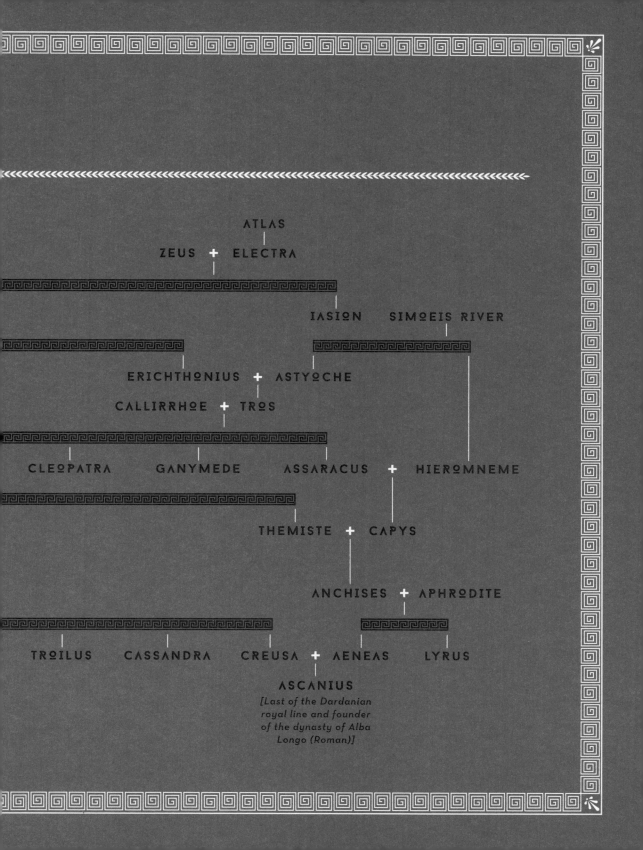

ATLAS

ZEUS ✚ ELECTRA

IASION   SIMOEIS RIVER

ERICHTHONIUS ✚ ASTYOCHE

CALLIRRHOE ✚ TROS

CLEOPATRA   GANYMEDE   ASSARACUS ✚ HIEROMNEME

THEMISTE ✚ CAPYS

ANCHISES ✚ APHRODITE

TROILUS   CASSANDRA   CREUSA ✚ AENEAS   LYRUS

ASCANIUS
[Last of the Dardanian
royal line and founder
of the dynasty of Alba
Longo (Roman)]

OEDIPUS Oedipus, whose name can be interpreted as meaning "swollen foot" or "foot-based knowledge," was the son of the Theban king Laius and his wife, the queen Jocasta. Since Laius had received a prophecy stating that his son was destined to kill him, baby Oedipus was exposed on the slopes of Mount Cithaeron with his ankles pinned together, this effort to cripple him being thought a deterrent to his rescue by a passing stranger. But the shepherd who had been instructed to expose the infant gave him to a member of the king of Corinth's staff who, in turn, delivered him to the Corinthian king Polybus and his wife, Merope. When, as a youth, Oedipus heard that he was not actually Polybus's son, he went to inquire about the truth of this rumor from the oracle at Delphi; the oracle's answer was not direct, its pronouncement being that Oedipus was destined to kill his father and marry his mother. So Oedipus left Delphi determined never to return to Corinth, in hopes of avoiding fulfillment of the prophecy. On the way he came upon a chariot driven by an elderly man. A dispute over right of way ensued at a crossroads, and Oedipus slew the stranger. This stranger, unbeknownst to Oedipus, was Laius, and Oedipus had accordingly killed his father. Oedipus, whose story is best known from the tragedian Sophocles's tragedies *Oedipus the King* and *Oedipus at Colonus*, then came to Thebes, where he was named king and given Jocasta as wife, as a consequence of ridding the land and its people of persecution by the Sphinx; this Oedipus did by solving the Sphinx's riddle, thus proving himself also to be the wisest human, as many had attempted to solve the riddle before him and paid with their lives. With Jocasta, Oedipus became father to two daughters, Antigone and Ismene, and two sons, Eteocles and Polyneices. All was well in Thebes until a plague descended on the city, and in order to counteract it, Oedipus sent his wife's brother, Creon, to Delphi in order to inquire after a remedy. The oracle declared that the murderer of Laius must be found and driven from the city. This, of course, was Oedipus himself, but not knowing his true identity, an important clue to which would have been the condition of his feet, his realization of the truth was not immediate. Jocasta guessed the truth first and hanged herself. A shattered Oedipus put out his own eyes but did not commit suicide, considering himself a source of pollution equally to the dead and to the living. He was subsequently exiled from Thebes and, wandering the countryside accompanied by his daughter Antigone, came to Colonus in the territory of Athens, where he unwittingly entered an area sacred to the Eumenides. The residents of Colonus wanted the polluted Oedipus to leave, and his challenges were compounded by the appearance of his brother-in-law, Creon, and his son Polyneices: Creon had come to take Oedipus back to Theban lands by force, as that city's safety depended on Oedipus's presence, and Polyneices, too, wished to have possession of Oedipus so that he might prevail in his assault on Thebes. As it happened, Thebes was under threat since Oedipus's sons, Eteocles and Polyneices, had agreed to rule in alternate years, but Eteocles refused to give up the throne, prompting Polyneices to muster an army against him. Fortunately, Oedipus was offered asylum by the Athenian king Theseus and subsequently vanished from the earth, with only Theseus knowing where he was buried. Thereafter Oedipus would safeguard Athens. Thebes, in turn, was repeatedly attacked, first by Polyneices and the Seven Against Thebes and later by the Epigoni, the surviving sons of the Seven. Eteocles and Polyneices, fulfilling Oedipus's curse upon them, killed each other in the first of these Theban conflicts.

(*See also* Antigone, Athens, Cithaeron [Mount], Colonus, Corinth, Creon, Delphi, Epigoni [the], Eteocles, Eumenides [the], Ismene, Jocasta, Laius, Merope [heroine], Polybus, Polyneices, Seven Against Thebes [the], Sphinx of Thebes [the], Thebes, *and* Theseus.)

OENEUS

Oeneus was a legendary king of Calydon in Aetolia. The most notable of his children with his first wife, Althea, were Deianeira and Meleager, and with his second wife, Periboea, it was Tydeus. The mythographers Apollodorus and Hyginus preserve a wide range of details about his life. Among other things, Oeneus reputedly recognized the god Dionysus's interest in his wife Althea and allowed the god to spend time with her; the result was Deianeira, who then was technically his stepdaughter. Dionysus, for his part, gave the gift of a grapevine to Oeneus, the first mortal to have received this valuable gift. As for Deianeira, she caught the eye of Hercules, to whom Oeneus gave her as a bride in a union that Hercules would live to regret. While a pious man, Oeneus had somehow overlooked the goddess Artemis when making sacrifice to the gods in thanks for the first fruits of harvest. In anger at him, the goddess sent a boar—the so-called Calydonian Boar—to ravage the land of Calydon and its orchards. In the course of this battle, Meleager killed Althea's brothers, in anger over which Althea caused Meleager's untimely death, followed by her own. Oeneus then married Periboea, who was either given to him as a prize or had been sent to him by her father with a decree that she should be put to death because her reputation had been tarnished. In any event, Periboea bore Oeneus two sons, one of them Tydeus, who would become father to the hero Diomedes.

(*See also* Althea, Artemis, Calydon, Deianeira, Diomedes, Dionysus, Hercules, Meleager, *and* Tydeus.)

OENOMAUS

Oenomaus was king of Pisa and a son of the god Ares, who gave him a pair of horses that were as swift as the wind. Oenomaus challenged all of the suitors of his daughter, Hippodamia, to a chariot race in the knowledge that he would win. Until the appearance of Pelops, Oenomaus had defeated, killed, and beheaded all of them. Pelops, however, defeated Oenomaus, doing so because he had bribed the king's charioteer, Myrtilus, to compromise Oenomaus's chariot. Having been fatally wounded when he was thrown from his chariot, Oenomaus was succeeded by Pelops, who took Hippodamia as his bride.

(*See also* Ares, Hippodamia, Myrtilus, *and* Pelops.)

OMPHALE
Omphale was a mythical queen of Lydia. According to the historian Diodorus Siculus, Hercules murdered Iphitus, brother of Iole, whose hand in marriage he had unsuccessfully sought. Consequently, Hercules became afflicted with an ailment that he could not shake. He consulted the oracle of Apollo, which instructed him to allow himself to be sold into slavery and to give the payment generated by his sale into slavery to the sons of Iphitus. It was Omphale to whom Hercules was sold, and he served her faithfully, ridding the land of the Cercopes, who were robbers and evildoers, killing some of them and taking others of them captive. He also killed Syleus, who had forced passersby to hoe his vineyard, with his own hoe, and, having sacked the city of the marauding Itoni, he enslaved its inhabitants. A delighted Omphale freed Hercules from obligation to her and with him bore a son by the name of Lamus.

(*See also* Apollo, Hercules, Iole, *and* Lydia.)

ORESTES
Orestes was the son of Agamemnon, king of Mycenae, and his wife, Clytemnestra. His siblings were Iphigeneia, Electra, and Chrysothemis, and his dramatic story, its details varying in each telling, lies at the core of plays written by all three great Athenian playwrights: Aeschylus, Sophocles, and Euripides. When Agamemnon left for Troy and Clytemnestra had taken Aegisthus as a lover, the baby Orestes was sent away to the court of King Strophius of Phocis, at least ostensibly for his own safety. When, after a ten-year absence fighting the Trojan War, Agamemnon returned to Mycenae and was murdered by Clytemnestra, Orestes, having consulted the oracle of Apollo at Delphi, was instructed by the god to make his way to Mycenae and avenge the death of his father. Accompanied by his Phocian friend Pylades, Orestes returned to Mycenae and, by some accounts with the support of his sister, killed Clytemnestra and Aegisthus. As a consequence of these murders, Orestes was relentlessly pursued by the Erinyes ("Spirits of Vengeance") until he stood trial for murder in Athens at the hallowed court of the Areopagus. There, according to Aeschylus, the goddess Athena exculpated him and pacified the Erinyes, making them goodly spirits now called the Eumenides. A variant tradition, which is the subject of Euripides's *Iphigeneia in Tauris*, portrays an Orestes who, as a result of relentless pursuit by the Erinyes, traveled to the barbarian land

of Tauris at Apollo's command. There he was to obtain an especially sacred wooden statue of Artemis that had fallen from the heavens and bring it to the territory of Athens. Again accompanied by Pylades, Orestes accomplished this task with the help of his sister Iphigeneia, who had become a priestess of Artemis in Tauris after being saved from human sacrifice by the goddess whom she now served. Orestes would eventually become the king of Mycenae and also of Sparta.

(*See also* Aegisthus, Agamemnon, Apollo, Athens, Chrysothemis, Clytemnestra, Delphi, Electra [heroine], Erinyes [the], Eumenides [the], Iphigeneia, Mycenae, Pylades, Sparta, Taurians [the], *and* Troy.)

ORION Orion was a noted hunter of enormous size who, upon his death, was raised to the heavens to become the constellation that bears his name.

(*See* Orion [prodigies].)

ORITHYIA Orithyia (or Oreithyia) was known to the poet Homer as a Nereid nymph but was more commonly known as a daughter of the Athenian king Erechtheus and his wife, Praxithea. Orithyia had caught the eye of Boreas, god of the north wind, as she danced along the banks of the Ilissus River, and he abducted her. Orithyia bore the god several children, among them the winged brothers Zetes and Calais, who would join the hero Jason on his quest for the Golden Fleece.

(*See also* Athens, Boreas, Calais, Erechtheus, Ilissus River [the], Jason, Nereids [the], *and* Zetes.)

ORPHEUS The renowned singer and musician Orpheus was a son of the Muse Calliope and the Thracian king Oeagrus or, alternatively, Apollo, who was said to have taught him how to play the lyre. Orpheus participated in the hero Jason's quest for the Golden Fleece but is best known for the events that led to the loss of his wife and his own death. Orpheus was married to a Naiad nymph named Eurydice, who was at one point pursued by the rustic deity Aristaeus and, in the course of her flight, was bitten by a serpent. The serpent's bite proved fatal, and a despondent Orpheus followed her into the Underworld, where, according to the Roman poet Ovid, he moved Hades, Proserpina, and all the sinners residing there to tears with his music. The regents of the Underworld permitted Orpheus a reprieve: he could lead Eurydice back up to the world of the living, but he must not look back until he emerged from the land of the dead. Overcome by worry, Orpheus did look back, and Eurydice was again taken from him. Now Orpheus was inconsolable and wandered the earth lamenting, moving animals, stones, and even trees with his plaintive songs. For three years he lamented, remaining true to Eurydice's memory and, by spurning their advances, angered some Thracian Maenads who tore him limb from limb. While the rest of him lay where he was killed, his still-singing head and sounding lyre were carried along the streams of the Hebrus River to the sea and eventually to the island of Lesbos, home of inspired poets. Now Orpheus's spirit passed to the world below, where he was reunited with Eurydice.

(*See also* Apollo, Aristaeus, Calliope, Eurydice [nymph], Hades [god], Jason, Maenads [the], Muses [the], Naiads [the], Proserpina, Thrace, *and* Underworld [the].)

PALINURUS
Palinurus was one of the Trojan refugees who accompanied Aeneas in his flight from Troy to Italy. Palinurus, however, met a tragic end on Italian shores. Overpowered by the god Somnus ("Sleep"), Palinurus, Aeneas's helmsman, fell overboard and, after washing up on the shore, was set upon by locals and killed. Aeneas encountered his ghost in the Underworld on the banks of the river Styx, which he could not cross because he had not received proper burial. The Sibyl, who had accompanied Aeneas, dispelled Palinurus's worries by telling him that he would receive burial in due course and that a land formation on the western coast of Italy would be named Cape Palinurus after him.

(*See also* Aeneas, Sibyl of Cumae [the], Somnus, Styx [the River], Troy, *and* Underworld [the].)

PALLAS
There were several characters in Classical mythology who were called Pallas, among them one of the Titans, one of the Giants, and the goddess Athena herself. The best-known human hero by that name appears in Virgil's epic the *Aeneid*. This Pallas was a son of the Arcadian king Evander, who had founded the town of Pallantium on what would later be known as Rome's Palatine hill. Evander was an important ally for Aeneas when he arrived in Italy from Troy and was faced with resistance by the native Italians. Evander entrusted his cherished son Pallas to Aeneas, and it was the Rutulian prince Turnus's killing of Pallas that caused Aeneas not to spare Turnus at the epic's end but rather to slay him brutally, calling his death a sacrifice to Pallas.

(*See also* Aeneas, Arcadia, Evander, Giants [the], Pallas [goddess], Rome, Rutulians [the], Titans [the], Troy, *and* Turnus.)

PANDARUS
Pandarus was a son of the Arcadian king Lycaon, a man with savage tendencies who was transformed into a wolf. Pandarus was an ally of the Trojans in the Trojan War and, through the intervention of the goddess

Athena, broke a truce established between the Greeks and Trojans by shooting an arrow at the Spartan king Menelaus, wounding him. Hostilities resumed, and Pandarus was eventually slain by the Greek hero Diomedes.

(*See also* Arcadia, Athena, Diomedes, Lycaon, Menelaus, *and* Troy.)

PANDORA Pandora, whose name means "giver of all things," was, according to the Greek poet Hesiod, the first woman. She was fashioned of earth and water by the god Hephaestus on Zeus's instruction, and she was created as retribution for Prometheus's assistance to humankind; Prometheus's assistance consisted of stealing fire from the gods, as well as tricking Zeus into accepting the lesser portion of a sacrificial animal on occasions when humans made sacrifice to the gods. The gods bestowed gifts on Pandora: Athena taught her how to weave and clothed her in lustrous garments, Aphrodite gave her grace and beauty, the Graces and Persuasion (Peitho) brought her necklaces of gold, and the Hours (Horae) crowned her head with floral wreaths, but Hermes made her shameless and deceitful and gave her the power of speech. Pandora was not offered to Prometheus, who, true to his name ("Foresight"), would have seen trouble coming, but to his brother Epimetheus, "Hindsight." No sooner did Epimetheus take possession of her than she opened a chest that she had been given and had been instructed not to open. Out flew many things that would be blessings for humankind but also sorrow, disease, and all manners of suffering that humans had not previously known. One thing only remained stuck under the chest's lid, that being Hope.

(*See also* Aphrodite, Athena, Epimetheus, Graces [the], Hephaestus, Hermes, Prometheus, *and* Zeus.)

PARIS Paris, who was known also as Paris Alexander or simply Alexander (or Alexandros, "Helper of Men"), was a son of Priam, king of Troy, and his wife, Hecuba. His many siblings included Hector, the staunch defender of Troy; the prophetic twins Cassandra and Helenus; and Polyxena, who would become the victim of human sacrifice. As the result of a disturbing dream indicating that their child would cause the destruction of Troy, Hecuba and Priam ordered the infant Paris to be exposed by one of the royal herdsmen on the slopes of nearby Mount Ida. When the herdsman returned to the site days later, he found Paris still alive, for he had been nursed by a bear, and took him in. Paris was later integrated into the royal family when he came to Troy and prevailed in every contest of funeral games (athletic contests held on the occasion of someone's death) that Priam had instituted; he was, in fact, on the verge of being killed by another contestant, his own brother Deiphobus, when

Cassandra recognized him. It later happened that, when Paris was tending his flocks on Mount Ida, he was visited by the goddesses Hera, Athena, and Aphrodite and was asked to award the famous Golden Apple to the fairest of them, having been selected for this task on the basis of his own beauty. This apple had been the goddess Eris's ("Strife's") gift to Peleus and Thetis at their wedding. None of the goddesses left Paris's decision to chance, each of them offering him a bribe: Hera offered him extensive rulership; Athena offered him victory in war; and Aphrodite, knowing him best, offered him the most beautiful woman in the world. For Paris, the choice was clear. He selected Aphrodite, and his prize would be Helen, wife of the Spartan king Menelaus. So, Paris set sail for Sparta, where he was hospitably entertained, and then, when Menelaus was summoned abroad, made off to Troy with Helen, who by some accounts went willingly, and by others not. As all the eligible nobles in Greece had vied for Helen's hand, her father had wisely asked all of them to swear an oath to abide by his (or, alternately, her) decision and to defend the selected groom should the need arise. Consequently, when Menelaus was in need, the Greeks assembled en masse, and a contingent of 1,000 ships, led by Menelaus's brother, King Agamemnon of Mycenae, set off for Troy in order to retrieve Helen and punish the Trojans. The Greeks and Trojans battled for ten years, and, according to Homer in the *Iliad*, it was in the tenth year that Paris at last faced Menelaus in single combat for the purpose of settling the conflict. However, when Paris was on the verge of being defeated and killed, he was saved by Aphrodite, and the battle raged on. At last Paris's brother Hector, who had been Troy's best hope for defense, was slain by Achilles. Paris later killed Achilles, shooting him with one of his arrows, and Paris himself was killed by the Greek hero Philoctetes, who wounded him with one of the poisoned arrows of Hercules.

(*See also* Achilles, Agamemnon, Aphrodite, Athena, Cassandra, Eris, Hector, Hecuba, Helen, Helenus, Hera, Ida [Mount], Menelaus, Mycenae, Peleus, Philoctetes, Polyxena, Priam, Sparta, Thetis, *and* Troy.)

PARTHENOPAEUS The hero Parthenopaeus was variously known as one of the Seven Against Thebes—an army led by seven commanders, including Oedipus's son Polyneices, against the city of Thebes—and brother of Argos's king Adrastus, or as a son of the fleet-footed huntress Atalanta and Meleager, who with Aphrodite's help was able to win Atalanta's hand.

(*See also* Adrastus, Aphrodite, Argos, Atalanta, Eteocles, Meleager, Oedipus, Polyneices, Seven Against Thebes [the], *and* Thebes.)

PATROCLUS Patroclus was the son of Menoetius and was born in the region of Locris in central Greece. When Patroclus was very young, he killed a boy with whom he had been playing dice and, as a consequence, he and his father went into exile. They came to the palace of King Peleus of Phthia, father of Achilles, whose faithful companion and friend Patroclus became. When Achilles withdrew from the fighting in the tenth year of the Trojan War, Patroclus, too, withdrew for a time but did re-enter the conflict as a surrogate for Achilles, whose armor he put on when he headed out to battle. Although Achilles warned him only to fight so long as to drive the Trojans back from the Greeks' camp, Patroclus stayed in the fray, fighting valiantly and killing, among many others, Zeus's son Sarpedon. Patroclus was eventually wounded by the god Apollo and a warrior named Euphorbus before being killed by Hector. It was the death of Patroclus that drove Achilles out of isolation and back into the war, his sole purpose being to exact vengeance for the death of his friend. This he did by killing Hector and then defiling his body until even the gods could stand it no longer.

(*See also* Achilles, Apollo, Hector, Peleus, Sarpedon, Troy, *and* Zeus.)

PELASGUS Pelasgus was the namesake of the Pelasgians, who were considered to be the original pre-Greek inhabitants of Greece. He was known variously as a king of Argos, Arcadia, and Thessaly, and his parents were said to be Zeus and Niobe, among others. According to the Greek poet Hesiod, Pelasgus was autochthonous, born of the soil. In Arcadia, Pelasgus was known as a culture hero, having taught the populace how to construct huts and make clothes from animal hides. With the Oceanid Meliboea (or, by some accounts, with the nymph Cyllene) he became the father of Lycaon, who, according to the Roman poet Ovid, was transformed into a wolf for his murderous tendencies.

(*See also* Arcadia, Argos, Lycaon, Niobe, Oceanids [the], Thessaly, *and* Zeus.)

PELEUS Peleus, who became king of Phthia in Thessaly, is perhaps best known as the father of Achilles, but he was certainly a warrior of note in his own right. He was a son of Aeacus, king of Aegina, and brother of Telamon. Since Peleus and Aeacus had killed their half brother, they were sent away from Aegina, and Peleus came to Phthia. There he wed Antigone, daughter of King Eurytion, but Antigone later killed herself, wrongly suspecting Peleus of not having been true to her. As for Eurytion, Peleus slew him by accident in the course of the hunt for the Calydonian Boar, in which he participated. Peleus also took part in Jason's quest for the Golden Fleece. On the grounds that he was the best man alive (or because neither Zeus nor Poseidon, who both desired her, wanted to risk fathering a son more powerful than themselves), the goddess Thetis was given to him in marriage. There was a tradition that Peleus had to work hard to gain physical possession of his bride, successfully wrestling with her as she changed shape from that of a woman to a beast and fire. All the gods attended the wedding, apart from Eris ("Strife"), who had not been invited, an exclusion that led to the beauty "contest" judged by the Trojan prince Paris and to the Trojan War.

By Peleus, Thetis became the mother of Achilles, whom she wanted to make immortal. This she did by holding the infant over burning embers, which Peleus witnessed in horror, causing her to abandon the effort and depart for the ocean; by another account, Thetis availed herself of a different method, namely dipping Achilles into the waters of the river Styx. In any event, Peleus outlived his son, since Achilles did not become immortal and was killed by the Trojan prince Paris at the end of the Trojan War.

(See also Achilles, Aeacus, Aegina, Calydon, Eris, Jason, Paris, Poseidon, Styx [the River], Thessaly, Thetis, Troy, and Zeus.)

PELIAS
Pelias was a king of Iolcos in Thessaly and a son of Poseidon and Tyro, whom the god had raped disguised as the river Enipeus. Tyro exposed both Pelias and his twin brother Neleus, but the boys were found and raised by herdsmen. As the mythographer Apollodorus reports, Pelias received his name from the mark (pelion) left on his forehead by one of the herdsmen's horses, who kicked him. When reunited with their mother, Pelias killed his stepmother Sidero, who had abused Tyro but had taken refuge in a precinct of Hera, which should have rendered her immune to any violence. This last act set Pelias on a course of enduring evildoing. He drove his half brother Aeson, who stood first in line to inherit the throne, from Iolcos and made himself king of that city. Later, when Aeson's son Jason came to claim the throne, Pelias sent him on a mission that he was sure would prove fatal, this mission being to retrieve the Golden Fleece from the barbarian land of Colchis. When, against all odds, Jason returned to Ioclos, he brought with him the Colchian princess Medea, who used her skills as a sorceress to end Pelias's life; this Medea did by convincing Pelias's daughters that she could make their father young again. Medea demonstrated how this could be done by rejuvenating an old ram that she first cut up and then tossed into a cauldron filled with a magic potion. Pelias's daughters agreed to subject their father to the same treatment, but Medea, exacting vengeance on behalf of Jason, threw Pelias's limbs into a cauldron filled only with water.

(See also Aeson, Colchis, Hera, Iolcos, Jason, Medea, Neleus, Poseidon, Sidero, Thessaly, and Tyro.)

PELOPS Pelops was the son of the goddess Dione and Tantalus, a man who greatly abused his privileged access to the gods. Tantalus's greatest sin consisted of chopping Pelops up and using his body parts as ingredients in a stew to be served to the gods. Almost all the gods realized what Tantalus had done in time. Only Demeter, who was distracted by grief over losing her daughter, Persephone, ate from the portion put before her, biting into Pelops's shoulder blade. When Zeus subsequently reassembled and revived Pelops, a piece of ivory in place of the shoulder blade was used to make him whole. When grown to maturity, Pelops set his sights on marrying the lovely Hippodamia, daughter of King Oenomaus of Pisa. Many had attempted to win her hand, and many had failed, their failure costing them their lives, for Oenomaus challenged them all to a chariot race that he was guaranteed to win and beheaded the losers. By bribing Myrtilus, Oenomaus's charioteer, to remove the linchpin from the wheel of his adversary's chariot, Pelops not only won the chariot race but also became the king of Pisa, since Oenomaus, thrown from his compromised chariot, had perished. But Pelops did not honor his promises to Myrtilus, whom he hurled from a cliff to his death; before expiring, Myrtilus was able to utter a curse against Pelops and his descendants. Among these descendants were the adulterous Theyestes and Atreus, who would become father to Agamemnon, later murdered by his wife, and to Menelaus, husband of the lovely Helen, all of them tragic figures. In spite of the curse, Pelops himself became a powerful ruler, extending his influence so far that the entire Peloponnese ("Island of Pelops") took its name from him. According to tradition, his chariot race with Oenomaus was the founding event of the Olympic Games, which took place at the sanctuary of Zeus at Olympia in what was formerly the territory of Pisa.

(*See also* Agamemnon, Atreus, Demeter, Dione, Helen, Hippodamia, Menelaus, Myrtilus, Oenomaus, Olympia, Tantalus, Theyestes, *and* Zeus.)

PENELOPE Penelope, daughter of the Spartan king Icarius, was the wife of Odysseus, mother by Odysseus of Telemachus, and a model of wifely fidelity. When Odysseus did not return home after the Trojan War and all of Ithaca's most eligible young men courted her, she put them off by stating that she would make her choice when she finished weaving a shroud for her father-in-law Laertes. Every night Penelope would undo the day's work, but eventually the suitors discovered her ruse and pressed her to finish. Fortunately, it was not long after this that Odysseus returned. Being as clever and circumspect as her husband, Penelope was unsure whether, after so many years, Odysseus really was who he claimed to be, and made trial of him: in Odysseus's presence, she told the nurse Eurycleia to move what had been her marriage bed for the newly arrived Odysseus to sleep in. Only Odysseus would know that this could not be done, for he had carved the bed from the stump of an olive tree around which he had built his palace.

(*See also* Eurycleia, Ithaca, Laertes, Odysseus, Sparta, Telemachus, *and* Troy.)

PENTHESILEIA Penthesileia was an Amazon and, as the Greek poet Quintus of Smyrna reports, a daughter of the war god Ares. After the death of Hector, she came to Troy as an ally of the Trojans, doing so by way of expiating a grievous sin: she had accidentally killed her own sister Hippolyta while hunting. She fought bravely, killing many Greeks, but she and her horse were felled by the great ash spear of Achilles. As she lay dying, Achilles, overcome by her loveliness, fell in love with her.

(*See also* Achilles, Amazons [the], Ares, Hector, Hippolyta, *and* Troy.)

PENTHEUS Pentheus was the son of the Theban king Cadmus's daughter Agave and Echion, one of the warriors (the so-called Sparti) who sprang from the dragon's teeth that Cadmus sowed. In Cadmus's advanced age, Pentheus became regent of Thebes, and it was then that Dionysus, Pentheus's cousin, came to Greece, arriving first in Thebes of all Greek cities, in order to introduce his worship to that land. Pentheus was skeptical of this supposed new god and attempted to imprison him together with those citizens of Thebes who joined his celebrants; the latter included Cadmus, the seer Teiresias, his own mother Agave, and his aunts, Ino and Autonoe. As was to be expected, the god was too powerful for Pentheus and would have his vengeance. While Pentheus was on the one hand disturbed by the god's effeminacy, he was also curious about it and was curious, too, about what the god's female celebrants (called Maenads or Bacchantes) were doing: it was later reported that they had taken to the wilderness, danced in ecstasy, and nursed the young of animals they had found. The Bacchantes' revels turned sinister when they caught sight of Pentheus spying on them. With Agave in the lead, the women tore Pentheus limb from limb, mistaking him for an animal and making him a victim of their *sparagmos* and *omophagia* (tearing apart and eating raw), known ancient ritual practices of the Bacchantes.

(*See also* Agave, Autonoe, Bacchantes [the], Cadmus, Dionysus, Ino [heroine], Teiresias, *and* Thebes.)

PERDIX Perdix was the great-grandson of the Athenian king Erechtheus and nephew of the craftsman Daedalus. As the Roman poet Ovid and others report, Perdix invented the saw and the compass, and an envious Daedalus hurled him from the Acropolis. But Minerva, patroness of all craftsmen, rescued him and transformed him into a partridge, the bird called *perdix* ("partridge" in Greek) after him.

(*See also* Acropolis [the], Athens, Daedalus, Erechtheus, *and* Minerva.)

PERSEUS The Greek hero Perseus was a son of the god Zeus and the princess Danae, daughter of Acrisius, king of the Greek city of Argos. Having learned from an oracle that he would be killed by his grandson, Acrisius sought to prevent access to his daughter by imprisoning her. According to the mythographer Apollodorus, this prison was an impenetrable buried chamber of bronze; for the poet Ovid, it was a brazen tower; and for the mythographer Hyginus, it was a bunker of stone. In any event, this prison was no deterrent for Zeus, who breached the prison in the shape of a stream of gold and lay with Danae, impregnating her. Alarmed but unwilling to assume the guilt of bloodshed, Acrisius set his daughter and her baby adrift in a chest to perish at sea. To no avail. When the chest and its passengers arrived safely on the island of Seriphus, mother and child were discovered and taken in by Dictys, a local fisherman. While in Dictys's care, Danae caught the eye of the fisherman's brother, the island's king Polydectes, who sought her hand in marriage.

Whether it was because Perseus, now grown, objected to the marriage or whether king Polydectes simply wished to have Danae for himself, he tricked Perseus into bringing him a wedding gift that, for any normal mortal, would be impossible to obtain: the head of the Gorgon Medusa. With the help of the gods Athena and Hermes, Perseus made his way to the Graiae ("The Old Ones" or "The Gray Sisters"), who, being the Gorgons' siblings, would be able to tell him how to find Medusa. They did not offer this information willingly, however, doing so only when Perseus contrived to seize the single eye and tooth that they shared between them. Perseus, they said, would have to find the nymphs of the north, who possessed equipment required to complete his task. From these nymphs Perseus received a leather satchel, winged sandals, and a magical cap that rendered those who wore it invisible. From Hermes he received a sickle, and from Athena a well-polished shield, essential as it could be used as a mirror with which to locate the Gorgons—scaly, horned, and snake-haired—who, if gazed upon directly, turned those looking at them to stone. After locating the Gorgons' lair, Perseus, unseen, severed Medusa's head while she was sleeping and placed it in his pouch. His winged sandals, then, conveyed him swiftly out of range of Medusa's sisters who, upon awaking, gave chase. From Medusa's neck, or from the blood that had been spilled, sprang the winged horse Pegasus and the relatively shadowy figure Chrysaor. Poisonous snakes swarmed in the lands over which he flew with the still-dripping severed head.

In the course of his journey back to Seriphus, Perseus stopped to visit Atlas, who had previously denied him hospitality and whom, in vengeance, he turned into the stony mountains that still bear his name by holding aloft Medusa's head. He also stopped in Egypt, where, being related to Danaus, he had ancestral ties and was later honored in cult. He also saw, and immediately desired, the princess Andromeda, who had been chained to a crag on the coast of Ethiopia. This was the doing of her father, King Cepheus: she was to be prey for a sea monster sent by Poseidon to range those waters, her sacrifice an atonement to the Nereid nymphs, whom his wife, Cassiopeia, had insulted, calling herself more beautiful than they. Having slain the monster as well as Andromeda's uncle and former suitor, Phineus, Perseus claimed her as bride and brought her to Seriphus. There Perseus again pulled out the Gorgon's head so as to turn Polydectes to stone for his ill treatment of Dictys and his mother. Having no further use for his winged sandals and magic cap, Perseus gave them to Hermes to return to the nymphs. The head of Medusa, however, he gave to Athena, who affixed it as an emblem on her breastplate or shield.

Perseus made Dictys regent of the island of Seriphus and, with his mother, Danae, set out in search of his grandfather, Acrisius, who, having learned of his grandson's survival and fearing that the oracle would be fulfilled, had left his kingdom in Argos. What the oracle had predicted did, nonetheless, come to pass, for Perseus unwittingly killed Acrisius with a discus while competing in athletic contests in the city of Larissa. Not wishing to return to Argos, Perseus made his cousin Megapenthes king and, in turn, assumed the latter's throne over Tiryns. By some accounts, Perseus established the city of Mycenae at the spot where he discovered water or where the cap of his sword's scabbard fell.

Perseus and Andromeda founded the Perseid Dynasty, becoming parents to seven children, among them Perses, from whom the kings of Persia claimed descent; Alcaeus, who fathered Amphitryon; Sthenelus, father of Eurystheus, who sent the hero Hercules on his labors; and Electryon, who sired Alcmena, the mother of Hercules.

The ancient travel writer Pausanias reports that in addition to being venerated as a hero in Egypt, Perseus received particular honors near Argos and Mycenae as well as in Athens and at Seriphus after his death. Upon their deaths, Cassiopeia, Cepheus, Andromeda, and Perseus all became constellations.

(*See also* Acrisius, Alcaeus, Alcmena, Andromeda, Argos, Athena, Atlas, Cassiopeia, Cepheus, Chrysaor, Danae, Dictys, Electryon, Ethiopia, Eurystheus, Gorgons [the], Graiae [the], Hercules, Hermes, Larissa, Medusa, Mycenae, Pegasus, Perses, Phineus, Polydectes, Seriphus, Tiryns, *and* Zeus.)

PHAEACIANS, THE The Phaeacians were a people beloved of the gods and lived on the island of Scheria. Having previously inhabited a land called Hyperia, these famed seafarers were brought to Scheria by Nausithous so that they might escape the neighboring Cyclopes, who harassed them. On Scheria, Nausithous established a well-ordered city, and he was succeeded as king by Alcinous, whose queen was Arete. Alcinous's daughter, the princess Nausicaa, guided Odysseus to her father's palace, where he was hospitably received. Although the Phaeacians were aware of a prophecy foretelling the destruction of their city if they generously continued to offer conveyance on their ships to all who needed it, they took Odysseus home to Ithaca. Upon their ship's return, it was turned to stone by Poseidon.

(*See also* Alcinous, Arete, Cyclopes [the], Ithaca, Nausicaa, Odysseus, Poseidon, *and* Scheria.)

PHAEDRA Phaedra was a daughter of Minos, king of Crete, and his wife, Pasiphae. Like her mother, Phaedra, too, fell victim to an inappropriate love. In Phaedra's case, she developed a passion for her husband Theseus's son, Hippolytus, a chaste devotee of the virgin goddess Artemis. Phaedra tried hard to suppress her feelings, but her old nurse perceived her suffering and compelled her to speak of what it was that ailed her. Promising to help, the nurse revealed Phaedra's passion to a horrified Hippolytus. Her reputation now beyond repair, Phaedra killed herself, but not before writing a note to her husband indicating that her death was a result of Hippolytus's having made unwanted advances upon her. This false accusation prompted Theseus to curse his son, causing his death.

(*See also* Artemis, Crete, Hippolytus, Minos, Pasiphae, *and* Theseus.)

PHAETHON The story of Phaethon ("The Gleaming One") and his tragic fate is vividly told by the Roman poet Ovid. Phaethon was a son of Helios, whom Ovid equates with Apollo, and the nymph Clymene. Wishing to know for certain that the Sun God was his father, Phaethon asked him for a favor that would yield the proof he needed. The otherwise all-seeing god acquiesced, inviting the youngster to ask any favor he liked. What Phaethon desired was to drive his father's chariot, and this he did with disastrous results. Driving it too high into the heavens, he was startled by the constellations, and, losing control of his horses, he scorched the clouds and all the Earth. As the universe was in turmoil, in danger of destruction, Jupiter himself intervened, striking down Phaethon with a lightning bolt. The boy fell to his death into the Eridanus River. His sisters, the Heliades, wept ceaselessly for him and turned into poplars yielding amber tears, while his lamenting kinsman Cycnus became a swan, forever singing a plaintive song.

(*See also* Apollo, Clymene, Cycnus, Eridanus River [the], Heliades [the], Helios, *and* Jupiter.)

PHILEMON Philemon was the husband of Baucis. The couple were Phrygian peasants who, in spite of their abject poverty, were the only ones in their village to offer the gods Jupiter and Mercury hospitality while they were traveling disguised as humans. For their generosity, Baucis and Philemon were rewarded by being appointed priests of the two gods. Their humble hut became a temple, and their village, which the gods utterly wiped out, became a lake. At the time of their deaths, occurring simultaneously at their request, the two became an oak tree and a linden.

(*See also* Baucis, Jupiter, Mercury, *and* Phrygia.)

PHILOCTETES Philoctetes was one of the many Greeks who sailed for Troy, but unlike most, he did not reach the shores of Troy at the inception of hostilities. When the Greeks stopped to make sacrifice on the island of Tenedos, Philoctetes was bitten by a snake. The wound was painful and festered, causing him to curse and cry out. Odysseus convinced the Greeks to abandon Philoctetes on the island of Lemnos on the grounds that his cries would bring them bad luck. Philoctetes then lived alone on Lemnos for ten years, armed with only the bow and arrow that Hercules had given him in thanks for lighting the pyre on which he wished to end his life; Hercules had been in agony, having been poisoned by his wife, Deianeira, with what she mistakenly thought was a love potion. The Greeks came to regret their abandonment of Philoctetes when it was revealed that Troy would not fall unless Philoctetes with Hercules's bow and arrow was present. Consequently, Odysseus and Achilles's son Neoptolemus went to retrieve Philoctetes, a thing they very nearly did not achieve, as Philoctetes was, justifiably, still angry. Nonetheless, Philoctetes was brought to Troy, and, his wound having been healed, he killed the Trojan prince Paris, whose abduction of Helen was the immediate cause of the war.

(*See also* Achilles, Helen, Hercules, Lemnos, Neoptolemus, Odysseus, Paris, *and* Troy.)

PHILOMELA Philomela ("Nightingale") was an Athenian princess who was imprisoned and repeatedly raped by her sister Procne's husband, King Tereus of Thrace. When Philomela threatened to reveal this ill treatment of her, Tereus cut out her tongue. But Philomela was able to tell her story nonetheless, for she wove it into a tapestry that was delivered to Procne, who had been led to believe that she was dead. The sisters plotted a terrible vengeance on Tereus, and as Philomela fled Tereus in his wrathful pursuit of her, she became a nightingale.

(*See also* Athens, Procne, Tereus, *and* Thrace.)

PHINEUS

Phineus was a blind seer whose parentage was disputed. Among those called his father were the god Poseidon, Agenor of Tyre, and Agenor's son Phoenix. Phineus married Cleopatra, a daughter of the wind god Boreas and Orithyia, and later took as wife Idaea, a daughter of Dardanus. Accounts of his blinding were various. Among those claimed as being responsible for this was Boreas (with help from the Argonauts), who, according to the mythographer Apollodorus, wished to punish Phineus for blinding his grandsons, which Phineus had done believing that they had made advances on Idaea. Alternatively, it was said that Zeus blinded him because he had revealed the future to humans, thus making too much knowledge available to them. In Apollonius of Rhodes's *Voyage of the Argo*, Phineus was being tortured by the Harpies, who snatched away what food he tried to eat and fouled the rest. He was saved, however, by Boreas's sons Zetes and Calais, who had joined Jason's crew of Argonauts, and in thanks for this, he revealed how the *Argo* could safely sail between the Symplegades ("Clashing Rocks").

(*See also* Agenor, Argonauts [the], Boreas, Calais, Dardanus, Harpies [the], Orithyia, Poseidon, Symplegades [the], *and* Zetes.)

PHRIXUS

Phrixus was a son of Athamas, king of Orchomenus in Boeotia, and Nephele. When his father, Athamas, later took Ino as wife, she devised a plot whereby to do away with Phrixus and his sister Helle, who, being born earlier than her own children, stood to become her husband's heirs. Ino thus caused the realm's stockpile of grain seed to become spoiled, with the result that when sown, the seed failed to germinate. Athamas then sent messengers to consult the Delphic Oracle regarding a remedy for this catastrophe. Ino, however, compelled the messengers to report falsely that the Oracle recommended the sacrifice of Phrixus and, by some accounts, Helle too. Nephele, however, was able to save her children, sending a golden fleeced and winged ram to carry them away to safety. In the course of the ram's flight, Helle lost her balance and fell into the waters below, which thereafter were called Hellespont, "Helle's Sea," and now are called the Dardanelles. Phrixus, for his part, was conveyed safely to the town of Aea in Colchis on the eastern shores of the Black Sea. The Colchian king Aeetes welcomed Phrixus, who sacrificed the ram in thanksgiving either to Ares, as the mythographer Hyginus writes, or to Zeus, according to Apollodorus. The ram's fleece was given to King Aeetes, who hung it in on the limbs of an oak in a grove sacred to Ares, where it was guarded by a dragon. It was this fleece that the hero Jason, accompanied by the Argonauts, was sent to retrieve. Meanwhile, Aeetes offered Phrixus his daughter Chalciope in marriage, but Aeetes came to fear Phrixus and his sons, having heard a prophecy that he would lose his kingdom to a foreigner. Aeetes thus contrived their murder, but Phrixus's sons, at least, were able to escape and were later rescued by Jason, who came upon them as castaways.

(*See also* Aeetes, Ares, Argonauts [the], Athamas, Boeotia, Colchis, Delphi, Helle, Hellespont [the], Ino, Jason, Nephele [heroine], *and* Zeus.)

PIERUS

Pierus was a Macedonian king who is perhaps best known as having been father to nine daughters, the Pierides. These young women had lovely singing voices and presumed themselves to be equal to or better vocalists than the Muses. The Roman poet Ovid recounts the contest between them. The Muses prevailed, as deities always did, and the daughters of Pierus, being sore losers, were transformed into chattering magpies for their continued insolence. Pierus was considered to be the namesake of Pieria, the birthplace of the Muses and of the bard Orpheus.

(*See also* Macedon, Muses [the], Orpheus, Pieria, *and* Pierides [the].)

PIRITHOUS

Pirithous (or Perithous and Peirithous) was a king of the Lapiths in Thessaly. He was called a son of Zeus by some but was also known as a son of Ixion, the sinner who would become fastened to a flaming wheel in the Underworld. Pirithous was reputedly involved in a wide range of adventures, among them attempted abductions, in which he was joined by the Athenian hero Theseus: the two first attempted to make off with Helen of Sparta, prior to her marriage to Menelaus, and, later, with Persephone, Hades's queen. Pirithous is best known for his battle with the Centaurs, who had been his neighbors. Pirithous invited them to his wedding, but the Centaurs became drunk in the course of the festivities and tried to make off with Hippodamia, Pirithous's bride, and the other Lapith women. A fierce battle ensued, and the Centaurs were driven from Thessaly.

(*See also* Athens, Centaurs [the], Hades [god], Helen, Hippodamia, Ixion, Lapiths [the], Persephone, Theseus, Thessaly, Underworld [the], *and* Zeus.)

PITTHEUS

Pittheus was a son of Tantalus's son Pelops and Hippodamia, daughter of Oenomaus of Pisa. Pittheus became a king of Troezen in the northeastern Peloponnese and played a significant role in the life of the hero Theseus. When King Aegeus of Athens came to Troezen and related what Apollo's oracle at Delphi had told him in response to his query about being childless, Aegeus understood its meaning, although it eluded Aegeus: the Athenian king was not to loosen his wineskin (goatskin container for wine) until he returned home. Pittheus accordingly arranged for his daughter Aethra to lie with Aegeus, and she became pregnant with Theseus, who would, when grown, make his way to Athens and claim that city's throne.

(*See also* Aegeus, Aethra, Apollo, Athens, Delphi, Hippodamia, Oenomaus, Pelops, Tantalus, *and* Theseus.)

POEAS Poeas was the father of Philoctetes, the friend who helped Hercules in his final hour by agreeing to light the funeral pyre that he mounted in order to end his life. Poeas joined the expedition of Jason and the Argonauts, and in the course of the return journey from Colchis, Poeas fatally wounded the Sicilian giant Talus.

(*See also* Argonauts [the], Hercules, Jason, Philoctetes, Sicily, *and* Talus.)

POLYBUS Perhaps the best-known Polybus was the Corinthian king who, with his wife, Merope (or Periboea), took in the infant Oedipus and raised him as his own child. When Oedipus learned from the Oracle at Delphi that he was destined to kill his father and marry his mother, he left Corinth but unknowingly killed his biological father, Laius, on the road. Oedipus became Laius's successor on the throne of Thebes and married his mother, who bore him several children.

The Corinthian Polybus became confused with a Sicyonian king of the same name who was father of Adrastus, one of the Seven Against Thebes.

(*See also* Adrastus, Corinth, Delphi, Laius, Merope [heroine], Oedipus, Seven Against Thebes [the], *and* Thebes.)

POLYDECTES Polydectes and his brother, Dictys, were grandsons of the wind god Aeolus and a Naiad (a water nymph). Polydectes became king of the island of Seriphus, and Dictys a fisherman. Polydectes became enamored of the hero Perseus's mother, Danae, when she and her baby Perseus arrived, adrift in a chest, on the island. Hoping to make Danae his bride, Polydectes contrived a plot whereby to rid himself of Perseus, who, by some accounts, stood in his way. Polydectes thus announced that he was planning to wed Hippodamia and requested fine horses specifically as a wedding gift. Perseus, who had been raised as a fisherman by Dictys, could never hope to purchase such a gift and, instead, offered (or was forced to offer) the head of the Gorgon Medusa instead, this being a "gift" that was seemingly impossible to obtain. When, contrary to expectation, Perseus returned to Seriphus with the Gorgon's head in hand, he turned Polydectes and his assembled courtiers to stone, petrification being the result of looking directly at Medusa. A kinder Polydectes is portrayed by the mythographer Hyginus, according to whom Polydectes took Danae as wife and raised Perseus in a temple of Minerva. When Acrisius arrived in pursuit of Danae and Perseus, his daughter and grandson, Polydectes interceded so as to reconcile grandfather and grandson. Although Perseus swore that he would never kill Acrisius, he did later kill him accidentally while throwing a discus.

(*See also* Acrisius, Aeolus, Danae, Dictys, Gorgons [the], Medusa, Minerva, Naiads, Perseus, *and* Seriphus.)

POLYDORUS

There were several heroes by the name of Polydorus ("Giver of Many Gifts"). One was a son of King Priam of Troy and his wife, Hecuba. As the Roman poet Virgil writes, in order to keep him safe from the Greeks during the Trojan War, his parents sent him to Polymestor, king of the Bistones in Thrace, but Polymestor, driven by greed, murdered the boy for the gold that had been sent along with him. When, after the fall of Troy, Hecuba had been taken captive by the Greeks and came to Thrace, she there discovered the corpse of her son and exacted vengeance upon Polymestor. On his way to Italy, the Trojan hero Aeneas, too, came to Thrace and discovered Polydorus's place of burial accidentally. When Aeneas picked some branches of myrtle and dogwood, the plants bled, and the voice of Polydorus was heard: Polydorus's ghost told Aeneas of his brutal murder. Aeneas subsequently made sacrifice to the deceased in order to ensure proper burial and quickly departed from Thrace.

Another Polydorus was the son of Cadmus and Harmonia and became father of Labdacus. By some accounts, he held the throne of Thebes for a short time but died while still a young man.

(*See also* Aeneas, Cadmus, Harmonia, Hecuba, Labdacus, Priam, Thebes, Thrace, *and* Troy.)

POLYIDOS

Polyidos (or Polyeidos), "The One Who Knows Much," was a Corinthian seer with very considerable powers to work miracles. According to the Greek poet Pindar, Polyidos assisted the hero Bellerophon, who had been tasked with slaying the Chimaera. The seer had instructed Bellerophon to go to sleep on an altar of Athena, where he dreamed that the goddess appeared to him, a golden bridle in hand. Bellerophon recounted the dream to Polyidos, who advised him to make sacrifice to Poseidon, as the dream-Athena had instructed to do; to make sacrifice to Athena; and to use the bridle, which had manifested itself in "real" form, in order to tame Pegasus. Polyidos also famously helped King Minos of Crete find his young son Glaucus and, after finding him, restore him to life: the child was found drowned in a vat of honey and was miraculously revived by Polyidos, who had observed a serpent reviving its dead companion.

(*See also* Athena, Bellerophon, Chimaera [the], Corinth, Crete, Glaucus, Minos, Pegasus, *and* Poseidon.)

POLYNEICES

Polyneices, whose name means "much strife," was the cause of much hostility in the city of Thebes. He was a son of Oedipus, king of Thebes, and the queen Jocasta. Together with his brother, Eteocles, he was cursed by his father; according to the playwright Sophocles, this was because the brothers had done nothing to prevent Oedipus from being exiled. Once they were of age, the brothers agreed to share the throne by ruling in alternate years, but Eteocles, who ruled first, refused to step down. As a result, Polyneices raised an army, which was led by his father-in-law, Adrastus, to march against Thebes. This contingent was known as the Seven Against Thebes, and in the ensuing battle, all the seven captains apart from Adrastus were killed. Polyneices and Eteocles killed each other, in this way fulfilling their father's curse upon them. Jocasta's brother Creon, who then became regent, forbade the burial of Polyneices on the grounds that he was an enemy of the city, a position with which Polyneices's sister Antigone disagreed at the cost of her life. The death of Polyneices's allies was later avenged by the so-called Epigoni, the sons of the fallen Seven.

(*See also* Adrastus, Antigone, Creon, Epigoni [the], Eteocles, Jocasta, Oedipus, Seven Against Thebes [the], *and* Thebes.)

POLYPHONTES

Polyphontes was a descendant of Hercules and usurper of the throne of Cresphontes, King of Messenia. Polyphontes, "Killer of Many Men," slew not only Cresphontes but also the king's two eldest sons. The youngest, Aepytus, was saved by the queen Merope and, when grown to manhood, avenged his father's death, subsequently becoming king in his place.

(*See also* Aepytus, Cresphontes, Hercules, Merope [heroine], *and* Messenia.)

POLYXENA

Polyxena was a daughter of King Priam of Troy and his wife, the queen Hecuba. Her best-known siblings were Paris (Alexander), Hector, Deiphobus, Helenus, Cassandra, Polydorus, and Troilus. Polyxena herself was known primarily for how she died. The most common account of her death is that the ghost of Achilles—appearing either above his tomb or in a dream—demanded her sacrifice upon his tomb, or he would prevent the Greeks from returning home from Troy. By some accounts, it was Achilles's son Neoptolemus who carried out the sacrifice.

(*See also* Achilles, Cassandra, Deiphobus, Hector, Hecuba, Helenus, Neoptolemus, Polydorus, Priam, Troilus, *and* Troy.)

PROCNE

Procne was a daughter of the legendary Athenian king Pandion. The best known of her siblings were Erechtheus and Philomela. Pandion gave Procne as bride to King Tereus of Thrace, and she bore him a son named Itys.

When Procne later discovered that Tereus had imprisoned and repeatedly raped Philomela, the sisters plotted a gruesome vengeance: they served Tereus his own son. When fleeing Tereus's rage, Procne became a swallow and her sister a nightingale.

(*See also* Athens, Erechtheus, Philomela, *and* Tereus.)

PROCRIS Procris was a daughter of the legendary Athenian king Erechtheus and was married to Cephalus, son of King Deion of Phocis. The Roman Ovid poet tells the best-known version of their tragic love story. While a newlywed Cephalus was out hunting, he was abducted by the goddess of the dawn, Aurora (Eos to the Greeks). Procris was anguished over his disappearance, but Cephalus was anguished, too, at being separated from his bride, a fact that angered the goddess. So Aurora released Cephalus and said to him in parting that he would come to wish that he had never been with Procris. The goddess's words planted a seed of doubt, and Cephalus wondered if Procris might have been unfaithful to him in his absence. Accordingly, he decided to test her by disguising himself and propositioning her, using money as a bribe. She refused him repeatedly until, at last, he offered an enormous fortune for a single night. When she relented, an angry Cephalus revealed himself, and she, in shame, departed for the woods to become a companion to Diana, goddess of the hunt. Cephalus apologized and won her back, and the two had happy years together. Later, however, when Cephalus was again out hunting, he took a break from the heat of the day. While resting in the shade, he called out to the cooling breeze, asking it to comfort him and restore his vigor. But someone overheard him addressing these tender words to Aura, which was a woman's name but also the word for "breeze." His alleged faithlessness was reported to Procris who, on the next day, followed her husband into the woods. When he heard a rustling, he shot what he thought was prey. What he found was no animal but his beloved Procris, fatally wounded.

The mythographer Apollodorus preserves a different version of the story, according to which Procris was successfully seduced by another man in Cephalus's absence. She subsequently fled to Crete, where King Minos desired her and offered her a hunting dog and javelin. In exchange for these gifts, she cured Minos of an illness that been causing his mistresses to perish, and she slept with him. Later fleeing the anger of Minos's wife, Pasiphae, Procris returned to Athens, where she was reconciled with her husband who, while the two of them were out hunting, killed her accidentally. Hyginus records a different version still that blends aspects of both others: Procris fled to Crete, where she became a devotee of Diana. She became reconciled to her husband in the guise of a young man with whom Cephalus agreed to spend the night in order to lay claim to the "youth's" fine hunting dog and javelin. When the two met at night, Procris's true identity was revealed, and although she was later killed in that fateful hunting accident, Procris bore to Cephalus one Arcesius, who sired Laertes, the hero Odysseus's father.

(*See also* Athens, Aurora, Cephalus, Crete, Diana, Erechtheus, Laertes, Minos, Odysseus, *and* Pasiphae.)

PROCRUSTES

According to the mythographer Hyginus, the miscreant Procrustes, whose name means "stretcher," was a son of Neptune. Whenever travelers came to him seeking lodging, Procrustes offered them a bed but would make them fit the bed exactly: he lopped off the limbs of those too tall and stretched the limbs of those too short. While making his way to Athens, a young Theseus came upon Procrustes and killed him by subjecting him to the very form of torture to which he had subjected others.

Procrustes was variously known also as Polypemon and Damastes.

(*See also* Athens, Neptune, *and* Theseus.)

PROTESILAUS

Protesilaus, whose name means "first among the people," was a son of Iphicles (or Actor) and Diomedea (or Astyoche). Having been one of Helen of Sparta's numerous suitors, he was obliged to go to Troy and went as commander of forty ships from Thessaly. According to the mythographer Hyginus, although an oracle had warned that the first man to touch the Trojan shore would be the first to lose his life, Protesilaus, whose real name was Iolaus, bravely leaped ashore. He was instantly killed by Hector. His new bride, Laodamia, daughter of Acastus, was grief-stricken at his loss and begged the gods that she be allowed to speak with him for just three hours. The gods granted this request, but when Protesilaus died a second time, Laodamia could not bear the sorrow, so she commissioned a bronze likeness of him and kept it in her chambers under the pretense that she was making sacrifice to it. Yet a servant saw her embracing the statue and, mistaking it for a live man, informed her father that she had a lover. Her father soon discovered the truth and, in order to put an end to her misery, cast the statue onto a pyre. Her sorrow compounded, Laodamia then threw herself on the pyre, too.

(*See also* Hector, Helen, Sparta, Thessaly, *and* Troy.)

PSYCHE

The story of Psyche, whose name means "soul," is told by the Roman author Apuleius in his novel *The Golden Ass*. Psyche was one of three princesses, all of them lovely, but Psyche was the loveliest of all. Her beauty became widely known, and people began to worship her as though she were an incarnation of the goddess Venus herself, leaving the goddess's altars empty of sacrifices. At this Venus was angered, and instructed her son Cupid to make Psyche fall in love with the lowliest of men. Meanwhile, Psyche's father had become frantic, as his daughter had no suitors; all admired her as though she were a statue and untouchable. The king consulted Apollo's oracle and was instructed to leave Psyche on a cliff, where she would become the bride of a monster. From that cliff, Psyche was wafted onto a beautiful meadow and found her way into a lovely palace where all her needs were attended to by handmaids whose voices she heard but whom she never saw. She had a husband, too: Cupid, who appeared to her only under cover of darkness. Although Cupid, whom she had never actually seen, advised her against it, Psyche allowed her sisters to visit her. Out of envy over her luxurious surroundings, they prompted her to find out what her husband looked like, leading her to believe that he might indeed be a monster. A worried Psyche then lit a lamp and illuminated her sleeping husband. She was enraptured by the sight, but oil from her lamp dripped on Cupid, and he woke, instantly taking flight. A now-pregnant Psyche wandered the earth in search of him, enduring every kind of hardship, and then became enslaved to Venus, who set her a series of what she thought would be impossible tasks. All these tasks, which included sorting vast quantities of grain, gathering wool from sheep with golden fleeces, and obtaining a sample of water from the river Styx, Psyche accomplished, the first with the assistance of ants, the second with assistance of a talking reed, and the third with the help of Jupiter's eagle. The last task consisted of obtaining a beauty cream from Proserpina, queen of the Underworld. In this case, too, Psyche had help: it came from the tower from which she intended to throw herself. Having faced the Underworld's countless dangers and having obtained a box of this cream, Psyche was overcome with curiosity and opened the container. Inside was no unguent but the sleep of death, from which Cupid saved her. Reunited with the young god, Psyche became immortal and bore him a child called Voluptas (Pleasure).

(*See also* Cupid, Jupiter, Proserpina, Styx [the River], Underworld [the], Venus, *and* Zeus.)

PYGMALION There are two notable Pygmalions in Greco-Roman mythology. One was a king of Cyprus who, as the Roman poet Ovid recounts, chose a life of celibacy in shock at the shameful lives led by women on the island. Possessing a sculptor's skill, he created an ivory statue of a girl so beautiful that he fell in love with her and showered her with gifts. On the occasion of the goddess Aphrodite's festival, he made an offering and a prayer to the goddess: he asked that he one day have a wife just like his ivory girl. His wish was granted: the statue became animate, a woman of flesh and blood. Post-classical authors called this woman Galatea. To Pygmalion she bore a girl named Paphos, whose son Cinyras later founded the city of (Old) Paphos, the site of Aphrodite's most hallowed sanctuary and the place where Aphrodite first stepped on land consequent to her watery birth.

The other Pygmalion was a king of Tyre in Phoenicia and, according to Virgil in his *Aeneid*, brother of Dido, who became one of the many casualties of the hero Aeneas's quest to reach the shores of Italy and establish the Roman race. Covetous of Dido's husband's wealth, Pygmalion murdered him and hid this fact from Dido. Yet the bloodied ghost of her husband, Sychaeus, appeared to her at night revealing her brother's murderous act and urging her to flee the country. This Dido did, taking with her a group of refugees who hated or feared the tyrant-king. As leader of these people, Dido traveled overseas to the land of Byrsa, in northern Africa, which she purchased with riches whose hiding place her husband's ghost had also disclosed.

(*See also* Aeneas, Aphrodite, Cinyras, Cyprus, Dido, Paphos, *and* Sychaeus.)

PYLADES
Pylades was the son of Strophius, king of Phocis in central Greece. He became a close friend and companion to the Mycenaean king Agamemnon's son Orestes, who by some accounts was his cousin and had been sent to the court of Strophius after his mother, Clytemnestra, and her lover, Aegisthus, had murdered his father, Agamemnon. Pylades accompanied Orestes when he returned to Mycenae to exact vengeance for his father's murder and was with him, too, when he traveled to the barbarian land of the Taurians in order to fetch a wooden statue of Artemis that, if brought to the territory of Athens, would ensure Orestes's release from pursuit by the Erinyes. Pylades was given Orestes's sister Electra as a bride and with her became father to two sons.

(*See also* Aegisthus, Agamemnon, Artemis, Athens, Clytemnestra, Electra [heroine], Erinyes [the], Mycenae, Orestes, *and* Taurians [the].)

PYRAMUS
Pyramus and Thisbe were young, star-crossed lovers who lived in the city of Babylon. According to the Roman poet Ovid, who vividly tells their tragic tale, the two met daily in secret, whispering to each other through a crack in the wall that separated their houses, for their parents objected to their special friendship, unwilling that they should meet or marry. At last they could stand separation no longer and planned to escape their parents by leaving their homes and the city under the cover of night. They agreed to meet at an easily recognizable landmark, the tomb of Ninus, father to the Babylonian

queen Samiramis. The tomb's location was marked by a mulberry tree heavy with white fruit. At the fall of darkness, Thisbe first made her escape, arriving alone at the place of meeting. As it happened, a lioness approached, her mouth bloodied from a recent kill. A terrified Thisbe fled, dropping her veil in flight, but the lioness did not pursue her, having come to this spot only for a drink. After mouthing Thisbe's veil, the lioness departed, and now Pyramus appeared. He did not see Thisbe, but instead caught sight of her bloodied veil. Believing his beloved to have been killed, he threw himself upon his sword. His blood stained the fruits of the mulberry red and also soaked its roots. Now Thisbe came out of hiding to discover the tree's color oddly changed and then quickly discovered the cause. In desperation she, too, threw herself upon the sword. The lovers' death was thereafter memorialized by the mulberry, its red fruit a constant reminder of their tragic end. In death, at least, their ashes were allowed to mingle, being kept in a single urn.

(*See also* Babylon, Semiramis, *and* Thisbe.)

PYRRHA Pyrrha was the daughter of the second-generation Titan god Epimetheus and Pandora, the first woman, who brought as a dowry the fateful Pandora's Box, filled with good and evil. Pyrrha married her uncle Prometheus's son, Deucalion, and with him survived the great flood brought on by Zeus, who was angered at all the human depravity he had witnessed and wished to eradicate humanity. When the couple's boat washed up on the summit of Mount Parnassus, which protruded from the waters covering the earth, Zeus pitied them and ordered the waters to recede. Pyrrha and Deucalion then repopulated the earth; receiving guidance from the goddess Themis, they cast stones over their shoulders, and these became the current, hardened human race. With Deucalion, Pyrrha would later become mother to six children, the best known of whom was Hellen, ancestor of the Hellenes, as the Greeks called themselves.

(*See also* Deucalion, Epimetheus, Hellen, Pandora, Parnassus [Mount], Prometheus, Themis, Titans [the], *and* Zeus.)

PYRRHUS Pyrrhus was another name for Neoptolemus, son of Achilles.

(*See also* Achilles *and* Neoptolemus.)

REMUS Remus was a son of the Vestal Virgin Rhea Silvia and Mars, and was the twin brother of Romulus, who became founder of Rome. After the twins had survived attempted drowning in the Tiber River and had grown to manhood, they desired to found their own city. As the brothers were the same age, there was no easy way to decide who would name and rule the city. In the course of a dispute between them, Remus, by way of mocking Romulus, leaped over the city's rising walls, causing his brother to slay him in anger.

(*See also* Mars, Rhea Silvia, Rome, Romulus, Tiber River [the], *and* Vesta.)

RHADAMANTHUS

Rhadamanthus (or Rhadamanthys) was a son of Zeus and the princess Europa. According to Homer, he was the brother of Minos, and according to Hesiod, he was brother of both Minos and Aeacus. Various traditions suggest that all three brothers became judges in the Underworld after their deaths. As for Rhadamanthus, the historian Diodorus Siculus records that on the island of Crete, which was the place of his birth, he became known for making the most just decisions and instituting appropriate punishments for malefactors. When he later resided in Asia Minor, islanders and mainlanders alike voluntarily subjected themselves to his rule because of his reputation for being a paragon of justice.

(*See also* Aeacus, Crete, Europa, Minos, Underworld [the], *and* Zeus.)

RHEA SILVIA

Rhea Silvia was the daughter of Numitor, a king of Alba Longa, the city that the Trojan hero Aeneas's son Ascanius had founded in Italy. Although Numitor was the elder son of King Procas and thus the latter's rightful heir, he was driven from the throne by his younger brother Amulius, according to the Roman historian Livy. Not stopping there, Amulius killed Numitor's sons and, so as to ensure that he would have no grandsons, made his daughter Rhea Silvia a Vestal Virgin; the Vestals, priestesses of Vesta, were required to remain celibate while serving the goddess, and indiscretions were punishable by death. In spite of all these measures, Rhea Silvia was impregnated by the god Mars. Amulius had Rhea Silvia imprisoned as a consequence, and he ordered her children, the twins Romulus and Remus, to be placed in a basket and set adrift in the Tiber River. Amulius, of course, expected that the twins would die, but they did not, famously being rescued by a she-wolf. As for Rhea Silvia, "mother" of the Romans, she was later released by her sons when they came of age.

(*See also* Aeneas, Alba Longa, Ascanius, Mars, Remus, Rome, Romulus, Tiber, *and* Vesta.)

RHOECUS

Rhoecus of Cnidus was said to have observed a particular oak ready to fall and ordered his slaves to prop it up. In gratitude for this, the Hamadryad nymph who inhabited the tree granted Rhoecus a wish. What he wished for was to lie with her, and she consented, stating that he must remain true to her and that she would send a bee as a messenger at the appropriate moment. When she did send the bee, Rhoecus happened to be engaged in a board

PLATE VI
Romulus and Remus: Twin brothers and founders of the city of Rome

game and was simply annoyed at the bee's presence, seemingly having forgotten what it could signify. In anger the nymph blinded him. According to Pindar, who offers a variant of the story, Rhoecus had been unfaithful and was stung.

(*See also* Hamadryads [the].)

ROMULUS Romulus and his twin brother, Remus, were children of Rhea Silvia, a priestess of Vesta, and the god Mars. Their birth was wholly unexpected, as Rhea Silvia's uncle, Amulius, had appointed her a Vestal precisely because the Vestals were to remain celibate, any breach of their vows of chastity being punishable by death. Upon the twins' birth, Rhea Silvia was imprisoned while Romulus and Remus were placed in a basket and set adrift in the Tiber River. When the waters receded, the basket and its precious contents were discovered by a she-wolf, who suckled the twins. A herdsman named Faustulus came upon them and brought them home, and he and his wife, Larentia, who were childless, raised the twins as their own. As the boys matured, they took to hunting and also to marauding, stealing from robbers and distributing the twice-stolen goods to their community of herdsmen. Remus was taken captive and delivered to Numitor, his grandfather, for punishment, but Numitor suspected his true identity. At the same time the herdsman Faustulus revealed to Romulus what he suspected the truth of his birth to be. Thus, Romulus and Remus each brought supporters with them to oust the usurper-king Amulius, and after Romulus killed Amulius, Numitor, the rightful king, was reinstated as ruler of Alba Longa. Romulus and Remus, for their part, now desired to build their own city, but as they were twins, it was not clear who should name and rule it. They accordingly decided to leave this question up to the gods, Remus positioning himself on the Aventine Hill and Romulus on the Palatine in order to await signs from above. Remus received a sign first, as six vultures appeared to him, but twelve then appeared to Romulus. The followers of each brother claimed their own champion victorious, and a quarrel ensued. In anger, Remus leaped over the city's rising walls by way of insult, and for this action Romulus killed him, thus becoming king and naming the city after himself: Rome. Romulus established laws as well as religious practices and priesthoods, and he increased the population by making his new city a sanctuary for all those desiring a new life. Still there was a problem, as the population consisted solely of men. Romulus sent envoys to neighboring cities to negotiate alliances and intermarriage, but the Romans were everywhere denied. Accordingly, Romulus devised a plan: the Romans would host a celebration in honor of Neptune and invite the neighboring peoples, including the Sabines. Pleased to attend, the neighboring peoples came, their women and children in tow. When their guests were engrossed in the spectacle, the Romans set upon the maidens and made off with them. This caused the outbreak of hostilities in which Romulus was at first victorious and dedicated Rome's first temple to Jupiter in consequence. Hostilities continued, however, and the Sabines, last among the neighboring peoples to do so, finally also attacked Rome. The Sabines went so far as to breach Rome's fortifications, since the Romans were betrayed by Tarpeia, daughter of a Roman commander, and hostilities raged on until the Sabine women entreated their new husbands and fathers to call a truce and make peace. This they did, making a single people out of two. After the death of the Sabine king Titus Tatius, Romulus ruled the combined peoples until his miraculous death and deification: while Romulus was reviewing the troops on the Campus Martius, a sudden storm enveloped him in clouds, and he disappeared from earth. Romulus, it was declared, had been carried to the heavens, and he was henceforth worshipped as the god Quirinus.

(*See also* Jupiter, Mars, Neptune, Quirinus, Rhea Silvia, Rome, Sabines [the], Tarpeia, Tiber, *and* Vesta.)

RUTULIANS, THE   The Rutulians were an Italian people residing in southern Latium. Their capital was Ardea, and their king, Turnus, had hoped to win the hand of Lavinia, daughter of Laurentum's king Latinus. When Aeneas arrived in Italy, Latinus promised Lavinia to Aeneas, and the Rutulians joined the other Latins in war against Aeneas and his allies.

(*See also* Aeneas, Latinus, Latium, Lavinia, *and* Turnus.)

SABINES, THE   The Sabines were an Italian people who lived northeast of Rome, the city founded by Romulus. At Rome's founding, their king was Titus Tatius, who later ruled jointly with Romulus after the Sabines and Romans resolved to become a single people. This union occurred subsequent to a bitter war resulting from the Romans' theft of the Sabines' women, a conflict that the Sabine women resolved by appealing to their new husbands and their fathers to make peace. Titus Tatius and Romulus ruled together for a period of five years until the former was murdered by a cohort from Laurentum, leaving sole rule to Romulus. After Romulus's passing, the Sabine Numa Pompilius became Rome's second king.

(*See also* Numa, Rome, *and* Romulus.)

SALMONEUS   Salmoneus's father was Aeolus, a son of Hellen and "founder" of the Aeolians. According to the mythographer Hyginus, Salmoneus first lived in Thessaly, but afterward came to Elis, where he founded a

city called Salmone. Salmoneus, in an excess of pride, wanted to be the equal of Zeus and went so far as to claim that he actually was this god, taking for himself sacrifices intended for Zeus and dragging behind his chariot kettles that produced a noise like thunder. He imitated Zeus's lightning bolts by hurling lit torches into the air. Consequently, Zeus struck him dead with one of his thunderbolts and wiped out the city of Salmone, inhabitants and all. The historian Diodorus Siculus adds to this tale the story of Salmoneus's daughter, Tyro. Salmoneus, who dishonored and disrespected all the gods, failed to believe that Tyro had been impregnated by Poseidon and treated her badly, this being another reason that he was struck down by Zeus. A variant of Tyro's saga makes Salmoneus's wife, Sidero, Tyro's tormentor and Tyro's sons her avenger.

(*See also* Poseidon, Sidero, Tyro, *and* Zeus.)

SARPEDON   There were two Sarpedons of note, one being the grandfather of the other. The elder Sarpedon was a son of Zeus either by Europa, daughter of Cadmus, or Laodamia, daughter of Bellerophon. Having been raised on the island of Crete, the elder Sarpedon fled from there to Asia Minor, where he fought the legendary Solymi, whose former lands he then ruled, doing so jointly with Lycus of Athens (from whom the Lycians took their name) at a later point. Sarpedon and his grandson Sarpedon became confused even in antiquity. In Homer's *Iliad* the younger Sarpedon was a son of Zeus and, with his cousin Glaucus, leader of the Lycians, who had come to fight on the side of the Trojans. In the course of the fighting, Sarpedon came face-to-face with Achilles's close friend Patroclus, and his father, Zeus, was grieved at the prospect of now losing his son. Zeus deliberated whether or not to save him and consulted Hera, who pointed out that all the gods had mortal children whom they would want to save, and that favoritism would bring with it strife. She suggested that he honor his son by having his body removed from the battlefield by Hypnos and Thanatos ("Sleep" and "Death") and brought to his home in Lycia for proper burial.

(*See also* Achilles, Bellerophon, Cadmus, Crete, Europa, Glaucus [hero], Hera, Hypnus, Lycia, Patroclus, Solymi [the], Thanatos, *and* Zeus.)

SCHOENEUS   Schoeneus was a Boeotian king, and a son of Athamas, who was also father of the ill-fated children Phrixus and Helle. Schoeneus is best known as the father of the swift-footed huntress Atalanta, whom no person could outrun, at least without resorting to trickery.

(*See also* Atalanta, Athamas, Boeotia, Helle, *and* Phrixus.)

SCIRON Sciron, by some accounts a son of Poseidon or grandson of Pelops, was a legendary outlaw who resided on the Scironian Cliffs on the Saronic Gulf at the eastern coast of the territory of Megara. Alongside these cliffs lay the road to Athens, and Sciron would ask passersby to wash his feet. While they were bent over, busy with the task, he would hurl them off the cliffs to their deaths in the sea, where, according to the mythographer Apollodorus, they were devoured by an enormous turtle. The hero Theseus rid the cliffs of this hazard by subjecting Sciron to the very treatment to which he had subjected others, his bones later fusing to the crags, according to the Roman poet Ovid.

(*See also* Athens, Megara [place], Pelops, Poseidon, *and* Theseus.)

SCYLLA Scylla was princess of the Greek city Megara and daughter of Nisus, that city's king. While Minos, king of Crete, was waging war upon Megara, Scylla fell in love with him at first sight. The way to win Minos's heart, she reasoned, was to ensure his victory over Nisus, a thing that, according to an oracle, could be achieved only if Nisus's single lock of purple hair were severed from his head. The Roman poet Ovid describes Scylla's treachery in detail: she cut the lock at night while her father was sleeping and offered it to Minos who, alarmed at this act of brazen betrayal, would have nothing to do with her. Minos set sail for Crete at first occasion, and Scylla leaped into the sea, swimming in pursuit. However, when she reached the Cretan vessel, her father, transformed into an osprey, dove at her, causing her to lose her grip. Now she, too, became a sea bird or, as mythographer Hyginus reports, a fish. The travel writer Pausanias's version of Scylla's end is different: he writes that Minos tied her by the feet to the ship's stern, thus causing her to drown.

This Scylla is to be distinguished from the nymph-turned-monster of the same name.

(*See also* Crete, Megara [place], Minos, Nisus, *and* Scylla [monster].)

SEMELE The lovely Semele distinguished herself by the manner of her death. She was a daughter of Cadmus, king and founder of Thebes, and his wife, Harmonia. As was the case with a number of lovely maidens, she caught the ever-roving eye of Zeus, by whom she became pregnant. Hera became aware of this affair and, disguising herself as Semele's old nurse, tricked Semele into doubting that her lover was divine. The goddess urged that she should ensure that he was not merely some mortal man claiming to be Zeus. The next time that Zeus visited her, a concerned Semele asked him for a favor, and he replied that he would grant her anything she desired. Being the guarantor of the sanctity of oaths, he could not deny her request: she asked that he appear to her in his full divine glory. So, he appeared to her as the god of storms and bearer of lightning. The pregnant Semele caught fire and perished, but Zeus was able to save her unborn fetus, the infant Dionysus, and sewed it into his thigh, from which the god was born when the period of gestation was complete. According to the playwright Euripides's tragedy *The Bacchae*, Semele's sisters Agave, Autonoe, and Ino, envious that their sister had become mother to a god, spread a rumor that Dionysus was no god and Semele's lover a mortal. For this the sisters were punished, being driven to murder Agave's son Pentheus. The Roman poet Ovid adds that Ino had actually served for a time as Dionysus's nurse, but that he was then given to the nymphs of Mount Nysa to raise.

(*See also* Agave, Autonoe, Cadmus, Dionysus, Harmonia, Hera, Ino, Nysa, Pentheus, Thebes, *and* Zeus.)

SEMIRAMIS The Assyrian queen Semiramis was a historical figure, accounts of whose life and achievements became steeped in legend. Reputedly a great beauty, Semiramis was said to have been born of the Near Eastern fertility goddess Derketo/Atargatis, nurtured by doves, and raised by shepherds. According to the historian Diodorus Siculus, while married to an Assyrian officer, Semiramis caught the eye of King Ninus, who wished to marry her. Under threat from Ninus, the officer committed suicide, and Semiramis then became queen. Later, after Ninus's death, she became sole regent and was credited with having built Babylon, as the Roman poet Ovid mentions in the tale of the star-crossed lovers Pyramus and Thisbe, as well as leading several successful military campaigns.

(*See also* Babylon *and* Pyramus.)

SEVEN AGAINST THEBES, THE The Seven Against Thebes were the seven captains assembled by King Adrastus of Argos to help Oedipus's son (and Adrastus's son-in-law) Polyneices in his bid to take the throne of Thebes from his brother Eteocles; the brothers had agreed to share the crown of Thebes by ruling alternately for a year, and Eteocles, who had assumed the kingship first, refused to step down. Although not all sources agree on the identity of the Seven, they are often listed as Adrastus; Polyneices; Tydeus, the brutal father of Diomedes; the prideful, godless Capaneus; Hippomedon; Parthenopaeus; and the seer Amphiaraus, who knew beforehand that the campaign would go badly. All the Seven apart from Adrastus were slain, and they were later avenged by their sons, the so-called Epigoni.

(*See also* Adrastus, Amphiaraus, Argos, Capaneus, Diomedes, Epigoni [the], Eteocles, Oedipus, Parthenopaeus, Thebes, *and* Tydeus.)

SIBYL OF CUMAE, THE Sibyls were prophetesses who, from birth, received divine inspiration and served the deities who inspired them throughout their very long lives. The Roman historian Varro notes known Sibyls from around the Greco-Roman world: Persia, Libya, Delphi, Cimmeria, Erythrea, Samos, Cumae, the Hellespont, Phrygia, and Tibur. The most famous of these was the Sibyl of Cumae, who resided in a mountain cavern at Cumae on Italy's Campanian coast. According to the Roman poet Virgil, there were one hundred entrances to the vast cavern, and from all of these the Sibyl's voice could be heard. The hero Aeneas was sent to consult the Sibyl, and, while possessed by the god Apollo, she told him of the wars he faced in Latium and that he must both pluck a certain golden bough as an offering for Proserpina and bury his fallen comrade Palinurus in order to gain access to the Underworld. Subsequently, she accompanied the hero all the way to the Elysian Fields, where he met his father, Anchises.

(*See also* Aeneas, Anchises, Apollo, Cumae, Delphi, Elysian Fields [the], Hellespont [the], Latium, Palinurus, Phrygia, Proserpina, *and* Underworld [the].)

SICHAEUS Sichaeus (or Sychaeus) was the murdered husband of Dido, queen of Carthage.

(*See* Carthage, Dido, *and* Sychaeus.)

SIDERO Sidero was the stepmother of Tyro, daughter of the sacrilegious Salmoneus, a king of Salmonia in Elis. For her ill treatment of Tyro, her grandson Pelias (or Pelias and his brother Neleus) killed her.

(*See also* Neleus, Pelias, Salmoneus, *and* Tyro.)

SINIS Sinis was a son of Poseidon, according to the Greek poet Bacchylides, and was a truly evil man who lived on the Isthmus of Corinth. Known as Pityokamptes ("Pine-Bender"), Sinis tied the arms and legs of passersby to pine trees that he had bent to the ground, and when he released the trees, his hapless victims were torn apart. On his way from Troezen to Athens, the young hero Theseus rid Greece of this plague by subjecting him to the same torture. A variant tradition preserved by the mythographers Hyginus and Apollodorus describes Sinis's preferred mode of torture differently: Sinis compelled passersby to bend, or to help bend, trees, which he released as the task was being completed, thereby launching his unsuspecting victims into the air.

(*See also* Athens, Corinth, Poseidon, *and* Theseus.)

SINON Sinon was a Greek whose treachery is vividly described in Virgil's *Aeneid*. A participant in the Trojan War, he pretended to have been designated by the Greeks for human sacrifice but to have escaped. The priest Laocoon had warned the Trojans to beware of the Trojan Horse, but Sinon told a lying tale that, together with Laocoon's death, convinced them that the horse was harmless. According to Sinon, the Greeks had departed for home and had left the horse as an offering to the goddess Minerva, whose anger at the Greeks for Ulysses and Diomedes's theft of her ancient statue, the so-called Palladium, had caused the Greeks to fare so poorly in the war.

(*See also* Athena, Diomedes, Laocoon, Minerva, Troy, *and* Ulysses.)

SISYPHUS
Sisyphus became one of the canonical sinners in the Underworld, his fate being to push a boulder up a hill only to have it always roll down again as he reached the top. Sisyphus was a son of Hellen's son Aeolus and grandfather of Bellerophon, and by some accounts, he was the founder of Corinth. Sisyphus became known as being cunning, and in the estimation of the gods, overly so. For example, when faced with repeated theft of his cattle by Hermes's son Autolycus, who had the ability to change the appearance of the cattle that he stole (from black to white, from horned to hornless, and so on), Sisyphus marked the bottom of his remaining cattle's hooves, thus making the animals identifiable. Among the reasons given by ancient sources for his eternal punishment in the Underworld were his taking captive Thanatos ("Death") himself, with the result that no person died until the god Ares intervened, releasing Thanatos and causing Sisyphus's death. The mythographer Apollodorus, by contrast, offers Sisyphus's betrayal of Zeus, who had secretly absconded with the river god Asopus's daughter Aegina, as a reason for his punishment in the Underworld.

(*See also* Aegina, Aeolus [hero], Bellerophon, Corinth, Hellen, Hermes, Thanatos, *and* Underworld [the].)

SOLYMI, THE
The Solymi were a warlike tribe that, as Homer and later authors recount, lived in eastern Lycia and were defeated by the hero Bellerophon, who, riding the winged horse Pegasus, attacked them on the orders of the Lycian king Iobates.

(*See also* Bellerophon, Iobates, Lycia, *and* Pegasus.)

SYCHAEUS Sychaeus (or Sichaeus) was the deceased husband of the Carthaginian queen Dido. According to Virgil's *Aeneid*, Sychaeus had been the wealthiest landowner in Phoenicia, and Dido's brother, Pygmalion, who was the king of Tyre, coveted his wealth. Driven by greed, Pygmalion murdered Sychaeus and hid his evil deed from Dido. Sometime later, the bloodied ghost of Sychaeus appeared to Dido in her sleep and revealed what he had suffered. Sychaeus's ghost also disclosed to Dido the location of a cache of hidden gold and silver and urged her to flee the country. This she did, gathering those who hated or feared the tyrant Pygmalion. With these refugees she set sail and arrived, ultimately, in Libya, where she founded a new city, Carthage. As a consequence of her disastrous love affair with the Trojan Aeneas, Dido committed suicide, but in the Underworld, she was reunited with her beloved Sychaeus.

(*See also* Aeneas, Dido, Carthage, Pygmalion, *and* Underworld [the].)

TANTALUS Tantalus was a legendary Lydian king who, with Sisyphus and Ixion, became one of the canonical sinners in Hades. Tantalus's eternal torture in the Underworld consisted of standing in a pool whose waters receded when he bent to drink, and branches hanging heavy with fruit above his head were blown out of his reach by breezes when he tried to pick their bounty. In addition to this, a boulder was suspended just overhead, always on the verge of falling, thus posing a constant threat. Though he was reputedly a son of Zeus who enjoyed the favor of the gods, it was a grave offense to them that occasioned his punishment, and this offense was variously described. The Greek poet Pindar recounts two reasons for his punishment. Tantalus had dined with the gods, who shared with him nectar and ambrosia, divine food that would make him immortal, but Tantalus subsequently shared this food with his mortal companions. Alternatively, in return for the meals that they had shared with him, Tantalus invited the gods to dine but, as a test of their wisdom, served them his son Pelops, of whom he had made a stew. Fortunately, all but one of the gods perceived that something was amiss; only Demeter, steeped in grief over her loss of Persephone, ate some of the stew, causing Zeus, who then reassembled and revived Pelops, to replace his nibbled-on shoulder blade with ivory. Pelops would become a tragic figure in his own right, as would Niobe, Tantalus's daughter.

(*See also* Demeter, Hades [place], Ixion, Lydia, Niobe, Pelops, Persephone, Sisyphus, Underworld [the], *and* Zeus.)

TARPEIA Tarpeia was the daughter of the Roman general Spurius Tarpeius, who had been charged with securing the Capitoline Hill against the attacking Sabines. Tarpeia betrayed the Romans by offering the Sabines entry into the Romans' fortifications in exchange for what they wore on their left arms. Presumably it was their heavy gold bracelets that Tarpeia was after, but the Sabines rewarded her instead with their shields, using these to crush her on the grounds that death was what a traitor deserved. Tarpeia gave her name to the Tarpeian Rock on Rome's Capitoline Hill from which later traitors were cast to their deaths.

(*See also* Capitoline Hill [the], Sabines [the], *and* Rome.)

TAURIANS, THE The Taurians were a people who inhabited the region now known as the Crimean Peninsula on the Black Sea. Among their kings were Perses, brother of the Colchian king Aeetes, and Thoas, who was king when Iphigeneia, having been saved from death at the hands of her father, Agamemnon, was brought to Tauris by the goddess Artemis. It was the custom of the Taurians to sacrifice strangers to Artemis, and Iphigeneia served as Artemis's priestess, her job being to prepare these human victims for sacrifice, until she was rescued by her brother Orestes.

(*See also* Aeetes, Agamemnon, Artemis, Colchis, Iphigeneia, Orestes, *and* Thoas.)

TEIRESIAS Teiresias (or Tiresias) was a Theban seer. He was descended from the Sparti, the "Sown Men" who sprang from the soil when Cadmus, founder of Thebes, sowed dragon's teeth. Like many of those who had received divine inspiration, he was blind, and the mythographer Apollodorus reports several causes of his blindness. Either he revealed the secrets of the gods to humans, saw the goddess Athena naked, or asserted that women receive greater pleasure from lovemaking than men, a statement that aroused Hera's anger. As it happened, Teiresias was uniquely qualified to judge in the last-mentioned matter as he had lived both as a man and as a woman: having one day stepped upon a female snake coupling with a male snake, he turned into a woman, and when he repeated this at a later point, now stepping on the male, he again became a man.

Teiresias served the Thebans faithfully for three generations. When Dionysus came to Thebes in order to introduce his worship to Greece, Teiresias wisely urged the young regent Pentheus to embrace the god as he and the aged Cadmus had done. Later, he revealed to Oedipus that the latter, and not some unknown brigand, was the murderer of Thebes's king Laius and thus, unknowingly, had committed incest with his mother. Teiresias knew, too, that Creon, who became regent of Thebes, was wrong to refuse burial to Oedipus's son Polyneices and that disaster would result. Even dead, Teiresias retained his prophetic powers, for his spirit appeared before Odysseus and prophesied all the trials that the hero would face in the future.

(*See also* Athena, Cadmus, Creon, Dionysus, Hera, Laius, Odysseus, Oedipus, Pentheus, Polyneices, *and* Thebes.)

TELAMON

Telamon was a son of Aeacus, king of Aegina, and brother of Peleus, who is best known as the father of Achilles. Telamon and Peleus joined together to kill their stepbrother Phocus and, as a consequence, were sent into exile by their father. While Peleus went to Thessaly, Telamon went to the island of Salamis, where he married the king's daughter, Glauce, and, after the king's death, became the island's regent. After Glauce's death, Telamon married Periboea (or Eeriboea), who bore Ajax (the Great or "Telamonian Ajax"), later to be one of the best warriors among the Greeks. Both Telamon and Peleus joined the hunt for the Calydonian Boar and Jason's quest for the Golden Fleece, but Telamon is perhaps best remembered for his assistance to Hercules when the latter attacked Troy in order to exact vengeance for an earlier wrong: as a reward for saving his daughter Hesione from a sea monster, the Trojan king Laomedon had promised to give Hercules the wondrous horses that he had received from Zeus but reneged on that promise. Telamon was the first to breach the walls of Troy, and for this, Hercules, never wanting to be outdone, came close to killing him. Telamon saved himself by claiming to be building an altar in honor of Hercules, and the latter awarded him Hesione, who would become the mother of Teucer by Telamon.

(*See also* Achilles, Aeacus, Aegina [place], Ajax [the Great], Calydon, Hercules, Hesione, Jason, Laomedon, Peleus, Salamis, Teucer, Thessaly, *and* Troy.)

TELEMACHUS

Telemachus, "Far-Fighter," was the son of Odysseus, king of Ithaca, and his wife, Penelope. When Odysseus left for Troy to fight in the Trojan War, Telemachus was just an infant, but when, after a twenty-year absence, his father returned, he had grown to become a suitable ally for him as he won back his home and kingdom from Penelope's lawless suitors. Homer's *Odyssey* recounts Telemachus's maturation process: asserting himself for the first time, he called an assembly of the Ithacans, a thing that had not occurred on the island for a very long time, and he traveled to mainland Greece in order to gather news of his father from old King Nestor of Pylos and Menelaus in Sparta. There was a tradition that Telemachus ultimately married the sorceress Circe, who made him and his mother, Penelope, immortal.

(*See also* Circe, Ithaca, Menelaus, Nestor, Odysseus, Penelope, Pylos, Sparta, *and* Troy.)

TELEPHUS Telephus was the son of Hercules and the princess Auge, a priestess of Athena and daughter of the Tegean king Aleus. As Auge had become pregnant out of wedlock, she abandoned her child, Telephus, in Athena's precinct, where he was later discovered by her father, Aleus. Aleus then ordered Telephus to be exposed on Mount Parthenius, where he was rescued by a doe who had a newborn fawn and nursed him until he was found by some shepherds. Auge, for her part, was sent away to be sold or drowned, but she escaped this fate, becoming the wife (or adopted daughter) of Teuthras, a king of Teuthrania in Mysia. According to an alternate tradition, Auge and Telephus were set adrift at sea in a chest by Auge's father and, contrary to expectation, survived, arriving in Mysia, where Telephus later became regent. When the Greeks arrived there on their way to Troy, Telephus was wounded by Achilles, and the wound would not heal. He learned from Apollo's oracle that only the source of his wound could cure him, so he went in search of Achilles, who was willing to help but claimed not to be a healer. According to the mythographer Hyginus, it was Ulysses who explained that Achilles's spear, not Achilles, was the required healer, and scraped some rust from its tip onto the wound, which instantly healed. In gratitude for this, Telephus showed the Greeks the way to Troy.

(*See also* Achilles, Apollo, Athena, Hercules, Troy, *and* Ulysses.)

TEREUS Tereus, reportedly a son of the war god Ares, was a Thracian king who was guilty of a terrible crime and, as a consequence, suffered terrible retribution. When the city of Athens was under attack, Tereus brought his forces to aid the Athenian king Pandion. For this kindness Pandion rewarded Tereus by offering him his daughter Procne as bride. When a period of five years had passed, Procne, who missed her sister Philomela, begged Tereus either to let her visit Athens or to let her sister come to visit her. Tereus acquiesced and set sail for Athens to fetch Philomela. However, the moment that he laid eyes on Philomela, he was gripped by passion. When, at last, Tereus and Philomela arrived in Thrace, he took her to a hut in the woods and raped her. When Philomela threatened to expose his crime, he grabbed his sword and cut out her tongue; Procne, meanwhile, was told that her sister had perished at sea. Although Philomela could not speak, she found another means of documenting her suffering: she turned to her loom, which she used to weave her story into a tapestry that she gave to the old woman who attended her. In this way, Tereus's crime was made known to Procne, who rescued her sister, and the two plotted their vengeance on Tereus. The sisters murdered Tereus's young son, Itys, and made a stew of him. They served this gruesome stew to Tereus, who ate with gusto until he asked for his son, and Philomela appeared with Itys's head. The full horror of what had transpired having been revealed, Tereus set upon the sisters with his sword. As they fled, Philomela became a nightingale and Procne a swallow. Tereus, for his part, became a hoopoe, a species of bird distinguished by its showy crown feathers.

(*See also* Ares, Athens, Philomela, Procne, *and* Thrace.)

TEUCER There were two heroes of note by the name of Teucer. The first of these was said to be a son of the river Scamander and Idaea, nymph of Mount Ida in the Troad (region surrounding the future site of Troy), but another tradition called him an immigrant from Crete. This Teucer was the first king of the Troad, and the Trojans were called Teucrians in acknowledgment of this fact. Teucer was succeeded by Dardanus, who had married Teucer's daughter. Both Teucer and Dardanus were ancestors of Troy's kings.

The other Teucer was a son of the hero Telamon and Hesione, daughter of the Trojan king Laomedon. His half brother was Ajax the Great, side by side with whom he fought in the Trojan War.

(*See also* Ajax the Great, Crete, Dardanus, Hesione, Ida [Mount], Laomedon, Telamon, *and* Troy.)

TEUCRIANS, THE The Trojans were sometimes called Teucrians after Teucer, an ancestor of the Trojan kings.

(*See* Teucer *and* Troy.)

THAMYRIS Thamyris is known as early as Homer's *Iliad* as a bard from Thrace who was exceedingly skilled in singing and playing the cithara. Yet Thamyris fell prey to hubris, foolishly boasting that he could outperform the Muses. For this presumption the Muses struck him blind and caused him to forget his art. Thamyris is also known as the first man to desire another male, the object of his affections being the Spartan youth Hyacinth.

(*See also* Hyacinth, Muses [the], Sparta, *and* Thrace.)

THERSANDER Thersander was a son of Oedipus's son Polyneices and Argea, daughter of the King Adrastus of Argos. Adrastus had led a contingent, the so-called Seven Against Thebes, that attacked Thebes in order to secure the throne for Polyneices. After the defeat of the Seven and the death of all seven captains but Adrastus, Thersander organized a second campaign against Thebes, the leaders of which were the sons, the so-called Epigoni, of the original Seven. Like his father before him, Thersander resorted to bribery in order to build his contingent: he offered the seer Amphiaraus's wife, Eryphile, the glorious, coveted robe (or necklace) of Harmonia in exchange for her convincing her son Alcmaeon to lead the campaign. When, as a consequence of this military effort, Thebes fell, Thersander became its regent. Thersander also reputedly participated in the Trojan War and was either killed by the Mysian king Telephus in the course of a raid or survived the raid and became one of the Greeks to hide in the belly of the Trojan Horse.

(*See also* Adrastus, Alcmaeon, Amphiaraus, Argos, Epigoni [the], Eryphile, Eteocles, Harmonia, Seven Against Thebes [the], Telephus, Thebes, *and* Troy.)

THESEUS
Theseus was a legendary king of Athens and the most important Athenian hero. His eventful life was recounted in detail by his ancient biographer Plutarch and by the mythographer Apollodorus. Theseus was reputedly the son of the Athenian king Aegeus and of Poseidon. His unusual parentage, which was similar to that of Hercules, resulted from Aegeus's consultation of the oracle at Delphi regarding his childlessness and subsequent visit to Troezen, where his friend Pittheus was king. Aegeus was baffled by the oracle's pronouncement that he should wait to open his wineskin (goatskin container for wine) until he got home, but Pittheus immediately grasped its meaning, ensured that Aegeus was drunk, and arranged for his daughter Aethra to sleep with him. The god Poseidon, as it happened, visited Aethra on the same night. When Aegeus departed for Athens the next day, he told Aethra that if she should be pregnant with a son by him, she should instruct the boy to retrieve a sword and sandals that he had hidden under a boulder and make his way to Athens. Aethra was indeed pregnant with a boy, and when he was strong enough to do so, he retrieved the items that Aegeus had hidden. According to Plutarch, it was either the stashing of these items (*thesis* in Greek) after which Aethra named the boy Theseus or Aegeus's later establishing him formally as his son and heir (*themenos*, "having established"). Admiring Hercules and wishing to emulate that distinguished hero, who had rid humankind of myriad banes, young Theseus set off for Athens not by sea, which would have been the shorter and easier route, but by land, across the Isthmus of Corinth. There he encountered an array of evildoers, all of whom he eliminated by subjecting them to the same treatment to which they had subjected others. Among them were Periphetes, who would strike travelers on the head with his bronze club, killing them; Sinis, who would tie his victims to a bent pine that, upon its release, would straighten and hurl them to their deaths; Sciron, who would push those so kind as to wash his feet from the cliffs by which he sat; and Procrustes, who offered travelers a bed but ensured that they fit its dimensions perfectly, either by stretching them or by lopping off protruding limbs. When

Theseus arrived in Athens, he was welcomed by Aegeus but was immediately disliked by Medea, whom Aegeus had married because she promised him an heir. She attempted to kill Theseus, offering him a cup of poisoned wine, but Aegeus, whom Medea had made suspicious of the youth, recognized Theseus's sword and, just as Theseus raised his cup to drink, dashed it to the ground. Theseus was declared Aegeus's heir, which pronouncement occasioned resistance on the part of the sons of Aegeus's brother, who rose up against him. Theseus vanquished his cousins' men, who had attempted to ambush him, and set out to win the favor of the Athenian people, first by capturing the Bull of Marathon that was ranging the countryside and wreaking havoc; the Bull of Marathon was the same bull with which Pasiphae, wife of King Minos of Crete, had become enamored and by which she had become mother of the Minotaur. At this time, the Athenians were under obligation to send seven young men and seven young women to Crete for the Minotaur to consume every nine years in atonement for the murder of Minos's son Androgeus. Now Theseus volunteered to be in their number, intending to slay the Minotaur. This he accomplished with the help of Minos's daughter Ariadne, who fell in love with him at first sight and gave him a ball of string to unravel as he made his way through the labyrinth that housed the Minotaur, thus ensuring that he could find his way out again. For her help, Theseus promised to make Ariadne his wife and take her back with him to Athens. But Theseus abandoned Ariadne on the island of Dia (Naxos), from where she was fortunately rescued by the god Dionysus—the abandonment being a point of controversy for Classical authors. Meanwhile, Aegeus had been awaiting Theseus's return anxiously, having instructed his son to raise a white sail to signal victory and a dark sail to signal his death. A distracted Theseus forgot to raise the white sail, causing Aegeus to leap from the Acropolis to his death. Theseus now became king and united all of the previously scattered settlements, in this way establishing Athens proper. While king of Athens, Theseus joined with Hercules in the latter's embroilment with the Amazons, which led to the Amazons' attack on the Acropolis itself. Theseus defeated the Amazons, and with the Amazon queen Hippolyta (or Antiope), became the father of Hippolytus, for whom Theseus's wife Phaedra, a daughter of Minos, developed a passion that led to her suicide and Theseus's calling a fatal curse upon Hippolytus. Things went from bad to worse when Theseus later attempted to abduct Helen of Sparta when she was just twelve years old and then decided to help his friend the Lapith king Pirithous abduct the Underworld's queen, Persephone, as his bride. Both Theseus and Pirithous were taken prisoner in the Underworld, but Theseus secured his release through the intervention of Hercules. Upon his return, Theseus found Athens in turmoil, his former allies having abandoned him. He therefore left Athens for the island of Scyros, where the king Lycomedes, having become worried about the presence of such a powerful person on his island, killed him. After his death, Theseus was elevated to the status of a demigod by the Athenians, whom he later assisted when they were threatened by the Persians in the course of the Persian Wars (499–449 BCE).

(*See also* Acropolis, Aegeus, Aethra, Amazons [the], Androgeus, Antiope, Ariadne, Athens, Corinth, Crete, Delphi, Dionysus, Helen, Hercules, Hippolyta, Hippolytus, Lapiths [the], Lycomedes, Medea, Minos, Minotaur [the], Naxos, Pasiphae, Persephone, Phaedra, Pirithous, Pittheus, Poseidon, Procrustes, Sciron, Scyros, *and* Sinis.)

THESTIUS

Thestius was a mythical Aetolian king, whose father was variously recorded as the god Ares or Agenor, a descendant of Dorus. According to the mythographer Apollodorus, Thestius had a number of children by one Eurythemis, daughter of Cleoboea. His daughters, who are all prominent figures in mythology, were Althea, mother of Meleager; Leda, mother of Helen of Sparta (and Troy), Clytemnestra, and the Dioscuri; and Hypermnestra, mother of the seer Amphiaraus. His sons participated in the hunt for the Calydonian Boar, and when Meleager awarded the boar's hide as a prize to the deserving huntress Atalanta, the brothers took it from her, thinking it a disgrace that this prize should be given to a woman. For this affront Meleager slew them, and it was in anger over the death of her brothers that Meleager's mother, Althea, cast a particular log that was the measure of his life into the fire.

(*See also* Agenor, Althea, Amphiaraus, Ares, Atalanta, Calydon, Clytemnestra, Dioscuri [the], Dorus, Helen, Hypermnestra, Leda, *and* Meleager.)

THEYESTES

Theyestes was a son of Pelops and his wife, Hippodamia. Since Pelops had won his wife's hand by treachery and, consequently, a curse had been called down upon him and his descendants, Theyestes's life was marked by tragedy. Theyestes and his brother, Atreus, had killed their stepbrother, Chrysippus, at their mother's request and were exiled from their home in Pisa as a result. Atreus wed Aerope, a princess from Crete, and with her became father to Agamemnon and Menelaus. Theyestes later seduced Aerope (or she fell in love with him), and she helped him obtain a golden fleece that Atreus had kept hidden instead of presenting it to the goddess Artemis as he should have. When the throne of Mycenae became vacant and that city's inhabitants were instructed by an oracle to select one of the sons of Pelops as their king, Theyestes, who was, unbeknownst to his brother, in possession of the fleece, said that possession of the fleece should be the deciding criterion. Thus,

Theyestes became king of Mycenae, but Atreus would have his vengeance. Claiming that there had been foul play, he suggested that the kingship should be given to that man who could reverse the course of the sun, a thing that he caused to occur with the help of Zeus. Now Atreus became Mycenae's king. He then invited Theyestes to a feast and fed him a meal made of his own children; the heads and hands of the victims were displayed to Theyestes as proof. Theyestes then went into exile and, perhaps unknowingly, fathered Aegisthus by his own daughter Pelopia. While Pelopia was pregnant, she was wed to Atreus, and the latter believed Aegisthus to be his own son. When a famine beset the land, the oracle at Delphi indicated that Atreus should find and bring back Theyestes. This he did and instructed Aegisthus to kill him, but Theyestes recognized Aegisthus's sword as his own, and Aegisthus's true paternity became known. Aegisthus then killed Atreus instead. Theyestes again briefly became king of Mycenae, but was driven from the throne by the Spartan king Tyndareus, who was acting on behalf of Atreus's sons Agamemnon and Menelaus.

(*See also* Aegisthus, Aerope, Agamemnon, Atreus, Crete, Delphi, Hippodamia, Menelaus, Mycenae, Pelops, Sparta, Tantalus, Tyndareus, *and* Zeus.)

THISBE Young Thisbe was the fairest girl in Babylon and was loved by her neighbor Pyramus. The dramatic tale of their forbidden, tragic love is an *aetion*, or explanation, for the reddening of the mulberry's fruit.

(*See also* Babylon *and* Pyramus.)

THOAS There were several characters by the name of Thoas in Classical mythology. One Thoas was a king of the barbarian people known as the Taurians. He was regent when Agamemnon's daughter Iphigeneia was brought to Tauris by the goddess Artemis. In Tauris Iphigeneia would become a priestess of Artemis, her particular task being to prepare strangers for sacrifice, for it was the custom of the Taurians to sacrifice visitors to their land.

Another Thoas was a king of the island of Lemnos, and was the only man to be spared when the island's women (the so-called Lemnian Women) killed all their male kin. Thoas was hidden by his daughter Hypsipyle and either escaped or, by some accounts, was later discovered and killed by the women.

A third Thoas was a king of Aetolia and a participant in the Trojan War, in which he fought bravely and which he survived.

(*See also* Agamemnon, Artemis, Hypsipyle, Iphigeneia, Lemnian Women [the], Lemnos, Taurians [the], *and* Troy.)

THYIADES, THE Thyiades (or Thyades), "Stormers," was another name for Maenads or Bacchantes, the female worshipers of Dionysus. This name is a reference to the women's wild dancing while possessed by the god.

(*See also* Bacchantes [the], Dionysus, *and* Maenads [the].)

TITHONUS Tithonus was a son of the Trojan king Laomedon and the brother of Priam, who would be Troy's king at the time of the Trojan War. The extremely handsome Tithonus was abducted by Eos, goddess of the dawn, and she was so taken with him that she asked Zeus to make him immortal, forgetting, however, also to ask that he remain ageless. Consequently, Tithonus wasted away with age, and Eos imprisoned him. At last there was nothing left of him but his chirruping voice. By some accounts, he had become a cicada (or grasshopper).

(*See also* Eos, Laomedon, Priam, Troy, *and* Zeus.)

TRIPTOLEMUS Triptolemus was a culture hero (bringer of civilization and culture) said to have been the first to sow seed for cultivation. He had a close connection with the goddess Demeter and her sanctuary at Eleusis. His parentage was variously recounted: he was known as a son of Celeus, a king of Eleusis, and his wife, Metaneira, and even as a child of Oceanus and Gaia. As the Roman poet Ovid writes, Ceres (the Roman Demeter) gave her chariot, which was drawn by two winged dragons, to Triptolemus and instructed him to sow the earth with grain, passing over both tilled and untilled lands.

(*See also* Celeus, Ceres, Demeter, Eleusis, Gaia, Oceanus [god], *and* Persephone.)

TROILUS Troilus was generally considered to be one of the many children of King Priam of Troy and his wife, Hecuba, although the mythographer Apollodorus writes that he was actually Hecuba's son by Apollo. Troilus is known in antiquity primarily for the manner of his death, the details of which vary from author to author apart from the fact that he died at the hands of the hero Achilles. For example, Troilus was said to have been captured by Achilles in a sanctuary of the god Apollo and killed on the god's very altar or to have been killed on the seashore while exercising his horses.

(*See also* Achilles, Apollo, Hecuba, Priam, *and* Troy.)

TROS Tros was the namesake of the Trojans and a son of Erichthonius, a king of Dardania, which was named after its founder, Dardanus. With Callirrhoe, daughter of the river god Scamander, he became the father of Ilus, who would establish the city of Troy. He was, by some accounts, also called the father of Ganymede, the handsome youth whom Zeus abducted to become his cup-bearer on Mount Olympus.

(*See also* Dardanus, Erichthonius, Ganymede, Ilus, Olympus [Mount], Scamander River [the], Trojans [the], Troy, *and* Zeus.)

TURNUS Turnus was the young and handsome king of the Rutulians, an Italian people living in southern Latium. Turnus had desired to marry Lavinia, daughter of the Laurentine king Latinus, and Latinus's wife, Amata, strongly favored this match. However, the union of Turnus and Lavinia was not to be, according to a prophecy that caused Lavinia's father to offer her instead to the Trojan Aeneas. Turnus, pressed by the goddess Juno, then led the other Latins in war against Aeneas. In the course of the fighting, Turnus killed Pallas, the son of Aeneas's ally Evander, and was brutally slain by Aeneas, who was seeking vengeance for Pallas's death.

(*See also* Aeneas, Amata, Evander, Juno, Latinus, Latium, Lavinia, Pallas, Rutulians [the], *and* Turnus.)

TYDEUS Tydeus was a son of Oeneus, king of Calydon, and became the father of Diomedes, one of the best and bravest of the Greeks fighting at Troy. Tydeus himself had been exiled from Calydon and came to Argos, whose king Adrastus promised to help him gain the throne of Calydon after first helping Polyneices with his bid for the throne of Thebes. Tydeus joined Adrastus and the famous campaign of the Seven Against Thebes, in the course of which he was fatally wounded. The mythographer Apollodorus reports that Tydeus had been a candidate for immortality but that when he demanded the head of Mela-nippus, who had wounded him, and sucked out his brains, a horrified Athena withheld this boon.

(*See also* Adrastus, Argos, Athena, Calydon, Diomedes, Polyneices, Seven Against Thebes [the], Thebes, *and* Troy.)

TYNDAREUS Tyndareus was one of the legendary kings of Sparta. His parents are variously recorded as the Spartan king Oebalus and a Naiad nymph by the name of Bateia, or as Perieres, grandson of Hellen, and the hero Perseus's daughter Gorgophone. According to the mythographer Apollodorus, after being driven from Sparta by his brother (or half brother), Tyndareus came to the court of Thestius, king of Aetolia, where he was given the princess Leda in marriage. With the help of Hercules, Tyndareus returned to Sparta and claimed the throne. As queen of Sparta, Leda bore children both to Tyndareus and to Zeus: Zeus was the father of the beautiful Helen (and, according to some sources, also Pollux and perhaps Castor), while Tyndareus was called the father of Clytemnestra, and perhaps Castor and Pollux (or just Castor). When it came time for Helen to wed, Tyndareus was presented with a real challenge, as all the eligible nobles of Greece came seeking her hand. The clever Odysseus advised him to ask all of the suitors to swear to defend the man selected if, in the future, he were to be subjected to some wrong with respect to his marriage. This way, there would be no strife between the suitors. It was either Tyndareus or Helen who chose Menelaus, the younger brother of Agamemnon, and Menelaus would succeed Tyndareus on the throne. As for the suitors' oath, that would prove to be essential when the Trojan prince Paris took Helen away with him to Troy, as all Helen's former suitors were bound to help Menelaus retrieve her. As for the rest of his best-known children (or stepchildren), Clytemnestra, a future husband-slayer, became the queen of Mycenae, and the twins Castor and Pollux became gods.

(*See also* Agamemnon, Castor, Helen, Hellen, Leda, Menelaus, Mycenae, Naiads [the], Odysseus, Paris, Perseus, Pollux, Sparta, Troy, *and* Zeus.)

TYRO

Tyro was the beautiful daughter of Salmoneus, who, in an excess of pride, had impersonated Zeus, for which crime he paid with his life. According to Homer, Tyro became the wife of Cretheus, a son of Aeolus and king of Iolcos, but she fell in love with the god of the river Enipeus. The god Poseidon desired her, and disguising himself as Enipeus, embraced her, becoming by her the father of Pelias, who would become king of Iolcos, and Neleus, a future king of Pylos. The mythographer Apollodorus adds that she exposed her children, and they were raised by the keeper of a horse that had kicked Pelias. When later reunited with their mother, they avenged Tyro's stepmother Sidero's ill treatment of her, killing Sidero even though she had sought refuge in a precinct of the goddess Hera. By Cretheus, Tyro became the mother of Pheres, who would become father to Admetus, and of Aeson, a future king of Iolcos and father of the hero Jason.

(*See also* Admetus, Aeolus, Hera, Iolcos, Jason, Neleus, Pelias, Poseidon, Pylos, Salmoneus, Sidero, *and* Zeus.)

ULYSSES

Ulysses (or Ulixes) is the Latin name for Odysseus, the Greek hero known for his great cunning as well as for his bravery and strength. He was credited with devising the Trojan Horse so that the Greeks, after a ten-year period, could at long last take the city of Troy, and he overcame numerous obstacles on his ten-year journey home to Ithaca from Troy.

(*See also* Odysseus *and* Troy.)

XUTHUS Xuthus was a son of Hellen, the legendary ancestor of all the Greeks, and the brother of Dorus and Aeolus. When Hellen entrusted each of his sons with regency over a portion of Greece, Xuthus was awarded the Peloponnese, but was driven away by his brothers for having designs on more territory. He arrived in Athens, where King Erechtheus gave him his daughter Creusa as a bride. With Creusa he became father to Ion, who would become the eponymous hero of the Ionians, and to Achaeus, who would found Achaea. According to the tragedian Euripides, Xuthus succeeded Erechtheus as king of Athens, but according to Pausanias, Xuthus selected Erechtheus's son Cecrops to assume that role.

(*See also* Achaeans [the], Achaeus, Aeolus, Athens, Cecrops, Creusa, Dorus, Erechtheus, Hellen, Ion, *and* Ionians [the].)

ZETES Zetes and his twin brother, Calais, were sons of Boreas, the north wind, and the Athenian king Erechtheus's daughter Oreithyia, whom Boreas had raped. As children of Boreas, they were known as "Boreads." The youths had wings, a physical feature inherited from their father, but, according to the Roman poet Ovid, they did not grow the wings until reaching puberty. The two accompanied Jason and the Argonauts on their quest for the Golden Fleece, and it was in the course of this adventure that they rescued the Thracian sinner Phineus from torture by the Harpies, who snatched away all his food. According to the poet Apollonius of Rhodes, the twins were loath to help Phineus when he asked them for help, as they feared retribution from the gods who had ordained Phineus's punishment. Heartened by the clairvoyant Phineus's claim that they had nothing to fear, they flew in pursuit of the Harpies, whom they very nearly caught, deterred only by the goddess Iris (or Hermes), who intervened and swore that the Harpies would no longer bother Phineus. The mythographer Apollodorus preserves a variant of the myth: while pursued by Zetes and Calais, one of the Harpies fell into a river in the Peloponnese to her death and another died of exhaustion. As for Zetes and Calais, the two perished at the hands of Hercules, who was angered to hear that it was they who had persuaded the Argonauts to leave him behind in Mysia, where he was searching for his young companion and lover, Hylas, who had been abducted by nymphs.

(*See also* Argonauts [the], Athens, Boreas, Erechtheus, Hercules, Hermes, Hylas, Iris, Jason, Oreithyia, *and* Phineus.)

ZETHUS Zethus and his twin, Amphion, were sons of Zeus and Antiope. The two were exposed after their birth but were found and raised by herdsmen.

Later reunited with their mother, Antiope, who had been imprisoned and tortured by Lycus, king of Thebes, and his wife, Dirce, they took vengeance upon the royal couple. Zethus and Amphion became joint regents of the city of Thebes, whose walls they built, Zethus by lifting the heavy stones and Amphion by charming them with his lyre. That city, which had previously been called Cadmeia after its founder, Cadmus, was now called Thebes after Zethus's wife, Thebe.

(*See also* Amphion, Antiope, Cadmus, Dirce, Lycus, Thebes, *and* Zeus.)

MONSTERS

PRODIGIES

AND

HYBRID

CREATURES

AEGAEON Aegaeon was another name for Briareus, one of the Hecatoncheires, hundred-handed and fifty-headed monsters born to the earth goddess Gaia. In Homer's epic the *Iliad*, it is explained that Aegaeon is the name that humans called him by but that the gods called him Briareus. In the passage of time, some monsters became conflated or confused with others. This was the case with Aegeaon/Briareus, whom the Roman poet Ovid describes as a sea deity, while Virgil, in his *Aeneid*, makes him a fire-breathing monster and one of the Giants who made an assault on Zeus and his siblings, the so-called Olympian gods. Aegaeon was even identified as one of the one-eyed Cyclopes.

(*See also* Briareus, Cyclopes [the], Gaia, Giants [the], Hecatoncheires [the], Olympus [Mount], *and* Zeus.)

ANTAEUS Antaeus was a Libyan giant and the son of Poseidon and Gaia ("Earth"). According to the mythographer Apollodorus, Antaeus would challenge travelers to his country to a wrestling match, in which he inevitably prevailed. The poet Pindar adds that he used the skulls of his victims to roof his father Poseidon's temple. Antaeus met his match when Hercules came to Libya on his way to retrieve the Hesperides' golden apples: in the knowledge that Antaeus derived his strength from contact with the earth (his mother), Hercules lifted him in the air and squeezed the life out of him.

(*See also* Gaia, Hercules, Hesperides [the], *and* Poseidon.)

ARGES Arges, "The Flashing One," was a Cyclops, one of the one-eyed giants born to the elemental gods Uranus ("Heaven") and Gaia ("Earth"). His brothers were Brontes and Steropes, according to the Greek poet Hesiod in his account of the origin of the gods.

(*See also* Cyclopes [the], Gaia, *and* Uranus.)

ARGUS The giant herdsman Argus (or Argos), the "Panoptes" ("All-Seeing One"), as he was called, was said to have as few as four eyes and as many as a thousand, according to the poet Hesiod and the tragedian Aeschylus, respectively. The mythographer Apollodorus adds that his eyes covered his entire body, and we learn from Ovid, for whom Argus had one hundred eyes, that only two of these rested shut at any given time. Just as there were divergent accounts of his appearance, there was no consensus about his parentage. Apollodorus lists four different potential human fathers, while for Aeschylus he was born directly from the earth and thus autochthonous. Argus is best known for his guardianship of the lovely maiden Io, whom Zeus pursued. To hide his amatory antics from his jealous wife, Hera, Zeus changed poor Io into a heifer. When Hera, suspecting trickery, asked

Zeus for the heifer as a gift, he could thus hardly refuse. Upon receiving Io, Hera tasked Argus with guarding her, though she was ultimately rescued by Hermes, who slew the monster. The killing of Argus is what earned Hermes the name "Argeiphontes," "Argos-Slayer." As a tribute to her devoted servant, Hera placed Argus's eyes on the tail feathers of the peacock, her sacred bird.

Other less-known exploits on Argus's part are recorded by Apollodorus, who reports that the exceedingly strong Argus killed the following: a bull that was ravaging Arcadia; a Satyr who was stealing the Arcadians' cattle; the monster Echidna, who was harassing passersby; and those guilty of murdering Apis, a king of the Peloponnese.

(*See also* Arcadia, Echidna, Hera, Hermes, Io, Satyrs [the], *and* Zeus.)

BRIAREUS Briareus ("The Mighty One"), also known as Obriareus or Aegaeon, was one of the three Hecatoncheires, hundred-handed and fifty-headed monsters born of the Earth goddess Gaia and Uranus. His siblings included the three one-eyed Cyclopes and the twelve Titan gods, according to the poet Hesiod. Of the Hecatoncheires, Briareus alone acquired somewhat of a personal mythology. For Homer, he is a son of Poseidon and was called upon by Thetis to prevent Poseidon, Hera, and Athena from revolting against Zeus and placing him in chains. Pausanias, on the other hand, repeats a tale explaining how the god Poseidon came to have special claim to the Isthmus of Corinth: when Poseidon and the sun god Helios were quarreling about control of the Isthmus, Briareus negotiated an agreement between them whereby Poseidon would maintain his interest in the isthmus while Helios would hold sway over the Corinthian acropolis, or Acro-corinth. Helios, in turn, would later transfer the Acrocorinth to Aphrodite.

(*See also* Aegaeon, Aphrodite, Corinth, Cyclopes [the], Gaia, Hecatoncheires [the], Olympus [Mount], Poseidon, Titans [the], Uranus, *and* Zeus.)

BRONTES Brontes, whose name means "the thunderer," was one of the brood of one-eyed Cyclopes born to the gods Uranus and Gaia. His brothers, according to the Greek poet Hesiod, were Arges and Steropes.

(*See also* Cyclopes [the], Gaia, *and* Ouranos.)

CACUS Cacus ("The Evil One," also spelled Kakos) was a bloodthirsty, fire-breathing, half-human giant and a son of the god Vulcan. In his epic the *Aeneid*, the Roman poet Virgil tells the only real story about him, a story repeated, but in slightly different detail, by other poets in the time of the emperor Augustus (indicating that Virgil might have been the story's original source). While Hercules was driving Geryon's cattle through Italy, Cacus contrived a ruse whereby to steal them.

While Hercules had stopped to pasture his cattle, Cacus, under the cover of night, grabbed eight cattle by the tail and dragged them to his cavern lair beneath the Aventine Hill at the future site of Rome; the cattle having been moved in this way, Hercules would be unable to track them. But, when Hercules later passed by the cave, one of the remaining cattle bellowed, and one of purloined cattle lowed in response, alerting Hercules to its whereabouts. In a rage, Hercules tore off the jagged peak that served as the cavern's roof and pelted the giant with arrows, branches, and rocks. Weakened, the monster could be strangled. His death was cause for celebration among the surrounding populace who, now rid of a scourge, revered Hercules as a hero and established the Great Altar of Hercules in his honor.

(*See also* Geryon, Hercules, *and* Vulcan.)

CECROPS Cecrops was known as the first king of Athens and its territory, Attica, which in his time was called Cecropia. He was reputedly autochthonous—literally being born from the earth—and hybrid in form, his lower body being that of a snake.

(*See* Cecrops [hero].)

CELAENO According to the Roman poet Virgil, Celaeno was one of the ghastly bird-woman Harpies who tortured the offending king Phineus as well as Aeneas's band of Trojan refugees by snatching away their food before it could be eaten. When the Trojans, swords in hand, attacked the Harpies, Celaeno terrified them by prophesying that they would eventually reach their goal, the shores of Italy, but that they would there suffer from grievous famine. Interestingly, Virgil describes Celaeno as a Fury, and thus as one of the Spirits of Vengeance with whom the Harpies may have been conflated. The Harpy Celaeno is to be distinguished from the Oceanid of the same name.

(*See also* Aeneas, Furies [the], Harpies [the], Oceanids [the], Phineus, *and* Trojans [the].)

CENTAURS, THE The Centaurs, literally "bull-slayers," are generally viewed as a tribe of hybrid creatures who had the torso of a human and body of a horse, but there was also a tradition—as, for example, recorded by the historian Diodorus Siculus—that they were a savage people who were the first to ride horses and who mated with mares to produce the first generation of "hippo-centaurs" ("horsey bull-slayers"). The Centaurs are described in some sources, including Diodorus, as being the direct offspring of the sinner Ixion and Nephele, a cloud goddess shaped by Zeus to resemble his wife, Hera, whom Ixion was pursuing. They are also called the children of Centaurus, a monstrous child of Ixion and Nephele, or of the god Apollo and Stilbe, a daughter of the river god Peneus and the Naiad Creusa. According to the poet Pindar, Centaurus sired the hybrid Centaurs by mating with mares. Still another tradition, preserved by the poet Nonnus, describes Zeus, having taken on the form of a horse, as being the father of the Centaurs with Ixion's wife, Dia.

The Centaurs are collectively best known for their battle with the Lapiths, a neighboring people whose prince, Pirithous, invited them to his wedding. Whether it was because they became inebriated and accordingly unruly, or because they resented the fact that Pirithous, another of Ixion's offspring, was going to inherit the latter's throne, the Centaurs tried to make off with the Lapith women at the wedding. A fierce battle ensued, in which the Lapiths prevailed. This famous battle was depicted both on the sculptures of the Parthenon and the Temple of Zeus at Olympia, where it symbolized the precedence of the Greeks over barbarians and culture over savagery. Several of the Centaurs had their own, distinct mythologies. These included the wise and educated Chiron, who raised the young Achilles, and Nessus, who assaulted Hercules's wife Deianeira.

(See also Achilles, Apollo, Chiron, Deianeira, Hercules, Ixion, Lapiths [the], Naiads [the], Nephele, Nessus, Parthenon [the], Pirithous, Olympia, and Zeus.)

CERBERUS
Cerberus, whom Homer calls "the hound of Hades," was one of the brood of monsters, which include the Hydra of Lerna and the Chimaera, spawned by Typhon and the half maiden, half serpent Echidna. He was variously described as having as many as fifty or one hundred heads and as few as three. The mythographer Apollodorus writes that Cerberus, the three-headed dog, had the tail of a dragon and snakes' heads growing from his back. For the poet Hesiod, Cerberus was an eater of raw flesh and had a bark like clashing bronze. Cerberus's duty was to allow the deceased to enter the House of Hades but to block the living from entering and the dead from leaving. On the instruction of the Sibyl of Cumae, the living hero Aeneas secured passage into Hades by throwing Cerberus a drugged honey cake. The best-known myth involving Cerberus is the tale of Hercules's twelfth and final Labor (or by some accounts, the tenth): Hercules was ordered to bring Cerberus up from the Underworld, a task that he accomplished by overpowering the beast without the use of weapons. As the poet Ovid writes, upon reaching the realm of the living, the distressed hound raged, foam from its mouth falling upon the earth to produce the poisonous plant aconite, which the sorceress Medea used in attempting to kill the hero Theseus.

(See also Aeneas, Chimaera, Echidna, Hades [god and place], Hydra of Lerna [the], Medea, Sibyl of Cumae [the], Theseus, Typhon, and Underworld [the].)

CERYNITIAN HIND, THE
The Cerynitian Hind, a golden-antlered deer sacred to the goddess Artemis, took its name from the Greek river

Cerynites, which rose in Arcadia and flowed through Achaea into the sea. Capturing this deer and bringing it alive to Mycenae constituted the third Labor of Hercules. According to the mythographer Apollodorus, Hercules, wishing neither to kill nor wound it, pursued it for a whole year. At last, the weary deer sought shelter on Mount Artemisius, and while making its way to the river Ladon, it was shot and wounded by Hercules, who carried it off on his shoulders. Along the way, Hercules encountered an angry Artemis, accompanied by her brother Apollo. The gods would have taken the deer from him but ultimately allowed him to continue with it to Mycenae when he explained that he had only been following orders from King Eurystheus who, accordingly, was to blame.

(*See also* Apollo, Arcadia, Artemis, Eurystheus, Hercules, *and* Mycenae.)

CHARYBDIS The whirlpool Charybdis, conceived of as a female monster, was located opposite Scylla in a narrow strait. According to Homer, a fig tree growing on the rocks above her signaled her exact location, thus allowing Odysseus safely to avoid her. Three times daily Charybdis would suck down waters so forcefully that even Poseidon could not rescue a ship caught in the maelstrom's powerful vortex. To avoid her, Odysseus resigned himself to the certain loss of men to Scylla, whose lair he would have to pass by closely. Jason, on his return journey from the land of Colchis, and Aeneas, on his way to Italy, were also able safely to avoid Charybdis. It was speculated even in antiquity that Charybdis actually existed and was located in the treacherous Straits of Messina.

(*See also* Aeneas, Colchis, Jason, Odysseus, Poseidon, *and* Scylla.)

CHIMAERA, THE The Chimaera was a hybrid female monster that, according to the poet Hesiod, was born of the half-maiden monster Echidna to Typhaon, a lawless monster confused or conflated by later writers with the hundred-bodied Typhon (also called Typhoeus). The Chimaera's siblings, all likewise monsters, included Orthus, the hound of Geryon; the hellhound Cerberus; and the many-headed Hydra of Lerna. For Hesiod, the Chimaera was fearsome, huge, swift-footed, and strong. She had three heads—one of a lion, another of a goat, and another of a dragon—being a lion in the front, a fire-breathing goat at her middle, and a serpent to the rear. The hero Bellerophon was sent by the Lycian king Iobates to kill this monster, which was ravaging the countryside. This Perseus did with the help of the winged horse Pegasus, whom he had tamed with the help of the gods, and from whose back he, flying aloft, slew the monster with his arrows.

(*See also* Bellerophon, Echidna, Geryon, Hydra of Lerna [the], Iobates, Lycia, Pegasus, *and* Typhon.)

PLATE VII

Cerberus: "The hound of Hades" that guards the gates of the Underworld

CHIRON Chiron was a Centaur, having the torso of a man and the body of a horse, but differed from the others of his kind in that he was wise, gentle, and cultured. He was skilled in the art of healing and, according to mythographer Hyginus, was the first to use herbs in the medical art of surgery. In addition to being an accomplished healer, Chiron was well versed in prophecy, music, and gymnastics, for he had received instruction in these arts by the divine twins Apollo and Artemis. Chiron is sometimes described as having the same parentage as all the Centaurs, thus being a child of the sinner Ixion and Nephele, the cloud goddess. Perhaps reflecting his elevated status, he was also known as a son of the god Cronus and the second-generation Titan Philyra, a daughter of Oceanus. According to the mythographers Apollodorus and Hyginus, as well as the poets Callimachus and Apollonius, when Cronus's dalliance with Philyra was discovered by his wife, Rhea, he transformed himself into a stallion, hence his child's half-equine form. Yet another tradition asserts that Zeus was Chiron's father. In any event, Chiron was renowned for his many skills and, accordingly, was given a number of heroes to rear and educate. The most notable of these were Achilles, Jason, Asclepius, Actaeon, and the twins Castor and Pollux.

For a long time, Chiron lived in a cave on Mount Pelion in coastal Thessaly, but he, together with the other Centaurs, was driven by their neighbors the Lapiths from Thessaly to Cape Malea in the Peloponnese. It was there that Hercules inadvertently caused Chiron's death, wounding him accidentally with one of his poisoned arrows. Chiron's suffering was so extreme that, although immortal, he wished to die. Of his end there are various accounts. The poet Ovid, for example, writes that Zeus, in pity, raised him—now the constellation Sagittarius—to the heavens. But it was also rumored that Chiron opted to swap destinies with Prometheus, who was suffering eternal torture in the Underworld.

(*See also* Achilles, Actaeon, Apollo, Artemis, Asclepius, Castor, Centaurs [the], Cronus, Hercules, Ixion, Jason, Lapiths [the], Nephele, Oceanus [god], Pelion [Mount], Prometheus, Rhea, Thessaly, Titans [the], Underworld [the], *and* Zeus.)

CHRYSAOR Chrysaor, whose name means "golden sword," was a warrior, and likely a monster, born of the god Poseidon and the Gorgon Medusa. He sprang fully grown from Medusa's neck when her head was severed by Perseus. Chrysaor, in turn, fathered the triple-headed (or by some accounts, triple-bodied) monster-king Geryon by Callirrhoe, a daughter of the god Oceanus.

(*See also* Geryon, Gorgons [the], Medusa, Pegasus, Perseus, Poseidon, *and* Oceanus [god].)

COTTUS Cottus, whose name means "wrathful one," was one of the three Hecatoncheires, hundred-handed and fifty-headed monsters born of the earth goddess Gaia and Uranus. His siblings included the three one-eyed Cyclopes and the twelve Titan gods.

(*See also* Cyclopes [the], Gaia, Hecatoncheires [the], Olympus [Mount], Titans [the], Uranus, *and* Zeus.)

CYCLOPES, THE
The Cyclopes, "Round-Eyed Ones," were godlike giants in appearance except that each had a single round eye on its forehead. In the earliest existing account of their birth, the poet Hesiod writes that three Cyclopes—named Arges, "The Flashing One," Brontes, "The Thunderer," and Steropes, "Lightning Bolt"—were born of the elemental gods Gaia and Uranus after the Titans. Their father, Uranus, found the Cyclopes and their brothers, the Hecatoncheires, so hideous that he thrust them back inside Gaia ("Earth") upon their birth. For this insult and injury Gaia would have her revenge, and she recruited her youngest Titan son, Cronus, to help her. This Cronus did by castrating his father and assuming kingship over the gods, until the eventual birth and rise of Zeus. Cronus released the Cyclopes from their prison in the Earth in order to help him in his coup, only to imprison them again. Zeus, too, asked for their assistance in his struggle for the throne against Cronus but released them. When freed, the Cyclopes were tasked with producing lightning bolts for Zeus, and their forge, according to the Roman poet Virgil, was located under Mount Etna in Sicily. The mythographer Apollodorus reports that the Cyclopes were eventually killed by Apollo in vengeance for Zeus's ending the life of his son Asclepius.

Most memorable of all Cyclopes was the monstrous shepherd Polyphemus, who imprisoned Odysseus and his men in his cave and would have eaten all of them had the clever Odysseus not devised a ruse to outsmart him. Polyphemus, and the other uncouth, uncivilized Cyclopes who lived near him on the island visited by Odysseus, had no clear relation to the thunderbolt-forging Cyclopes of which Hesiod and others tell: they were, instead, lawless, uncultured cave-dwellers who lived off the land without practicing agriculture, relying as they did on the gods to supply them with an abundance of grain and grapes while, at the same time, disdaining them.

(*See also* Apollo, Asclepius, Cronus, Gaia, Hecatoncheires [the], Odysseus, Polyphemus, Sicily, Titans [the], Uranus, *and* Zeus.)

ECHIDNA
According to the poet Hesiod, the cave-dwelling Echidna was half lovely maiden and half serpent. Her parents are variously given as the sea god Phorcys and his sister Ceto; Chrysaor and Callirrhoe; and Tartarus and Gaia. With the monstrous Typhon (also called Typhaon or Typhoeus), she herself was mother to an array of other monsters. These included Orthus, the two-headed guard dog belonging to the triple-bodied Geryon; Cerberus, the triple-

headed dog that guarded Hades; the many-headed Hydra of Lerna, which Hercules later slew; and the many-headed dragon Ladon. To her own son Orthus, Echidna reputedly bore the Nemean Lion, which Hercules famously killed, and the Sphinx of Thebes, which Oedipus outwitted, causing its death. The cave-dwelling monster Scylla, to whom Odysseus lost some of his companions; the vulture that eternally feasted on Prometheus's liver; and the composite-beast Chimaera, slain by Bellerophon, were also known as her offspring.

(*See also* Bellerophon, Cerberus, Chimaera, Chrysaor, Gaia, Geryon, Hades [place], Hercules, Hydra of Lerna [the], Ladon, Nemean Lion [the], Odysseus, Oedipus, Phorcys, Prometheus, Scylla, Sphinx of Thebes [the], Tartarus, *and* Typhon.)

ENCELADUS Enceladus was one of the Giants (Gigantes) who waged war on Zeus and his siblings. Enceladus was killed in this battle by the goddess Athena, who was said either to have thrown the entire island of Sicily or just Mount Etna onto him. His fiery breath is still emitted from Etna's mouth.

(*See* Athena, Giants [the], Sicily, *and* Zeus.)

EPHIALTES Ephialtes and his twin brother, Otus, were exceedingly handsome and tall (well over 50 feet, 15 meters) but also filled with hubris. Together they committed several outrages against the gods, going so far as to attack them, and for this they were duly punished.

(*See also* Otus.)

ERYMANTHIAN BOAR, THE The Erymanthian Boar was an enormous creature that ranged the wooded slopes of Mount Erymanthus in Arcadia and ravaged the lands belonging to those who lived in the town of Psophis. It was Hercules's fourth Labor to capture this bull alive, which he did by chasing the animal into deep snow. When Hercules appeared in Mycenae with the boar over his shoulders, a terrified king Eurystheus hid in a large storage jar.

(*See also* Arcadia, Erymanthus [Mount], Eurystheus, Hercules, *and* Mycenae.)

EURYALE Euralye, the "Wide-Strider," was one of Medusa's two immortal sisters and a Gorgon. The tragedian Aeschylus describes the three sisters as having snakes as hair and being detested by humankind.

(*See also* Gorgons [the] *and* Medusa.)

FAUNS, THE Fauns were Roman woodland spirits, or demigods, who came to be viewed as having hybrid human-animal characteristics and to be equated or confused with Satyrs. Like Satyrs—and like the prophetic rural god

Faunus, of whom they constitute a plurality—they were thought to inhabit the forests and mountains, to be associated with goats and sheep, and to be lovers of the Nymphs. As for their appearance, they were predominantly anthropomorphic but having goats' tails, ears, and horns.

(*See also* Faunus, Nymphs [the], *and* Satyrs [the].)

FAUNUS
Faunus was an Italian nature deity who was associated with forests and wild places and was responsible, too, for the fertility of flocks and fields. He became conflated or identified with the Greek god Pan, borrowing the latter's goatlike physical features as well. In addition to being a nature and fertility deity, Faunus possessed prophetic powers.

(*See* Faunus [god].)

GERYON
Geryon was the triple-headed (or triple-bodied) regent of the mythical island Erythia ("the Red Island"), located in the far west, by some accounts lying beyond the Pillars of Hercules. Geryon was the child of Medusa's son Chrysaor and the Oceanid Callirrhoe, and he was famous for his fine herd of crimson-colored cattle. To lay claim to and drive away these cattle was the hero Hercules's tenth Labor.

On his way to the Red Island, Hercules erected the two pillars that bear his name: one on the European and one on the African continent. Since the sun was beating down on him relentlessly while erecting the pillars, an exasperated Hercules shot an arrow at the sun god Helios. Admiring Hercules's spirit, the god supplied him with a magic chalice in which to transport the cattle, once captured. Hercules slew both the herdsman and the double-headed dog that had been charged with guarding the herd. As for Geryon, Hercules killed him with one of his arrows.

(*See also* Chrysaor, Erythia, Helios, Hercules, Medusa, *and* Oceanids [the].)

GIANTS, THE
There were quite a number of notable giants in Classical mythology, among their number being Talus, the bronze giant; Otus and Ephialtes, who stormed the heavens; the Cyclops Polyphemus; and the hunter Orion. Nontheless, these are distinct from "the Giants" (in Greek, Gigantes), brothers, according to the Greek poet Hesiod, born from the blood that fell upon the earth when Cronus, avenging the grievous wrong done to his mother Gaia ("Earth"), castrated his father Uranus. Other beings that were born from the blood of Uranus were the Erinyes (spirits of vengeance), while Aphrodite was born from the foam produced when Uranus's severed testicles fell into the sea. Hesiod describes the Giants as large in size, and having gleaming armor and long spears. The mythographer

Apollodorus would later say that they were unsurpassed in size and so strong that they were invulnerable. They were terrifying to look at, having long hair and beards as well as serpents' scales covering the lower part of their bodies.

Exploits attributed to the Giants (Gigantes) were several. The most famous of these was the Gigantomachy, the famous battle between the gods and Giants, in which the Giants unsuccessfully battled Zeus and his siblings. Classical authors eventually confused and conflated this battle with the earlier battle between the Olympian gods (Zeus and his siblings) and the Titans (an older generation of gods) for control of the world. As for the Gigantomachy, this power struggle was occasioned by the Giant Alcyoneus's theft of the cattle of the sun god Helios and Gaia's attempt to make Alcyoneus immortal, both of which things were a direct threat to the gods. Having learned that they required a mortal to help them vanquish the Giants, Zeus and his siblings enlisted the aid of Hercules, who killed Alcyoneus as well as others of the Giants. Apart from Alcyoneus, the best known of the Giant brothers were Enceladus and Porphyrion. According to the mythographer Apollodorus, Porphyrion made an assault on both Hercules and the goddess Hera, for whom he had developed unbridled passion. When he attempted to rape the goddess, Zeus struck him with a thunderbolt and Hercules slew him with an arrow. The goddess Athena dealt with Enceladus by throwing the island of Sicily on him.

(*See also* Aphrodite, Athena, Cronus, Cyclopes [the], Enceladus, Erinyes [the], Gaia, Hera, Hercules, Orion, Otus, Polyphemus, Talus, Titans [the], Uranus, *and* Zeus.)

GORGONS
The Gorgons were three monstrous sisters whose lair was in the territory of Libya. Their names were Stheno, Euryale, and Medusa, and they were said to be the offspring of the sea deity Phorcys and his sister Ceto. According to an alternate tradition, they sprang from the earth goddess Gaia, who produced them to be her allies in the battle between the gods and Giants. Of the Gorgon sisters only Medusa was mortal, and for that reason Perseus was sent to fetch her head. According to mythographer Apollodorus, the Gorgons had serpents as hair, large tusks like a boar's, hands of bronze, and golden wings. Indeed, they were so hideous in appearance that they turned to stone all who looked upon them directly.

(*See also* Medusa, Perseus, *and* Phorcys.)

GRAIAE, THE
The Graiae (or Graeae), whose name means "the old ones" or "the gray-haired ones," were, like the Gorgons, children of the sea god Phorcys and his sister Ceto. As Phorcys's offspring they were known collectively as the Phorcydes, and Apollodorus reports that they were old from birth. Their names are given as Enyo (translated as "Horror"), Pemphredo (or Pephredo, "Alarm"), and Deino ("Dread" or, according to Hyginus, Persis, "Ruin"). Between

them they had a single eye and tooth, which they shared. Perseus stole this eye and tooth as a means of forcing the sisters to reveal the location of their siblings, the Gorgons. The Graiae resided in Libya, in the far west of the world as it was known to the Greeks.

(*See also* Enyo, Gorgons [the], Perseus, *and* Phorcys.)

GRIFFINS, THE
Griffins were Libya, hybrid creatures having the head of a bird of prey and the body of a winged lion. These monsters "originated" in the ancient Near East, from where they were imported and absorbed into Greek thought and material culture. Classical authors ranging from poets to historians and geographers mention the griffins as tasked with guarding vast resources of gold to be found in the northern mountains near the lands of the Hyperboreans and the Scythians (a historical nomadic people based in the Black Sea and Caucasus region). This gold, it was said, was coveted by the Arimaspi, a tribe of one-eyed horsemen, who repeatedly attempted to steal it.

(*See also* Arimaspi [the], Caucasus Mountains [the], *and* Hyperboreans [the].)

GYGES
Gyges (or Gyes), whose name means "son of the earth," was one of the three Hecatoncheires, hundred-handed and fifty-headed monsters born of the earth goddess Gaia and Uranus. His siblings included the three one-eyed Cyclopes and the twelve Titan gods.

(*See also* Briareus, Cyclopes [the], Gaia, Hecatoncheires [the], Olympus [Mount], Titans [the], Uranus, *and* Zeus.)

HARPIES, THE
The Harpies, whose name means "snatchers" or "grabbers," were two or (according to some sources) three monstrous female *daímones*, or spirits—technically deities—that personified the demonic, unpredictable, grasping forces of storm winds. For the poet Hesiod, they were two in number and the daughters of the Oceanid Electra and Thaumas, a son of the primordial elemental gods Pontus ("Sea") and Gaia ("Earth"). Hesiod gives their names as Aello ("Storm Wind") and Ocypete ("Swift Foot"). Homer speaks of a Harpy named Podarge, which also means "swift-footed," who was the mother of Achilles's miraculous horses. Later authors provide other names as well, including Celaeno ("The Dark One") and Nicothe ("Swift Victor").

The Harpies were originally ill-defined physically but, over time, came to be viewed as winged monsters with human heads. Thus in Homer's *Odyssey*, the Harpies are merely forces that cause the disappearance of Odysseus, while for Virgil, there is "no monster more awful or savage," for they are creatures that have "the faces of maidens and avian bodies, bellies that ooze the most fetid gore, clawed hands, and faces pallid from starvation." The Harpies are best known for their persecution of the Thracian king Phineus, whom they had been sent to punish for abusing the oracular powers given him by the god Apollo: the Harpies would snatch away Phineus's food with their beaks or talons, and on the occasions that they left him any food, what food they did not take was rendered inedible by their foul stench. The heroes Jason and Aeneas, together with their respective cohorts, both encountered the Harpies. In the case of Jason's crew, the swift sons of the north wind Boreas, Zetes and Calais, were persuaded by Phineus to help him, and they pursued the Harpies when they appeared. Had the goddess Iris not intervened, the brothers would have overtaken and killed the monsters. From this point on, the Harpies ceased to plague Phineus. As for the Trojan hero Aeneas, he and his men were themselves plagued by the Harpies, who twice succeeded in stealing food from them while on their long journey to Italy. When Aeneas and his men turned their swords upon them, one, Celaeno, angrily uttered terrifying prophetic words: the Trojans would, at long last, reach Italian shores but they would there be beset by famine so great that they would resort to chewing their very tables.

(*See also* Achilles, Aeneas, Boreas, Calais, Celaeno, Iris, Jason, Oceanids [the], Odysseus, Phineus, Thrace, Trojans [the], *and* Zetes.)

HECATONCHEIRES, THE

The three Hecatoncheires ("Hundred-Handers"), Cottus, Briareos, and Gyges (or Gyes), were monstrous siblings of the Cyclopes and Titans, all of them being the offspring of the earth goddess Gaia and Uranus. According to the poet Hesiod, the Hecatoncheires each had one hundred arms and fifty heads, and they were hideous, strong, and filled with hubris. Uranus detested them from the first moment and thrust them back deep inside their mother, Gaia, after their birth, causing her great pain—pain she would not bear. Gaia made a sickle and asked her Titan children to avenge her for the violence she had suffered. Only the youngest, Cronus, came forward. Armed with the sickle, he waited until his father came to lie with Gaia at night and, ambushing Uranus, castrated him. Yet the Hecatoncheires were still not released from their prison in Tartarus, as the depths of Earth were known. This did not occur until Zeus, needing help battling Cronus and the other Titan gods, released the Hecatoncheires, only later, after the battle, to return them there again. The mythographer Apollodorus adds that when they were returned to Tartarus, the Hecatoncheires were made guards of the vanquished Titans, whom Zeus imprisoned there.

(*See also* Cronus, Cyclops, Gaia, Tartarus, Titans [the], *and* Uranus.)

HYDRA (OF LERNA), THE

The Hydra was an enormous serpent with nine heads—or as many as fifty or one hundred—one of which was immortal. Its parents were the giant Typhon and Echidna, half maiden and half serpent, the so-called "mother of all monsters." The Hydra's haunts were the marshes of Lerna, near the city of Argos. The second of Hercules's Labors was the slaying of the Hydra. But each time that Hercules would cut off one of its heads, two would grow in its place. Not only this, but a giant crab that kept the Hydra company appeared and joined the fray. Hercules's clever nephew and companion Iolaus proposed a remedy: the moment Hercules severed a head, Iolaus would cauterize the stump with a firebrand. This the two did until only the Hydra's immortal head remained. Hercules then cut off this head, and after burying it beneath a boulder, dipped his arrows in the Hydra's lethal venom. Both the Hydra and the crab, which Hercules had also slain, were placed in the heavens by the goddess Hera as constellations.

(*See also* Argos, Echidna, Hercules, Lerna, *and* Typhon.)

LADON The hundred-headed serpent, or dragon, Ladon was variously known as the offspring of the sea god Phorcys and his sister Ceto, or as the child of the monstrous Typhon (or Typhoeus) and Echidna. Alternatively, he was said to have sprung from the earth. Having no need for sleep, and thus able to be ever watchful, he became guardian of the Hesperides' golden apples. After being slain by Hercules, whose eleventh Labor consisted of fetching the golden apples, Ladon became the constellation Serpentarius.

(*See also* Echidna, Hercules, Hesperides [the], Phorcys, *and* Typhon.)

LAESTRYGONS, THE The Laestrygons (or Laestrygonians) were a mythical people, or more properly, group of cannibalistic giants, whom Odysseus and his men encountered on their perilous, ten-year return voyage from Troy after the Trojan War. When Odysseus caught sight of the Laestrygons' town of Telepylos, which had been founded by a son of Poseidon, they believed that they had come upon a place whose inhabitants were likely to welcome them. The first of the Laestrygons whom the Greeks came upon was the Laestrygonian king Antiphates's daughter, who had gone out from the city to fetch water. She showed the men the way to her father's palace, where they found a terrifying woman, the queen, who was as large as a mountain. The queen summoned her husband, who snatched up two of the Greeks and prepared to eat them. The other Greeks ran to their ships. Only the ship of Odysseus and his own crew escaped the island, however, for the Laestrygons came running in the tens of thousands, hurling boulders that smashed the other ships and killed many of their crew. What men were not crushed were speared like fish.

(*See also* Odysseus, Poseidon, *and* Troy.)

MARSYAS Marsyas was a Phrygian Satyr (or Silen) whose misfortune it was to come upon a flute that the goddess Athena had cast aside: the goddess was displeased at the appearance of her face—cheeks puffed out—which she saw reflected in a pool while playing this instrument. Marsyas was so pleased at his newfound skill that he challenged the god Apollo to a musical contest. Inevitably, the god, who was playing his cithara, was designated the winner, though it is variously reported how he achieved his victory: either by stipulating that both parties were required to play their instruments upside down, which Marsyas was unable to do, or by singing to accompany his cithara, thus enhancing his song. In any event, the outcome of the contest was a gruesome one. Apollo hung Marsyas from a lofty tree and flayed him alive for daring to challenge a deity. Marsyas's stripped skin was said either to have been made into a wineskin or to have been left suspended. So terrible was the sight of his skinned, still-living body, writes the poet Ovid, that all the countryfolk and rustic gods wept, their tears forming the river that thereafter bore the Satyr's name.

(*See also* Apollo, Athena, Phrygia, Satyrs [the], *and* Silens [the].)

MEDUSA Medusa was one of the three Gorgon sisters, creatures so hideous that they turned all who looked at them to stone. Medusa alone of the three was mortal, and once had been a beautiful maiden whom the god Poseidon pursued. She was transformed into a snake-haired monster by Athena, either out of envy of the girl's beauty or out of anger at the fact that Poseidon had lain with her in Athena's shrine, defiling it.

When Perseus beheaded Medusa, Pegasus and Chrysaor, Medusa's children by Poseidon, sprang fully grown from her severed neck. According to the tragedian Euripides in his play *Ion*, Athena gave two drops of Medusa's blood to the Athenian king Erichthonius: one drop could cure disease, and the other was lethal. In another version of the tale, Athena gave a portion of the blood to the healing god Asclepius to be used as a cure for illness and as a means to restore life.

According to Roman tradition, Medusa and the god Vulcan were the parents of the fire-breathing giant Cacus.

(*See also* Asclepius, Athena, Cacus, Chrysaor, Erichthonius, Gorgons [the], Pegasus, Poseidon, *and* Vulcan.)

MINOTAUR, THE

The Minotaur, or Minotauros ("Bull of Minos") in Greek, was a hybrid monster, with the head of a bull and the body of a man, that lived on the island of Crete. The Minotaur was the offspring of the Cretan queen Pasiphae and a handsome white bull for which she developed a consuming passion. The bull had been sent to Crete by the god Poseidon in answer to a prayer by the island's king Minos, who, boasting that the god would do whatever he asked, promised to sacrifice the bull to the god upon its appearance. Yet Minos did not keep his promise, and in vengeance for this slight, Poseidon caused Minos's wife, Pasiphae, to fall in love with it. Unable to quell her passion, a desperate Pasiphae asked the craftsman Daedalus, then residing on the island, to help her consummate her desire. To this end, Daedalus constructed a hollowed wooden cow to enclose Pasiphae for the amorous encounter. The result was the monstrous Minotaur, which Minos could not bring himself to kill and, instead, kept enclosed in a mazelike prison, the Labyrinth, constructed by Daedalus.

When Minos's son Androgeus was later killed in Athens, a plague was sent upon that city. Apollo's oracle at Delphi advised the Athenians to send seven youths and seven maidens to Crete every nine years, where they would be fed to the Minotaur by way of atonement for Androgeus's death. It was the Athenian king Aegeus's son Theseus who put an end to this terrifying tribute. Volunteering as one of the seven youths, Theseus traveled to Crete and, with the assistance of Minos's daughter Ariadne, was able to escape the Labyrinth after slaying the Minotaur; falling in love with Theseus at first glance, Ariadne had offered him a ball of yarn that he was to unravel as he entered the Minotaur's treacherous lair. Though Theseus promised to take Ariadne back to Athens with him, he abandoned her on the island of Naxos, from where she was rescued by the god Dionysus, who made her his bride. Theseus, meanwhile, did not escape punishment for his actions. Upon his arrival home, he forgot to raise a white sail of victory, which caused his father, Aegeus, anxiously awaiting his son's safe return, to hurl himself into the sea in grief.

(*See also* Aegeus, Ariadne, Athens, Crete, Daedalus, Dionysus, Minos, Naxos, Pasiphae, Poseidon, *and* Theseus.)

NEMEAN LION, THE

Killing the invulnerable Nemean Lion was the first and one of the best known of the Labors of Hercules. This lion, which resided at Nemea in the eastern Peloponnese, was variously said to be the offspring of the serpent-maiden Echidna and either Typhon or her own son Orthus, the two-headed dog that guarded the giant Geryon's herds. According to the Greek poet Hesiod, the goddess Hera raised the lion and set him loose upon the hills of Nemea, where he proceeded to prey on the inhabitants. Hercules attempted to shoot the lion with his bow and arrow but quickly learned that the lion's pelt could not be penetrated. Overcoming the lion ultimately required both trickery and a show of strength: Hercules ambushed the lion by stealthily entering the cave in which it had gone to hide and wrestled with it to its death. Upon accomplishing this task, Hercules skinned the lion and thereafter always wore its pelt. It is the pelt and his famous club that make Hercules easily recognizable in Classical art.

(*See also* Echidna, Geryon, Hercules, Nemea, *and* Typhon.)

NESSUS The Centaur Nessus is best known for his assault on Hercules's wife, Deianeira, and for indirectly causing Hercules's death. When Hercules and his wife came to the Evenus River, Nessus offered to carry Deianeira across the forceful currents. With Deianeira in his grasp, Nessus attempted to rape her, but Hercules stopped him with a lethal arrow shot. As Nessus lay dying, he succeeded in convincing Deianeira to keep a sample of his blood to use as a love charm that, he claimed, would ensure her husband's everlasting love. Tragically, Deianeira did keep and use the Centaur's blood, which was no love charm, for it was tainted by toxic poison from Hercules's arrow—poisonous venom from the dread Hydra of Lerna that Hercules had earlier slain.

(*See also* Centaurs [the], Deianeira, Hercules, *and* Hydra of Lerna [the].)

ORION Orion was a noted hunter of enormous size who, upon his death, was raised to the heavens to become the constellation that bears his name. There were various accounts of his birth and also widely varied accounts of the adventures that marked his life. He was known as a son of Poseidon and Euryale, a daughter of King Minos of Crete, but also, indirectly, a son of the childless Hyrieus of Thrace, who had asked the gods Zeus, Poseidon, and Hermes for a son; as the Roman poet Ovid writes, the gods obliged Hyrieus by urinating in a bull's hide that was buried and, after a nine-month period of gestation, yielded Orion. According to the mythographer Apollodorus, who outlines Orion's life, the god Poseidon gave him the gift either of being able to walk on the oceans' water or of being able to stride through it. His first marriage was to Side, whom the goddess Hera sent to the Underworld since she believed herself to be the goddess's rival in beauty. Orion later pursued Merope, daughter of Oenopion, the king of Chios. When Oenopion sought to delay the union, an impatient and intoxicated Orion raped Merope. For this the king blinded him as he slept, but Orion made his way to the sun god Helios, who restored his sight. Among his loves was the goddess Eos, who took him to the island of Delos. There were various accounts of how he met his end, among them a fatal game of quoits (ring toss) with the goddess Artemis, attempted rape of a Hyperborean maiden by the name of Opis, and the bite of a scorpion. According to this last version, both the scorpion and Orion became constellations.

(*See also* Artemis, Crete, Eos, Helios, Hera, Hermes, Hyperboreans [the], Merope, Minos, Poseidon, Underworld [the], *and* Zeus.)

OTUS Otus and his twin brother, Ephialtes, were, according to Homer, not only the most handsome men ever to grace the earth (after Orion) but also the tallest, and thus giants. When just nine years of age they measured nine forearm-lengths in breadth (about 22.5 feet, or 7 meters) and nine arm spans in height (approximately 54 feet, or 16 meters). The twins were called Aloads, "sons of Aloeus," Aloeus being a son of Poseidon and Canace, daughter of Aeolus, Lord of the Winds. Aloeus, however, was not their real father, for their mother, Iphimedeia, had been impregnated by the god Poseidon, with whom she was in love. The mythographer Apollodorus adds that Iphimedeia had become so infatuated with Poseidon that she frequented the seashore where she filled her lap with water; consequently, Poseidon came to meet her.

These marvelous twins, regrettably, were too prideful and committed a series of outrageous acts. They took Ares, the fierce god of war, captive and kept him in a bronze cauldron bound in chains for thirteen months. The god had become so faint and broken, as Homer affirms, that had the twins' new stepmother, Eeriboeia, not interfered by alerting Hermes, who released him, Ares would have perished. The Aloads even aspired to attack the gods in their safe dwelling place in the heavens, which they intended to reach by piling the mountains Olympus, Ossa, and Pelion one upon the other. As a final outrage against the gods, each of the twins made advances on a goddess: Otus on Artemis and Ephialtes on Hera. Their punishment for this offense was swift and final: the goddess Artemis disguised herself as a deer and leaped between them. In their eagerness to kill this deer, they accidentally killed each other on the island of Naxos.

Curiously, the travel writer Pausanias notes a tradition according to which the two giants were the first to worship the Muses on Mount Helicon.

(*See also* Aeolus, Aloeus, Ares, Artemis, Canace, Helicon [Mount], Hera, Hermes, Muses [the], Naxos, Olympus [Mount], Orion, Ossa [Mount], Pelion [Mount], *and* Poseidon.)

PEGASUS The winged horse Pegasus was a child of the Gorgon Medusa by Poseidon. Pegasus and his brother, the giant Chrysaor, were not born by normal means but rather sprang fully grown from Medusa's severed neck when Perseus cut off her head. The poet Hesiod says of Pegasus that his name is derived from the springs, *pegai*, of Oceanus near which he was born and that he eventually went to live among the gods, with Zeus, for whom he carried thunder and lightning.

Pegasus is best known for his adventures with the hero Bellerophon. According to the poet Pindar, Bellerophon tamed the horse with a golden bridle given him by the goddess Athena, who instructed him also to sacrifice a white bull to Pegasus's father, Poseidon, in order to ensure his success in breaking the horse. Mounted on Pegasus's back, the young hero attacked the Amazons, killed the fire-breathing Chimaera, and defeated the Solymi, a belligerent tribe dwelling in Lycia. In another of Pindar's works, Bellerophon is presented as an example of hubris; Pegasus threw Bellerophon when he attempted to reach the dwelling places of the gods so that he might keep company with Zeus. Less dramatic but nonetheless notable details about Pegasus involve his creation of several springs where he struck the earth with a hoof. These were the Hippocrene Spring, a spring on Mount Helicon that was sacred to the Muses, and also the spring of Pirene, which marked the spot where Bellerophon first bridled him and which was of immeasurable importance to the city of Corinth. Not coincidentally, Pegasus, as a symbol of the city, was depicted on coins minted by the city of Corinth and her colonies, for Bellerophon was the son of Corinth's king, Glaucus.

(*See also* Amazons [the], Athena, Chimaera, Chrysaor, Corinth, Gorgons [the], Helicon [Mount], Hippocrene, Medusa, Muses [the], Oceanus [place], Perseus, Pirene, Poseidon, Solymi [the], *and* Zeus.)

POLYPHEMUS

According to Homer's *Odyssey*, from which he is best known, Polyphemus was the most powerful of the Cyclopes and the son of the god Poseidon and the nymph Thoosa, daughter of the sea deity Phorcys. Like the other Cyclopes, he was a giant—as Odysseus describes him, "a mountain of a man"—and had a single, round eye in the middle of his forehead. Also like the other Cyclopes, he was a lawless, cave-dwelling loner. When Odysseus and his men came to the island of the Cyclopes, he was curious to find out what sort of people lived there, so, accompanied by twelve men, he made his way inland from the shore to come upon the cave of Polyphemus, which was fitted out with a fenced yard and pens for the keeping of goats and sheep. While the Cyclops was out pasturing his flocks, Odysseus and his men helped themselves to cheese in the Cyclops's cave. His men now wanted to leave, but Odysseus wished to stay, hoping for the gifts that, in the Greek world, one would typically expect to receive from a person whose house one was visiting; such gift giving was the norm, regardless of whether visits were made by chance or whether either party was previously known to the other. But the Cyclops, having no regard for custom or culture, kept the Greeks imprisoned in his cave and, grabbing two of Odysseus's men, dashed them together and ate them. After Polyphemus had made himself another such meal, Odysseus contrived a plan whereby to escape the cave. Odysseus offered the Cyclops strong, undiluted wine, which he greedily drank in abundance; a civilized man in the Greek world would have cut his wine with water. Only now did Odysseus offer his name, but it was a false one: "Nobody." With the Cyclops soon in a drunken slumber, Odysseus and his comrades put out his single eye with a massive, sharpened branch of olive, its tip aglow from being held in the Cyclops's fire. Polyphemus cried to his neighbors for help, but they turned away laughing when he shouted that "Nobody" was hurting him. Odysseus and his men were able to escape the sealed cave by fastening themselves to the underbellies of the Cyclops's largest, wooliest rams. It was the blinding of Polyphemus that earned Odysseus the hatred of Poseidon, who proceeded to torment him and further delay his return to Ithaca.

Polyphemus arguably showed a marginally "softer" side in his amorous pursuit of the Nereid nymph Galatea. In order to win her favor, he took pains to improve his appearance and sang of his love for her to the accompaniment of a flute. Galatea, however, loathed the monster as much as she loved handsome Acis, son of the woodland deity Faunus and a sea nymph. In a rage at finding the lovers together, Polyphemus threw a massive rock at Acis, crushing him. In answer to Galatea's prayer that Acis somehow be saved, the earth split open to reveal him reincarnated as a river god.

(*See also* Acis, Cyclopes [the], Faunus, Galatea, Nereids [the], Odysseus, Phorcys, *and* Poseidon.)

PORPHYRION

Porphyrion was one of the Giants (Gigantes), fierce, serpent's tail–legged giants who waged war on Zeus and his siblings and were born from the blood generated by the castration of Uranus. Porphyrion appears to have been among the strongest of his brothers, and the Greek poet Pindar calls him their leader or king. He acquired a passion for Hera and attempted to rape her, apparently through Zeus's devising, whereupon Zeus struck him with a lightning bolt and Hercules then killed him with one of his arrows.

(*See also* Giants [the], Hera, Hercules, Uranus, *and* Zeus.)

PYTHON

Python was as an enormous dragon or serpent that resided by a spring at Delphi. The Roman poet Ovid writes that the monster was born from a sludge-covered Gaia ("Earth") after the Great Flood that nearly eliminated all humankind. According to so-called *Homeric Hymn* to the god Apollo, Python was female and had been given the dreadful monster Typhon to rear. She was reputedly a bane to humans, to whom she brought death in great numbers until Apollo killed her with his weapons, a bow and arrows. The monster's corpse lay rotting in the sun, and in a story repeated by the geographer Strabo and others, it was the putrefaction (*pythesthai* means "to rot" in Greek) of its body that was the source of the monster's name as well as of Pytho, the name of the area where it died; Pythian, an epithet for Apollo; and Pythia, the name of the priestesses of Apollo's oracle at Delphi.

The travel writer Pausanias and others preserve the legend that Python had been posted at Delphi by Gaia or by Themis to guard the oracle at Delphi and that by slaying Python, Apollo gained ownership of this most famous of sites of prophecy. The god was said to have instituted the Pan-Hellenic Pythian Games, which were held every four years, to commemorate his slaying of this monster.

(*See also* Apollo, Delphi, Gaia, Hera, *and* Themis.)

SATYRS, THE
Satyrs were male hybrid creatures who were part horse and part human. They stood and walked upright, unlike the quadruped, half-horse Centaurs to whom they were akin, and in their original, traditional form, they had horses' tails, long hair and beards, horses' ears, bulbous foreheads, and snub noses. Artistic representations also showed them sometimes with the legs and hooves of a horse as well as with enlarged, erect penises. It was only in the Hellenistic Period (after 323 BCE, the death of Alexander the Great) that Satyrs, in an assimilation to the rustic god Pan, took on a goatlike appearance, having shorter tails and sprouting horns. Satyrs, who in earliest times were indistinguishable from Silens, were woodland spirits or daemons that lived in the wild, being found in mountains, forests, and caves alongside Nymphs with whom they cavorted and whom these lusty creatures amorously pursued. Lustfulness, enthusiasm for wine, and a propensity for mischief were characteristic of them. Silens, on the other hand, came to be viewed as elderly Satyrs. Alongside Nymphs, both Satyrs and Silens formed the typical entourage of the shape-shifting god Dionysus. The best-known Satyr in Classical mythology was also the most tragic of them. This was Marsyas, who had found the flute cast aside by the goddess Athena, and, when he discovered that he had a talent for playing the instrument, he made the terrible mistake of challenging Apollo to a music contest. As a consequence of his pridefulness, he was flayed alive.

Another Satyr, his name unknown, pursued the Danaid Amymone, but was driven off by Poseidon, who then took up in the pursuit of the maiden himself.

(*See also* Amymone, Apollo, Athena, Centaurs [the], Dionysus, Marsyas, Nymphs [the], Poseidon, *and* Silens [the].)

SCYLLA Scylla was a sea nymph turned monster. She was variously described as a daughter of an otherwise shadowy Crataeis or Lamia, of the sea goddess Echidna, or of Hecate, goddess of witchcraft, and the sea god Phorcys (or Typhon or Triton). According to the Roman poet Ovid, Scylla had many suitors but shunned all of these, taking refuge among the nymphs of the sea. But the sea god Glaucus caught sight of her and pursued her, to no avail. She fled in fear of him, so Glaucus went to the abode of the sorceress Circe in order to obtain a cure for his lovesickness and to find a way to punish Scylla. Circe duly obliged him by tainting Scylla's favorite pool, the place she went to bathe, with poisons. As she waded, waist-deep, into the tainted water, the submerged parts of her body altered gruesomely, her loins now fixed with the snarling heads of dogs. Ultimately, Scylla was further transformed into a bristling crag. Alternate versions of the story claim that she was transformed into a monster by Amphitrite or Poseidon. In Homer's *Odyssey*, the earliest literary mention of Scylla, she is a monster who yelps like a young dog and has twelve feet as well as six necks with three rows of gnashing teeth. She lived her days in a cave from which perch she reached out to snatch fish and hapless sailors, among them six of Odysseus's crew. Jason and his heroic crew the Argonauts escaped her with the help of the sea goddess Thetis, and the Trojan hero Aeneas, too, was able to avoid her on his way to Italy.

Even in antiquity there were attempts to locate the mountainous rock or promontory that was Scylla's lair and that lay opposite the great rock beneath which the whirlpool Charybdis could be found; according to the historian Thucydides, for example, the rocks of Scylla and Charybdis were situated to either side of the Straits of Messina, the waterway between Rhegium and Messana, which was narrow, rough, and offered treacherous passage to ships.

The monster Scylla is to be differentiated from the treacherous Megarean princess who betrayed her homeland out of love for King Minos of Crete.

PLATE VIII
The Sirens: Hybrid female monsters who lure sailors to their deaths

---

(See also Aeneas, Argonauts [the], Charybdis, Crete, Echidna, Glaucus [god], Hecate, Jason, Megara [place], Minos, Odysseus, Phorcys, Poseidon, Scylla [heroine], Triton, *and* Typhon.)

SILENS, THE
Silens were originally indistinct from Satyrs, woodland spirits who were half human and half horse. Over time, however, Silens came to be seen as elderly Satyrs, the most prominent of their group being Silenus.

(*See also* Satyrs [the] *and* Silenus.)

SILENUS
Silenus was an elderly Satyr and the most notable of the Silens, woodland daemons who were half horse but who, over time, became more goatlike. Silenus was represented in literature and art as jovial, rotund, and balding. Like other Silens and Satyrs, he was fond of wine, music, and dance. There were various accounts of his birth: the poet Nonnus describes him as autochthonous, born literally from Gaia ("Earth"), but according to rhetorician Aelian, he was the immortal son of a Nymph. Silenus was a fixture in the entourage of the god Dionysus, with whom he had a particularly close relationship: there was a tradition that it was Silenus to whom the infant Dionysus was given by Zeus to rear after the tragic death of his mother, Semele, and the historian Diodorus Siculus notes that Silenus was Dionysus's attendant, advisor, and instructor. The Phrygian king Midas was said to have had an encounter with Silenus, either when taking him captive in a miraculous garden, where he was then asked to prophesy the future, or when coming to his rescue after he had become separated from Dionysus in a drunken state. For his rescue of Silenus, Dionysus rewarded Midas by granting him a wish, and what Midas wished was that everything he touched would turn to gold.

(*See also* Dionysus, Gaia, Midas, Nymphs [the], Phrygia, Semele, Silens [the], *and* Zeus.)

SIRENS, THE
The Sirens were hybrid female monsters with human heads and the bodies of birds. Sometimes they were also represented as having human arms with which to hold their musical instruments. The particular hazard that they posed was to lure sailors to their deaths with their enchanting songs. For Homer, the Sirens were two in number, and he does not describe their appearance, while later authors (and artists) indicate that there were three of them and that they were bird women. The Sirens are best known from Odysseus's encounter with them. The goddess Circe warned Odysseus that the Sirens' irresistible songs caused all those who heard them to forget their homecomings and, as a consequence, their island's beach was covered with their victims' glistening bones. Odysseus was instructed to place softened wax in his men's ears while passing the Sirens and to have himself lashed to the boat's mast, so that he could

enjoy the Sirens' song about the Trojan War without succumbing to their fatal enticements. It was a good thing that Odysseus listened to Circe, for he was so overcome by the Sirens' voices that he begged his men to release him, a request that they, fortunately, did not hear or heed. According to the epic poet Apollonius of Rhodes, the hero Jason and his companions, too, encountered the Sirens. On their way back from Colchis with the Golden Fleece, Jason and his men passed the island Anthemoessa, where the Sirens resided. The bard Orpheus sang to the accompaniment of his lyre so loudly that he drowned out the Sirens' song, and all of Jason's men were saved except one, who leaped overboard.

Apollonius and others call the Sirens daughters of the river god Achelous and of the Muse Terpsichore (or Melpomene). The Sirens were said to have been companions of the goddess Demeter's daughter, Persephone, before she was abducted by Hades. The Roman poet Ovid adds that the Sirens had golden feathers and were transformed into bird-maidens so that they could move as quickly as possible in their search for Persephone.

(*See also* Achelous [god], Circe, Colchis, Demeter, Hades [god], Jason, Melpomene, Muses [the], Odysseus, Orpheus, Persephone, *and* Terpsichore.)

SPHINX OF THEBES, THE
Sphinxes were hybrid monsters introduced to the Greek world from Egypt and the Near East. Represented as winged lions with human heads, they featured in Greek art as early as the Bronze Age (circa 3000–1150 BCE) but entered the literary tradition as we know it much later. In Greek texts, sphinxes are female, though in art there are also males. Classical authors offer varying accounts of these monsters' origins. The poet Hesiod refers to the Sphinx (in the singular) as the offspring of the serpent-maiden Echidna (or the Chimaera) with the monstrous dog Orthus. Assuming that there were more than one Sphinx, the infamous Sphinx of Thebes was the only one really to distinguish herself, and when ancient authors mention "the Sphinx," it is the monster that plagued the city of Thebes that they speak of. Thus, the mythographer Apollodorus writes that the Sphinx, born of Echidna and the monstrous Typhon, had a woman's face; the breast, feet, and tail of a lion; and a bird's wings. He goes on to relate the story well known from the playwright Sophocles's masterpiece, *Oedipus the King*, adding some background detail. The Sphinx had been sent by the goddess Hera as a plague upon the populace of the city of Thebes, whom she terrorized by posing a riddle that none could solve, failure to answer correctly resulting in death. The city's regent, Creon, offered his sister, the queen Jocasta, as bride to

whoever might successfully
solve this riddle and rid the
city of the Sphinx. This Oedipus
did, reasoning correctly that the
creature that walked on four feet in
the morning, on two at noon, and on three in
the evening was a human (as crawling baby, biped adult, and staff-as-
sisted elder). Oedipus's unanticipated response caused the Sphinx to
throw herself from a cliff to her death. Oedipus then became king of Thebes
and unwittingly married his mother, who was Jocasta.

(*See also* Chimaera [the], Creon, Echidna, Hera, Jocasta, Oedipus, Orthus, Thebes,
and Typhon.)

STEROPES Steropes, whose name means "lightning bolt" or "lightener,"
was a Cyclops, a one-eyed giant born of the elemental gods Gaia and Uranus.
His siblings were Brontes ("The Thunderer") and Arges ("The Flashing One").
The Cyclopes' names reflect the nature of their service to Zeus, for whose use
they forged lightning bolts.

(*See also* Cyclopes [the], Gaia, Uranus, *and* Zeus.)

STHENO The Gorgon Stheno, the "Strong One," was one of Medusa's
two immortal sisters.

(*See also* Euryale, Gorgons [the], *and* Medusa.)

STYMPHALIAN BIRDS, THE According to the mythogra-
pher Apollodorus, the infamous Stymphalian Birds roosted in a dense growth
of trees by Lake Stymphalus near the town of Stymphalus in Arcadia. The travel
writer Pausanias adds that they were man-eating, and Hyginus writes that the
birds discharged their feathers as missiles. Whatever their particular threat,
Hercules was ordered to kill or drive away these birds as the sixth of his famous
Labors. This he did with the help of the goddess Athena, who supplied him
with a bronze rattle that he used to startle the birds from their hiding places so
that he could shoot them with his arrows once they took flight.

(*See also* Arcadia, Athena, Hercules, *and* Stymphalus.)

TALUS The bronze giant Talus (or Talos) has been described as a living
statue or something of a robot, but he was a sentient, living being. The poet
Apollonius of Rhodes says of him that he was descended from the ancient Race
of Bronze and had been given by Zeus to Europa so that he might keep watch

over the island of Crete, which he circuited three times daily; according to tradition, there had been five successive ages or races of humans, the Race of Gold, the Race of Silver, the Race of Bronze, the Race of Heroes, and the present, deeply flawed Race of Iron. Talus's body and his limbs were of bronze and thus invulnerable, except for a place at his ankle, where blood coursed through a single vein. Talus is best known for his encounter with Jason and the Argonauts, who were accompanied by the sorceress Medea. When, in the course of their return voyage from fetching the Golden Fleece, the Argonauts attempted to seek shelter in a harbor on the island of Crete, Talus pelted them with rocks. Medea, however, put a hex on him, and while hoisting more rocks, he grazed his ankle and thus was fatally wounded.

The mythographer Apollodorus offers a slightly different account of his origins and his physiognomy: after creating Talus, the god Hephaestus made a gift of him to the Cretan king Minos. Hephaestus's creation had a single vein extending from his neck to his ankles that was sealed at its end with a nail of bronze. He perished when Medea either drove him mad or when she, as a trick, convinced him that she could make him immortal and pulled out the nail that sealed his vein.

(*See also* Argonauts [the], Crete, Europa, Hephaestus, Jason, Medea, Minos, *and* Zeus.)

THESPIAN LION, THE
The Thespian Lion once ranged the slopes of Mount Cithaeron. The lion was a bane, as it preyed on the flocks both of Amphitryon, Hercules's stepfather, and of Thespius, king of Thespiae. According to the mythographer Apollodorus, when Hercules was just eighteen years old, he undertook to kill the troublesome lion. He stayed with Thespius for fifty days and nights until he was finally able to slay the lion. Thespius, well aware of Hercules's more-than-mortal strength and desiring Hercules's offspring, sent a different one of his daughters to the hero every night, and somehow Hercules was fooled, thinking that he had all the while been sleeping with the same maiden.

(*See also* Amphitryon, Cithaeron [Mount], *and* Hercules.)

TITYUS
The giant Tityus was a son of Zeus and Elara, daughter of the Boeotian hero Orchomenus. According to the mythographer Apollodorus, Zeus, wishing to keep his indiscretion secret from his wife, Hera, hid Elara under the earth

after impregnating her. After a period of gestation, Tityus emerged from the earth, and for this reason was called earth-born. In time, however, Tityus would commit a sin that would cause him to return underground, this time, however, taking up residence in Tartarus, the part of the Underworld reserved for sinners. His sin was to have attempted raping Leto, mother of the divine twins Apollo and Artemis, who consequently killed him with their arrows. It was in the Underworld that Odysseus, and later Aeneas, saw him, his enormous body sprawled over nine acres, his liver being eternally eaten by vultures.

(*See also* Aeneas, Apollo, Artemis, Boeotia, Leto, Odysseus, Tartarus, Underworld [the], *and* Zeus.)

TYPHOEUS Typhoeus was another name for Typhon, an enormous hybrid monster produced by Gaia and sired by Tartarus.

(*See* Gaia, Tartarus [god and place], *and* Typhon.)

TYPHON The monstrous Typhon (also called Typhoeus) was early on confused and conflated with Typhaon. According to the Greek poet Hesiod, Gaia ("Earth") produced Typhon/Typhoeus with Tartarus, a personification of the deep, dank parts of Hades deep within Earth. Typhon was a terrible monster with prodigious strength. He had a hundred serpents' heads that had dark, flickering tongues and produced the sounds of every kind of animal: a lion, bull, dog, snake, and more. His eyes flashed fire. With the she-monster Echidna, Typhon/Typhaon became father to a host of other monsters: Orthus, the hound of triple-bodied Geryon; Cerberus, the hound of Hades; the many-headed Hydra of Lerna; and the fire-breathing Chimaera. Zeus correctly perceived Typhon as a threat to his realm and shook the heavens and seas alike with his thunder. God and monster engaged in a terrible battle that caused the earth, sky, and sea to seethe with powerful winds, earthquakes, and fire. Even Hades trembled beneath the earth's crust. Eventually, Zeus felled his rival, striking him with a blazing thunderbolt, and cast him into the depths of Tartarus. The mythographer Apollodorus provides a more detailed physical description of the giant: he was so enormous in size that his head reached beyond the mountains to the stars. A hundred serpents' heads projected from his arms, and this winged giant had hissing, coiling vipers in place of legs. According to Apollodorus, Pindar, Ovid, and others, when Zeus overcame Typhon, he cast him beneath Mount Etna on the island of Sicily, which fact accounts for that mountain's volcanic activity.

(*See also* Cerberus, Chimaera [the], Echidna, Gaia, Geryon, Hades [god and place], Hydra of Lerna [the], Sicily, Tartarus [god and place], *and* Zeus.)

PART

IV

PLACES
AND
LAND-
MARKS

ABYDUS Abydus was a city located on the narrowest part of the Dardanelles, or Hellespont, as it was called in antiquity. This city, founded in the seventh century BCE, was situated on the Asian side of the strait, and as the Greek historian Herodotus noted, it was there that the Persian king Xerxes constructed a bridge spanning the Hellespont so as to facilitate passage for his massive army to Greece. Abydus was notable in Classical mythology as the home of Leander, a young man whose beloved Hero, a priestess of the goddess Aphrodite, lived in Sestus, on the Hellespont's opposite shore. Leander would swim to meet her at nightfall until their liaison took a tragic turn, his drowning occasioning Hero's suicide.

(*See also* Aphrodite, Hellespont [the], Hero, *and* Leander.)

ACHELOUS RIVER, THE The Achelous River, Modern Greek Akheloos Potamos, is one of the longest rivers (approximately 137 miles, or 220 kilometers) in Greece. Rising in the Pindus Range, it flows into the Ionian Sea and, in antiquity, formed a natural border between the regions of Aetolia and Acarnania in central Greece. This river was of such importance that its deified personification, the river god Achelous, could be invoked as the deity of all rivers, and both the river and its god featured in a number of myths. For example, Achelous was reputedly the father of Castalia, namesake of the Castalian Spring, which was sacred to the Muses; Alcmaeon, son of one of the Seven Against Thebes, purified himself in this river's waters after killing his mother, Eriphyle, for her repeated treachery; and Hercules wrestled with Achelous in order to win the hand of his last wife, Deianeira. In the course of the wrestling match with Hercules, Achelous was said to have assumed the form of a serpent and then of a bull. The geographer Strabo explains these myths by relating them to physical features of the river itself: its serpentine course and the bull-like roar generated by its rushing waters.

(*See also* Alcmaeon, Castalian Spring [the], Deianeira, Hercules, Muses [the], *and* Seven Against Thebes [the].)

ACHERON, THE RIVER Acheron was believed to be one of the main rivers in the Underworld, the geography of which shifted over time. In fact, the name of the river was sometimes used to refer to the Underworld in its entirety. According to Homer, who is the earliest source of information about the location and nature of this river, Acheron lay beyond the river Oceanus, which encircled the world of the living, and by the Grove of Persephone. It was there, at the point where the rivers Phlegethon and Cocytus, a branch of the river Styx, flowed into Acheron, that Odysseus dug a pit from which he conjured the souls of the dead. In Virgil's *Aeneid,* by contrast, Acheron is identified with the Styx and is the river over which Charon ferried the souls of the dead.

(*See also* Aeneas, Charon, Cocytus [the River], Oceanus [god and place], Odysseus, Persephone, Phlegethon [the River], Styx [the River], *and* Underworld [the].)

ACROPOLIS, THE

The Acropolis is a massive, flat-topped, limestone outcropping in the Attic plain that served as Athens' old citadel and later its religious center. It rises to a height of approximately 492 feet (150 meters) and has a greatest length and width of about 885 feet (270 meters) and 512 feet (156 meters), respectively. The term "acropolis," which means "high city" or "highest part of the city," can refer to the upper town of any city in Greece. For purposes of defense, there was a tendency to build settlements on hilltops, often fortified, and when populations expanded, to build in the areas surrounding the original town center. In the case of Athens, whose acropolis is the best known, the upper city was fortified in the Bronze Age (thirteenth century BCE) and, in that period, contained a palatial building. After the destruction of the palace and the close of the Bronze Age, the Acropolis, having become the symbolic center of the city, saw several phases of temple and monument construction, the most ambitious being undertaken by the tyrant Peisistratus in the sixth century BCE and the statesman and general Pericles in the fifth century BCE. Ruins of the monuments now visible on the Acropolis stem from the building program of Pericles, whose aim was to make Athens a showcase and "school" for all of Greece.

As the goddess Athena was the patron goddess of Athens, she figured heavily in the symbolism of the Acropolis monuments. The Parthenon, constructed in the years 447–432 BCE in Athena's honor and dedicated to her as maiden goddess (*Parthenos*), contained a monumental (38 feet, or 11.5 meters, tall) cult statue of gold and ivory that depicted Athena as warrior-goddess wearing a helmet, which was decorated with a sphinx, griffins, and Pegasus, and wearing a breastplate, the latter bearing the head of Medusa. With her left hand, the Parthenos statue supported a shield bearing scenes from the legendary battle of the Athenians, led by Theseus, against the Amazons and from the battle of the gods and Giants, and in her right hand held a small winged Nike (personification of victory). On her sandals appeared scenes from the battle of the Lapiths and Centaurs, and on the statue's base, the myth of Pandora. At her feet lay curled a serpent, a depiction of the early Athenian king Erechtheus. Myths featured on the statue reappeared on the sculptural decoration of the Parthenon itself, in particular the battles of the Lapiths and Centaurs, the Athenians and Amazons, and the gods and Giants, which, together with scenes from the Trojan War, have been interpreted as symbolizing the victory of the

Greeks over the Persians in the Persian Wars (492–449 BCE) and, as a consequence, the god-sanctioned victory of civilized Greece over "the barbarian" writ large. The temple's pediments, for their part, featured the spectacular birth of Athena from the head of Zeus and her triumph over Poseidon in the contest for patronage of Athens.

Another Athena, made of bronze and allegedly visible to sailors as far away as Sounion (Sunium), stood outside the Parthenon by the formal entrance to the upper Acropolis precinct and represented Athena, again armed, as Promachos, defender of the city and leader of the battle ranks. The Acropolis also housed the temple known as the Erechtheum, which is distinguished by its caryatid porch and was sacred to Athena Polias (guardian of the city) and to the legendary Athenian kings Erechtheus and Cecrops, as well as to Poseidon, the mark of whose trident striking the Acropolis's rock could be seen in the temple. In close proximity to the Erechtheum stood the olive tree that Athena produced in her contest with Poseidon. The Acropolis also housed the small temple of Athena in the guise of goddess of victory, Nike, and a shrine of Artemis. At the base of the Acropolis lay the theater of Dionysus who, in addition to being the god of wine, was the patron god of the theater.

(*See also* Amazons [the], Artemis, Athena, Athens, Attica, Cecrops, Centaurs [the], Dionysus, Erechtheus, Giants [the], Gorgons [the], Griffins [the], Lapiths [the], Medusa, Nike, Pandora, Parthenon [the], Pegasus, Poseidon, Sphinx, Theseus, Troy, *and* Zeus.)

AEAEA Aeaea is the mythical island inhabited by the enchantress goddess Circe, who detained Odysseus for a full year in the course of his ten-year journey home from Troy. According to Homer's *Odyssey*, she resided there with a group of nymphs and an entourage of tamed wolves and lions. The hero Jason, accompanied by the barbarian princess Medea, also visited this island in search of Circe, who was Medea's aunt and from whom they sought purification from the pollution of murder. In antiquity, the island was variously believed to be in the Far East, at the edge of the known world, or in the West, according to the Roman poet Virgil, located somewhere off the Italian coast between Cumae, where the Sibyl resided, and Latium, where the Trojan hero Aeneas and his band of Trojan refugees would eventually settle.

(*See also* Aeneas, Circe, Cumae, Jason, Latium, Medea, Odysseus, Sibyl of Cumae [the], *and* Troy.)

AEGEAN SEA, THE The Aegean Sea lies between the coast of Greece and Turkey, extending from the Hellespont to Crete, as defined by the Greek historian Herodotus. Among the legendary etymologies for the sea's name is derivation from the name of the Athenian king, Aegeus, who plunged to his death in this body of water because he thought his son, Theseus, had perished while attempting to kill the Minotaur.

(*See also* Aegeus, Athens, Minotaur [the], *and* Theseus.)

AEGINA The island of Aegina lies in the Saronic Gulf approximately 13 miles (20 kilometers) southwest of Athens. This island, which was settled as early as the fourth millennium BCE, is notable among other things for the imposing remains of its temple of the fertility goddess Aphaea, the sculptural decoration of which depicted scenes from the first and second Trojan wars, both of which had connections with the island's mythology. According to legend, the island took its name from the nymph Aegina, whom Zeus abducted to the island of Oenone, which he subsequently renamed after her. By Zeus, Aegina became the mother of Aeacus, a later king of the island who would repopulate his plague-decimated island with ant-people. Aeacus, for his part, was the father of Peleus, later Achilles's father, and Telamon, who would become the father of the Ajax the Great. Achilles and Ajax fought in the second and best known Trojan War, while Telamon helped Hercules in his battle, an earlier Trojan war, against Troy's king Laomedon.

(*See also* Achilles, Aeacus, Ajax [the Great], Hercules, Laomedon, Peleus, Telamon, Troy, *and* Zeus.)

ALBA LONGA The town of Alba Longa was located in the region of Latium on Mount Albanus, modern Monte Cavo, southeast of Rome. According to legend, Alba Longa was founded by Ascanius, the son of Aeneas, who had brought a group of Trojan refugees to Italy after the fall of Troy to the Greeks in the Trojan War. Alba Longa would remain the capital of Latium until the founding of Rome by Romulus and was allegedly destroyed in the middle of the seventh century BCE by the Roman king Tullus Hostilius.

(*See also* Aeneas, Ascanius, Latium, Rome, Romulus, *and* Troy.)

ALPHEUS RIVER, THE Alpheus, Modern Greek Alfios, is the largest river in the Peloponnese and one of the largest in Greece. Rising in southern Arcadia and flowing by Olympia into the Ionian Sea, its course is some 70 miles (110 kilometers) in length. The Alpheus is featured in the Labors of Hercules, who diverted its course in order to clean the stables of Augeas, and as in the case of all rivers, the Alpheus was conceived of not only as a place but also as a deity, the river god Alpheus, who was a personification of this river. The god Alpheus was one of the many children of Oceanus and developed a passion for the nymph Arethusa, whom he pursued to Sicily, where she became a spring and their waters mingled.

(*See also* Alpheus [god], Arcadia, Arethusa, Augeas, Hercules, Oceanus [god], *and* Sicily.)

ARCADIA Arcadia was a rugged, mountainous region in the central Peloponnese more suited to hunting and animal husbandry than to agriculture. Its boundaries were largely defined by mountains (clockwise from the northeast, by Mount Erymanthus, Mount Cyllene, Mount Aroania, Mount Oligyrtus, Mount Parthenius, the foothills of the Parnon and Taygetos ranges, Mount Nomia, and Mount Elaeum), and it was slightly smaller in area than the modern regional unit of the same name. Arcadia's most important river, the Alpheus, is also the principal river in the Peloponnese. Other Arcadian bodies of water well known from mythology are Lake Stymphalus, home of the dangerous Stymphalian Birds, and even the Underworld's river Styx, which made a short aboveground appearance in the region. The Arcadians claimed that they were descendants of the most ancient inhabitants of Greece, the Pelasgians, who were named after Pelasgus, the culture hero responsible for teaching the Arcadians how to build huts and make clothing from animal hides. The namesake of Arcadia was said to be Arcas, a son of Zeus and the bear-woman Callisto. In keeping with the region's rustic character, Arcadia was considered the home of the god Pan, the birthplace of Hermes, and a favorite hunting ground of the goddess Artemis.

(*See also* Alpheus River [the], Arcas, Artemis, Callisto, Erymanthus [Mount], Hermes, Pan, Pelasgus, Stymphalus, Styx, *and* Zeus.)

ARETHUSA Arethusa, Fonte Aretusa in Italian, is a spring on the Sicilian island of Ortygia, which is the historic center of Syracuse. The spring is said to have taken its name from the Peloponnesian nymph Arethusa who fled the amorous pursuit of the river god Alpheus to arrive on Ortygia, where she became a spring. The nymph Arethusa, who personified this spring, appeared as the emblem of Syracuse on coinage issued by that city in antiquity.

(*See also* Alpheus [god and place], Ortygia, *and* Sicily.)

ARGOS Argos, which is sited about 3 miles (5 kilometers) from the coast, was the principal city in the Argolis region of the eastern Peloponnese and is the site of a modern town of the same name. According to the Greek geographer Strabo (64 BCE–19 CE), the greater part of Argos was situated in a plain, and it had a citadel called Larisa, a moderately fortified hill upon which there was a temple of Jupiter. Argos was reputedly the oldest city in Greece, and its mythology was complicated and confused even in antiquity. By some accounts, Argos was originally inhabited by the ancestors of Pelasgus, namesake of the pre-Greek, aboriginal inhabitants of Greece called Pelasgians and a descendant of the local Argive river god Inachus. As the mythographer Apollodorus writes, Argus, who gave his name to Argos, was a brother of Pelasgus. There are physical remains of a Bronze Age settlement and fortifications at Argos that point to the city's importance in that period, especially the late fourteenth to thirteenth centuries BCE, but its height of power and influence came later, beginning in the middle of the eighth century BCE through the sixth century BCE, in the so-called Archaic Period, when its territory extended along the eastern coast of the Parnon peninsula to the island of Cythera. While Argos lost territory and power to its neighbor Sparta, it did control the sites of Mycenae, Tiryns, and Lerna, all of which, including Argos, play a significant role in mythology. Among Argos's most notable legendary figures are Io, Inachus's daughter, who was transformed into a cow; the selfless and heroic Cleobis and Biton; Danae, whose prison the god Zeus accessed in the form of a golden shower and with her became father of the Gorgon-slayer Perseus; Adrastus, leader of the Seven Against Thebes; and Eurystheus, the king for whom Hercules performed his Labors. Among the gods, it was Hera to whom Argos was most sacred.

(*See also* Adrastus, Cleobis, Danae, Eurystheus, Gorgons [the], Hera, Hercules, Inachus, Io, Lerna, Mycenae, Pelasgus, Perseus, Seven Against Thebes [the], Sparta, Tiryns, *and* Zeus.)

ATHENS Athens, which according to legend was named after its patron goddess Athena, was and still is the principal city of the region of Attica. The city lies on a plain that is surrounded by the Aegaleos, Parnes, Pentelicon, and Hymettus mountains. Piraeus, the city's port, lies on the northeastern edge of the Saronic Gulf, and was connected by a system of long walls (a walled access "corridor" approximately 4 miles (6 kilometers) to the walls of Athens proper, on either side of which ran the Ilissus and Eridanus rivers. Athens is dominated by the Acropolis, the ancient city's citadel and religious center, which houses Athena's most important temple, the Parthenon. Already in antiquity, the Acropolis became a museum of sorts to Athenian mythological history, containing structures that alluded to the many roles assumed by the city's patron goddess as well as to the city's legendary founders and early kings, among them the earth-born Cecrops, the snake-man Erechtheus, and the hero Theseus, notable for reputedly slaying the Minotaur of Crete, uniting the various settlements in Attica, and repulsing an attack on his city by the Amazons.

(*See also* Acropolis, Amazons [the], Athena, Attica, Cecrops, Crete, Erechtheus, Ilissus River [the], Minotaur [the], *and* Theseus.)

ATTICA Attica, modern Attiki, is the territory of Athens. In antiquity, Attica could be defined as the triangular peninsula at the eastern edge of central Greece, being separated from Boeotia to its north by Mount Parnes and Mount Cithaeron and from Megara to the west by Mount Cerata. Modern Attica is somewhat larger, including Megara, the Saronic Islands, the island of Cythera, and a portion of the Peloponnese.

Prior to the ascendancy of Athens, Attica contained a number of separate communities that, according to tradition, were twelve in number at the time of the legendary king Cecrops. These eventually united to form a single Athenian state, which development was attributed to the Athenian hero Theseus. The sanctuary of Eleusis (modern Elefsina), sacred to the goddess Demeter and her daughter Persephone, and the sanctuary of Artemis at Brauron (modern Vraona) were located in Attica, the former northwest of Athens's center and the latter to its southeast. Another mythologically significant site in Attica is Colonus, which was situated just outside the walls of Athens and was the site of the death and heroization of Oedipus as well as of the sacred grove of the Eumenides.

(*See also* Artemis, Athens, Cecrops, Cithaeron [Mount], Colonus, Demeter, Eleusis, Eumenides [the], Megara [place], Oedipus, Persephone, *and* Theseus.)

AULIS Aulis was a town on the eastern coast of Boeotia just south of the Euripus channel, which separates the island of Euboea from the Greek mainland. The travel writer Pausanias visited Aulis and intimates that it was named after the daughter of Ogygus, a legendary Boeotian king. He saw there both a temple of Artemis containing two marble statues of the goddess, one holding torches and the other shooting an arrow, and the very plane tree that, at the time of the Trojan War, had become the locus of an important omen: a snake appeared before the Greeks gathered there and, winding its way up the tree's trunk, proceeded to devour a sparrow's eight nestlings and the mother sparrow herself. As Homer writes, the Greek seer Calchas interpreted this as a sign that the Greeks would be victorious at Troy, but that the war would last a full nine years, with Troy falling in the tenth. Indeed, Aulis is best known as the gathering point of the Greek forces bound for Troy, and as the site where the Mycenean king Agamemnon's daughter Iphigeneia was sacrificed at the bidding of Artemis.

(*See also* Agamemnon, Artemis, Boeotia, Calchas, Euboea, Iphigeneia, *and* Troy.)

BABYLON The ancient city of Babylon was located on the Euphrates River in what is now southern Iraq. Situated in the Fertile Crescent, Babylon was settled from at least the third millennium BCE and, rising to prominence during the reign of Hammurabi (1792–1750 BCE), famed for his code of laws, the city served during his reign as the political, religious, and cultural center of the ancient Near East. Babylon's Hanging Gardens, called one of the Seven Wonders of the ancient world, but not yet found by archaeologists, were reputedly created over 1,000 years later by the king Nebuchadnezzar II (reigned 604–562 BCE), under whom the city again flourished and, according to the Greek historian Herodotus, became the most splendid city in the known world. Nebuchadnezzar's extensive building campaign also produced (in rebuilt form) the Marduk temple Esagil and the ziggurat Etemanaki that served as the axis connecting heaven and earth and that came to be known as the Tower of Babyl. In the Roman poet Ovid's tale of the star-crossed Babylonian lovers Pyramus and Thisbe, which is the best-known Classical myth involving the city, the legendary Assyrian queen Semiramis is credited with building Babylon and its remarkable walls.

(*See also* Pyramus, Semiramis, *and* Thisbe.)

BOEOTIA   Boeotia is a region of central Greece, the modern regional unit (Viotia) of this name being slightly larger than the district was in antiquity. Ancient Boeotia lay northwest of Athens and was divided from the territory of Athens and Megara by Mount Cithaeron and Mount Parnes. It was separated from Phocis on its western border by Mount Helicon, and was further delimited geologically by the Gulf of Corinth to the southwest and the Gulf of Euboea to the northeast. Boeotia was settled as early as the Paleolithic Age (Old Stone Age), and enjoyed prominence first in the Bronze Age (the second millennium BCE), being the site of two notable Mycenaean palace centers, one at Orchomenos and the other at Thebes. Of these two cities, it was Thebes that became the most powerful in the region, and for this reason, the city has an extraordinarily rich mythological tradition: for example, it was the city populated by warriors sprung from dragon's teeth sown by Cadmus and home, too, of Oedipus. As regards the region more broadly, Boeotia was the birthplace of Narcissus, who loved no one but himself, and it was the site of Mount Helicon, which was sacred to the Muses.

(*See also* Cadmus, Cithaeron [Mount], Helicon [Mount], Megara [place], Muses [the], Narcissus, Oedipus, Thebes, *and* Zeus.)

BOSPHORUS, THE   The Bosphorus (or Bosporus) is the narrow strait connecting the Black Sea, called the Euxine Sea in antiquity, with the Sea of Marmara, the ancient Propontis. The Bosphorus and Hellespont separate the European and Asian continents and allow passage for ships between the Mediterranean and Black Sea. According to the Greek tragedian Aeschylus, the Bosphorus took its name from the heroine Io who, having been transformed into a cow as a result of the goddess Hera's jealousy of her, was driven by a gadfly from Greece to Egypt, the Bosphorus being her point of crossing.

(*See also* Hellespont [the], Hera, Io, *and* Zeus.)

CALYDON The city of Calydon was located on the banks of the Evenus River in the ancient region of Aetolia in west-central Greece. According to legend, the city was named after its founder, Calydon, a son of Aetolus, after whom the region of Aetolia is named, and grandson of Endymion, a king of Elis who became the lover of the moon goddess Selene. A later regent of Calydon, Oeneus, failed to make sacrifice to the goddess Artemis, who sent a boar to ravage the land. This resulted in the famous Calydonian Boar hunt, as a consequence of which the hero Meleager met an early death, his mother having thrown the log that constituted the measure of his life into the fire.

(*See also* Aetolia, Aetolus, Artemis, Endymion, Meleager, Oeneus, *and* Selene.)

CAPITOLINE HILL, THE The Capitoline Hill is one of the Seven Hills of Rome, and although it is the smallest of these, it was the most important, evolving from the original settlement's citadel to the later city's religio-political center. Its northeast summit was known as the Arx, and was the location of the citadel proper, while the southwest summit, which overlooked the Roman Forum, was called the Capitol (Capitolium). According to the Roman historian Livy, the Temple of Jupiter Feretrius was the first temple to have been built on the Capitoline, and it was Romulus himself, Rome's founder, who was responsible, commissioning the temple in order to commemorate a military victory that he attributed to the assistance of Jupiter. The most important temple on the Capitoline was that on the Capitolium dedicated to Jupiter Optimus Maximus, Juno, and Minerva, the so-called Capitoline Triad of deities. It was at this temple that victorious generals celebrating a triumph as well as magistrates assuming office made sacrifice. The temple and the entire hill came to be called "Capitolium," a name that, according to the Roman historian Livy, was derived from the discovery on the site of an oversize human skull by those constructing the temple; this discovery was interpreted as a sign of the future greatness of Rome, the citadel being destined to become the "head" (*caput* in Latin) of a world empire. In addition to other shrines and monuments, the Capitoline Hill was the location of the Tarpeian Rock, the precipice that was named after the treacherous Tarpeia and from which traitors were thrown to their deaths. At the foot of the Capitoline in the Forum stood the majestic temple of Saturn, to whom the entire hill had once belonged.

(*See also* Juno, Jupiter, Minerva, Rome, Romulus, Saturn, *and* Tarpeia.)

CARTHAGE According to tradition, the city of Carthage was founded in the late ninth century BCE by Phoenician colonists on what is now the Tunisian coast of North Africa. Because of its strategic position, Carthage became a rival to Rome and, inevitably, these two powers clashed in the Punic Wars (264–146 BCE). In the course of the conflict, the Carthaginian general Hannibal marched over the Alps into Italy, much to the horror of Rome. Carthage was annihilated by the Romans in 146 BCE, only to rise again a century later but now firmly under the Roman thumb as capital of the Roman province of Africa.

The Roman rivalry with Carthage was powerfully reflected in the tale of the Phoenician queen Dido, legendary founder of Carthage, who lost her dignity and her life as a consequence of her fateful love affair with the Trojan Aeneas, who was destined to travel to Italy where he would become the ancestor of the Romans. Hannibal, according to the Roman poet Virgil, would be Dido's avenger.

(*See also* Aeneas, Dido, Rome, *and* Troy.)

CASTALIAN SPRING, THE The Castalian Spring on the slopes of Mount Parnassus near Apollo's sanctuary at Delphi reputedly took its name from the spirit that inhabited it, namely the nymph Castalia, a daughter of the river god Achelous. Castalia had leaped into the spring's waters in order to escape pursuit by the god Apollo. The spring was sacred to the Muses and, for those who imbibed its waters, was thought to be source of musical and poetic inspiration. The travel writer Pausanias describes the spring as both sweet to drink and pleasant to bathe in. Those wishing to consult the oracle at Delphi purified themselves with the spring's water.

(*See also* Achelous [god], Apollo, Delphi, Muses [the], *and* Parnassus [Mount].)

CAUCASUS MOUNTAINS, THE The Caucasus Mountains, a range 684 miles (1,100 kilometers) in length and up to 37 miles (60 kilometers) wide, extend from the Black (Euxine) Sea to the Caspian Sea, forming what was considered a natural barrier between Europe and Asia. As these mountains constituted what the Greeks viewed as the northern edge of the civilized world, the Caucasus region was believed to be the home of a variety of mythological creatures and legendary "barbarian" tribes or peoples such as the Griffins, hybrid creatures that were part bird and part lion; the warlike Amazons; the mysterious Arimaspi; and the Hyperboreans, who enjoyed a felicitous existence. It was in

the Caucasus Mountains, too, that the Titan Prometheus was said to have been shackled and his continually regenerating liver eaten by a vulture as punishment for helping humankind.

(*See also* Amazons [the], Arimaspi [the], Euxine Sea [the], Griffins [the], Hyperboreans [the], Prometheus, *and* Titans [the].)

CEPHISSUS RIVER, THE There were several rivers by the name of Cephissus in Greece, among them one in Boeotia, two in the territory of Athens, and one in the territory of Argos. The deity personifying the Boeotian Cephissus was said to be the father of the lovely youth Narcissus, who pined away out of love for himself. The deity of the Argive Cephissus, for his part, was reputedly one of the judges in the contest between Hera and Poseidon for patronage of Argos, a contest in which Hera prevailed.

(*See also* Argos, Athens, Boeotia, Hera, Narcissus, *and* Poseidon.)

CHIOS The Greek island of Chios lies in the Aegean Sea in relatively close proximity to the coast of Asia Minor (4 miles, or 7 kilometers). There was a tradition that Chios was colonized by Greeks from the island of Euboea in the ninth century BCE. The island had a reputation for being a rich, fertile land and a good source of pine: the Greek historian Thucydides remarks on its prosperity, the island's inhabitants being the wealthiest people in Greece. It was Oenopion, a legendary king of this island, who was said to have put out the eyes of the enormous Orion for violating, or wooing, his daughter Merope.

(*See also* Aegean Sea [the], Merope, *and* Orion.)

CITHAERON, MOUNT Mount Cithaeron (or Kithairon) is a mountain, or, more properly, a mountain range north of the Isthmus of Corinth and separating the territory of Athens (Attica) and Megara from Boeotia. Cithaeron was sacred to a host of deities, among them Zeus, Dionysus, Hera, and Pan, and was the location of numerous myths associated with these deities and others. It was in a cave on Cithaeron that Dionysus was said to have been reared, and the infant Oedipus was left to die on this mountain's slopes. Oedipus survived, but Actaeon, one of his ancestors, met his gruesome end while hunting on this mountain, as did Pentheus, Dionysus's cousin.

As for the mountain's name, the travel writer Pausanias notes that it was named after a legendary Boeotian king who, being quick of wit, helped Zeus when confronted, as he often was, with the jealousy of his wife, Hera. Cithaeron advised the philandering Zeus to place a wooden effigy of his new love interest in a wagon, seeing to it that Hera would discover it. Pulling the veil from its head, Hera was relieved to discover a statue, and not a woman, in her husband's possession.

(*See also* Actaeon, Dionysus, Hera, Megara [place], Oedipus, Pan, Pentheus, *and* Zeus.)

CLASHING ROCKS, THE
"Clashing Rocks" is a translation of the Greek "Symplegades," name of the great rock formations that were believed to lie to either side of the northern end of the Bosphorus and that would quickly move together and clash, crushing ships between them.

(*See also* Bosphorus [the] *and* Symplegades [the].)

CNOSSUS
Cnossus (or Knossos), site of the famed palace of King Minos, is located in a fertile valley just southeast of the modern city of Heraklion on the island of Crete. The site itself was occupied as early as 7000 BCE (the Neolithic Period), and the expansive, multilevel palace, which was subsequently repeatedly modified until its destruction around 1300 BCE, saw its initial phase of construction in the early second millennium BCE. The first systematic excavations of the palace were conducted in the early twentieth century by Sir Arthur Evans and published in his multivolume work *The Palace of Minos at Knossos*. The efforts of Evans and his successors established Cnossus as the political, religious, and artistic center of the so-called Minoan civilization of Crete. In mythology, the palace at Cnossus was not only King Minos's seat of power but also the location of the labyrinth that Minos compelled the Greek craftsman Daedalus to construct as a prison for the Minotaur, Minos's wife Pasiphae's monstrous child by a bull for which she had developed an unquenchable passion.

(*See also* Crete, Daedalus, Minos, Minotaur [the], *and* Pasiphae.)

COCYTUS
Cocytus was one of the rivers of the Underworld, its name traditionally derived from the ancient Greek *kokyein* "to wail," making it the River of Wailing. According to Homer, the Cocytus was branch of the river Styx and, together with the river Phlegethon, fed the river Acheron. The Roman poet Virgil adds details that heighten the horror of the hero Aeneas's descent into the Underworld: in the Underworld's antechamber, Aeneas and the Sibyl who guides him come to a path leading to the river Acheron and a point where the Acheron's tributaries converge in a vast, seething whirlpool that belches forth the thick sludge carried by the dark waters of Cocytus.

(*See also* Acheron River [the], Aeneas, Phlegethon [the River], Sibyl, *and* Underworld [the].)

COLCHIS
Colchis was a fertile, natural-resource-rich region that lay at the eastern end of the Black (or Euxine) Sea and was hemmed in by the Greater

and Lesser Caucasus ranges. Settlements existed in the region as early as the third millennium BCE, and the Greeks sent colonists there in the sixth century BCE. For the Greeks, Colchis was a mysterious, barbarian land, and in mythology it was known as the destination of young Phrixus, who escaped becoming the victim of human sacrifice on the back of a golden-fleeced ram. At that time, Colchis was the kingdom of King Aeetes, a son of the god Helios and father of the sorceress Medea. It was to Aeetes's kingdom that the Thessalian hero Jason traveled in order to retrieve the Golden Fleece that, after the ram was sacrificed, hung in a sanctuary of the god Ares.

(*See also* Aeetes, Ares, Euxine Sea [the], Hera, Jason, Medea, Phrixus, *and* Thessaly.)

COLONUS Colonus, taking its name from the Greek for a small hill (*kolonos*), was a region that formed part of the territory of the city of Athens and lay just north of the city in close proximity to the famous Academy, the location of Plato's school of philosophy. Colonus was the birthplace of the tragedian Sophocles, and it was there that the blind Oedipus, accompanied by his daughter Antigone, stumbled upon a grove sacred to the Eumenides and ultimately met his mysterious end, becoming thereafter honored in cult by the Athenians as their protector and benefactor.

(*See also* Antigone, Athens, Eumenides [the], *and* Oedipus.)

CORINTH The ancient city of Corinth was located at the western end of the isthmus separating the Peloponnese from Boeotia and is about 2 miles (3 kilometers) removed from modern Corinth. This city, which possessed an imposing citadel on the heights of Acrocorinth, was strategically positioned and important, being located at a point where roads from the north led into the Peloponnese and ships passed from east to west, and vice versa, through the isthmus.

The mythological history of Corinth is a complicated one, varying in its details from author to author. According to the mythographer Apollodorus, Sisyphus, son of Aeolus, founded Corinth, which was formerly called Ephyra (or Ephyraea). The travel writer Pausanias adds that Corinth received its first name, Ephyra, from a daughter of Oceanus who had lived in that place, but that at a later point, the city was renamed Corinthus after a descendant of the sun god Helios.

As regards the more extended mythology of Corinth, Sisyphus was said to have married Merope, daughter of Atlas, with her having a son named Glaucus, who would become father to the hero Bellerophon, slayer of the monstrous Chimaera. In order to accomplish this feat, Bellerophon needed to tame the winged horse Pegasus, who with his hoof created the Corinthian spring of Pirene. Corinth also had a strong connection to the myth of Oedipus, as it was the

Corinthian king Polybus and his wife, Merope, who adopted the infant Oedipus when his birth parents left him to die. Herself a descendant of Helios, the sorceress Medea likewise had ties to Corinth and brought the hero Jason there, only to have him seek an alliance with the Corinthian king Creon through marriage to his daughter Creusa (or Glauce, as she was also known).

(*See also* Aeolus, Atlas, Bellerophon, Chimaera [the], Creon, Creusa, Glauce, Glaucus [hero], Helios, Jason, Medea, Merope [nymph and heroine], Oceanus [god], Oedipus, Pegasus, Pirene, Polybus, *and* Sisyphus.)

CRETE Crete, which has a total area of some 3,219 square miles (8,336 square kilometers) is the largest of the Greek islands and lies approximately 99 miles (160 kilometers) south of the Greek mainland. The island's terrain is varied and mountainous, and its strategic location in the Mediterranean on trade routes from Egypt, Cyprus, and Asia Minor was a major factor in the island's rise to a position of cultural and political prominence in the Bronze Age (roughly 3000–1150 BCE). The Bronze Age civilization on Crete, which was called Minoan after the legendary Cretan king Minos, flourished, with a number of palace centers being built on the island around 2000 BCE at Phaistos, Malia, Zakro, and Cnossus, which is the best known of these. It was Cnossus that was reputedly the center of Minos's power, and there that the famed craftsman Daedalus constructed the labyrinth that housed the dreaded Minotaur. The island's mountains Ida and Dicte, meanwhile, both were credited with being the birthplace of the god Zeus.

(*See also* Cnossus, Daedalus, Ida [Mount], Minos, Minotaur, *and* Zeus.)

CUMAE Cumae was a city located on Italy's Campanian coast. Founded in the middle of the eighth century BCE, it was the first Greek colony to have been established on the Italian mainland. In mythology, Cumae featured principally as the site of a mountain cave that housed the prophetic Sibyl, who led the Trojan hero Aeneas to the Underworld. The Sibyl's cave was located in close proximity to the deep, sulfurous Lake Avernus, which served as a gateway to the depths of Hades.

(*See also* Aeneas, Hades [place], Sibyl of Cumae [the], Troy, *and* Underworld [the].)

CYNTHUS, MOUNT Cynthus is a mountain on the island of Delos. A temple sacred to the goddess Hera was located at the mountain's foot, and a sanctuary of Zeus and Athena on its peak. Since, according to legend, Cynthus was the birthplace of Apollo and his sister Artemis, they both could be referred to as "Cynthian" ("of Mount Cynthus").

(*See also* Apollo, Artemis, Athena, Cynthia, Delos, Hera, *and* Zeus.)

CYPRUS The island of Cyprus, now the Republic of Cyprus, is the third-largest island in the Mediterranean, having a surface area of 3,572 square miles (9,251 square kilometers), and is located at the eastern edge of the Mediterranean, south of Turkey, west of Syria and Lebanon, northwest of Israel and Palestine, and north of Egypt. As a consequence of its strategic position, bridging East and West, Cyprus saw an influx of settlers from Anatolia, Greece, and Phoenicia, among others, and was absorbed into the empires of Assyria, Egypt, Persia, Macedonia (under Alexander the Great), and Rome. In mythology, Cyprus is notable for its connection with Aphrodite, whose most important sanctuary was located on Cyprus at Paphos, reputedly the place where she first stepped on land after her watery birth. Aphrodite's beloved Adonis was the son of Myrrha, princess of Cyprus, by her own father, the Cypriote king Cinyras. Pygmalion, another king of Cyprus, fell in love with his statue, who became animate through the powers of Aphrodite. It is because of her connection with Cyprus that Aphrodite was called "Cyprian."

(*See also* Adonis, Aphrodite, Cinyras, Myrrha, Paphos [place], Pygmalion, *and* Rome.)

CYRENE The town of Cyrene was founded by Greek colonists from Thera in 61 BCE on the eastern coast of Libya near the Cyre spring, which was deemed sacred to Apollo. A tradition arose according to which the city was named after Cyrene, granddaughter of the river god Peneus, who was abducted by Apollo and who at that place gave birth to the god's son Aristaeus, bringer of the agricultural arts to humans.

The region surrounding Cyrene, which was rich in grain, olive oil, and silphium, a plant used as a spice, perfume, and medicine, was called "Cyrenaica" and became part of both the Roman and Byzantine empires.

(*See also* Apollo, Aristaeus, Cyrene [heroine], *and* Peneus [god].)

CYTHERA Cythera (or Kythira) is a Greek island that lies off the southeastern tip of the Peloponnese, between mainland Greece and Crete. Having good harbors and strategically located for trade, this island was coveted by Argos, Sparta, Athens, and Rome, becoming in succession part of the territory of all of these. In myth, Cythera is principally known for its association with the goddess Aphrodite, since Cythera, which was the location of an important sanctuary to the goddess, claimed to be the place where she first stepped ashore after her birth from the sea, a distinction claimed also by the island of Cyprus.

(*See also* Aphrodite, Argos, Athens, Cyprus, Rome, *and* Sparta.)

DELOS The now uninhabited small island of Delos, having a surface area of just 1.3 square miles (3.4 square kilometers), lies in the Aegean Sea at the center of the circle of islands called the Cyclades. In antiquity, the island was one of the most sacred places in the Greek world, as it was considered to be the birthplace of the god Apollo and, by most accounts, also of his twin sister, Artemis. There was a tradition according to which Delos was earlier known as Asteria and/or Ortygia ("Quail") after the second-generation Titan goddess Asteria, who was pursued by Zeus and, in order to escape him, plunged into the sea in the form of a quail, thereafter becoming this island. It was reputedly the case that Delos was ungrounded and floated in the sea until Asteria's sister, Leto, arrived there to give birth to the divine twins Apollo and Artemis. While Hera, Zeus, and Athena all had identifiable cult sites on the island, religious activities here centered on Leto, Artemis, and, in particular, Apollo.

In terms of its political history, the island is best known for having become the center and treasury of the defensive confederacy of Greek city states organized in the wake of the Persian Wars, the so-called Delian League (formed 478 BCE). The Athenians, under the statesman and general Pericles, would move the Delian treasury to Athens and transform the confederacy into their empire, which actions occasioned the Peloponnesian War (431–404 BCE) and the political demise of Athens.

(*See also* Apollo, Artemis, Asteria, Athena, Athens, Hera, Leto, Ortygia, Titans [the], *and* Zeus.)

DELPHI As the most important sanctuary and oracle of the god Apollo, Delphi was one of the most sacred places in ancient Greece. Dramatically situated, Delphi is located on the lower part of the steep southwestern slope of Mount Parnassus in the region of ancient Phocis, central Greece. The sanctuary looks out over the Pleistos Gorge at the Kirphis Mountains lying opposite it. The Gulf of Corinth, which is only 6 miles (10 kilometers) distant, is also visible from the site. Habitation on the site has been traced to the Bronze Age (fifteenth century BCE), and the active presence of a cult of Apollo there is attested by dedications dating to the eighth century BCE. The roughly rectangular sacred area of the sanctuary itself, the *temenos*, is enclosed by a wall inside of which were located an array of monuments and small, temple-like treasuries erected by the various city-states of Greece;

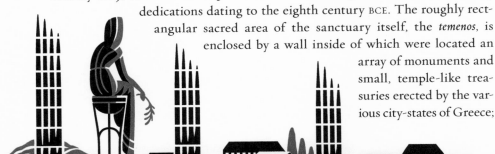

a theater; the so-called Rock of the Sibyl, perched upon which the first priestess of Apollo was said to have chanted her prophecies; and the Temple of Apollo, to which the Sacred Way wound up the slope. The oracle itself was located inside the Temple of Apollo, where the Pythia, Apollo's priestess, was seated on a tripod over a fissure from which gas vapors rose, causing the ecstatic "inspiration" or trance that marked her possession by the god. Pilgrims traveled to Delphi from Greece and beyond to put questions to Apollo via the Pythia, his mouthpiece. The Pythia's responses were uttered in verse and were interpreted by priests. The oracle's responses were famously misunderstood, as in the case of Oedipus.

The site of Delphi was steeped in lore: the oracle reputedly lay at the center of the world, its location having been chosen by Zeus, who released an eagle from each end of the earth, and the place where their flight paths converged was Delphi. As the world's center, it was consequently the world's *omphalos*, Greek for "navel," and a sculpted, oversized *omphalos* resided in the god's temple. According to legend, the oracle belonged first to the goddess Gaia and was guarded by a serpent, the Python (or Pytho), which Apollo slew. The Python gave its name to the site, which was called Pytho before Delphi, and Apollo's priestess was consequently called the Pythia. According to the *Homeric Hymn to Pythian Apollo*, the name of Delphi is to be derived from the word for dolphin in Greek, *delphis*, since the god assumed the shape of a dolphin to board the ship of a certain crew of men from Crete whom he would make his priests. As for Apollo's temple, there were said to have been six iterations of it, the first being made of laurel branches from the Vale of Tempe; the second of feathers and wax; the third of bronze, being the handiwork of Hephaestus; the fourth of stone, designed by Trophonius and Agamedes; the fifth a stone replacement erected upon the destruction of the fourth in 548 BCE; and the sixth (completed 320 BCE), again of stone, replacing the damaged fifth. This last temple endured until it was destroyed in 390 CE on the orders of the Roman emperor Theodosius I, who wished thereby to eradicate this potent Pagan threat to Christianity.

(*See also* Apollo, Crete, Gaia, Oedipus, Parnassus [Mount], Pytho, Tempe [Vale of], *and* Zeus.)

DODONA
Dodona was the site of the most famous oracle of Zeus. The sanctuary of Dodona, which contained this oldest of the Greek oracles, was located in the ancient region of Epirus, part of which now belongs to Greece and part to Albania. At Dodona, oracular responses issuing from Zeus were reputedly delivered by the fluttering of the leaves of the god's sacred oak tree and by the flight or cooing of doves settling in the tree's branches. The Greek

historian Herodotus recounts two alternative accounts of the oracle's founding and the role of the doves. He heard at Dodona that two black doves had flown from Thebes in Egypt, one settling at Dodona in an oak where it assumed a human voice, and one settling in Libya, future site of the oracle of Zeus Ammon. By contrast, Herodotus continues, Theban priests maintained that the Phoenicians absconded with two Theban priestesses, one being taken to Libya and the other to Greece, each later founding a place of divination at their new home; it was because the women spoke a language unintelligible to the people among whom they settled that they were called "doves."

(*See also* Ammon *and* Zeus.)

ELEUSIS Eleusis (Modern Greek Elefsina), which formed part of the territory of Athens (Attica), was about 12.5 miles (20 kilometers) west of the city of Athens and situated on the road from Athens to the Isthmus to Corinth on a low hill close to the sea. Eleusis was famous primarily as the site of a sanctuary of Demeter and Persephone, in whose honor the famed Eleusinian Mysteries were celebrated, attracting initiates from throughout the Greek world. Tradition underscored the deep links of Eleusis with Demeter. The Eleusinian king Celeus, who had taken Demeter in when she was roaming the earth in search of Persephone, reputedly was responsible both for building the sanctuary of the goddess in his kingdom and for instituting the Mysteries. The travel writer Pausanias records a tradition to the effect that Eleusis was named after the hero Eleusis, a son of the god Hermes and of Daeira, a daughter of Oceanus. By some accounts, according to the mythographer Apollodorus, Eleusis was the father of Triptolemus, a culture hero (bringer of civilization and culture) closely associated with Demeter, but a variant tradition casts Triptolemus, who sowed grain over all the earth from a winged chariot given him by Demeter, as a son of the Eleusinian king Celeus.

(*See also* Athens, Attica, Celeus, Corinth, Demeter, Hermes, Oceanus [god], Persephone, *and* Triptolemus.)

ELYSIAN FIELDS, THE (*See* Elysium.)

ELYSIUM The conception of Elysium (or Elysian Fields) changed over time, beginning as a paradisiacal land inhabited by heroes as an alternative to entering the House of Hades (in other words, to dying) and evolving into a region of the Underworld reserved for those who had led noble, virtuous lives. Elysium is first described by Homer in his *Odyssey*, where it is prophesied that the hero Menelaus will not die but, in the course of time, will be conveyed by the gods to the Elysian Fields that lie at the ends of the earth, at the western edge of the river Oceanus. This Elysium is a land free from snow and winter's cold, cooled by breezes from Oceanus's streams and by the west wind, Boreas. In this land, where life is easy for mortals, Rhadamanthus presides. Homer's view of Elysium coincided and became conflated with beliefs in a region called the Isles of the Blessed, which were likewise believed to lie at the edges of the earth. According to the Greek poet Pindar, the Isles (or Island) of the Blessed are flooded with the light of the sun, and those who resided there lived free of toil. This land is cooled with breezes and graced with drifts of golden flowers and groves of trees. The inhabitants, who wear wreaths and garlands, include the heroes Peleus, Cadmus, and Achilles. These earlier traditions of Elysium were fused and transformed by Virgil, who, in his epic the *Aeneid*, offers the most developed picture of the Underworld. There Elysium is a region of the Underworld, and it is gated, lying apart from the dank and terrifying region of Tartarus, which is reserved for sinners. Virgil's Elysium is a region bathed in roseate light, with its own sun and stars. Its residents engage in sport or sing, dance, and feast, moving freely throughout the region's shady groves and sun-drenched, grassy, well-watered meadows. It is in Elysium that Aeneas, ancestor of the Romans, meets his father, Anchises, who had died on the journey from Troy to Italy.

(*See also* Achilles, Aeneas, Anchises, Boreas, Cadmus, Hades [god and place], Menelaus, Oceanus, Odysseus, Peleus, Rhadamanthus, Rome, Troy, *and* Underworld [the].)

EREBUS   Erebus became synonymous with the Underworld, but originally connoted darkness in the earth's depths, as in the Greek poet Hesiod's account of the origins of the world, where Erebus is represented in quasi-personified form as the father, with Nyx (Night), of Hemera (Day) and Aether (Upper Air).

(*See also* Underworld [the].)

ERIDANUS RIVER, THE   The Eridanus River features significantly in the myth of Phaethon, the son of Apollo (Helios) who drove his father's sun-chariot so erratically that he threatened the very existence of the earth and the heaven's constellations. Phaethon plunged to his death in the Eridanus River, and it was on this river's banks that his sisters, the Heliades, were transformed into poplar trees that, in eternal grief, shed tears of amber. The hero Hercules also came to the Eridanus and asked the god of that river for guidance when seeking the Garden of the Hesperides.

For all its legendary renown, the Eridanus and its location were controversial even in antiquity, some authors doubting its very existence, among them the geographer Strabo and the historian Herodotus. Key in the attempted identification of the river was its reputedly being a source of amber; for that reason the river Po

PLATE IX
The Elysian Fields: A prophesied paradise of the afterlife

was identified as a likely candidate, but even the Granicus, Ebro, Rhine, Nile, and the fabled world-river Oceanus were posited as the Eridanus of myth.

(*See also* Apollo, Heliades [the], Helios, Hercules, Hesperides [the], Oceanus [place], *and* Phaethon.)

ERYMANTHUS, MOUNT Erymanthus is a mountain range located in what was southwestern Arcadia in antiquity but belongs now to the regions of Achaea and Elis. It was in the thick forests of Erymanthus that the goddess Artemis would hunt and there, too, that the giant Erymanthian Boar ranged and brought destruction to those who lived in the region. Capturing the boar alive was the fourth Labor of Hercules, a task that he accomplished by driving the animal into deep snow.

(*See also* Arcadia, Artemis, Erymanthian Boar [the], *and* Hercules.)

ERYTHIA The mythical island Erythia (or Erythea), "Red Island," was known as the kingdom of the triple-bodied Geryon. The island was thought to lie in the far west, where the sun sets in the streams of the river Oceanus, thereby "reddening" the island, and to have been named after one of the daughters of Hesperus, the evening star, or of Geryon himself. Hercules famously went to this island in order to seize the cattle of Geryon as his tenth Labor, traversing Oceanus in an enormous cup given him by the sun god Helios. According to the Greek geographer Strabo, Erythia could be identified with Gades (modern Cadiz) and nearby islands in southwestern Spain.

(*See also* Geryon, Helios, Hercules, Hesperus, *and* Oceanus [place].)

ETHIOPIA In antiquity, Ethiopia (or Aethiopia), the "gleaming" or "burnt" region, was a land south of Egypt extending roughly from the Nile's first cataract and including the territory of ancient Meroe north from modern Khartoum in Sudan. A different, shifting vision of Ethiopia emerges from mythology. In the *Odyssey*, Homer speaks of two groups of Ethiopians, both living at the ends of the world: one group residing where the sun sets and the other where it rises. Ethiopia figures most notably in the tale of the hero Perseus and the Ethiopian princess Andromeda, whom her father had shackled to a jagged cliff at the sea's edge as prey for a dread sea monster.

(*See also* Andromeda *and* Perseus.)

ETRURIA Etruria was a region of Italy inhabited by the Etruscans, a pre-Roman people whose origins were disputed even in antiquity, being called both indigenous Italians and immigrants from Lydia in the Near East. According to the

Roman statesman Marcus Porcius Cato, the Etruscans once controlled nearly all of Italy, and they were undisputedly a major power and a significant cultural influence on Rome, their presence having been verified archaeologically in an area extending from the northern Italian Alps (the Po Valley) to Salerno, though the center of their power was northwestern Italy between the Arno and Tiber rivers. The Romans were indebted to the Etruscans for certain religio-political practices and architectural forms, and were governed by a series of kings of Etruscan origin until the elimination of kingship and the foundation of the Republic in 510 BCE. Rome and Etruria were also political or imperial rivals, periodic hostilities ending with Etruria's absorption into the Roman state at the close of the Social Wars of 91–87 BCE.

In terms of mythology, a culture of conflict between the Romans and Etruscans is preserved even in Rome's foundation myth, beginning with the alliance between the Etruscan king Mezentius and the Rutulian prince Turnus against Aeneas, ancestor of the Romans, and his band of refugees from Troy, with whom king Latinus of Latium had joined forces.

(*See also* Aeneas, Latinus, Latium, Mezentius, Rome, Rutulians [the], Troy, *and* Turnus.)

EUXINE SEA, THE
Euxine Sea was the name by which the Black Sea was known in antiquity. The name "Euxine," which means "hospitable" or "friendly to strangers" in Greek, has been interpreted as a euphemism, as this body of water was subject to severe storms and was encircled by barbarian tribes. The historian Strabo tellingly explains that this sea was once actually called "Axenos," "inhospitable," and notes the threat posed especially by the Scythians, who sacrificed strangers, ate their flesh, and made drinking cups of their skulls. He adds that in a later period, when the Ionian Greeks had created settlements along its shores, the sea was called Euxine. According to legend, it was the hero Jason and his crew of Argonauts who first accessed the Euxine Sea by ship, having been the first to pass through the Symplegades ("Clashing Rocks").

(*See also* Argonauts [the], Jason, *and* Symplegades [the].)

FIELDS OF MOURNING, THE
The Fields of Mourning (Campi Lugentes in Latin), a region of the Underworld, appear to have been a creation of the Roman poet Virgil. After the hero Aeneas and his guide, the Sibyl, passed the threshold of Hades guarded by the triple-headed Cerberus, they came to this expansive region of the Underworld, which housed those who died from broken hearts. It was in the Fields of Mourning that Aeneas came upon his former lover, the Carthaginian queen Dido, whom he had cruelly spurned. As Virgil writes, this region's inhabitants included the tragic heroines Phaedra, Procris, and Pasiphae, among many others.

(*See also* Aeneas, Carthage, Cerberus, Dido, Hades [god and place], Pasiphae, Phaedra, Procris, Sibyl of Cumae [the], *and* Underworld [the].)

HADES
Hades, the "Unseen," was the Greek name for the Underworld and for the god who reigned there, though it might be more accurate to state that Hades was the name for the Land of the Dead, wherever it was thought to be located, and the king thereof. In Homer's epic the *Odyssey*, one of the earliest extant literary works from antiquity, the Underworld geography is unclear: Odysseus is told that he must travel to the "House of Hades" in order to consult the seer Teiresias. Access to the House of Hades appears to lie just beyond the streams of the river Oceanus, which encircles the earth. Spirits of the dead rise from a pit in the earth, having come from the depths of Erebus, to speak with Odysseus. The House of Hades appears at one moment to lie at the edges of the earth and at another to lie beneath it, where Odysseus sees Minos, Judge of the Dead; the Giant Orion, ranging the fields of asphodel; Tityus, his liver being torn out by vultures; Tantalus, trying vainly to reach water below him and fruit growing overhead; Sisyphus, pushing his stone uphill; and the shade of Hercules. In the works of later authors, however, Hades is underground, and the Underworld's geography becomes more developed.

(*See also* Erebus, Minos, Oceanus [place], Odysseus, Orion, Tantalus, Teiresias, Tityus, *and* Underworld the].)

HEBRUS RIVER, THE
The Hebrus, now called Maritsa (or modern Greek Evros), was a principal river of Thrace, originating in the Rhodope Mountains and discharging into the Aegean Sea. The Hebrus, taking its name from the Greek word "wide" (*eurus*), was notable in mythology as the river that carried the singing head of Orpheus along its currents after he was dismembered by Thracian celebrants of the god Dionysus.

(*See also* Aegean Sea [the], Dionysus, Orpheus, *and* Thrace.)

HELICON, MOUNT
Helicon is a mountain range in southwestern Boeotia, central Greece. It was a principal site of worship for the Muses; this was where, as the Greek poet Hesiod writes, the Muses were accustomed to dance and where, as he was herding his flocks, they presented him with a laurel staff, a source of poetic inspiration. There were two springs sacred to the Muses on Helicon: the Hippocrene, created by the winged horse Pegasus, and Aganippe, both of which, as the travel writer Pausanias states, were situated near the Grove of the Muses.

(*See also* Boeotia, Hippocrene Spring [the], Muses [the], Pegasus, *and* Zeus.)

HELLESPONT, THE The Hellespont is the narrow strip of water, or strait, now known as the Dardanelles. Of strategic importance throughout history, the Hellespont, which divides the European and Asian continents, connects the Aegean Sea with the Sea of Marmara and allows passage, via the Bosphorus, to the Black Sea. The strait took its name from little Helle, who was drowned in its depths. Helle's stepmother, Ino, had conspired to have her and her brother Phrixus killed, but the children's own mother, Nephele, tried to save them by seeing to it that they were carried out of harm's way by a winged, golden-fleeced ram. As the ram made its way through the heavens to Colchis on the eastern shores of the Black Sea, Helle lost her balance and fell into the strait's waters below them. In terms of mythology, the strait also figured significantly in the tragic tale of the star-crossed lovers Hero and Leander, both of whom lost their lives in the Hellespont's currents.

(*See also* Colchis, Helle, Hero, Ino, Leander, Nephele, *and* Phrixus.)

HIPPOCRENE SPRING, THE The Hippocrene spring on Boeotia's Mount Helicon, a mountain held sacred to the Muses, was thought to have inspired the poetic endeavors of those who drank from it. According to tradition, the Hippocrene, which means "horse's spring," was created by the winged horse Pegasus when he struck the ground with his hoof.

(*See also* Boeotia, Helicon [Mount], Muses [the], *and* Pegasus.)

IDA, MOUNT There were two mountains by the name of Ida that featured significantly in Classical mythology. One is Mount Ida (Modern Greek Idi) on the island of Crete, and the other, modern Kazdağı, in what is now northwestern Turkey. The Cretan Ida is the tallest peak, 8,057 feet (2,456 meters) high, of the mountain range crossing the island from west to east, and was known as the birthplace of Zeus. The Greek historian Diodorus Siculus notes that the truth of this tale could be substantiated by physical remains, one such piece of evidence being the existence of a substantial cave on the slopes of Ida that had continued to be sacred to Zeus: it was in a cave that the goddess Rhea was said to have given birth to Zeus and to have left him to be raised by nymphs and the Curetes. As for the Asian Ida, this mountain, too, had links with Zeus but had manifold other associations as well. Its summit reaching a height of 5,820 feet (1,770 meters), Asian Ida was the site of the ancient city Dardania that dominated the region before the founding of Troy by one of the descendants of Dardanus, Dardania's founder. Mount Ida was deeply entrenched in the story of Troy. It was from this mountains that Zeus snatched the prince Ganymede to become his cup-bearer, and it was there, too, that the Trojan prince

Paris sat in judgment of the goddesses Hera, Athena, and Aphrodite, awarding the last of these the title of "fairest," and setting in motion the events that would lead to the Trojan War. It was also on Ida's slopes that Aphrodite seduced Anchises, becoming by him mother of Aeneas, ancestor of Rome's founders Romulus and Remus. Mount Ida appears to have given its name to a mountain nymph, Idaea, who resided there and, again according to Diodorus Siculus, was impregnated by the local river god Scamander, later giving birth to Teucer, the first to rule as king over the land of Troy.

(*See also* Aeneas, Anchises, Aphrodite, Athena, Curetes [the], Dardanus, Ganymede, Hera, Paris, Rhea, Romulus, Scamander River [the], Teucer, Troy, *and* Zeus.)

ILION   Ilion (or Ilium and Ilios) was another name for Troy, whose founder was said to be Ilus.

(*See also* Ilus *and* Troy.)

ILISSUS RIVER, THE   The Ilissus, Modern Greek Ilisos, is a small river that rises from springs on Mount Hymettus in Attica, the territory of Athens. The river, which was channeled underground in the first half of the twentieth century, flows southeast and south of Athens's ancient, central, fortified area and, prior to the diversion of its course, used to be a tributary of the Cephissus (modern Kifisos) River. As one of the two major rivers of Athens, Ilissus featured in tales of the city's legendary past. Notably, the banks of the Ilissus were the site of the abduction of Orithiya, daughter of the Athenian king Erechtheus, to Thrace by Boreas, god of the north wind. According to the historian Herodotus, the Athenians were instructed by an oracle to call upon their son-in-law, Boreas, to help them in the Persian Wars, and, since Boreas obliged them by sending a storm to decimate the barbarian fleet, the Athenians established a sanctuary in the god's honor by the Ilissus River.

(*See also* Athens, Boreas, Erechtheus, Orithyia, *and* Thrace.)

IOLCOS   Iolcos (or Iolcus), modern Volos, was a Thessalian town near the Anaurus (Anavros) River, whose waters flow from Mount Pelion into the Gulf of Pagasae. Iolcos featured significantly in the legends surrounding the hero Jason, who, with his crew of Argonauts, sailed to the barbarian land of Colchis in order to retrieve the Golden Fleece, a task that he completed with the assistance of the princess Medea. Iolcos was rightfully the kingdom of Jason's father, but he had been deposed by his half brother Pelias. Correctly viewing Jason as a threat, Pelias sent Jason to Colchis. It was from the Gulf of Pagasae that the Argonauts launched their ship the Argo, and it was the Anaurus

River that Jason had earlier helped the goddess Hera cross, thus earning her continued protection.

(*See also* Argonauts [the], Colchis, Hera, Jason, Medea, Pelias, *and* Thessaly.)

IONIA   The central part of the western coast of Asia Minor became known as Ionia, as cities in this region were founded by Greeks of the Ionian tribe who, according to tradition, were descended from the Athenian king Ion. Ionia extended roughly southward from Smyrna, modern Ismir, to Miletus, which lay close to the mouth of the Meander River (Turkish Buyuk Menderes) and near the modern village of Balat in Turkey.

(*See also* Athens, Ion, *and* Ionians [the].)

ITHACA   The island of Ithaca, modern Ithaki, is one of the seven Ionian Islands off the western coast of Greece. This small island, with a total area of just 37 square miles (96 square kilometers), has been and still is identified as the island kingdom of Odysseus. In the *Odyssey*, Homer describes it as sunny, surrounded by close-lying islands, having rugged terrain, and being well suited to rearing young men. It was from Ithaca that Odysseus set out for Troy leading a contingent that manned twelve ships. Of these men he alone returned after ten years of fighting at Troy and a further ten years of adventure-ridden sea travel as he made his way home.

(*See also* Odysseus *and* Troy.)

LARISSA   Larissa was one of the most important cities of Thessaly, a district of northeastern Greece. Larissa was located on the southern bank of the Peneus River and, in mythology, was the site of the accidental death of the Argive king Acrisius at the hands of his grandson Perseus, the Gorgon-slayer.

(*See also* Acrisius, Argos, Gorgons [the], Peneus River [the], Perseus, *and* Thessaly.)

LATIUM   The region of Italy called Latium was the territory inhabited by the Italic tribes known as the Latins (Latini in Latin), who gave their name to the Latin language. While the Latium inhabited by the historical early Latins was bounded by the Apennine Mountains to the east and by the Anio and Tiber rivers to the north, mythological Latium appears to have had more indeterminate boundaries. According to the Roman poet Virgil, Latium had been ruled by the god Saturn, who brought a Golden Age to Italy, and subsequently by the rustic deities Picus and Faunus, followed by King Latinus, whose daughter the Trojan Aeneas would wed and, by this union, become founder of the future race of Romans.

The origin of the name "Latium" is uncertain, being variously derived from the verb "to hide," *latere* in Latin, in reference to Saturn's hiding in this region, as well as from the Latin *latus,* "wide," a possible reference to the breadth of the plain at the foot of the Alban hills.

(*See also* Aeneas, Faunus, Latins [the], Latinus, Picus, Rome, Saturn, Troy, *and* Turnus.)

LEMNOS Lemnos is an island lying in the northern Aegean Sea. The island had a special connection with Hephaestus, god of the forge, as it was there that he landed, and was well cared for, when Zeus cast him from Olympus for aiding his mother, Hera. In myth, Lemnos was also important as the home of the Lemnian Women, all but one of whom, the princess Hypsipyle, had killed their male kin, and as the island on which the Greeks abandoned the snake-bitten hero Philoctetes on their way to fight the Trojan War.

(*See also* Hephaestus, Hera, Hypsipyle, Lemnian Women [the], Olympus [Mount], Philoctetes, Troy, *and* Zeus.)

LERNA Lerna, which was an important settlement in the Bronze Age (roughly 3000–1200 BCE), lay south of Argos in the Peloponnese. According to Greek tradition, Lerna was the location of a spring produced by the god Poseidon when the territory of Argos was suffering from drought and the lovely Amymone, whom the god pursued, had come in search of water. This spring would become the home of the Hydra of Lerna, a many-headed serpent that Hercules slew as the second of his twelve labors.

(*See also* Amymone, Argos, Hercules, Hydra of Lerna [the], *and* Poseidon.)

LYCIA Lycia was a region of southwestern Asia Minor on what is now the southwestern coast of Turkey. According to the Greek historian Herodotus, who in this case is relating myth-history, Lycia was settled by immigrants from Crete led by Sarpedon, a brother of the Cretan king Minos. Both Sarpedon and Minos, Herodotus writes, were sons of Europa by Zeus, who had abducted her from Phoenicia by taking on the shape of a handsome white bull. Herodotus adds that Lycus, son of the Athenian king Pandion, came to join Sarpedon in that land upon being banished from Athens by his brother, Aegeus, and that the inhabitants of the region were subsequently called Lycians after him, their territory then being called Lycia. The Lycians were among those who fought on the side of Troy in the Trojan War, and, although Zeus considered interfering to prevent it, Sarpedon lost his life in that war. Apart from Sarpedon, another hero of note who traveled to Lycia was Bellerophon, slayer of the Chimaera, the monster that was terrorizing the Lycian countryside.

(*See also* Aegeus, Athens, Bellerophon, Chimaera [the], Crete, Europa, Sarpedon, Troy, *and* Zeus.)

LYDIA   Lydia was a region of western Asia Minor, having Mysia to the north, Phrygia to the east, and Caria to the south. Its borders with Phrygia and Caria shifted over time, and at the height of its power, Lydia controlled all of Asia Minor west of the River Halys, except Lycia. The region was not only rich in natural resources, as the legends surrounding the historical and wealthy king Croesus (reigned circa 560–547 BCE) attest, but lay on important trade routes between the sea and the rest of Anatolia, factors that contributed significantly to its wealth and influence on Greek and Roman culture. The coveted territory of Lydia was absorbed in succession by the Persians (546–334 BCE), Alexander the Great, and the Romans, under whom it became part of the Province of Asia in 129 BCE.

Lydia featured heavily in classical mythology. For example, in the playwright Euripides's tragedy *The Bacchae*, the god Dionysus claims to have come from his home in Lydia to Greece, bringing with him his religion and a band of Lydian worshippers. Tantalus, who became one of those undergoing eternal torture in the Underworld, was said to have been a king of Lydia. One of Tantalus's children was Pelops, who gave his name to the Peloponnese, and another was Niobe, who tragically boasted that she was more fortunate than the goddess Leto because she had more children. This boast, an affront to the goddess, led to the death of all Niobe's children at the hands of Apollo and Artemis, Leto's two children. In her grief, Niobe became a weeping rock. Lydia was also the home of Arachne, a skilled weaver, who made the mistake of challenging the goddess Athena and, as a consequence, lived the rest of her life as a spider.

(*See also* Apollo, Arachne, Artemis, Athena, Croesus, Dionysus, Leto, Lycia, Niobe, Pelops, Phrygia, Tantalus, *and* Underworld [the].)

MACEDON   Macedon, or Macedonia, was the territory of the Macedonian tribes, who, according to the Greek poet Hesiod, inhabited Pieria and Mount Olympus, essentially the region north of Thessaly, west of the Axius River (modern Vardar), and south of Thrace. Historically, the Macedonians first became significant under the rule of Philip II (reigned 359–336 BCE), father of Alexander the Great, who united the area politically.

There were various mythological derivations of the name Macedon: from a son of the Arcadian king Lycaon, a son of Zeus, or a son of Aeolus. Among Macedon's legendary kings was Pierus, father of the Pierides, who rivaled the Muses in singing.

(*See also* Aeolus, Arcadia, Lycaon, Muses [the], Olympus [Mount], Pierides [the], Pierus, Thessaly, Thrace, *and* Zeus.)

MEGARA

Megara, which is situated just less than a mile (1.5 kilometers) from the Saronic Gulf, is still a settlement site and lies on the Isthmus of Corinth between the cities of Corinth and Athens. Megara's territory was known as the Megaris and was delimited physically to the south by the sea, to the west by the Gerania Mountains, and to the northeast by the mountains Cerata, Pateras, and Cithaeron.

The most colorful myth associated with Megara is the tale of the princess Scylla, who became infatuated with the Cretan king Minos and sacrificed her family, her honor, and her existence in human form for the sake of her misguided passion. As for how the city got its name, there were various accounts. According to the travel writer Pausanias, "Megara" is a reference to two temples built in the city by a legendary king in honor of Demeter, each of which was a *megaron* (temple or hall). Alternatively, as the Boeotians believed, Megareus, a son of Poseidon, brought an army of Boeotians to help Nisus, Scylla's father, wage the war against Minos; Megareus lost his life in that war, and the city, previously called Nisa, was renamed Megara in his honor.

The place Megara is, of course, to be distinguished from the heroine of the same name.

(*See also* Athens, Boeotia, Corinth, Crete, Demeter, Megara [heroine], Minos, Nisus, *and* Scylla.)

MESSENIA

The region of Messenia was the southwestern part of the Peloponnese, being bounded on the north by Elis and Arcadia, and on the east by Sparta. Messenia was fertile, as it had both rich soil and an adequate supply of water from springs, rivers, and precipitation, and it was the site of important settlements at least as early as the Bronze Age. Especially notable was the so-called Palace of Nestor at Pylos, the last phase of which dates from approximately 1400 to 1150 BCE. Much of Messenia's later history was dictated by relations with Sparta, which absorbed a large part of Messenia and reduced its inhabitants to helots, indentured servants or "public slaves," as the geographer Strabo calls them.

In terms of mythology, the region's association with the wise king Nestor of Pylos, who features significantly in the epic poems of Homer, is especially important. Messenia also had ties with Hercules, as it was said to have been ruled by Cresphontes, one of Hercules's numerous descendants and then by Cresphontes's son Aepytus.

(*See also* Arcadia, Cresphontes, Hercules, Nestor, Pylos, *and* Sparta.)

MOURNING, THE FIELDS OF (*See* Fields of Mourning [the].)

MYCENAE Mycenae looms large in Classical mythology as the site of the palace of Agamemnon, leader of the combined Greek forces that sailed to Troy with 1,000 ships. The imposing ruins of the Bronze Age palace, built circa 1400 and destroyed circa 1200 BCE, are situated on a rocky hill in the northeastern corner of the plain of Argos in the Peloponnese and lies about 8 miles (13 kilometers) from the sea. The location of the palace was strategic, as the surrounding territory is readily visible from the hilltop, and, as can be deduced from the site's massive fortification walls—individual stones being so large that they were said to have been put in place by Cyclopes—defensibility was clearly a priority. While there are traces of settlement at Mycenae dating to the Early Bronze Age (the third millennium BCE), it was in the later Bronze Age (starting 1600 BCE) that Mycenae witnessed what appears to be a sudden explosion of wealth and power, burials having been discovered dating to this period that were filled with precious objects confirming Homer's description of Mycenae as "rich in gold." The nineteenth-century excavator of the site, Heinrich Schliemann, named one of the elaborate beehive tombs outside the city walls the Tomb of Atreus (Agamemnon's father), another the Tomb of Clytemnestra (Agamemnon's wife), and a third the Tomb of Aegisthus (Clytemnestra's lover). In one of the two grave circles at the site, Schliemann found what he believed to be the gold death mask of Agamemnon himself, though all of these identifications are speculative. Finds from Mycenae were so rich that the entire culture of Bronze Age Greece has been called Mycenaean.

(*See also* Aegisthus, Agamemnon, Argos, Atreus, Clytemnestra, Cyclopes [the], *and* Troy.)

NAXOS The Greek island of Naxos is one of the largest (166 square miles, or 430 square kilometers) and most fertile of the Cyclades island group in the Aegean Sea. Even in antiquity, the island was famed for its grapes and wine, so it is not surprising that, in mythology, the island had a particular link to the god Dionysus. The island was one of several places that, according to the historian Diodorus Siculus, claimed to be the place where the god was born or raised. It was on this island that Dionysus found his bride, Ariadne, daughter of King Minos of Crete, whom the Athenian hero Theseus had ignobly abandoned there although she had helped him in his quest to slay the Minotaur. It was also on Naxos that the hubristic giants Otus and Ephialtes were said to have met their end through a stratagem devised by the goddess Artemis.

(*See also* Aegean Sea [the], Ariadne, Artemis, Crete, Dionysus, Giants [the], Minos, Minotaur [the], Otus, *and* Theseus.)

NEMEA Ancient Nemea was a sanctuary sacred to Zeus and located in the northeastern Peloponnese, just east of the modern town of Nemea. The site was said to have derived its name from the nymph Nemea, daughter of the local river god Asopus. The Nemean sanctuary was the site of the Panhellenic Nemean Games, which, according to tradition, were established by the hero Adrastus. Nemea was also the location of the first Labor of Hercules: killing the invincible Nemean Lion, whose skin the hero wore as a trophy subsequent to his victory over the beast.

(*See also* Adrastus, Hercules, Nemean Lion [the], *and* Zeus.)

NYSA Nysa is best known in mythology as the place where the Hyades, also called the Nysaean Nymphs, raised the baby Dionysus after his father, Zeus, rescued him from the incinerated remains of his mother, Semele. The location of Nysa, and even its precise nature—whether mountain, city, plain, or valley—was a matter of debate in antiquity. In Homer's *Iliad* Nysa is not a mountain, and in the Homeric *Hymns* it is a plain. The historian Herodotus places the town of Nysa in Ethiopia, Arrian locates it in India, and Diodorus Siculus proposes Arabia and Phoenicia. The Roman encyclopedist Pliny, meanwhile, refers to Nysa as a town in the Transjordan region, what is now southern Syria and northern Palestine. The sixth-century CE geographical writer Stephanus of Byzantium adds to these locations Mount Helicon, Naxos, Thrace, and the Caucasus Mountains. These various mythological towns of Nysa are to be distinguished from the town of that name in Caria, which prospered due the proximity of a sanctuary of Pluto and Cora (Kore) as well as a therapeutic sulphur spring and a cave for restorative incubation.

(*See also* Caucasus Mountains [the], Cora, Dionysus, Ethiopia, Helicon [Mount], Hyades [the], Pluto, Semele, *and* Thrace.)

OCEANUS Oceanus, also called the River Ocean, was the cosmic river believed to flow around the disc of the earth, separating earth from the heavens. According to the Greek poet Hesiod's account of the origin of the world, Oceanus was a child of Gaia ("Earth") and Uranus ("Heaven"). Homer describes Oceanus as having deep-running waters and as the source of all rivers, springs, and seas, and insofar as Oceanus was personified, these rivers and bodies of water were his children. It was thought that the sun god Helios rose from the streams of Oceanus in the east and, at an opposite point, also set in them, being subsequently conveyed back to the east at night in his floating golden cup. Since Oceanus defined the limits of the earth, it was on this river's shores that an array of monsters and mythical peoples were said to reside, among them the

Ethiopians, the grasping Harpies, triple-bodied Geryon, and the golden apple–tending Hesperides, according to the poets Homer and Hesiod. In an early period, even Elysium and the Underworld were said to be located there.

As, through time, geographic knowledge increased, Oceanus was reconceived as a world ocean, or outer sea, lying beyond the Strait of Gibraltar.

(*See also* Elysium, Ethiopia, Gaia, Geryon, Harpies [the], Helios, Hesperides [the], Oceanus [god], Underworld [the], *and* Uranus.)

OETA, MOUNT

Mount Oeta, Modern Greek Iti, is a branch of the Pindus Range in southern Thessaly, central Greece. It was on this mountain that Hercules met his end when, wishing to end the agony induced by poison, he climbed there onto his funeral pyre.

(*See also* Hercules *and* Thessaly.)

OLYMPIA

The pan-Hellenic sanctuary of Olympia, together with Delphi the most significant religious center of ancient Greece, is located in the northwestern Peloponnese in the regional unit of Elis. Olympia, which was primarily dedicated to Zeus, chief of the gods dwelling on Olympus, lies in a valley watered by the Cladeos and Alpheus rivers, and is sited on the northern bank of the latter. Olympia's walled sacred precinct, which was called the Altis, contained a host of structures that included the Temple of Zeus (erected 470–456 BCE), a temple of Hera, altars, and dedicatory statues. The Temple of Zeus contained a monumental statue (36–39 feet, or 11–12 meters) of Zeus seated on his throne and created by the famed sculptor Phidias of gold and ivory. The statue was called one of the Seven Wonders of the Ancient World, and the Greek geographer Strabo notes that if the sculpted Zeus had stood, he would have burst through the temple's roof. The temple was decorated with an array of scenes from myth that were all related to the site of Olympia. The temple's east (main) pediment depicted the tense moment before the hero Pelops's chariot race with King Oenomaus of Pisa, a race that, according to tradition, was the founding event of the Olympic Games, which were held every four years after their establishment in 776 BCE. The western pediment depicted the battle between the Lapiths and Centaurs, which has been understood as symbolizing the defeat of the Persians by the Greeks in the Persian Wars. Meanwhile, the Twelve Labors of Hercules were depicted over the Temple's front and back porches; it was Hercules, according to the Greek poet Pindar, who measured out the Altis for his father, to whom he consecrated the sanctuary, and established the Olympic Games.

(*See also* Centaurs [the], Hera, Hercules, Lapiths [the], Oenomaus, Pelops, *and* Zeus.)

OLYMPUS, MOUNT

Mount Olympus is the highest mountain in Greece, its summit reaching 9,570 feet (2,917 meters). Since the mountain rises between the plains of Thessaly and Macedon, Olympus was variously considered to be part of Thessaly, as according to the Greek historian Herodotus, and of Macedon, as the geographer Strabo opines. The Greek poet Homer repeatedly describes Olympus as tall, rugged, having many folds, and, at its summit, being free from disturbance by rain, wind, and snow. Given its imposing height, Olympus, fittingly, was considered to be the dwelling place of the third and "last" generation of gods, among whom Zeus, the weather god, was king. Although there was a tradition that there were twelve Olympian gods, the number of deities who resided on Olympus varied and could include all but the gods of the Underworld. The typical cohort of Olympian gods included the siblings Zeus, Hera, Hestia, and Poseidon; as well as Zeus's children Athena, Hebe, Artemis, Aphrodite, Hermes, Ares, Apollo, and Hephaestus. Demeter and Dionysus could also be included in this group, however, and even the Muses and Hercules, among others, spent time on Olympus. Each of the Olympian gods was said to have his or her own palace, outfitted with furnishings created by the skilled Hephaestus. As the mountain's summit was so lofty, it was believed to be inaccessible to humans and thus sometimes indistinguishable in myth from the heavens.

(*See also* Ares, Aphrodite, Apollo, Artemis, Athena, Demeter, Dionysus, Hebe, Hephaestus, Hera, Hercules, Hermes, Hestia, Macedon, Muses [the], Poseidon, Thessaly, Underworld [the], *and* Zeus.)

ORTYGIA

Several places in the Greek world were known as Ortygia, "Quail's Land," and all had links to the goddess Artemis. Among them was the island of Delos, whose earlier names Asteria and Ortygia were explained by a myth according to which Asteria, sister of the Titan goddess Leto, was pursued by Zeus and, in order to escape him, transformed herself into a quail and plunged (or was flung by Zeus) into the sea. According to the mythographer Hyginus, a floating island was created from Asteria's body, and it was this island, later called Delos, on which Leto gave birth to the twin deities Apollo and Artemis. According to an alternate tradition regarding Artemis's birth, her brother Apollo was born on Delos, but she was born at a different place called Ortygia, which was identified as a sacred grove near the city of Ephesus.

A third Ortygia that featured in mythology is the island of this name that lies off the Syracusan coast of Sicily. It was on this island that Arethusa, becoming a spring, emerged from her subterranean flight from the river god Alpheus, who was in hot pursuit. It was Artemis who assisted her in her escape.

(*See also* Alpheus [god and place], Apollo, Arethusa, Artemis, Asteria, Delos, Leto, Sicily, *and* Zeus.)

OSSA, MOUNT Ossa (modern Kissavos) is a mountain in Thessaly located between Mount Pelion, which lies to its southwest, and Mount Olympus to the north, being separated from the latter by the famed Vale of Tempe. According to legend, the giants Otus and Ephialtes threatened to pile Mount Ossa on Olympus, and Mount Pelion on Ossa, in order to reach the heavens so that they could make an assault on the Olympian gods.

(*See also* Giants [the], Olympus [Mount], Otus, Pelion [Mount], Tempe [Vale of], *and* Thessaly.)

PACTOLUS RIVER, THE The Lydian Pactolus River (modern Sart Çayi) is a tributary of the Hermus River (the modern Gadiz) in what is now western Turkey. The River originates in the Tmolus Mountains, which are now called Bozdag, and flows along the ruins of the ancient city of Sardis. The Pactolus was famous in antiquity as a source of gold, which was said to have resulted from the legendary King Midas's washing his hands in its waters.

(*See also* Lydia *and* Midas.)

PAPHOS The town of Paphos, specifically Old Paphos near the modern town of Kouklia on the island of Cyprus, was the site of the goddess Aphrodite's most important sanctuary and was heavily associated in mythology with that goddess. It was on Cyprus that the goddess, born of the sea's foam, was said first to have stepped ashore, in close proximity to the town of Paphos. There were various related but conflicting tales about the foundation of Paphos itself. For example, the mythographer Apollodorus writes that a foreign prince, Cinyras, came to Cyprus, founded Paphos, successfully won the daughter of the island's king, Pygmalion, in marriage, and sired the handsome Adonis, who later would win the goddess's heart. Pygmalion, meanwhile, is known to readers of Ovid's *Metamorphoses* as the creator of an ivory statue in female form so lovely that, although having publicly eschewed the pleasures of the flesh, he became utterly enamored of her. Aphrodite heard his fervent prayers for the statue's animation, and a daughter, who would give her name to Paphos, was ultimately born of their union. For the mythographer Hyginus the aforementioned Cinyras was the son of Paphos.

(*See also* Adonis, Aphrodite, Cinyras, Cyprus, *and* Pygmalion.)

PARNASSUS, MOUNT Parnassus is a mountain range in the territory of ancient Phocis that separates northern and central Greece. The portion of Parnassus best known in Classical mythology is the highest peak of the range, the southwestern slope of which is the location of Delphi, the famed sanctuary and oracle of Apollo, and also of the Castalian Spring, which was

PLATE X

The Parthenon: Greek temple dedicated to the goddess Athena

sacred to the Muses. It was on the peak of this mountain that the boat of Deucalion and Pyrrha washed up on the occasion when Zeus unleashed a Great Flood intended to eradicate wicked humanity. While Parnassus had a particularly close association with Apollo, that god shared the mountain with Dionysus, who, as the god of disorder, blurred distinctions, and transgression, was the opposite of Apollo, the god of clarity, order, and light.

(*See also* Apollo, Castalian Spring [the], Delphi, Deucalion, Dionysus, Muses [the], Pyrrha, *and* Zeus.)

PARTHENON, THE
The Parthenon, erected between the years 447 and 432 BCE on the Athenian acropolis and constructed of marble from the local mountain Pentelicus, was dedicated to Athena as maiden goddess (Parthenos). The temple's architects were Ictinus and Callicrates, and the famed sculptor Phidias oversaw the Parthenon's extensive sculptural decoration, all portraying scenes from myth: the birth of Athena, the victory of Athena over Poseidon for patronage of Athens, and the battles between the Lapiths and Centaurs, Greeks and Amazons, gods and Giants, and Greeks and Trojans. Phidias was also responsible for the monumental (38 feet, or 11.5 meters, tall) cult statue of gold and ivory that depicted Athena as warrior-goddess and was housed inside the temple, which was viewed as the earthly dwelling place of Athena. The Parthenon was an integral part of the overarching symbolism conveyed by structures on the Acropolis, which even in antiquity became a museum of sorts to the heavily mythologized history of the city.

(*See also* Acropolis [the], Amazons [the], Athena, Athens, Centaurs [the], Giants [the], Lapiths [the], Parthenos, Poseidon, *and* Troy.)

PELION, MOUNT
Mount Pelion, Modern Greek Pilio, lies in southeastern Thessaly in close proximity to Mount Ossa, which is located between it and Mount Olympus. Indeed, as Homer notes, the giants Otus and Epialtes planned to stack Mount Ossa on Olympus and Mount Pelion atop the both of these in order to attack the gods in their heavenly abodes. Also according to Homer, the densely wooded Pelion yielded the spear of ash that the Centaur Chiron gave to Peleus, father of Achilles, and that Achilles himself used as a weapon in the Trojan War. The Greek epic poet Quintus of Smyrna adds that it was on Mount Pelion that Peleus and Thetis, parents of Achilles, had wed. Pelion was further known as the very birthplace of the Centaurs and the location of the cave of Chiron, who raised the infant Achilles and, by some accounts, the hero Jason as well.

(*See also* Achilles, Centaurs [the], Chiron, Giants [the], Jason, Olympus [Mount], Ossa [Mount], Otus, Peleus, Thessaly, Thetis, *and* Troy.)

PENEUS RIVER, THE There were two Peneus (also spelled Peneius and Peneios, Modern Greek Pinios) rivers in Greece. One was located in Thessaly, a region of northern Greece. This large river, which originates in the Pindus mountains and, flowing into the Thermaic Gulf through the scenic Tempe Valley (Vale of Tempe) between Mount Olympus and Mount Ossa, irrigated most of the region. In mythology, Peneus, the god of this river, was the father of the huntress Daphne, who was desired by the god Apollo and escaped the god's aggressive pursuit by being transformed into a laurel tree.

The other Peneus River is located in the Peloponnese, arising from the mountains of Arcadia and flowing west into the Mediterranean opposite the island of Zakynthos. This river supplied water to the city of Elis, which had athletic facilities comprising gymnasia and palaestras (wrestling grounds), running tracks, bathing facilities, and other buildings for athletes who came to the neighboring sanctuary of Olympia to compete in the Olympic Games.

(*See also* Apollo, Arcadia, Daphne, Olympia, Olympus [Mount], Ossa [Mount], Peneus [god], *and* Tempe [Vale of].)

PHERAE Pherae was a city in Thessaly that, according to the mythographer Apollodorus, was founded by Pheres, a son of Cretheus, king of Iolcos. Pheres was succeeded as king by his son Admetus, and the city is best known in myth for its association with the latter. For a time, Admetus served as the god Apollo's master and, as a consequence of his kind treatment of the god, Apollo allowed him to find a substitute when faced with early death. Tragically, Admetus did not foresee that his wife, Alcestis, would volunteer to die in his place.

(*See also* Admetus, Alcestis, Apollo, Iolcos, Pheres, *and* Thessaly.)

PHLEGETHON, THE River Phlegethon ("Blazing River"), also known as Puriphlegethon, "Fire-Blazing River," was one of the rivers of the Underworld. According to Homer, it was one of the tributaries of the river Acheron, but in the imagination of the Roman poet Virgil, writing centuries later, Phlegethon encircled the triple-wall-bounded region of the Underworld called Tartarus, which was reserved for the greatest sinners.

(*See also* Acheron [the River], Tartarus, *and* Underworld [the].)

PHRYGIA Phrygia is the Greek name of an ancient geographic region of western-central Anatolia (modern Turkey) that was inhabited by the Phrygians, a people speaking an Indo-European language who likely immigrated there from the Balkans in Europe perhaps in the ninth century BCE. For the Greeks and Romans, Phrygia formed part of the exotic, "barbarian" but seductive East. While the boundaries of Phrygia are difficult to define, the Phrygians had a more or less cohesive religion and culture. The rich city of Gordium, founded by the quasi-historical king Gordius, emerged as the kingdom of Phrygia's center, and King Midas of the "golden touch" appears to have ruled there in the eighth century BCE. Gordium was said to have been destroyed by a nomadic tribe called the Cimmerians around 800 (or 700) BCE. Phrygia itself was later conquered by the Lydians from the west, and then incorporated into the empires of Persia, Alexander the Great, and Rome in succession. The Phrygian mother-goddess Cybele was introduced both to Athens and to Rome, and Phrygia had a significant presence in Classical mythology, being the home of not only Gordius and Midas but also the Satyr Marsyas and of the devout Baucis and Philemon, for example.

(*See also* Athens, Baucis, Cybele, Gordius, Lydia, Marsyas, Midas, Rome, *and* Satyrs [the].)

PIERIA   Pieria was a region of Greece that in antiquity lay between Mount Olympus and what is now called the Thermaic or Macedonian Gulf. According to the Greek poet Hesiod, it was in Pieria that the Muses, patron goddesses of the arts, were born, and it was here, too, that Orpheus was born and, after his violent death, most of his dismembered body parts laid to rest. The legendary namesake of the region was the Macedonian king Pierus, whose nine daughters would rival the Muses in singing. Both the Muses and Pierus's daughters could be called Pierides—in the case of the Muses, this being a nod to their birthplace, and in the case of the daughters of Pierus, an acknowledgment of their parentage; however, the name was usually reserved for the Muses alone.

(*See also* Muses [the], Olympus [Mount], Orpheus, Pierides [the], *and* Pierus.)

PILLARS OF HERCULES, THE   The Pillars of Hercules, rocky promontories to either side of the Strait of Gibraltar, were said to have been shaped or set in their current location by the hero Hercules. One of the pillars is the Rock of Gibraltar, or rock of Calpe, which is located near the southern tip of the Iberian Peninsula, and the other is Abyla, modern Jebel Musa in Morocco, which is situated on the African continent opposite the Rock of Gibraltar. The Greek historian Diodorus Siculus recounts several alternate versions of Hercules's creation of the pillars, though in all instances the hero was in the far west while completing his tenth Labor, seizing the famed cattle of triple-bodied Geryon. According to Diodorus, Hercules may have set the pillars in place as a means to commemorate his journey to the far west, which was the edge of the world then known to the Greeks, or to make the strait narrower so that sea monsters could not pass from the sea beyond (the Atlantic) into the Mediterranean. Diodorus also mentions that the rocks may have resulted from Hercules's cleaving what was once a continuous land mass, thus creating a separation between Europe and Africa and a means for ship passage. Diodorus offers no opinion regarding which of the versions he offers is correct. Instead, he invites his readers to decide.

(*See also* Geryon *and* Hercules.)

PIRENE Pirene (or Peirene) was the name of an important spring that, according to the geographer Strabo, supplied the ancient city of Corinth with water. Strabo also notes that its water was clear and good for drinking, and it is not surprising, therefore, that this spring was said to be a favorite watering ground of the winged horse, Pegasus, and the place where Bellerophon was able to catch him. As for the origins of this spring, the travel writer Pausanias notes that it was named after a nymph of the same name who, in grief over the accidental death of her son at the hands of the goddess Artemis, dissolved in her own tears.

(*See also* Artemis, Bellerophon, Corinth, *and* Pegasus.)

PYLOS According to Homer, Pylos was the kingdom of the elderly, wise king Nestor who features in the *Iliad* as a trusted advisor of the Greeks fighting at Troy. In the *Odyssey*, Odysseus's son Telemachus visits Nestor at Pylos in order to gather information about the fate of his father, who had been away from home for twenty years. Homer describes Nestor's palace as "well-built" and the kingdom as being both "sandy" and having the river Alpheus in close proximity. Taken together, these descriptions caused confusion regarding the actual location of Nestor's Pylos even in antiquity. Consequently, the geographer Strabo notes that, in his time, there were three candidates, all in the Peloponnese and all claiming to be Nestor's Pylos: one in the area of Triphylia near modern Kakovatos; another in Messenia (near modern Ano Englianos), where richly fresco-decorated remains of a Mycenaean Bronze Age palace (destroyed circa 1200 BCE) have been found; and a third in the territory of Elis.

According to legend, Pylos was founded by Neleus, who, together with eleven of his twelve sons, was slain by Hercules, leaving his twelfth son, Nestor, as king.

(*See also* Alpheus [place], Mycenae, Neleus, Nestor, Odysseus, Telemachus, *and* Troy.)

ROME The ancient city of Rome lay on the left (eastern) bank of the Tiber river about 19 miles (30 kilometers) from the sea. A character in the Roman historian Livy's monumental history of Rome extolls the site chosen for the city's foundation, praising it for its healthful air, wide river, and distance from the sea, being close enough to ensure ease of commodity transfer but far enough away to ensure defensibility. Further, there was sufficient open space to allow for expansion. According to Roman tradition, Rome was a colony of the Latin city of Alba Longa, which had been founded by Ascanius (Iulus), son of the Trojan Aeneas. Rome itself was founded by Romulus and Remus, Alban princes who had been left to die in the Tiber as newborns but were rescued by a she-wolf. As the new city began to rise on the Palatine Hill, Romulus killed his brother in a dispute and became Rome's first king and namesake. Rome's population expanded, in part as a result of forcible recruitment, as in the case of the Romans' "theft" of women from the neighboring Sabines. Also according to tradition, Rome came to comprise settlements on the remaining of the seven hills (the Capitoline, Aventine, Esquiline, Quirinal, Viminal, and Caelian) that would form the ancient city's core, a union that required draining the swamp that lay in their midst and its transformation into the Roman Forum. In broad strokes, this tradition has been substantiated by archaeology. Traces of human habitation, or at least presence, have been found dating to the Bronze Age (circa 1400 BCE) on the Palatine, Capitoline, and Esquiline. Remains of huts, a clear indicator of settlement, on the Palatine Hill date to as early as the late tenth or early ninth centuries BCE, and the eighth century, in agreement with the traditional date of 753 BCE, witnessed expansion and fortification of the Palatine site. The Capitoline, later Rome's most sacred hill, appears also to have been inhabited in these periods. As the Palatine settlement expanded, burial sites shifted to the Esquiline and Quirinal, and the swampy area at the Palatine's base was partially drained to accommodate an early Forum. From its humble beginnings, Rome would evolve from a city in Italy to a world city and the center of a seemingly "limitless empire," in the words of the Roman poet Virgil. That increasingly unwieldy empire would begin its decline from at least the fourth century CE and fall in the late fifth.

(*See also* Alba Longa, Capitoline Hill [the], Romulus, Sabines [the], *and* Tiber River [the].)

SALAMIS The island of Salamis, best known for being the site of a decisive naval battle (480 BCE) in which the Greeks defeated the Persian king Xerxes and his forces, lies in the Saronic Gulf off the coast of Attica, the territory of the city of Athens. Now known as Salamina, this island was reputedly named after Salamis, daughter of the god of the river Asopus in the Peloponnese. By the god Poseidon, Salamis became the mother of Cychreus, who, according to the travel writer Pausanias, first settled the island after liberating it from the threat of a particular snake, thus making it habitable, and named it after his mother.

Cychreus, the island's first king, had no sons and made Telamon, from the island of Aegina, his successor, giving him his daughter Glauce in marriage. This Telamon and Glauce would become the parents of Ajax (the Great), one of the foremost fighters of the Greeks in the Trojan War. Pausanias adds that Philaeus, a grandson of Ajax, gave the island over to the Athenians, after being granted Athenian citizenship. As for Cychreus, there was, in fact, a sanctuary dedicated to him on the island where he was worshipped in the form of a snake-man, part human and part snake. It was reported that a snake, a manifestation of the hero Cychreus, appeared to help the Athenian forces in the Battle of Salamis.

(*See also* Ajax [the Great], Athens, Attica, *and* Telamon.)

SCAMANDER RIVER, THE
The Scamander River, modern Karamenderes, rises from Mount Ida in what is now Turkey and flows into the Hellespont (Dardanelles). The Scamander played a significant role in the legends surrounding the city of Troy. The god of the river, who was a personification of it, was said to have been the father of Teucer, first king of the Troad, the region controlled by Troy after that city's founding. Scamander's children reputedly included Callirrhoe, grandmother of Ilus, founder of Troy, which he originally called "Ilium" after himself. The importance of the river to Troy was underscored by the fact that the Trojan prince Hector's son Astyanax was also called Scamandrius.

(*See also* Asytanax, Hector, Hellespont [the], Ida [Mount], Ilus, Teucer, *and* Troy.)

SCHERIA
Scheria (or Scherie) was the mythical island kingdom of the Phaeacians, who, according to Homer's *Odyssey*, had been brought there by their former king Nausithous, so that they might escape continued harassment by the neighboring Cyclopes. When Odysseus arrived on Scheria, he encountered a well-ordered society and was hospitably received by the king Alcinous, his family, and the people over whom he ruled. It was from Scheria that Odysseus returned to Ithaca, the former being the last foreign place to which he traveled on his ten-year journey home. Later Classical authors identified Homer's Scheria as Corcyra (Corfu).

(*See also* Alcinous, Cyclopes [the], Ithaca, Odysseus, *and* Phaeacians [the].)

SCYROS
Scyros (or Scyrus), modern Greek Skiros, lies in the Aegean Sea and is part of the Sporades island group east of Euboea. The island had important links with the heroes Achilles and Theseus. It was to this island that a young Achilles was sent by his mother, the goddess Thetis, so as to avoid being taken to fight at Troy, where she knew he would be killed. Achilles, disguised

as a girl, lived among the daughters of the island's king, Lycomedes, until Odysseus came to find him and tricked him into revealing himself. While on the island, Achilles impregnated one of Lycomedes's daughters, becoming with her the father of Neoptolemus, who would also go to fight at Troy, where he displayed both skill as a warrior and extraordinary cruelty. As for the Athenian hero Theseus, he reputedly fled to this island when, after his attempted abduction of Helen and Persephone, the Athenians had turned against him and no longer wanted him as king. According to the mythographer Apollodorus, King Lycomedes eventually killed Theseus, throwing him to his death from a cliff. In historical times (476/5 BCE) the Athenians transferred what were reputedly Theseus's bones to Athens from Scyros after the ghost of Theseus appeared to assist the Greeks as they fought in the Battle of Marathon (490 BCE) against the Persians, as the Greek historian and biographer Plutarch reports.

(*See also* Achilles, Aegean Sea, Athens, Helen, Lycomedes, Neoptolemus, Odysseus, Persephone, Theseus, Thetis, *and* Troy.)

SERIPHUS

The island of Seriphus is one of the group of Aegean islands known as the Cyclades ("Circlers") that encircled Apollo's sacred island of Delos. It was on this island that Danae, whom Zeus had impregnated by assuming the form of a shower of golden rain, and her infant son Perseus washed ashore, thus escaping death at sea. When the island's king Polydectes later wished to marry Danae, he sent Perseus to fetch the head of the Gorgon Medusa in the expectation that Perseus would certainly perish, thus ceasing to constitute an obstacle to his intended marriage.

(*See also* Aegean Sea [the], Apollo, Danae, Delos, Medusa, Perseus, Polydectes, *and* Zeus.)

SICILY

Sicily, which has a surface area of 9,927 square miles (25,711 square kilometers), is the largest island in the Mediterranean and played a significant part in the geography of myth. The name Sicily is derived from the Sicels, inhabitants of the island who are thought likely to have arrived on the island from the Italian mainland at the end of the second millennium BCE. Trinacria, the mythical island housing the cattle of Helios, became identified with Sicily, and, according to the Roman poet Virgil, the Trojan Aeneas stopped on Sicily on his way to Italy, leaving some of those who had followed him from Troy on that island to live with King Acestes. The craftsman Daedalus was said to have fled to Sicily from Crete, where he had been held captive by King Minos, and the nymph Arethusa fled to the island of Ortygia, off the coast of Syracuse, in her effort to escape the amorous pursuit of the river god Alpheus. Enceladus, one of the giants who had attacked the gods on Mount Olympus, was thought to lie buried under Mount Etna, still to this day breathing fire through that mountain's open crater. Another source of Etna's flames was the forge of the Cyclopes, who, deep under the earth, made the lightning bolts of Zeus.

(*See also* Acestes, Aeneas, Alpheus [god and place], Arethusa [nymph and place], Crete, Cyclopes [the], Daedalus, Enceladus, Giants [the], Helios, Minos, Olympus [Mount], Ortygia, Trinacria, Troy, *and* Zeus.)

SIDON

SIDON Sidon was the most important city in Phoenicia, modern Lebanon, until it was overshadowed politically and economically in the early first millennium BCE by the Phoencian city of Tyre. Indeed, Sidon could be invoked to refer to all of Phoenicia. Among the best-known mythological characters hailing from Phoenicia were King Agenor, who was known variously as a king of Tyre or Sidon, Europa, and Cadmus. Agenor was the father both of Europa, whom Zeus, in the guise of a tame, beautiful white bull, abducted, and of Cadmus, the founder of the city of Thebes, a city that he populated by sowing dragon's teeth.

(*See also* Agenor, Cadmus, Europa, Thebes, *and* Zeus.)

SPARTA

SPARTA The Greek city of Sparta was the principal city of Laconia in the southern Peloponnese. The region of Laconia had Messenia to the west, Arcadia and Argos to the north, and the sea to the south and east. The city of Sparta itself was located on the Eurotas River in the valley between Mount Taygetus and Mount Parnon. Though Sparta became the dominant land power in Greece in the seventh century BCE, the historian Thucydides (fifth century BCE) noted that if Sparta, which was also called Lacedaemon, were to become depopulated and only the temples and foundations of the public buildings were left, posterity would be suspicious of Sparta's renowned power. Yet, he continued, the Spartans occupied two-fifths of the Peloponnese, led the rest of it, and had numerous allies in addition. Since Sparta was neither densely built up nor adorned with magnificent temples and public buildings, but rather was composed of a collection of villages, its remains would not create much of an impression. If, on the other hand, Athens were to suffer the same misfortune, that city would, because of the grandeur of its buildings, appear to be twice as powerful as it actually was.

The mythographer Apollodorus provides a brief summary of Sparta's geographic mythology: Taygete, one of the daughters of Atlas, was impregnated by Zeus and gave birth to a son named Lacedaemon, who became the king and namesake of the territory that Sparta would control. Lacedaemon married Sparta, after whom he named his capital. Sparta, for her part, was a daughter of the hero Eurotas and granddaughter of Lelex, who was born of the soil and one of the first inhabitants of Laconia. Lacedaemon and Sparta became the parents of a son, whom they called Amyclas, and a daughter, Eurydice, whom King Acrisius of Argos married. Amyclas, in turn, became father to the fair youth Hyacinth, whom the god Apollo loved and accidentally killed with a throw of his discus.

The legendary kings of Sparta included Tyndareus, father of the Dioscuri Castor and Pollux as well as of Clytemnestra, the murderous wife of Agamemnon, and stepfather of the beautiful Helen, Sparta's future queen. It was by virtue of marriage to Helen that Agamemnon's brother Menelaus became king of Sparta, and it was while he was king that the Trojan prince Paris arrived and made off with Helen, prompting the Trojan War.

(*See also* Acrisius, Agamemnon, Apollo, Argos, Castor, Clytemnestra, Dioscuri [the], Eurydice [nymph], Helen, Hyacinth, Menelaus, Paris, Pollux, Troy, *and* Tyndareus.)

STYMPHALUS Stymphalus was the name of a town and also a lake in that town's vicinity. The travel writer Pausanias visited Stymphalus in the second century CE, remarking that an older town of Stymphalus had been replaced by a new one, and that the town was in his time part of a league of cities in the territory of Argos. Pausanias adds that Stymphalus clearly had been part of Arcadia originally, as its founder, Stymphalus, was a grandson of Arcas, Arcadia's legendary namesake, who was the son of Callisto, one of Zeus's ill-fated love interests. Pausanias notes of Stymphalus's geography that in the town's territory, there was a spring that formed a small lake in winter. According to legend, Lake Stymphalus was home to the feather-shooting (or, by some accounts, flesh-eating) birds that Hercules was sent to chase off as his sixth Labor.

(*See also* Arcadia, Arcas, Argos, Callisto, Hercules, *and* Stymphalian Birds [the].)

STYX, THE RIVER According to Classical mythology, the Styx, or as Homer calls it Stygos Hydor ("Water of Horror"), was the principal river of the Underworld. For the early Greek poet Hesiod, the quasi-personified Styx was the most important (and/or eldest) among the older generation of the daughters of Oceanus, who had 3,000 watery daughters in total. Hesiod notes, too, that she became the mother of Zelus ("Emulation"), Nike ("Victory"), Cratos ("Strength"), and Bia ("Force"). For her assistance to him in his battle with the Titan gods, Zeus made Styx the patron goddess, and thus guarantor, of oaths, which were henceforth sworn by her waters. In the Roman poet Virgil's vision of the Underworld, the depersonified Styx winds nine times around the realm of the dead, and it is this river (or sometimes the Acheron) over which the ferryman Charon conveyed the souls of the dead in their passage from the world of the living to that of the dead.

The Styx, flowing in a thin stream of poisonous waters, was believed to have emerged above ground for a short distance in Arcadia, according to the ancient authors Strabo and Pliny the Elder. There was speculation in antiquity that it was water from the Arcadian Styx—having been carried in a hollowed hoof, this being the only material able to withstand the waters' chill and corrosiveness—that was used to kill Alexander the Great in Babylon at the age of thirty-two in the year 323 BCE.

(*See also* Acheron, Arcadia, Babylon, Charon, Nike, Oceanus [god and place], Titans [the], *and* Zeus.)

SYMPLEGADES, THE

The Symplegades, "Clashing Rocks," were two rock formations identified even in antiquity with the Cyanean Rocks, two rocky islands located just west of the point where the Bosphorus joins the Euxine (Black) Sea. According to the Greek poet Apollonius of Rhodes, the *Argo*, which belonged to the Thessalian hero Jason, was the first and only ship to pass through these rocks successfully. As the seer Phineus told Jason and his crew, these rocks were not rooted to the sea's bottom and often collided. As it was necessary for the *Argo* to pass through these rocks on its way to Colchis, the location of the Golden Fleece, Phineus advised Jason and his Argonauts to allow a dove first to pass through the rocks, and if the dove should make it through, then to pass through as swiftly as possible, rowing with all their might. The dove was successful, losing only the tips of its tailfeathers, and thus the *Argo*, too, secured safe passage, losing only a bit of the stern. As a consequence of the *Argo*'s passage, with which the goddess Athena had assisted, the Symplegades became fixed, separated for all time.

(*See also* Argonauts [the], Athena, Bosphorus [the], Colchis, Euxine Sea [the], Jason, Phineus, *and* Thessaly.)

TARPEIAN ROCK, THE

The Tarpeian Rock was a precipice on the southeastern side of Rome's Capitoline Hill. It was from this rock that murderers and traitors were reputedly thrown to their deaths. The Tarpeian Rock was named after the treacherous Tarpeia, daughter of the Roman commander Spurious Tarpeius, who, out of greed, betrayed Rome to the Sabines and was the first to be hurled from the rock.

(*See also* Capitoline Hill [the], Sabines [the], Tarpeia, *and* Rome.)

TARTARUS Tartarus was the deepest, darkest, most terrifying part of the Underworld. According to the Greek poet Hesiod, Tartarus came into being very early on in the creation of the universe, arising from Chaos's great primordial void together with Gaia ("Earth") herself. It was in Tartarus that Zeus imprisoned the Titan gods who challenged his authority, their prison lying as far beneath the earth as heaven is above it. According to Hesiod, an anvil of bronze dropped from the heavens would fall for a full nine nights and days before reaching the earth upon the tenth; dropped from the earth's surface into the earth's depths, it would require a further nine days and nights to arrive in Tartarus. For Hesiod, Tartarus was bounded by a fence of bronze, and dark night wrapped itself around the region in triple bands like a necklace. It was the location of the House of Hades guarded by the hellhound Cerberus, and there, too, resided Hypnus ("Sleep"), Thanatos ("Death"), and the river Styx. Above it had grown the roots of the earth and unfruitful sea. The Roman poet Virgil expands on this vision of Tartarus, making it a distinct, well-defined region of the Underworld and the counterpart of Elysium (Elysian Fields). For Virgil, Tartarus lay at the base of a bristling crag, was ringed by three walls, and was surrounded by the flaming river Phlegethon. The walls had impenetrable gates of adamant and an iron tower from which the Fury Tisiphone kept watch. From inside the walls could be heard the sinners' groans as well as the clanking and dragging of the chains that bound them. The region's portals were guarded by the monstrous Hydra, and Tartarus itself gaped widely, being twice as deep as the distance from earth to the heavens. In Tartarus resided the Titans, the giants Otus and Ephialtes, and the sinners Tantalus, Sisyphus, and Ixion; it was the region reserved for murderers, cheaters, liars, misers, adulterers, warmongers, and all manner of other evildoers.

(*See also* Cerberus, Chaos, Elysium, Furies [the], Gaia, Giants [the], Hades [god and place], Hypnus, Ixion, Otus, Phlegethon [the River], Sisyphus, Somnus, Styx [the River], Tantalus, Thanatos, Tisiphone, Titans [the], *and* Zeus.)

TEMPE, VALE OF The Vale of Tempe, Modern Greek Tembi, is a gorge, 6 miles (10 kilometers) long and 89–164 feet (27–50 meters) wide, in Thessaly situated between Mount Olympus and Mount Ossa. The Peneus River flows through Tempe into the Aegean Sea, and it is the story of the river god

Peneus's daughter Daphne that is perhaps the best-known myth associated with this lush, narrow valley. As the god Apollo ran in pursuit of her, Daphne called to her father for help and was transformed into a laurel tree, which would remain Apollo's sacred tree. The valley had other associations with Apollo, too, as it was in the waters of Peneus that the god reputedly cleansed himself after slaying Python, the serpent or dragon that had guarded the oracular site of Delphi.

(*See also* Aegean Sea [the], Apollo, Daphne, Delphi, Olympus [Mount], Ossa [Mount], Peneus [god and place], Python, *and* Thessaly.)

THEBES
The ancient city of Thebes, site of the modern village of Thiva, was located in the plains of southern Boeotia in central Greece and separated from the territory of Athens, its rival, by the Cithaeron range. The scant remains of the ancient city are a poor indicator of the city's importance in antiquity from the Bronze Age (roughly middle of the fourteenth century BCE) onward; the rich mythology of Thebes suggests otherwise, however. The city's legendary founder was Cadmus, who populated Thebes by sowing dragon's teeth. Cadmus was a brother of Europa, the Phoenician princess abducted by Zeus, who had transformed himself into a handsome bull in order to lure her. With Harmonia, Cadmus became the father of Semele, the mother of Dionysus by Zeus. Cadmus also was the grandfather of Pentheus, who met a gruesome end on Mount Cithaeron due to his disparagement of his divine cousin. At Thebes, Dirce, evil wife of the Theban king Lycus, likewise met a terrible end, being dragged to her death by a bull; her punishment was devised in part by Zethus, after whose wife, Thebe, the city was named, according to the mythographer Apollodorus. The clever Oedipus became a ruler of Thebes before his tragic demise, which was occasioned by unknowingly murdering his father and marrying his mother. Oedipus's kingdom then became the object of strife between his sons, Polyneices and Eteocles, again with tragic results extending to their descendants. Significantly, Thebes was also the birthplace of Hercules.

(*See also* Athens, Boeotia, Cadmus, Cithaeron [Mount], Dionysus, Dirce, Europa, Harmonia, Hercules, Lycus, Oedipus, Pentheus, Polyneices, Semele, Zethus, *and* Zeus.)

THESSALY
The modern Greek administrative region of Thessaly (Thessalia) in northern Greece is largely coterminous with ancient Thessaly, which was bounded by a series of lofty mountains: Ossa and Pelion to the east, Olympus to the north, Pindus to the west, and Othrys to the south. Of these mountains, Olympus, Ossa, and Pelion loomed especially large in myth. Olympus was home of the Olympian gods; the giants Otus and Ephialtes planned to pile Olympus, Ossa, and Pelion on top of one another as a means to attack the gods; and Pelion was home of

the Centaur Chiron. Other important physical features of Thessaly are the lovely Vale of Tempe and the river Peneus, whose god was the father of the ill-fated Daphne.

Thessaly is known to have been inhabited by hunter-gatherers as early as the Paleolithic (circa 9000 BCE) and to have been densely populated, especially in its fertile eastern lowlands, in the Neolithic period (roughly 4000–2000 BCE) by people practicing farming. From a mythological perspective, it comes as no surprise that Iolcos, home base of Jason and his Argonauts, emerged as a significant palace center in the subsequent Bronze Age. Thessaly was also the home of Achilles, best of the Greeks who fought at Troy; of Admetus, kind master to the god Apollo; and of the hybrid Centaurs.

(*See also* Achilles, Apollo, Argonauts [the], Centaurs [the], Chiron, Daphne, Iolcos, Olympus [Mount], Ossa [Mount], Otus, Pelion [Mount], Peneus [god and place], Tempe [Vale of], Troy, *and* Zeus.)

THRACE   The Thrace of antiquity, being considered to be coterminous with the northern edge of the known world, had indeterminate boundaries, essentially comprising all of Europe to the north and east of Macedon to the edges of the Aegean and the Black Sea. Although much or most of Classical mythology is marked by violence, it appears to be the case that this reputedly strange, barbarian land accrued some of the most violent legends. Among the mythical kings of Thrace were Tereus, who raped and mutilated his sister-in-law; Diomedes, who fed his horses human flesh; Polymestor, who murdered the young Trojan prince Polydorus for his money; and Lycurgus, who attacked the god Dionysus and his nurses. And it was a group of Thracian women that dismembered the gifted singer Orpheus, who, in grief over the death of his wife, had refused their attentions.

(*See also* Aegean Sea [the], Diomedes, Dionysus, Lycurgus, Macedon, Orpheus, Polydorus, Tereus, *and* Troy.)

TIBER RIVER, THE   The Tiber is the most important river in central Italy. The Tiber's waters rise from the Apennine Mountains and flow some 250 miles (400 kilometers) to the Tyrrhenian Sea, carrying along the way a significant amount of silt, giving them a brown tinge that the Roman poet Virgil described as *flavus* (yellow). Its waters were not potable, but the river was navigable from its mouth at Ostia to the city of Rome itself. Since Rome rose along the Tiber's banks, spreading to either side, the Tiber, logically, plays a significant role in the mythology of the city. It was in the Tiber's stream that the twins Romulus and Remus, Rome's founders, were set afloat after their birth to Rhea Silvia by the god Mars. It was there, too, that the twins failed to meet their end, being rescued by a she-wolf. Although the source of the river's name is uncertain, the Roman grammarian Festus notes that the river had once been named Albula because of the white color (*albus*) of its water, but it was later given the name Tiber after Tiberinus Silvius, a king of Alba Longa, who perished in it.

(*See also* Alba Longa, Mars, Remus, Rhea Silvia, Rome, *and* Romulus.)

TIRYNS

The center of the ancient city of Tiryns was located on a low, rocky hill in the Argolid, a region of the northeastern Peloponnese that encompassed Argos, which ultimately became its dominant city; Tiryns; Mycenae; Epidaurus; and Nauplion (modern Nafplio). Situated just 1 mile (1.5 kilometers or so) from the sea, Tiryns achieved particular prominence in the Bronze Age, when it became the site of a notable, fresco-decorated, fortified palace (1400–1200 BCE) and certainly one of the most powerful mainland palace centers in that period along with Mycenae. Tiryns declined greatly in power at the end of the Bronze Age and fell increasingly under the thumb of the neighboring city of Argos, which destroyed the city around 470 BCE.

In mythology, Tiryns had a connection with an array of Greece's most important heroes, among them Bellerophon, Perseus, and Hercules. Proetus, king and founder of Tiryns, sent Bellerophon to Lycia, where the latter would be tasked with killing the Chimaera; Perseus became a king of Tiryns before founding Mycenae; and Hercules performed his Labors for Eurystheus, another king of Tiryns.

(*See also* Bellerophon, Chimaera [the], Eurystheus, Hercules, Lycia, Mycenae, *and* Perseus.)

TRINACRIA

Trinacria (or Thrinacria), "Three Points," was the mythical island in the vicinity of Scylla and Charybdis that, according to Homer, housed the cattle and sheep, 350 each, of the sun god Helios. It had been prophesied that if Odysseus and his men could abstain from slaughtering any of these, they would return home, albeit after much suffering. They could not, and all but Odysseus perished. In antiquity, Trinacria became identified with the three-pointed island of Sicily, its points being at the cities known as Lilybaeum, Pachynus, and Peloris in antiquity.

(*See also* Charybdis, Helios, Odysseus, Scylla, *and* Sicily.)

TROY

The remains of Troy are located on the mound of Hisarlik, which overlooks the plain along the Turkish Aegean coast in ancient Anatolia. The site is about 4 miles (6.5 kilometers) from the coast, 3 miles (4.8 kilometers) from the southern entrance to the Dardanelles (the ancient Hellespont), and near the modern city of Canakkale, Turkey. The city lay on a bay that has become filled with silt over the centuries by the Scamander and Simois rivers, a fact that obscures the reality of what must have been Troy's enormous importance as a cultural bridge between the Balkans, Anatolia, and the Aegean and Black Sea regions. As such, it was a coveted site and, as it turns out, likely subjected to war and destruction not once but several times. Hisarlik was first identified as the location of Troy in 1820 by Charles Maclaren, who was followed by Frank Calvert in 1863 and 1865, and, most famously, by Heinrich Schliemann, who excavated the site in a series of campaigns between 1870 and 1890. Notably, the site has undergone archaeological exploration continuing to the present day. Nine major settlement layers have been discovered on Hisarlik, each built upon an earlier one. Troy I, the oldest stage of building, dates to the early Bronze Age (circa 3000–2500 BCE). Troy II (circa 2550–2300 BCE) yielded finds that prompted Schliemann to conclude that this was Homer's Troy: remains of several grand houses or structures as well as an abundance of artifacts made of gold, electrum, silver, carnelian, and lapis lazuli. As Homer's Trojan War is thought to have taken place considerably later, the well-fortified Troy VI (circa 1750–1300 BCE) became a candidate for Homer's Troy, though its dates, too, have been deemed too early. Although more humble, Troy VIIa (circa 1300–1180 BCE) has appeared to be the most likely choice, unless Homer's Troy is a conflation of several Troys, which may well be the case.

In ancient literary sources, Troy, named after the hero Tros (a son of Erichthonius), was variously called Ilios and Ilion (or Ilium) after its founder Ilus. The Trojans, meanwhile, were called Dardanians and Teucrians after Dardanus and Teucer (a son of the god of Scamander River and a nymph of Mount Ida), legendary early kings of the Troad (region around Troy). Ilus's city was said later to have been ruled by Laomedon and, later still, by Priam, in the course of whose reign the Trojan War took place and whose son Paris caused the war by abducting the lovely Helen from her home in Sparta. Among the best-known heroes who fought at Troy were Achilles, Agamemnon, Menelaus, Ajax, and Odysseus on the Greek side, and Prince Hector on the side of the Trojans. After ten years of fighting, it was through a ruse devised by Odysseus—a massive, hollow, warrior-filled wooden horse left ostensibly as an offering for Athena—that the city fell.

(*See also* Achilles, Agamemnon, Ajax [the Great], Athena, Dardanus, Erichthonius, Hector, Helen, Ida [nymph and Mount], Ilus, Laomedon, Menelaus, Odysseus, Paris, Priam, Sparta, Teucer, *and* Tros.)

UNDERWORLD, THE
The Underworld was variously known as Hades, the House of Hades, Acheron, and Tartarus in Classical mythology, and just as beliefs surrounding death and the afterlife changed over time, so too did conceptions of the Underworld's geography. The geography that emerges from the hero Aeneas's visit to the Underworld in the Roman poet Virgil's epic the

Aeneid is the most complete and colorful, though not without its ambiguities. Near the cave of the prophetic Sibyl at Cumae was the stagnant, gloomy, vaporous lake of Avernus, which was an entrance to the Underworld. Passage to the House of Hades itself was achieved through a cave, and in the antechamber of Hades were clustered an array of horrors: Cares, Disease, Old Age, Fear, Famine, and Sleep, the brother of Death. Beyond these was located an enormous elm tree swarming with false dreams, as well as War, the Eumenides's iron chambers, crazed Discord, Centaurs, Scyllas, Gorgons, Harpies, a Hecatoncheir ("Hundred-Hander"), and the Hydra, all being monsters so terrifying that Aeneas drew his sword in fear. Just beyond, the waters of Cocytus and Acheron converged in a sludgy, belching vortex, and the souls of the dead, eager for passage over the river Styx, thronged the river's banks. The squalid, flame-eyed ferryman, Charon, could take only the souls of the buried dead, while the unburied were consigned to roam for one hundred years. Beyond the Styx was stationed the watchdog Cerberus, serpents bristling at his neck, who, in his cave, guarded the Underworld proper. Not far from Cerberus could be found wailing infants who had died no sooner than their lives began, those wrongfully condemned to death, suicides, and Minos sitting in judgment over all the souls in order to determine their proper place in the afterlife: Tartarus or Elysium. Here, in a neutral zone, lay the Fields of Mourning, in which resided those who died of broken hearts, among them the Carthaginian queen Dido, as well as places inhabited by more of those prematurely dead. Beyond these regions the road led in two directions, one to Tartarus and one to Elysium. Dreaded Tartarus lay at the base of a cliff, was bounded by a triple wall, and was surrounded by the fiery streams of the river Phlegethon. The Fury Tisiphone stood watch there, whips in hand and ready to strike the wicked, their punishments having been determined by the judge Rhadamanthus. Within its walls, Tartarus gaped black and deep, holding in its maw the likes of Sisyphus, Tityus, and Ixion. As for Elysium, this was the afterlife paradise of those who had lived good and virtuous lives. This region was as open and lush, bright and flower-filled, as Tartarus was dark and cheerless.

(*See also* Acheron [the River], Aeneas, Carthage, Centaurs [the], Cerberus, Charon, Cocytus [the River], Dido, Elysium, Eumenides [the], Furies [the], Gorgons [the], Harpies [the], Hecatoncheires [the], Hydra of Lerna [the], Ixion, Minos, Phlegethon [the River], Rhadamanthus, Scylla, Sisyphus, Styx [the River], Tartarus, Tisiphone, *and* Tityus.)

APPENDIX OF GODS

GREEK PRINCIPAL GODS / ROMAN EQUIVALENTS

Zeus / Jupiter
Hera / Juno
Poseidon / Neptune
Demeter / Ceres
Athena / Minerva
Apollo / Apollo
Artemis / Diana
Ares / Mars
Aphrodite / Venus
Hephaestus / Vulcan
Hermes / Mercury
Hestia / Vesta
Dionysus / Bacchus
Hades or Pluto /
    Dis or Pluto

PRIMORDIAL GODS

Chaos (void)
Gaia (earth)
Uranus (sky)
Ourea (mountains)
Pontus (sea)
Tartarus
    (underworld)
Erebus (darkness)
Nyx (night)
Aether (light)
Hemera (day)
Eos (dawn)
Helios (sun)
Selene (moon)
Aeolus (wind)

WIND GODS

Boreas (north wind)
Notus (south wind)
Zephyrus (west wind)
Eurus (east wind)

MUSES

Calliope (epic poetry)
Clio (history)
Erato (love poetry)
Euterpe (music)
Melpomene (tragedy)
Polyhymnia (sacred
    poetry)
Terpsichore (dance)
Thalia (comedy)
Urania (astronomy)

GRACES (CHARITES)

Aglaia (Resplendent One)
Thalia (Blooming One)
Euphrosyne (Good
    Cheer)

FATES (MOIRAI)

Clotho (Spinner)
Lachesis (Caster of Lots)
Atropos (Unturnable
    One)

FURIES (THE ERINYES)

Tisiphone (Avenger
    of Murder)
Megaera (Envious One)
Alecto (Implacable One)

THE TITANS

Asteria, 2nd generation
Astraeus, 2nd
    generation
Atlas, 2nd generation
Clymene, 2nd
    generation
Coeus, 1st generation
Crius, 1st generation
Cronus, 1st generation
Dione, 2nd generation?
Eos, 2nd generation
Epimetheus, 2nd
    generation
Eurynome, 2nd
    generation
Hecate, 3rd generation
Hyperion, 1st
    generation
Iapetus, 1st generation
Leto, 2nd generation
Menoetius, 2nd
    generation
Metis, 2nd generation
Mnemosyne, 1st
    generation
Oceanus, 1st generation
Perses, 2nd generation
Phoebe, 1st generation
Prometheus, 2nd
    generation
Rhea, 1st generation
Selene, 2nd generation
Styx, 2nd generation
Tethys, 1st generation
Theia, 1st generation
Themis, 1st generation

GLOSSARY OF
ANCIENT SOURCES

AELIAN [Claudius Aelianus] (circa 170–235 CE)—a Roman rhetorician and author of *Historical Miscellany*, a cultural-historical work in Greek that is filled with moralizing anecdotes and short biographies of illustrious personages as well as descriptions of the world's natural wonders and diverse cultures.

AESCHYLUS (525/4?–456/5 BCE)—together with Sophocles and Euripides, one of the most famous Greek tragedians. He reputedly authored seventy to ninety plays, only seven of which have survived: *Agamemnon*, *Libation Bearers*, *Eumenides*, a trilogy known as *The Oresteia*; *Suppliants*; *Persians*; *Seven Against Thebes*; and *Prometheus Bound*.

ALCMAN (mid? to late seventh century BCE)—a Greek lyric poet who worked in Sparta but was possibly born in Lydia, modern Turkey. His works, short poems performed to the accompaniment of the lyre (or other instrument), are now known in only fragmentary form.

ANTONINUS LIBERALIS (second or third century CE)—a grammarian and author of a collection of myths written in Greek and known as the *Collection of Tales of Metamorphosis*. The details of his life have not been preserved, and the *Collection* is his only surviving work.

APOLLODORUS (first or second century CE)—the name that, likely in error, has become associated with an encyclopedic summary in Greek of Greco-Roman myth and legend. That work is entitled *The Library*.

APOLLONIUS OF RHODES (first half of the third century BCE)—author of the Greek epic poem *Argonautica* (*Voyage of the Argo*), centered on the hero Jason's quest for the Golden Fleece.

APULEIUS [Lucius Apuleius] (circa 125–? CE)—a Roman author and rhetorician born in Madaura, a Roman-Berber city in what is now Algeria. His best-known work is the only complete novel in Latin to have survived from antiquity. This work, known under the titles *The Golden Ass* and *Metamorphoses*, presents a first-person account of the adventures of the tale's hero, who is named Lucius and is transformed into a donkey.

ARATUS (315?–240 BCE)—a Greek poet born in Cilicia, the southern coast of Asia Minor (modern Turkey). His only surviving work is a 1,154-hexameter verse poem entitled *Phenomena* on the positions, risings, settings, and mythology of the most important stars and constellations.

ARRIAN [Lucius Flavius Arrianus] (circa 86–160 CE)—a Greek historian as well as military commander and public official of the Roman Empire. Born in Bithynia, central-northern Turkey, his work *The Anabasis of Alexander* is an important source on the campaigns of Alexander the Great.

ATHENAEUS (active circa 200 CE)—author of a fictional account in Greek of one or more dinner parties in Rome. Its title variously translated as *The Connoisseurs in Dining* or *Learned Diners*, the work recounts the guests' conversations on food and a variety of other subjects.

BACCHYLIDES (520?–450? BCE)—a Greek lyric poet from the island of Ceos, now known as Kea or Tzia. According to Greek tradition, he was one of the foremost nine composers of lyric poetry, short poems performed to the accompaniment of the lyre or other instrument.

CALLIMACHUS (circa 310/305–240 BCE)—a notable Greek poet and scholar who was born in Cyrene in what is now northeastern Libya and became a major literary figure in Alexandria, Egypt. While he was reputedly very prolific, most of his works, which included poems on mythological subjects, have been entirely lost or survive only in fragmentary form.

CATO, MARCUS PORCIUS (218–202 BCE)—Roman statesman and military figure who rose to prominence in Rome's wars against Hannibal and Carthage. A staunch advocate of traditional lifestyles, morality, and government, his writings include a work *On Agriculture* that covers topics including the cultivation of olives, grapes, and other fruit as well as pasturage for domesticated animals. Cato's historical work *Origins*, begun in 168 BCE and incomplete at the time of his death, describes the early history of Rome until the year 149 BCE.

CATULLUS [Gaius Valerius Catullus] (84?–55? BCE)—a Roman poet from the Italian town of Verona, whose slim book of poems, a *libellus* (little book), as he calls it, reveals that he was a member of the Roman Republic's "high society," and includes references to the orator and statesman Cicero, Julius Caesar, and Caesar's rival the general Pompey the Great, among others.

DIODORUS (active circa 60–20 BCE)—known as Diodorus Siculus, "the Sicilian." He authored *The Library of History*, an extensive history of the known world from mythical times to Caesar's conquest of Gaul. His work, written in Greek, includes discussions of Egypt, Mesopotamia, India, Scythia, Arabia, North Africa, Greece, and Europe.

DIONYSIUS OF HALICARNASSUS (circa 60 BCE–7? CE)—a Greek historian and rhetorician who came from Halicarnassus to Rome at some time after 30 BCE, living and working there in the reign of the emperor Augustus. Dionysius's major work was the twenty-book (or chapter) *Roman Antiquities*, a history of Rome from the city's mythical origin to the first Punic War (264 BCE).

EURIPIDES (485?–406 BCE)—together with Aeschylus and Sophocles, one of the most famed Greek tragedians. He authored some ninety plays on mythological subjects, eighteen of which survive: *Alcestis, Medea, Hippolytus, Andromache, Hecuba, Trojan Women, Phoenician Women, Orestes, Bacchae, Helen, Electra, Heraclidae (Children of Hercules), Hercules, Suppliant Women, Iphigenia at Aulis, Iphigenia among the Taurians, Ion,* and *Cyclops.*

FESTUS [Sextus Pompeius Festus] (late second century CE)—scholar and author of an abridged version of the grammarian Verrius Flaccus's (55 BCE?–20? CE) *De Verborum Significatu (On the Meaning of Words).*

HELLANICUS (480?–395? BCE)—a chronicler, mythographer, and ethnographer from the Greek island of Lesbos. Among his works, which survive only in fragmentary form, were a complete history of Athens, *Atthis,* as well as the *Troica,* a myth-history of Troy. His ethnographic writings covered a wide geographic range, from Greece to Egypt, Cyprus, Scythia, and Persia.

HERODOTUS (480?–425 BCE)—known as the "father of history," he was the first to make the events of the past the subject of investigation. His history in Greek of the Greco-Persian Wars (490–479 BCE), *The Histories,* contains a wealth of geographical, mythological, political, and ethnographic information.

HESIOD (active circa 725 BCE)—according to Greek tradition, the author of two highly influential, instructional epic poems: the *Theogony,* which treats the origins of the universe and of the gods, and the *Works and Days,* which includes reflections on social and religious conduct as well as a farmer's calendar.

HOMER (eighth century BCE)—according to Greek tradition, author of the *Iliad* and *Odyssey*, together constituting the earliest extant examples of literature in the Western world. The so-called *Homeric Hymns*, a collection of poems celebrating the Greek gods and of unknown authorship, are wrongly attributed to him.

HYGINUS (second century CE?)—known, probably falsely, as the author of a handbook of mythology compiled from a variety of Greek sources and a manual of astronomy, also with mythological content: *Fabulae* (*Stories*) and *Astronomica* (*Poetical Astronomy*), respectively.

JUVENAL [Decimus Iunius Iuvenalis] (active late first and early second centuries CE)—a noted Roman satirist about whose life little is now known. His sixteen satirical poems are collected as *Satires*.

LIVY [Titus Livius] (59 BCE–17 CE)—author of a history of Rome from the origins of the city to the time of Augustus. Published in installments, his 142-chapter work, *Ab Urbe Condita* (*From the Founding of the City*), won immediate acclaim.

NONNUS (active third quarter of the fifth century CE?)—a Greek poet from the city of Panopolis (Akhim) in Egypt. His epic poem *The Dionysiaca* (*Things about Dionysus*) centers on the life and exploits of the god Dionysus.

OVID [Publius Ovidius Naso] (43 BCE–18 CE)—among the best known and highly acclaimed of Latin poets. His work includes the *Metamorphoses*, that epic poem which for centuries has been the primary source of Greek and Roman myth and legend. His other works include the controversial *Ars Amatoria* (*Art of Love*), a manual on the arts of seduction; *Heroides* (*Heroines*), a series of fictional letters in verse from heroines in mythology to their lovers; and *Fasti* (*Calendar*), a poetic work that goes through the official Roman calendar month by month, indicating festival days as well as their origins and mythology.

PARTHENIUS (first century BCE)—a Greek scholar and poet from Nicaea, a Greek city in northwestern Anatolia, modern Turkey. A war captive brought to Italy and later freed, he greatly influenced important Roman poets such as Virgil. His works are known only in fragmentary form apart from the *Erotika Pathemata* (*Sufferings from Love*), a work in prose collecting stories told in the works of Greek poets.

PAUSANIAS (circa 115–180 CE)—author of a description in Greek of mainland Greece based on his own travels. Cast as a travel guide, *The Description of Greece* provides a wealth of information regarding many now-lost sites, monuments, and artworks as well as the customs and beliefs of those regions that he visited.

PINDAR (active circa 498–446 BCE)—Greek lyric poet known chiefly for his commemoration of victors at the Olympic and Pythian Games, which were held in a religious context at the sanctuaries of Olympia (sacred to Zeus) and Delphi (sacred to Apollo) respectively.

PLATO (428/7–348/7 BCE)—Athenian philosopher and founder of the philosophical community or school that came to be called the Academy. Among Plato's many writings is *The Republic*, a discourse on the ideal state, which features Socrates (by whom Plato had been deeply influenced) as a character.

PLINY THE ELDER [Gaius Plinius Secundus] (23/24–79 CE)—Roman statesman, admiral, and scholar who was among the victims of Mount Vesuvius's eruption. A prolific writer on topics that included grammar, oratory, military science, and biography, he is chiefly remembered for his extensive encyclopedic work on natural history, *The Natural History*, which encompasses topics including astronomy, botany, geology, horticulture, medicine, mineralogy, and zoology.

PLUTARCH [Lucius? Mestrius Plutarchus] (45?–125 CE)—biographer and moral philosopher. A prolific writer, he is remembered primarily for his work on morality and his biographies of eminent Greek and Roman political and military figures. His *Lives of the Noble Greeks and Romans*, which is also known as the *Parallel Lives* or *Plutarch's Lives*, included fifty biographies of prominent figures including Alexander the Great, the legendary Athenian king Thesius, and Numa, one of the legendary kings of Rome and the reputed successor of Romulus.

PROPERTIUS [Sextus Propertius] (second half of the first century BCE)—a Roman elegiac poet born in the Italian town of Assinium (modern Assisi). He enjoyed the patronage of the emperor Augustus and is best known as an author of poetry on the theme of love. His surviving work consists of four books of *Elegies*.

QUINTUS OF SMYRNA (third or fourth century CE)—author of a surviving epic poem in Greek entitled *The Things that Happened Between the Iliad and Odyssey*, in Greek *Ta meth' Homeron*.

SAPPHO (late seventh century BCE)—a lyric poet of such high repute that she was called the "Tenth Muse" in antiquity. Sappho was born and lived on the Greek island of Lesbos; apart from that, details of her life are uncertain. She is known for the passionate, female-centered nature of her poetry. Of her collected poems, it is largely only fragments that survive.

SENECA [Lucius Annaeus Seneca] (4? BCE–65 CE)—a Roman statesman, philosopher, and dramatist. Born in Cordoba, Spain, Seneca was educated in Rome and became first tutor and then political advisor to the emperor Nero. Among his works are a group of tragedies on mythological themes: *Hercules Furens* (*The Madness of Hercules*), *Troades* (*The Trojan Women*), *Phoenissae* (*The Phoenician Women*), *Medea, Phaedra, Oedipus, Agamemnon,* and *Thyestes.*

SERVIUS [Marius Servius Honoratus] (active circa 400 CE)—a Roman grammarian and commentator best known for his extensive commentary on the works of Virgil.

SOPHOCLES (495/495?–406/405 BCE)—an Athenian playwright, and the most popular in his day. He was the author of 120 plays, among them *Antigone, Oedipus the King, Oedipus at Colonus, Philoctetes, Ajax, Women of Trachis,* and *Electra.*

STATIUS [Publius Papinius Statius] (second half of the first century CE)—a Roman poet whose surviving works are an epic entitled *Thebaid*, focusing on the campaign of the Seven Against Thebes; an unfinished epic entitled *Achilleid*, centering on the life of Achilles; and *Silvae*, a collection of poems on assorted subjects.

STESICHORUS (active circa 600–550 BCE)—a Greek lyric poet who was a contemporary of the poetess Sappho of Lesbos. Stesichorus's poems, which were known in antiquity to have been numerous, have survived only in fragments. Of considerable fame in antiquity, Stesichorus is thought to have been born either in Sicily or in southern Italy.

STRABO (circa 65 BCE–25 CE)—historian and geographer. He is known primarily for his wide-ranging work in Greek on geography, inclusive of Spain, Gaul, Italy, the Balkans, Asia Minor, India, Egypt, northern Africa, and more. His seventeen-part work is known simply as *Geographia* (*Geography*).

TACITUS [Publius? Cornelius Tacitus] (55?–117 CE)—a Roman historian and statesman. He was born in Gaul, but came to Rome by 75 CE. His surviving works are: *Agricola* (*The Life of Agricola*); *Germania; Dialogus de oratoribus* (*Dialogue on Oratory*); *Historiae* (*Histories*), focusing on the reign of the Roman emperors from Galba to Domitian; and the *Annales*, a history covering the ascendancy of the emperor Tiberius to that of Nero.

THEOCRITUS (early third century BCE)—a Greek author of pastoral poems entitled the *Idylls*. Theocritus, who is called the creator of the bucolic genre of poetry, was likely born in Syracuse and then spent time working on the island of Cos as well as in Alexandria, Egypt. While thirty of the *Idylls* attributed to him have survived, not all were actually authored by him nor are all of the poems pastoral (dealing with the charms of country life) in content.

THUCYDIDES (460?—400 BCE)—an Athenian general and historian, known as the author of the first fact-based historical work, *The Peloponnesian War*.

VIRGIL [Publius Vergilius Maro] (70?–19 BCE)—illustrious author of the *Aeneid*, an epic poem recounting the founding of Rome and the origins of the Roman people. Virgil, who enjoyed the patronage of the emperor Augustus, was also the author of the *Eclogues*, a group of pastoral poems, and the *Georgics*, a didactic poem as much about agriculture as it is about the social and political concerns of the day.

VITRUVIUS [Marcus Vitruvius Pollio] (circa 80/70–15 BCE)—Roman architect and engineer who lived and worked during the regimes of Julius Caesar and the emperor Augustus. He is known chiefly for his *De Architectura* (*On Architecture*), the earliest known and vastly influential work on architecture and the art of building.

INDEX

Main entry is in **bold**.
Illustrations are in *italics*.